Colonization and Its Discontents

Colonization and Its Discontents

Emancipation, Emigration, and Antislavery in Antebellum Pennsylvania

BEVERLY C. TOMEK

New York University Press

NEW YORK AND LONDON

NEW YORK UNIVERSITY PRESS
New York and London
www.nyupress.org

LIBRARY OF CONGRESS CATALOGING-IN-PUBLICATION DATA

Tomek, Beverly C.
   Colonization and its discontents : emancipation, emigration, and antislavery in antebellum Pennsylvania / Beverly C. Tomek.
      p.   cm. — (Early American places)
   Includes bibliographical references and index.
   ISBN 978-0-8147-8348-1 (cl : acid-free paper)
   ISBN 978-0-8147-8349-8 (e-book)
   1. Antislavery movements—Pennsylvania—History.   2. Slaves—Emancipation—
Pennsylvania—History.   3. Free African Americans—Pennsylvania—
History.   4. Pennsylvania Society for Promoting the Abolition of Slavery—
History.   5. Pennsylvania Colonization Society—History.   6. Pennsylvania
Anti-Slavery Society—History.   I. Title.
E449.T658   2010
326'.809748—dc22

                                                        2010037511

References to Internet Web sites (URLs) were accurate at the time of writing. Neither the author nor New York University Press is responsible for URLs that may have expired or changed since the manuscript was prepared.

New York University Press books are printed on acid-free paper, and their binding materials are chosen for strength and durability. We strive to use environmentally responsible suppliers and materials to the greatest extent possible in publishing our books.

Manufactured in the United States of America
10 9 8 7 6 5 4 3 2 1

To R. J. M. Blackett,
. . . an all-around great guy.

Contents

Illustrations

Abbreviations

AASS	American Anti-Slavery Society
ACS	American Colonization Society
HSP	Historical Society of Pennsylvania
LCP	Library Company of Philadelphia
PAS	Pennsylvania Abolition Society
PAAS	Pennsylvania Anti-Slavery Society
PCS	Pennsylvania Colonization Society
YMCSP	Young Men's Colonization Society of Pennsylvania

Prologue

On the evening of May 17, 1838, at least nine Philadelphia fire companies stood by and watched as the four-day-old, $40,000 Pennsylvania Hall burned to the ground. In contemporary accounts of the blaze, some said the firemen were complicit in the destruction and worked only to prevent the fire from spreading to the surrounding buildings. Others reported that at least one fire company tried to save the hall but was prevented from doing so by an angry mob.[1] The extent of the effort made by Philadelphia's mayor and police force to protect the building is also unclear. What is certain is that by morning the once grand structure was reduced to smoldering rubble.

Pennsylvania Hall was built with funds collected by Philadelphia's abolitionists and managed by the Pennsylvania Hall Association. The ambitious venture was a practical as well as a symbolic response to the anti-abolitionist sentiment that permeated Philadelphia society in the 1830s. Unwelcome in most halls and meetinghouses in the city, abolitionists and their supporters created a space dedicated to the freedom of thought, speech, and human equality. They advertised the new hall as such, and the keynote speaker dedicated it as a "Temple of Liberty." The two speakers who followed focused on temperance. Under those terms, the public could tolerate the building and paid little mind to the new structure, perhaps giving the reformers a false sense of security. Once the abolitionists began to speak specifically about slavery and civil rights, however, the hall became a threatening symbol of the wrong kind of liberty, and the attack commenced.[2]

FIGURE 1. "Destruction of the hall" by John Sartain. (Courtesy of the Library Company of Philadelphia.)

The abolitionists who came together to build the hall were members of one or both of two abolitionist groups in the state: "gradualists" and "immediatists." The gradualists of the Pennsylvania Abolition Society (PAS) wanted to end slavery through legal means while maintaining peace throughout the nation and preparing blacks to function as productive free citizens. The "immediatists," represented nationally by the American Anti-Slavery Society and locally by the Pennsylvania Anti-Slavery Society (PASS), argued that slavery was a sin and should end immediately without compensation for slave owners and regardless of how "prepared" the slaves were to enjoy their freedom.

Most immediatists wanted to end slavery at once and force a complete overhaul of the American racial system; they hoped that impassioned speeches and displays of black and white unity would awaken whites to the immorality of racial hatred and make them willing to accept their black neighbors on equal terms. The PAS was as deeply opposed to slavery as the immediatists were, but most members feared that radical confrontation would only fan the flames of racial intolerance and thereby prove detrimental to the cause. The rash of anti-abolitionist violence throughout the late 1830s lent credence to these concerns, making it increasingly difficult for abolitionists of either group to peacefully coexist with mainstream institutions and organizations.

Although the lines between these types of abolition have been clearly drawn by some historians, the fact is that, in Pennsylvania at least, they were actually quite blurry. Many names appear on the roster of both groups, and most members of the Pennsylvania Hall Board of Managers belonged to both the PAS and PASS.[3] Philadelphia abolitionists had formed an immediatist group in 1835, but not until 1837 was the PASS founded to coordinate efforts on the state level. Indeed, just a little more than a year before the hall was built, the PAS deliberated over whether to send delegates to the Harrisburg convention that founded the PASS. Deciding in the end not to send delegates, the gradualists made it clear that they did not "intend to express any sentiment adverse to the objects of that convention" and that they held "the right of free discussion to be sacred and inherent in every human being and cannot but view every attempt to prevent it, as an infringement of the liberty and rights of the citizens of this commonwealth."[4]

By the time of the dedication the right of free discussion had taken on a new significance. Between 1835 and 1837, a number of newspapers had been attacked, starting with an attempt by a mob to tar and feather William Lloyd Garrison, the nationally known Massachusetts immediatist newspaper editor. Garrison narrowly escaped, but the violence continued as presses were attacked throughout the northern United States. An attack in Alton, Illinois, took an even more violent turn, producing the first martyr to the abolitionist cause: Elijah P. Lovejoy was shot to death defending his press from a second mobbing. Closer to home, an abolitionist lecturer and Presbyterian minister, J. M. McKim, a correspondent for Philadelphia's abolitionist *National Enquirer and Constitutional Advocate of Universal Liberty*, was attacked while lecturing in a New Jersey community approximately seven miles from Philadelphia. The general violence against abolitionists in Philadelphia prompted the *Enquirer* to issue a statement calling for an end to mob action.[5] In this hostile climate it is perhaps surprising that the hall managers did not foresee the mobbing, especially since the *Enquirer* was to be housed in the basement, but there is no indication that they did.

During the four days it was open, a number of reform groups used the hall, but it was the abolitionists who drew the wrath of the Philadelphia public. The keynote speaker, David Paul Brown, was a respected member of the Philadelphia antislavery community. A member of the PAS since 1818 and a delegate to the American Convention of Abolitionists during the gradualist heyday, he was a lawyer who fought against slavery on a case-by-case basis. In 1835 he had joined the Philadelphia Anti-Slavery Society, but he maintained his ties to the gradualist PAS. During his keynote address, he called Pennsylvanians to task for the recent constitutional convention of 1837–38 that had deprived blacks of the right to vote, and he denounced the mob action and southern assault on northern states' rights. "We do not threaten secession from the South, if they do not conform to our views. We do not attempt intimidating them with nullification. . . . We do not instruct or authorize our representatives to bluster or bully them into our measures." Instead, "we pursue the even and direct tenor of our way, to the great object of emancipation,—unseduced by blandishments, and undismayed by threats." He then denounced the idea that free blacks should be colonized to Africa, and he called for the passage of laws that would provide for the education of slaves to prepare them for freedom. Finally, trying to unite gradualist and immediatist, he called for "the passage of a law rendering all colored children born after a given time, free, upon their arrival at a certain age," but he added that "to effectuate this great object, immediate means must be adopted."[6]

The next day Garrison, the Boston immediatist known for just the type of fiery oratory and incendiary actions the PAS warned against, came to the floor, and the meetings took a radical turn. Less interested in the kind of abolitionist unity Brown sought, Garrison criticized him for his gradualist stance and censured the hall's managers for failing to include black speakers in the dedication ceremonies. "It has appeared to me, as well as to others, that there is a squeamishness with regard to coming out boldly in favor of the doctrine of *immediate* emancipation, and letting the public understand, distinctly, the object of our assembling together." Familiar enough with the Pennsylvania antislavery climate, he recognized that Brown's words were "adapted to please all parties—to allay, in some measure, the prejudice that prevails against us and our holy cause." Calling gradualists men of "'caution' and 'prudence,' and 'judiciousness,'" he took on a confrontational tone by saying that he had "learned to hate those words." Finally, he insisted that "there is too much colonizationism here" and took the managers to task over handbills he had seen posted throughout the city advertising a debate to be held in the hall the next week over that subject. "Sir, let every advocate of the colonization society, who maintains the propriety or duty of transporting our colored countrymen to Africa, on account of their complexion, be regarded as an enemy to his species and a libeler of God."[7]

Garrison's stance was considered extreme, even by many Pennsylvanians who opposed slavery. First, he had not only spoken out against Brown's speech but he had also admitted to hating some of the most important traits of gradualism: caution, prudence, and judiciousness. Finally, in his parting statement, he had attacked one other antislavery group that had gained a great deal of support in Pennsylvania—the colonizationists.

By 1838 the American Colonization Society (ACS) had managed to nourish a strong auxiliary chapter in the Keystone state. Made up largely of Quakers and current and former members of the PAS, the Pennsylvania Colonization Society (PCS) raised money to buy slaves conditionally freed upon their agreement to settle in Liberia, a colony founded by the ACS in west Africa. It also raised money to outfit voyages of freed blacks to the colony and to provide for their initial support on arrival. In later years the group would shift focus and become an agency that sought to foster the emigration of free blacks from the state, but at this point its efforts centered on slaves who would not be freed by other means.

In the light of the growing tension, hall managers tried to keep the peace by leaving room for all voices. As the immediatists Charles C. Burleigh and Alvan Stewart took up Garrison's cause, criticizing Brown and colonization, respectively, Samuel Webb, the treasurer of the

Pennsylvania Hall Association, tried to regain order. He rose and said, "As there appeared to be a diversity of opinion in regard to the best mode of abolishing slavery, he was authorized by the Managers of the Hall (who had just conferred together) to say, that there would be a discussion in that place on the ensuing morning, when all who chose to participate might have an opportunity of explaining their views, whether in favor or against *immediate* or *gradual* abolition, *colonization*, or *even slavery itself.*"

Though a group met to discuss slavery and its remedy the next morning, the tension was not resolved. Most of those who asked to speak were immediatists, and Elder F. Plummer, a member of none of the societies, rose and asked for more representation from the colonizationists. The day before, Garrison had supposedly mentioned Elliott Cresson, the city's leading colonizationist, in his attack on the movement, but there is no evidence that Cresson or any of his supporters attended the debate.[8]

It is difficult to know whether Garrison's presence was *the* catalyst that transformed generalized public disdain into full-out mob violence. There is no question, however, that the morning after his provocative speech, handwritten placards appeared throughout Philadelphia alerting citizens of his (and by extension all abolitionists') "avowed purpose of effecting the immediate emancipation of slavery throughout the United States" and calling for "all citizens entertaining a proper respect for the right of property and the Constitution of these sates to interfere, *forcibly if they must*, and prevent the violation of pledges heretofore held sacred."

Despite this very public threat, scheduled antislavery sessions continued at Pennsylvania Hall. It wasn't until the fourth day, when the National Anti-Slavery Convention of American Women was scheduled to meet, and anti-abolitionists had begun assaulting African Americans on nearby streets, that managers temporarily put a stop the proceedings. With support from the mayor the meetings scheduled for Thursday evening at Pennsylvania Hall were suspended, in the hope that the violence would not escalate.[9]

There are conflicting accounts of the actual mobbing. What is known is that the building came under serious attack during the first meeting of the Anti-Slavery Convention of American Women on the evening of the third day, but the women remained calm and concluded their meeting. On the fourth and final day, supporters of the Free Produce movement held a Requited Labor Convention, and the Anti-Slavery women met one last time. At this time, a large crowd began to gather, and the managers began to fear for the safety of the building, so they appealed to the mayor and the sheriff. The mayor then took custody of the keys to the hall and went there to address the mob. He told the mob to keep Philadelphia's reputation in mind and promised that no meetings would be held there that night. Oddly, he then told the mob *We never call out the military here! We do not need such measures. Indeed, I would, fellow citizens, look upon you as my police, and I trust you will abide by the laws, and keep order. I now bid you farewell for the night.* Around 10 p.m. the fire alarm went out. The mob had broken into the abolitionist bookstore in the basement and then stormed the rest of the building, piling benches, books, and papers in rooms and setting them on fire.[10]

Five months after the building was destroyed, a grand jury returned bills against Samuel Yeager and Edgar Kimmey for their role in destroying the hall. They returned the bills only to discharge a "necessary duty," and they felt compelled to restate what they saw as the cause of the unrest: "For several days before the acts of open violence occurred . . . the whole community was agitated and excited by transactions which originated on the very spot. . . . Passions were necessarily to be excited. Tumult and irregularity could scarcely fail to ensue." In other words, they blamed the radical abolitionists.

Interestingly, Elliott Cresson was the chair of this jury. Although Cresson wanted to see an end to slavery, he didn't endorse the broader ideals of those who worked to build Pennsylvania Hall. He was an anti-slavery man of a different sort. He had been a member of the PAS until he discovered the African colonization movement in the late 1820s and joined the Pennsylvania Colonization Society. He ultimately became the state's most active advocate of resettlement.[11]

The PCS shared the gradualist outlook and belief in working through the system to end bondage. Many colonizationists, including Cresson, would have liked a peaceful end to slavery, but they had stopped believing that racial harmony was a realistic possibility in America. Given their conservative racial stance, colonizationists organized around the goal of returning blacks to Africa. Unsurprisingly, the colonizationists felt disdain for the immediatist abolitionists, whom they considered too radical to effect any change in the condition of the slaves. This contempt for immediatists was shared by most Pennsylvanians, and it was also reflected in the grand jury, which, though it returned indictments in the assault on the hall, nonetheless felt compelled to blame the abolitionists for adopting "injudicious measures" that offended the public's sensibilities.[12]

Each of these groups—the PAS, the PASS, and the PCS—fought to abolish slavery, but they differed in ideology and in the tactics employed to achieve that end, as evidenced by the tensions inside Pennsylvania Hall. Crucially, they also disagreed about how they saw the nation's black population. This book tells the story of how these three distinct but overlapping abolitionist groups collectively, though not always cooperatively, fought to end slavery in the United States. It also reveals the central role that black Americans played in these organizations. Much has been written about each of these groups individually, but they have not until now been placed together in one narrative. Indeed, many abolitionists and historians of the immediatist movement would leave the colonizationists out of the antislavery picture entirely. Thus, in order to put them more firmly into the overall story, I have given colonizationists center stage in this narrative.

* * *

In the course of completing this book, I incurred a number of debts, for assistance, moral support, and funding. A number of people offered advice and assistance. First and foremost, Richard Blackett has been an outstanding and understanding mentor. He helped me narrow my topic, refine my focus, and sharpen my writing. He read each chapter several times and has always been pleasant and cheerful, even when being asked to look at something "just one more time." He refused to allow me to slack off, even in the face of some unique challenges. Deborah Gershenowitz at NYU Press showed an early interest in the project and worked hard to get it not only on the NYU list but also in the Early American Places series. Gabrielle Begue has also been a supportive and friendly contact at NYU. I was also fortunate to have excellent readers who offered very detailed and thoughtful criticism. I thank them sincerely. I also thank Tim Roberts, managing editor with the Early American Places Initiative, and Teresa Jesionowski, an outstanding copy editor.

Staff members at many archives have offered useful ideas and pointed me to important sources in their collections. Phil Lapsansky showed genuine interest in the project from the first moment I ventured into the Reading Room of the Library Company of Philadelphia in 2001, and he has since that moment been a great mentor who has always had time to answer my emails with friendship as well as scholarly advice. James Green also welcomed me into the Library Company community warmly and offered valuable help, especially on the Mathew Carey chapter. Connie King was also helpful on many occasions and, even more important, has become a true friend beyond the LCP walls. Rachel D'Agostino, Linda August, and Edith Mulhern have been wonderful allies in the Reading Room, just as Nicole Joniec, Sarah Weatherwax, Erika Piola, Linda Wisniewski, and Charlene Peacock have been great to work with in the Print Room. Not only have they cheerfully accepted countless call slips, but their kindness at the end of the day has made it easier to be so far from my family for relatively long periods of time. Tamara Miller, Lee Arnold, and Dana Lamparello at the Historical Society of Pennsylvania did the same. They are all very knowledgeable about the history of Philadelphia, and Pennsylvania in general. Perhaps even more important, though, they make the Library Company and the HSP comfortable and pleasant places to work. Susan Pevar at Lincoln University in Oxford, Pennsylvania, was equally pleasant and helpful. Finally, my work could not have been completed without the help of the interlibrary loan staffs at the University of Houston's M. D. Anderson Library and the Victoria College/University of Houston-Victoria Library, especially Lou Ellen Callarman and Garry Church.

Many other friends and acquaintances offered advice and moral support as well. Immanuel Ness read the entire manuscript, offering much-needed encouragement in the final stages, and Alice Taylor gave the Prologue and Introduction a thorough critique that greatly improved the overall quality of the manuscript. Important mentors at the University of Houston included Eric Walther, Karl Ittmann, Anthony Dworkin, Landon Storrs, James Kirby Martin, and Bob Buzzanco. Angela Murphy offered encouragement, ideas, and companionship during trips to Philadelphia and Memphis, and Theresa Jach, Marjorie Brown, and Daphyne Pitre were always there when I needed a friend. David Smith, Wayne Ackerson, Vernon, Georgeanne, and Bea Burton, Hal Smith, Judy McArthur, Iris Tamm, Sandra Woods, Victoria Bynum, Gregg Andrews, Jim Selcraig, Mary Ellen Curtin, Dwight Watson, and Ken Margerison all offered guidance and friendship. Dan Horowitz suggested sources that helped me flesh out some of my broader arguments, and James Brewer Stewart offered insightful comments on the Elliott Cresson chapter, parts of which I presented at the Organization of American Historians meeting in 2008 and published in *Pennsylvania History* (75, no. 1 [Winter 2008]: 26–53) as an article titled "Seeking 'an immutable pledge from the slave holding states': The Pennsylvania Abolition Society and Black Resettlement." I am grateful to the editors of *Pennsylvania History* for permission to include that research here. I also thank *American Nineteenth Century History* for allowing me to reprint portions of my article "'From motives of generosity, as well as self-preservation': Thomas Branagan, Colonization, and the Gradual Emancipation Movement" (6, no. 2 [June 2005]).

My friends at Wharton County Junior College, especially Amanda Shelton, G. G. Hunt, Elizabeth McLane, JoAnn Taylor, Ed Hume, and Liz Rexford, have made life pleasant with their friendliness and congeniality. Ken Woodruff read part of the manuscript and helped me refine my argument about cognitive dissonance, and Margaret Sherrod provided helpful input on the James Forten chapter.

Finally, I could not have made it without my family. My husband, Bobby, had to take on many household responsibilities when I was buried deep in my writing, or when I was away on research trips. He also worked many long days, weekends, and holidays to pay the bills at times when I offered little financial help. He has been supportive from the very beginning to the very end, and he shared his valuable and much-appreciated photo editing skills. Joey, my oldest son, helped out a great deal by watching his little brothers and knowing just when to offer one of his insightful and funny social commentaries. My twins, Grady and Andrew, brought beauty and humor to my world, but, most important, their bravery in the face of premature birth and numerous medical obstacles taught me that nothing is impossible and that no excuse is valid for giving up. My parents, Alberta Titus and Hal Scull, and my siblings, Bruce Scull and Brenda Hermes, offered a great deal of support as well. Brenda drove an hour each way every weekend to come to my home and help me catch up on housework, help me entertain the boys, or keep the boys busy while I wrote. Perhaps even more important, she knew when to make me stop and take some time away from the computer.

Other family members, and friends who are basically extended family, offered support in numerous ways. Special thanks go to Vlasta Tomek, Victor and Evelyn Svoboda, Myra Lampley, Katelin Kombos, and David Tewes.

Finally, I could never have conducted the research without financial support. Professor Blackett provided funds from the John and Rebecca Moores Endowed Chair to support travel to Philadelphia, and Joe Pratt, former chair of the history department at the University of Houston, funded a preliminary research trip to Philadelphia while my work was still in the planning stages. The Library Company of Philadelphia and the Historical Society of Pennsylvania also funded research in their collections by awarding me an Andrew Mellon Fellowship, and the Library Company generously granted me an Albert M. Greenfield Foundation

Fellowship. The Pennsylvania Historical Association, the University of Houston-Victoria, and Wharton County Junior College provided travel funding as well.

Life is a complicated mix of things professional and things personal. I dedicate the beautiful moments in life to my family—the time we spend together playing games, watching sunsets, fishing at the creek, traveling, or just watching movies on a lazy weekend. These things, often done as a happy diversion to get away from work, I dedicate to my men—Bobby and Joey, Andy and Grady. This book, which has been the centerpiece of my academic life for almost a decade, I dedicate to my mentor, who has read every word multiple times with great patience and care. A simple "thank you" is simply not enough.

Introduction

Pennsylvania offers an excellent lens through which to view the changes that took place within the American antislavery community from the founding era to the ultimate achievement of emancipation during the Civil War. First is the fact that unlike other antislavery strongholds such as Massachusetts and New York, Pennsylvania contained strong chapters of three major antislavery groups—the "gradualists" of the Pennsylvania Abolition Society (PAS), the colonizationists of the Pennsylvania Colonization Society (PCS), and the "immediatists" or "modern" abolitionists of the Pennsylvania Anti-Slavery Society (PASS). Second, the state's abolitionist legacy and its geographical location as a northern border state created an intellectual and social environment that gave its colonization chapter a particularly strong support base.

What resulted from these two factors was a complicated antislavery network that interacted on a regular basis. Though some historians have described gradualists as "emancipationists" rather than ""abolitionists," none has questioned the sincerity of either gradualist or immediatist efforts to end human bondage. The historical assessment of colonizationists, in contrast, has been mixed. Thus, my first goal in describing the complexities of the overall antislavery movement is to show that colonization, at least in Pennsylvania, was undoubtedly an antislavery movement, and it remained a key part of the antislavery landscape throughout the nineteenth century.

Colonization drew antislavery support from two main sources. First, some reformers who followed the movement did so because they saw

FIGURE 2. "Abolition Hall. The evening before the conflagration," by Zip Coon. (Unidentified origin. Courtesy of the Library Company of Philadelphia.)

growing white resistance to abolition and resentment of free blacks as evidence that emancipation alone would never solve the country's racial dilemma. As abolitionists and free blacks came increasingly under attack, starting as early as the second decade of the nineteenth century, as I will show, some PAS members who had fought for black uplift began to see the goal as impossible in the face of white resistance and became attracted to the idea of African colonization. These colonizationists, whom I describe as "humanitarian" throughout this book, saw their work with the colonization society as a logical corollary to gradual abolition.

A second group of reformers, more politically minded, supported colonization for reasons that stemmed more from Pennsylvania's location than its reform legacy. This group followed a political agenda that emphasized the ideas embodied in what came to be known as Henry Clay's American System. Like Clay, a longtime American Colonization Society supporter and president, the members of this group believed that slavery jeopardized the potential political and industrial greatness of the United States. They did not oppose slavery primarily for the benefit of the slave, but they opposed it nonetheless, as I will show. Although different historians have looked at these sides of the colonization movement, no one before has put the two together and then placed them collectively within the framework of American antislavery.

Part of the problem has involved word choice. There has been much debate over the meanings of the terms "abolitionist" and "antislavery." Using their own title, we would call gradualists "abolitionists." Indeed, they called their group the Pennsylvania Abolition Society. Once the immediatists entered the picture, however, they appropriated the name abolitionist for those who agreed that slavery must be abolished immediately. Many historians followed this trend. Because the PAS fought for gradual emancipation rather than immediate abolition, they argued, PAS supporters were technically "emancipationists" rather than "abolitionists." Either way, both groups were clearly "antislavery," and they worked together in Pennsylvania to a large extent, as the cooperative effort to build Pennsylvania Hall shows.

In fact, a close look at PAS and PASS records reveals an informal coalition much like the one described by Doug Rossinow in *Visions of Progress*. Rossinow describes a cooperative reform environment in which a "left-liberal tradition" led to a "political zone where liberalism and radicalism overlapped." Together, leftists and liberals worked to champion "the validation of free speech and free conscience and the imperative of racial equality." Though he was concerned with the sixty-year period

from the 1880s to the 1940s, his work aptly describes the relationship between various groups of Pennsylvania antislavery advocates in the early
to mid nineteenth century. As this book will show, the most radical immediatists came to see themselves at odds with gradualists, and even the
less radical eventually dismissed colonizationists altogether, but many
gradualists and colonizationists felt that they were all fighting for the
same goal, even if they did not always agree on tactics.[1]

One other area in which terminology needs clarification involves a
general tendency among some social historians to see "antislavery" as
always benevolent. By bringing in the political side of the movement,
we will see the ways in which "antislavery" can take on a selfish, even
racist, meaning. Not all who opposed slavery did so because they cared
about slaves. Instead, some opposed slavery because they saw slaves as
a threat to the republic they were trying to create. They believed bound
workers posed a constant threat of uprising and an inefficient labor force
that, little by little, was feeding into a growing free black population.
These free blacks, they argued, created a subculture of uneducated, often
criminal, citizens unequipped to participate in the republican experiment. Of course, this viewpoint is unfair to blacks and quite racist. Yet it
is still an antislavery stance. To illustrate these different antislavery ideas
this book will make clear distinctions between political antislavery and
the social movement known as abolition. It will also show how colonization as a movement relied on both of these currents in order to thrive in
Pennsylvania.

In making the claim that colonization was clearly an antislavery
movement I am addressing a debate that arose within decades of the
American Colonization Society's founding in 1817. Abolitionist criticism
of the ACS, spearheaded by black leaders such as James Forten and white
immediatists such as William Lloyd Garrison, was organized around
the assertion that colonization was a racially driven ruse to remove
free blacks from the United States. This plan, they argued, would not
weaken but rather strengthen the bonds of slavery by removing a powerful segment of the abolitionist community. This critique of the ACS took
a while to solidify, but once it did it became deeply entrenched in the
historical record and featured heavily in scholarly assessments of abolitionism between the 1960s to the 1990s. Social historians whose work
focused primarily on black and white immediatists were persuaded by
the Garrisonian argument that antebellum African Americans clearly
recognized colonization as a proslavery movement and therefore fought
from the beginning to defeat it.

Writers who have agreed with abolitionist accusations that the ACS was both racist and proslavery usually stress the southern origins of the movement. Although a number of men played key roles in the founding of the American Colonization Society, those who focus on the southern origins give the primary role in the ACS's founding to Charles Fenton Mercer. Mercer was a Virginia congressman who argued that voluntary resettlement was a means of dealing with his constituents' fears of a growing free black population. What southerners feared was that free blacks in the South would encourage slaves to fight for their own liberation, revolting and seeking violent retribution. They also argued that freedmen would become lazy and live off of public resources. Historians in this camp have generally relied heavily on abolitionist sources and contended that northern philanthropists who joined the colonization society were tricked by southern slaveholders into supporting a proslavery movement.[2]

Other historians have strongly disagreed with the assessment of the colonization movement as proslavery and have generally focused on the role of northern evangelicals and missionaries such as Robert Finley and Samuel J. Mills in founding the ACS. Finley was a Presbyterian minister from Princeton, New Jersey, and Mills was the founder of the American Bible Society and the American Board of Commissioners for Foreign Missions. Both men had clear credentials in the missionary and reform communities of their day, and both saw colonization as an antislavery endeavor that would encourage individual masters to free slaves, foster emancipation at the state level, and perhaps even more important to their broader agenda, help take Christianity and civilization into Africa. Seeing benevolent founders as evidence of humanitarian motivation, many in this camp have portrayed colonization as an antislavery movement that appealed to the less radical members of the reform community.[3]

The most recent works in this tradition are Hugh Graham Davis's biography of Leonard Bacon, a Connecticut minister and social activist, and Eric Burin's examination of the American Colonization Society and southern manumissions. Davis shows that for Bacon and other New England colonizationists, the movement was first and foremost "a missionary and humanitarian enterprise," which would ensure "emancipation and black improvement at home" as well as "civilization for Africa." As Davis clearly illustrates, Bacon became for many of his generation the symbol of benevolent colonization, and, as I show, he had considerable influence on the Pennsylvania colonization movement. He gained the support of a number of Pennsylvania antislavery colonizationists who had a long history of participating in the state's moral reform groups, including the PAS.[4]

Humanitarians were drawn to the colonization movement for two main reasons. First, they wanted to take Christianity to Africa, and, second, they saw colonization as a way of securing freedom for slaves who would otherwise have been subjected to a lifetime of bondage. Eric Burin has described the efforts of the Pennsylvania philanthropists who worked diligently to raise money to send conditionally freed blacks to Liberia, and I will trace this idea even further by looking at the PCS's efforts to secure the freedom of slaves on a case-by-case basis and its campaign to force the ACS as a body to adopt a strong antislavery stance.[5]

Finally, another important avenue of colonization studies is the political assessment of the movement. This body of scholarship reinforces the claim that colonizationists were deeply opposed to slavery, even if their opposition was fueled by self-interest. Studies of this nature have shown that colonization was a nationalist movement whose primary concern was in creating a racially pure (translation "white") republic. Taking the debate beyond the realm of abolitionist studies and into the political arena, Douglas Egerton has contributed the most to this field by showing that although Mercer led in the organization's founding, he, like many colonizationists of the border South, wanted ultimately to end slavery. The plan was to remove free blacks as a first step to ridding the country of all African Americans. According to Egerton, "It was not that the free black was a danger to slavery; it was that his skin made him a part of the permanent lower class, and thus a danger to an industrializing society." Egerton contrasted the "pre-modern" Deep South with the industrializing North, concluding that colonization was most popular in the North and border South and that it faced its greatest challenge not from the abolitionists, but from the planters of the lower South. He argued that southern opponents of the scheme realized that the ACS's plan could have been economically viable and genuinely feared the threat it posed to the slave economy. This political antislavery was indeed the type that ultimately appealed to a larger constituency through the Whig, Free Soil, and Republican parties.[6]

* * *

Beyond arguing that colonization was an antislavery movement, this book shows exactly how resettlement—the desire to transport free blacks from the United States to Africa—fit into Pennsylvania antislavery. My work is the first to draw clear connections between the PAS, the PCS, and the PASS. First, I illustrate that the PAS and PCS shared, to varying degrees, a desire to control the black population. This tradition of control began with Pennsylvania's first abolitionists, as revealed in future PAS president Benjamin Franklin's 1755 warning that "the number of purely white people in the world is proportionably very small." He insisted that for the colonies to reach their potential they had to remain white, and he lamented the growth in both the German and African populations. The forced immigrants from Africa especially made Franklin and his fellow intellectuals uneasy, not only because of their complexion, but also because they believed the violent circumstances in which slaves were brought to the New World left them resentful.[7]

Franklin and his associates in the PAS had a number of goals. First and foremost, they hoped to curtail further importation of slaves into the state. Second, they hoped to ameliorate the conditions of, and in Franklin's word, "Anglify," the blacks in their midst. They hoped this would lead to peaceful relations between whites and free blacks as well as make the enslaved fit for eventual freedom. Members of the PAS hoped to convince slave owners to help prepare their slaves for independence and then free them. They worried that bound labor and the resulting racial stratification of American society would put the young republic in great peril and threaten blacks and whites alike.

Though later generations of whites would develop a proslavery ideology that bondage was a means of civilizing blacks, most men of the founding era knew and readily admitted that the system was wrong. They argued that bondage fostered resentment, hampered the intellectual, emotional, and social development of the enslaved, and left them degraded and unable to function productively in free society. Thus, slavery was no way to "Anglify" anyone, as Thomas Jefferson warned when he equated slavery to having a "wolf by the ear." The basic problem was that slavery had created a biracial populace that threatened the ultimate goal of creating a homogenous republic.[8]

During the founding era, however, the outlook remained positive, as many whites agreed that emancipation could solve the dilemma. The colonial assembly had limited slave importation to keep the black population small from the beginning so that, once freed, the small black population would have no choice but to blend in with the Anglo society and adopt European culture. With proper help they could be taught to function independently and contribute to the overall success of the new nation. Thus, early abolitionists, who believed strongly in the need to educate free blacks for the sake of the republic, insisted that emancipation must be a gradual process so that the emancipated could be trained and thoroughly prepared to function as free persons before being released into society.

Quakers took a leading role in these efforts, so most historians have attributed Pennsylvania's early antislavery endeavors to the benevolence of the Quakers and the PAS. Though gradualists have not received the amount of attention that the immediatists have, those who study the PAS point to its efforts at amelioration and its use of mild tactics calculated not to stir the South. At the same time, some have admitted that Quakers were sometimes as concerned with the ways slavery harmed whites by encouraging slothfulness and greed. This assessment introduces some important points. First, Quaker efforts to strengthen their abolition crusade resulted from a desire to save their own souls from God's wrath as well as a hope of freeing the enslaved. Also, much of their antislavery effort revolved around the desire to limit the importation of slaves rather than to free all blacks held in bondage. When viewed together, these studies reveal that though Pennsylvania antislavery was influenced by Quaker humanitarianism, many abolitionists wanted to protect their society from an evil system as well as the presence of an unwanted population. Once blacks were brought into the colony, antislavery advocates hoped to keep them under tight control with legislation such as taxes on manumission. When that failed, they struggled to guide free blacks by teaching them to behave "properly." This, as the first chapters of this book show, left the state's emancipation movement ripe for colonizationist arguments.[9]

My description of the self-interested side of Pennsylvania antislavery efforts also supports the findings of a growing number of scholars who examine the role of race in the antebellum North and its connection to republican ideology and white identity formation. For some Americans of the early Republic and antebellum years, colonization provided the only solution for freeing the slaves without leveling American society. This attitude effectively tied republicanism to the hardening attitudes against free blacks in the North.[10] In this racial climate, many white Americans, even early abolitionists, became convinced that sending America's blacks to Africa would solve the country's racial dilemma.

* * *

Already at the forefront of America's antislavery movement, Pennsylvanians would play a leading role in bringing colonization into the broader antislavery agenda. Indeed, as this book reveals, the border states, particularly Pennsylvania, played a crucial role in the growth and development of the colonization movement because of their unique geographic and demographic positions. The antislavery movement had grown internationally, led largely by British reformers who campaigned first to end the slave trade (1807) and then to abolish slavery in the British West Indies (1833, 1838), but a crucial difference between the British and American abolitionists was that British reformers fought against a system that had little day-to-day relevance for them, since the slaves they fought to free lived thousands of miles away. Opponents of slavery in the United States were forced to contend not only with the issue of slavery but also with the question of what role blacks would play in a nonslaveholding republic.

Residents of the northern border states faced a different situation. They had a black population that was much larger than that in England yet much smaller than that in any southern state. Yet, their proximity to slave states made them inviting havens for escaped slaves and manumitted blacks seeking a new start. Their fight to abolish slavery, if won, would leave them with what they hoped would be a manageable number of free black neighbors, and most hoped that keeping that number small would allow for peaceful race relations and successful assimilation of the black population into white society.

Thus, although more and more southerners chose to hold as tightly as possible to the wolf's ear for as long as they could, Pennsylvania gradualists chose to loosen their grip slowly and let the wolf go once they persuaded it not to bite. From the very beginning this choice contained elements of humanitarianism mixed with white self-preservation through racial control. Many opposed slavery for the sake of the enslaved, and the system's abuse, exploitation, and destruction of families truly disturbed some whites morally. Yet, even those who cared about the slaves wanted equally to protect white Pennsylvanians. They fought to end slavery in their state so they could avoid both divine retribution and race war.

This cautious, decidedly patriarchal approach provided a common ground between early abolitionists and colonizationists. Though the PAS as a body never endorsed colonization, some Pennsylvania abolitionists had long considered removing free blacks to the western territories or other areas distant from the white population. Before the Revolution some Quakers, including Anthony Benezet, toyed with the idea, and between the war and the founding of the American Colonization Society in 1817, a handful of abolitionists pondered the issue, as I will show in the early chapters of this book.[11]

For many early advocates of relocating free blacks, British colonization at Sierra Leone provided an important model. This project began
as an extension of the general policy of the English to remove unwanted
populations from the British Isles. It began in 1584 when the explorer
Richard Hakluyt pointed out that British prisons were full of convicts
and suggested they be sent to distant parts of the empire. Not only did
Queen Elizabeth agree to send "rogues, vagabonds and sturdy beggars"
to North America, she also considered taking the additional step of sending "blackamoores" to Africa. Though African repatriation did not gain
support for two more centuries, the removal of criminals and paupers
did. The result was the 1718 Transportation Act, which set into motion
a system that resulted in thousands of vagrants and convicts being sent
first to North America and later to Australia. Although the movement
was clearly designed to rid Britain of undesirable subjects, some advocates of removal stressed the possibility of reforming criminals and giving settlers a fresh start. This same mix of motives influenced the Sierra
Leone project.[12]

Historians of British colonization in Sierra Leone have engaged in
many of the same debates as those who study American colonizationists'
efforts in Liberia. On the one hand, some have highlighted the British
government's desire to limit the relief rolls by removing the poor and unwanted. The poor laws were inadequate in dealing with white indigents,
and they were not expanded to deal with the growing black population.
This situation worsened once Britain ended the slave trade and had to
deal with the issue of "recaptives," or Africans rescued from the illicit
trade. British humanitarians such as Granville Sharp, Thomas Fowell
Buxton, and the reformers of the Clapham Sect became involved, lending their antislavery and reform credentials to the endeavor. Describing
Buxton in ways that sound similar to Hugh Davis's characterization of
Bacon, Howard Temperley has contributed much to understanding the
role of evangelical conscience in British African colonization. He argued
that Buxton and his fellow abolitionists believed that Britain had a duty
to uplift the continent their government had been exploiting for centuries by creating a new Africa based on Christianity, civilization, and
commerce. On the other hand, Mavis Campbell, although conceding the
role of the humanitarians, has added that there was a more sinister motive behind government involvement in the scheme. She argued that the
government began to listen to ideas put forth by philanthropists to "regenerate" Africa only after realizing that the growing black population,
fueled largely by the arrival of recaptives and black loyalist refugees from

the American Revolution, would be "dependent on public support." Finally, some have argued that ultimately Sierra Leone served as an important base of operations from which to combat the slave trade and gave New World blacks a chance for freedom and independence.[13]

American reformers could take what they wanted from British colonization and apply it to their own efforts. Given the level of transatlantic contact, especially among the Quaker community, early American abolitionists saw the Sierra Leone project through the lens of abolition and moral reform. At the same time, the politically minded antislavery nationalists saw government involvement as crucial and sought to duplicate British efforts by bringing colonization clearly into the American political program. On the reform side, the PAS as a body even considered resettlement and did not completely reject it until the late 1830s.

Indeed, the late 1820s saw many PAS members join the colonization society, seeing it as an extension, rather than a rejection, of their previous antislavery work. To begin with, gradualists and colonizationists both sought to change society by working through the system. PAS members, mostly doctors, lawyers, and other elites in Pennsylvania society, fought the institution of slavery through the courts on a case-by-case basis, choosing to sue for the liberty and rights of individual black clients. Likely influenced by the radical turn taken by the French Revolution, as well as the social turmoil among the lower orders in their own state, they feared that too much agitation at the grassroots level would alienate lawmakers and encourage disruption of the fragile union. Thus, they chose their battles and their tactics carefully.[14] The state's colonizationists agreed on most of these points. They shared faith in elite leadership, respect for the existing system, and willingness to work within it, a belief that successful emancipation must be gradual and include a program to prepare the freedmen, respect for property rights, and a desire to win over, rather than alienate, slaveholders. Thanks partly to the gradualist legacy, and partly to geography, both strains of the colonization movement drew support in Pennsylvania.

Humanitarian colonizationists dominated the PCS by the mid-1830s. Even as they continued antislavery work, they generally maintained that white Americans would never accept free blacks, and they found immediatist efforts to force the issue distasteful. The problem with their plan was that rather than fighting the prevailing racial tension, it actually increased it. Any scheme that relied on targeting and removing a specific group of people would by nature rest on, and even increase, bias. In this case, the bias was based on what had come to be seen as racially specific characteristics, and even the most humanitarian colonization-ists became increasingly obsessed with the idea of blacks' "degraded condition" and believed that American racial antipathy was a permanent hindrance to racial equality. By not giving up completely on black uplift efforts, especially in the field of education, however, they provided the main bridge connecting all three movements. As we will see, they even forced the ACS to reorganize in the late 1830s in an effort to return the parent society to what they saw as its true principles.[15]

As the humanitarians fought to retain control of the movement, they were forced to work with colonizationists who supported the endeavor as part of a political movement to create a homogenous white republic. Like many who embraced Free Soil and political antislavery in the 1840s and 1850s, politically motivated colonizationists saw antislavery more as part of a specific political agenda than as a traditional reform movement. Focusing on politics over humanitarian reform, they shared Mercer's vision of resettlement as the way to rid the country of a population that they believed stifled American progress. According to this view, slavery was an antiquated and inefficient labor system that hampered the nation's overall development and left the United States with a racially divided population.

Supporters who focused on colonization as part of a broader political agenda embraced resettlement to prevent a permanent lower class from threatening national progress. Even if they wanted freedom for both races, they placed most of their concern with the political future of the young republic. They wanted to preserve their white country by keeping blacks from challenging racial and national purity. Hoping to avoid divine retribution, race war, racial mixing, and sectional tension, this group saw racial homogeneity as a crucial characteristic of a strong nation, so they embraced colonization.[16] As we will see, this idea would live on through the Free Soil and Republican parties of the antebellum years.

Whereas some southern planters had supported colonization early on as a means of removing only free blacks and thus strengthening slavery, by the 1830s more had begun to understand the antislavery implications of both strains of the movement, and fewer and fewer were willing to support colonization. Though colonization remained popular in the North and border South, it began to face greater opposition not just from immediatists but from the planters of the lower South, especially as the cotton gin made slavery increasingly profitable.

* * *

Although this southern opposition was strong, the outcry of black Americans and white members of the immediatist abolition movement also helped ensure colonization's failure in Pennsylvania and throughout the country. Thus, this book would be incomplete without addressing the rise of the immediate abolition movement.

The best study of the emergence of immediatism to date is Richard S. Newman's *The Transformation of American Abolitionism*. Newman contrasts the gradualists, whose main base of support was Pennsylvania, with the immediatists, who were strongest in Massachusetts. He shows how the more elite tactics of PAS supporters were largely replaced in the 1830s by the more vocal, grassroots tactics of the immediatists. Crucial to this transformation was the willingness of the latter to include African Americans and women in their organizations and their campaign. These tactics, he argues, gave the immediatists a commanding presence, leaving Americans to "ever remember the aggressive post-1830s movement as the essence of organized antislavery."[17]

In many ways, I agree with Newman's assessment, but my study shows that, though the Massachusetts immediatists may be remembered as the most vocal among the abolitionists, the epicenter of American antislavery did not necessarily shift from Pennsylvania to Massachusetts. At the same time, my focus on Pennsylvania reveals that the relationship between different types of abolitionists was not necessarily as tense as has been implied. When all three groups—gradualists, colonizationists, and immediatists—are added into the equation at the same time, Pennsylvania antislavery remains vibrant and active throughout the 1830s and beyond. After all, as the 1838 Pennsylvania Hall incident reveals, Garrison himself knew that Pennsylvania immediatists were reluctant to criticize their gradualist cohorts, and when they did speak out against colonization it lacked the vigor he desired. He realized that if he wanted to push the national antislavery movement in a more radical direction he would have to force Pennsylvania reformers to join his immediatist crusade wholeheartedly. Although many joined the immediatists in the 1830s, others sought to maintain ties to multiple organizations and to build coalitions throughout the 1840s and 1850s.

In this atmosphere, even the immediatists and colonizationists learned from each other and shared common features. To begin with, colonizationists pioneered some of the tactics immediatists later used. Most important, they began the process of bringing antislavery to a broader audience. The ACS and its auxiliaries drew leadership from the same elite ranks that provided the key players in gradualist circles, but they also employed traveling agents to enlist financial and moral support from all levels of society. They celebrated and publicized even small contributions of money, clothes, books, and many other goods and services offered to aid their cause, and they employed the press in both pamphlet and periodical form. Significantly, they also tried to reach out to women and blacks for support. By introducing antislavery to all strata of society, the colonization society awakened many men and women who would later make up the main body, and leaders, of the immediatist groups.[18] Despite these similarities, immediatists and colonizationists often found themselves at odds, primarily because the former were more willing to take into account the fears and desires of black Americans.

* * *

All facets of the antislavery movement contained these competing yet sometimes reinforcing lines of thought. Humanitarian colonizationists often crossed the line into what has been described as abolitionist territory, even if tepidly. At the same time, many abolitionists eventually turned to the Free Soil and Republican agendas, which focused on exclusion of slaves, and often free blacks, from the new territories and states in the American west to keep the new lands open to whites only.[19] By using individual Pennsylvania colonizationists as case studies, we can better understand all three avenues of the state's antislavery movement. By opening a window into both strains of the colonization movement, each of which accorded well with the state's antislavery legacy, we can examine the elements of control—both social and political—that were so crucial to both gradual abolitionists and colonizationists.

As Chapter 1 will show, Pennsylvania antislavery, like American antislavery in general, proceeded from several motives, one of which was an effort to limit the black population from the beginning. When that did not work, gradual abolitionists urged the freeing of those slaves who had been brought into the colony. Once the slaves were freed, the PAS immediately began efforts to train them as useful members of American society. Its efforts gained for the state a reputation as a beacon of liberty, though by the turn of the century an influx of escaped slaves and black migrants caused it to question its efforts. At the same time many of the PAS's white neighbors began to blame it for the state's growing black population. The drive to secure removal of blacks fit into this overall scheme, and by 1817 the PAS and other gradualist groups were meeting to question, and try to come to terms with, their declining status at virtually the same time the ACS was being founded in Washington, D.C. Thus, I begin by looking at the state of the PAS in 1817 and trace the history of the organization to that date.

Next, I examine the growth of the colonization movement. The American Colonization Society initially received a lukewarm reception in Pennsylvania, but within a decade of its 1817 founding national ACS leaders were desperately seeking the support of the middle states and began to agitate in earnest for converts to the cause. Chapter 2 shows how, through an effective marketing plan, the organization tapped into Pennsylvanians' existing fears of retribution and racial mixing, while emphasizing the humanitarian aspects of colonization in an all-out push to win support in Pennsylvania. By the end of the 1820s the ACS had gained many important members.

Chapters 3 and 4 tell the stories of two of the most vocal of these converts—former PAS members Mathew Carey and Elliott Cresson. Carey was a Philadelphia printer and Catholic exile from Ireland who opposed bondage and oppression of any class of people. At the same time, however, he was an ardent supporter of the political aspects of colonization and was enticed by the movement's promise that it would be a modernizing force for the young republic. The story of his life, and of his work for the ACS, illustrates the political side of the movement. At the same time, Cresson saw something entirely different in colonization. He joined the PCS in the hopes of redeeming the African continent by attacking the slave trade at its source and encouraging missionary work, as well as uplifting the black population in the United States. His story shows just how sincerely some gradualists and colonizationists opposed slavery for more humanitarian and less selfish reasons, though, as we will see, even he sought to control those he hoped to help. For both of these men, colonization was an extension of emancipationist efforts, though each joined out of different motives.

Since some have portrayed black resistance to colonization as swift and strong, I will next turn to a case study of one of the most famous black leaders of the time, the wealthy Philadelphia sailmaker and community leader James Forten. His story will reveal the way in which the state's free black population played a number of important roles in the drama that unfolded as the three branches of antislavery interacted. Though appreciative of PAS efforts, black leaders such as Forten were never willing to be controlled. His story bolsters the claims of historians

Floyd J Miller, Dickson D. Bruce Jr., and Mary Tyler McGraw that a number of black Americans were interested in emigration when they thought it would offer true leadership opportunity. Once they saw that blacks would not be granted the level of respect they had hoped for, though, they changed their minds and became suspicious of white-led colonization efforts. This independent spirit was what led to most blacks' ultimate rejection of the ACS.[20] By studying Forten's life, we can see the changes in Pennsylvania's racial climate through the lenses of the black community and evaluate the hopes and failures of both gradual abolition and colonization. Through Forten we can also catch a glimpse of the renewed hope that came with the growth of immediatism.

My last case studies take the ACS and PCS into the Civil War years and show another dimension—the self-help side of colonization—by examining the contributions of Philadelphia's Benjamin Coates and Pittsburgh's Martin R. Delany. Both of these men saw potential for African colonization to lead to commercial success for African American colonists. Coates, a young white Quaker who shared most of Cresson's vision, played an important role in shifting Pennsylvania colonization's focus from freeing slaves to uplifting the black race through the Free Produce movement. He also provided an important bridge between gradualism and colonization because he, unlike Cresson and others who chose to join one organization or the other, remained an important figure in both the PAS and PCS, fighting for black education and uplift through each organization. He also brought an economic agenda into the colonization movement, combining a dream of cotton cultivation in Africa with Cresson's emphasis on spreading Christianity.

Finally, I conclude the case studies by returning to the African American perspective and examining another commercial colonization venture put forth by Delany. Like Forten, Delany saw a possibility that African colonization could create the opportunity for black leadership and self-determination, and his ideas were much like those proposed by Coates. He wanted to found an African colony independent of the ACS that would grow cotton and thus compete with slave-grown southern cotton. Like Coates, he wanted to end slavery but focused on proving racial equality to benefit free blacks as well, and I conclude the book by showcasing an emigration scheme he developed in the late 1850s.

* * *

Gradual emancipation, colonization, and immediate abolition all competed for support among Pennsylvania's antislavery community during the first half of the nineteenth century. White and black supporters of each agenda contributed ideas and dreams in the larger effort to somehow solve America's racial dilemma. This book reveals how complicated and multifaceted antislavery was by showing that the movement contained elements of exclusion and limitation as well as racial improvement and black uplift all along. It also shows that colonization's antislavery appeal had a dual character that gained support from a number of followers for very different reasons. A study of ideas, this book seeks to understand the leaders and intellectuals who supported colonization and emigration. Only by examining the broad range of arguments through the eyes of those who believed the rhetoric can we begin to understand what colonization, abolition, and, most important, "antislavery" meant to the very people who participated in the movements. Because these terms could have different meanings for each person who uttered them, it is important to place these characters into the context of their own cultural and intellectual worlds. The case studies that follow provide a better understanding of the overall antislavery movement by doing just that. The story ends as I assess the legacies of gradualism, colonization, and immediatism and trace exclusionary efforts into the political arena of Civil War America.

1 / "Many negroes in these parts may prove prejudissial several wayes to us and our posteraty": The Crucial Elements of Exclusion and Social Control in Pennsylvania's Early Antislavery Movement

America's antislavery movement underwent a sea change in 1817. The oldest champion of black freedom reported to the annual convention of American abolition societies that year that "the number of those actively engaged in the cause of the oppressed Africans is very small." Struggling since 1804 to gain a quorum at many of their scheduled meetings, the Pennsylvania Abolition Society blamed this apathy on the retirement of many of its seasoned leaders, combined with "a mistaken impression that the work is nearly accomplished." Their effort to lead the freed along a path of social conditioning was wilting as well. Instead of unquestioningly accepting white advice and guidance, free blacks were taking their destiny into their own hands and trying to enjoy their liberty on their own terms. The PAS agenda of slowly but steadily fighting for the rights of African Americans while serving as liaison between the black and white communities was failing, and the group was being forced to re-evaluate its role in the struggle for freedom.[1]

That same year the American Colonization Society (ACS) appeared on the national antislavery scene to compete with the gradualists for the spotlight. A close look at the gradualist legacy will illuminate the role colonization would later play in the antislavery movement after the 1820s. Examining the gradualists' goals and tactics, as well as the challenges they faced by this pivotal year, will reveal much about both movements and their common characteristics, most important of which was a need to oversee and control the free black population. It will also shed light on how gradual abolitionists interacted with the growing free black

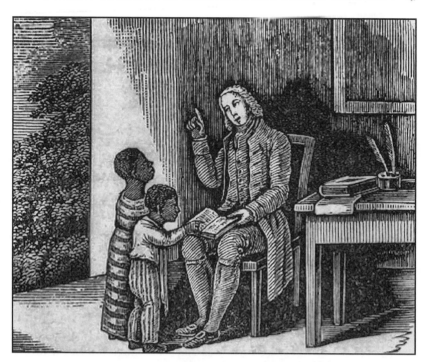

FIGURE 3. Anthony Benezet Reading to Colored Children. (This is a public domain image from Wiki Images.)

leadership and how their efforts to limit the black population from the beginning set a precedent for later efforts to remove those who had found asylum in the state.

Pennsylvania has long been celebrated not only as the birthplace of American liberty but also as the home of the antislavery movement. German Mennonites and Quakers first protested North America's system of human bondage in 1688, and Philadelphia Quakers banned slave ownership among members in 1774. A year later, they formed the first abolition society in the colonies. This group, called the Society for the Relief of Free Negroes Unlawfully Held in Bondage, was short-lived. It was resurrected in 1784 with the help of non-Quakers, including Benjamin Franklin and Benjamin Rush. Three years later it became the Pennsylvania Society for Promoting the Abolition of Slavery, and the Relief of Free Negroes, Unlawfully Held in Bondage. Still composed mostly of Quakers, this group took up the crusade to end slavery in the state, and in the meantime, the Pennsylvania legislature passed a gradual abolition act in 1780. Few slaves remained in the state by 1800.[2]

Though Pennsylvania's founders made no real effort to prohibit slavery in the beginning, resistance to human bondage began by the end of the seventeenth century. Benjamin Furly, a Quaker agent of William Penn, may have made the first attempt to keep slaves out by proposing a law that would "let no blacks be brought in directly." According to Furly's wishes, any slaves who had been brought to Pennsylvania from Virginia, Maryland, "or elsewhere" would have been declared free after eight years. Apparently the agent thought the West Jersey Constitution contained a similar provision, but no such law existed in Jersey, and none was adopted in Pennsylvania. Indeed, 150 Africans arrived in the colony just three years after the Quaker founders and were eagerly purchased and employed in the work of clearing land and building the city of Philadelphia. Between 1682 and 1705 about one of every fifteen Philadelphia families managed to acquire one or more enslaved laborers, and the situation began to bother some Quakers almost immediately.[3]

The result was an attack on the slave trade, which began with a petition from Germantown in 1688. The Germantown petition, like most protests that followed, appealed to both religious conscience and white self-interest. The authors cited three reasons for opposing slavery. First, it was morally wrong. Not only was slavery a tragic violation of the Golden Rule, it also forced God's creatures to commit adultery by tearing families apart and making people live together in forced situations in the New World. Also, the moral taint of human bondage discouraged European immigration to the colony. Finally, the system posed a dangerous threat to both Quaker souls and the physical safety of whites. The petitioners asked if slave owners would be willing to violate their nonviolent principles and defend themselves in the face of insurrection. "If once these slaves (which they say are so wicked and stubborn men) should join themselves, fight for their freedom and handel their masters and mastrisses, as they did handel them before; will these masters and mastrisses tacke the sword at hand and warr against these poor slaves?" They added that such a situation was likely and perhaps justified: "Have these negers not as much right to fight for their freedom, as you have to keep them slaves?"[4]

A group of Quakers led by George Keith issued a similar protest five years later. This group also used moral and religious justification while appealing to white self-interest. To begin with, the group warned that buying slaves was the same as buying stolen goods, yet worse, since it would be "accounted a far greater crime under Moses' Law" to buy stolen people than stolen property. Like the previous petition, the Keithians warned fellow Quakers to abide by the Golden Rule, and they quoted Deuteronomy and Exodus to argue against the cruel treatment of slaves and the ripping apart of slave families. They concluded by issuing a stern warning that would appear in many antislavery tracts that followed— all men were created by God, and He would eventually seek justice for His abused children. Turning to the book of Revelation, they cautioned: "*Brethren*, let us hearken to the voice of the Lord, who saith, *Come out of* Babylon, *my people, that ye be not partakers of her sins, and that ye receive not her Plagues; for her sins have reached unto Heaven, and God hath remembered her Iniquities; for he that leads into Captivity shall go into Captivity.*" The solution? Quakers should not buy slaves except to set them free. Those who already had slaves should let them go after they had worked long enough to repay the owner for their purchase price or, in the case of babies born into slavery, the cost of their upbringing. Finally, those who had slaves should "teach them to read, and give them a Christian Education."[5]

Other Quakers added their voices to this budding antislavery crusade, focusing mostly on importation. In 1696, the Yearly Meeting cited "several" papers, including those by William Southeby and Cadwalader Morgan, as influencing their decision to advise Friends to "be careful not to encourage the bringing in of any more Negroes." As a result, the Pennsylvania Quakers wrote to Friends and suppliers in the West Indies asking them to stop sending slaves. This did not work, because two years later the Philadelphia meeting asked members to write to Friends in Barbados and ask them to "forbear sending any negroes to this place, because they are too numerous here." A group of Friends, including Southeby, drafted the letter, explaining that the Yearly Meeting had concluded that "many negroes in these parts may prove prejudissial several wayes to us and our posteraty" and had agreed that "endeavors should bee used to put a stop to the Importing of them." If the letter had any effect, it was temporary. In 1711 Chester Monthly Meeting protested the buying of slaves brought into Pennsylvania, and leaders reminded Friends about their 1696 advice. Four years later a Philadelphia Quaker merchant, Jonathan Dickinson, wrote to a relative in Jamaica to "intreat" him "not to send any more" slaves because "the generality of our people are against any coming into the country."[6]

Banning the importation of slaves was central to this early phase of the antislavery movement. Chester Monthly Meeting played a large role in this endeavor, petitioning the Yearly Meeting in 1711, 1715, and 1716, but because 60 percent of Yearly Meeting leaders owned slaves, they only cautioned Quakers against the practice. The petition drive continued, however, with Quaker farmers and artisans calling for a ban on the further importation of slaves several times between 1711 and 1729, and the Yearly Meeting strengthened its early statement in 1730. Again, this was merely a caution rather than a directive.[7]

The Pennsylvania Assembly tried to provide a stronger response to these pleas. They attempted to prohibit slave importation by levying duties beginning in 1700. In most cases the Crown repealed such taxes, but the colonists eventually found a way to avoid this interference by passing acts and not telling the government until enough time had passed that they had already become law. After the famous New York slave insurrection of 1712, the assembly passed a high import tax of twenty pounds per slave, but by 1729 the tax had dwindled to two pounds. In 1761 they raised the tax to ten pounds, and when this tax reached twenty pounds again in 1773, the traffic in human labor in Pennsylvania halted.[8]

These efforts mirrored similar action taken throughout the North American colonies as British slave imports to these colonies grew from 37,400 in the period between 1701 and 1725 to 116,900 in the years between 1751 and 1775. South Carolina and Georgia began trying to limit imports in 1698, and the former tried to prohibit the slave trade altogether in 1760, but the Privy Council forbade this action and reprimanded the governor. North Carolina imposed prohibitive duties in 1786, and Virginia made similar efforts from 1710 to 1772 when the House of Burgesses tried to petition the king to stop the trade to their state. In these planting colonies, opposition to the trade was most often based on fear of insurrection, as historian W. E. B. Du Bois showed long ago. He claimed that similar efforts were made in the farming colonies of New York, Delaware, New Jersey, and Pennsylvania because the system was not as profitable in those states, but the fear factor applied in these colonies as well. Finally, Du Bois contended that opposition to the slave trade in the New England colonies was "from the first based solely on moral grounds, with some social arguments."[9]

Motives for focusing on the slave trade before attacking slavery itself were complicated. Many Quakers realized that traffic in human beings relied on force and thus violated their principle of nonviolence. Also, concentrating on the trade allowed these abolitionists to express their qualms about slavery yet earn respect for moderation. At the same time, many believed that without fresh slave imports from abroad, slavery would eventually die out. In contrast, calling for immediate release of all slaves would have branded them as radicals and offended those whose consciences they hoped to awaken, so they used limited, short-term goals in order to make their overall agenda of emancipation more easily attainable. Finally, by arguing against the slave trade, Quakers managed to ease their consciences without causing financial problems for the slave owners in their ranks.[10]

At the same time, the focus on importation reveals an element of self-interest. Even the most benevolent whites feared the growing black population and the threat of insurrection. Stopping the trade as soon as possible limited the threat by keeping the black population relatively small. Quaker abolitionists attacked slavery at times of high importation because the larger the enslaved population, the greater the danger. The legislature shared the fear and joined the effort to limit importation. In seeking import duties, they listed as their main motivations concern for the spread of disease, alarm at the news of slave revolts in other areas, and dread over the prospect of an increase in the number of runaways and petty criminals.[11]

Both the legislature and abolitionists agreed that the enslaved population needed to be kept as small as possible because the system presented a number of threats to white society. First, if the system was indeed morally wrong, then it must at some point invoke the wrath of God. Indeed, many Quakers saw the Seven Years' War as evidence of God's displeasure, and they renewed their antislavery efforts in response. Also, slavery encouraged owners to be lazy and greedy, two major areas of contention among Quakers. As if that were not bad enough, it put whites in peril. What if, as the Germantown group warned, slaves did rise up? Whites would either be killed or forced to disregard the church's nonviolent tenets in order to defend themselves. Though they hoped to eventually do away with slavery altogether, Quaker abolitionists had to first focus on the short-term solution of ending the trade. If they succeeded, when they turned to general emancipation, they would be dealing with as small a population of freedmen as possible.

Anthony Benezet's works illustrate this connection. Benezet was the quintessential Quaker abolitionist. He joined the crusade in 1750 and soon began publishing antislavery tracts. He ultimately played a large role in bringing abolition beyond the bounds of the Quaker meeting and into the larger society. He convinced the Philadelphia Yearly Meeting to accept abolition, and he managed to persuade them to publish his 1754 *Epistle of Caution and Advice, Concerning the Buying and Keeping of Slaves.* He also influenced non-Quaker abolitionists in both Britain and the colonies, including Granville Sharp, John Wesley, Thomas Clarkson, and Benjamin Rush. And when the state legislature was considering the gradual abolition bill, he personally visited each member to seek support for the measure.[12]

Like the petitioners before him, Benezet saw the slave trade as both morally wrong and dangerous to white interests. He described the slave trade as murder and insisted that Europeans deliberately caused African nations to war with each other and take captives for the market. Not only did this encourage murder, it was also "manstealing" and a gross violation of God's law, and it provided a flimsy excuse for participating in the trade. Countering arguments that the captives were better off toiling in the Americas than being executed at home, he asked if fighting a just war would make it acceptable for the English to enslave and sell the French. He also used firsthand accounts to describe in sad detail the violence of the trade and the abuse of slaves, pointing out that blacks were just "as susceptible of Pain and Grief" as whites, and calling on his readers to put themselves in the slaves' shoes. He asked, "What Distress can we conceive equal to the Alarms, and anxiety, and Wrath, which must succeed one another in the Breasts of the tender parents, or affectionate children, in continual Danger of being torn one from another and dragged into a state of cruel Bondage!" To further illustrate his point about family destruction, he described a tragic case in which a family lost its father figure and provider to the trade, showing how slavery hurt not only those taken captive but also those who managed to avoid getting kidnapped.[13]

Whether they realized it or not, slavery put whites in great peril. Benezet pointed out that the system made slave owners feel themselves "more consequential" than others and encouraged them to become lazy and greedy. At the same time it left laboring people and tradesmen feeling "slighted, disregarded, and robbed of the natural opportunities of Labour common in other countries." As a result it discouraged white European immigration. But these problems were fairly minor. The real threat lay in the form of retribution at the hands of either God or the enslaved. Because of the violence and theft inherent in the system, it greatly displeased God, and he would eventually make things right. Benezet, who introduced the argument that many of the calamities the colonies were facing were products of divine retribution, warned that it would only get worse. Slaveholders must free their slaves and help them find jobs "not only as an Act of Justice to the Individuals, but as a Debt due, on Account of the Oppression and Injustice perpetrated on them . . . and as the best means to avert the judgements of God." Either God or the enslaved would eventually punish not only the slave owners but also their white neighbors, and he pointed to the unrest in Barbados to show that the larger the black population became, the greater the danger.[14]

Benezet proposed a four-step plan to end slavery and thus prevent such a disaster. First, "all farther Importation [must] be absolutely prohibited." For most this would have been enough, because this step solved the issue of violence inherent in the trade. For Benezet, however, it was just the beginning, since keeping slaves was as morally wrong as owning them. Therefore, once the slaves already in the colonies had served long enough to repay the owner for money he had spent on their purchase or rearing, they should be freed. Like indentured servants, slaves guilty of willfully neglecting their duty could be required to serve additional time. He proposed that the freed be treated in a manner consistent with English poor laws, suggesting that they be "enrolled in the County Court, and obliged to be a resident during a certain Number of Years within the said County, under the Inspection of the Overseers of the Poor." Benezet's last step called for restitution in the form of land grants. He argued that giving the freed land would make them taxable citizens and give them a stake in society.[15]

For Benezet's plan to work, the black population would have to be small, and before they could be freed, slaves would have to be carefully prepared. For this reason, Benezet joined fellow gradualists in pushing first for an end to the slave trade by supporting the efforts to tax imports. Aware of public concern over the idea of emancipation, he addressed the fears of his white neighbors by insisting that the freed should not be sent to Africa because "that would be to expose them, in a strange Land, to greater Difficulties than many of them labour under at present." Yet, "to set them suddenly free here would be perhaps attended with no less difficulty, for undisciplined as they are in Religion and virtue, they might give a loose to those evil Habits, which the Fear of a Master would have restrained." The solution was to teach the slaves Christianity and prepare them to take care of themselves so they could prove to doubters that they deserved their freedom. He believed this plan would work as long as Pennsylvania, and the other North American colonies for that matter, did not become the type of large-scale slave societies found in the Caribbean.[16]

Once Quaker abolitionists managed to convince the Yearly Meeting to forbid Friends to buy or sell slaves, they began phase two of their agenda—a push for emancipation. Keith's followers had emancipated a small number of slaves, and beginning in 1735 a few Philadelphia Quakers had started using their wills to this end. In the 1740s this trend grew, but most manumissions were gradual, requiring additional years of indenture. By the 1750s, however, fewer wills stipulated additional service, and more slaves were freed outright. Indeed, the Yearly Meeting took its first real stand against slaveholding in 1754 and warned Friends not to import or buy slaves in 1755. Also that year they suggested for the first time that slaveholding, not just participation in the slave trade, violated Christianity. Issuing Benezet's *An Epistle of Caution and Advice, Concerning the Buying and Keeping of Slaves*, the Yearly Meeting reminded Friends of the role of theft and war in providing captives for the slave trade. This document also asked owners to treat their slaves kindly and prepare them for freedom. After issuing this statement, the Yearly Meeting began a crusade to convince slaveholding Friends of the error of their ways.[17]

More than twenty years elapsed before the Yearly Meeting declared itself free of slaveholding. After all, the commitment to not acquire more slaves carried no financial loss, but agreeing to release valuable property would lead to great financial sacrifice. The Seven Years' War contributed greatly to effecting this change. Two years after the war began, the Quaker organization moved from opposing the slave trade to crying out against slavery itself. For the first time, leaders formally called for sanctions against members who imported, bought, or sold slaves. Seeing the war as the divine retribution early abolitionists had warned about, Quaker reformers included antislavery in their push for moral revitalization of the church and called for at least partial disowning of those who refused to give up their slaves. Two years after the Yearly Meeting adopted its new stance, it received a boost in gaining support from non-Quakers, including Benjamin Franklin, one of Pennsylvania's most famous abolitionists.[18]

By 1760 slave importation into the colony reached its peak, and by the end of the Seven Years' War, the black population exceeded 1,400. This was a small proportion of the colony's overall population of roughly 183,703 in 1760, but it was enough to concern whites, who began to fear the possibility of violence and the strange customs of the new residents. As a result, a "number of inhabitants" of Philadelphia sent the assembly a remonstrance against "the mischievous consequences attending the Practice of importing slaves into this Province" and asked for a law against further importation. The Pennsylvania assembly responded by increasing import duties until they were high enough to prevent further traffic in humans.[19]

In 1780 Pennsylvania became the first state to pass an abolition law, but the law had a number of limitations. It provided for gradual freedom so that slaveholders could recapture their investment rather than forcing them to release the enslaved outright. Owners were allowed to keep their current slaves and free their offspring after periods of indenture. Also, lawmakers exercised great care in preventing a situation that would shift the burdens of emancipation to nonslaveholders by requiring owners to post bonds of thirty pounds each on all manumitted slaves to provide for their care in the case of indigence. They also passed special laws regulating the conduct of blacks by prohibiting vagrancy, interaction with slaves, and racial mixing. Further legislation required that all children of free blacks and those of mixed heritage be bound out until their twenties.[20]

At this point abolitionists began to think about the future of race relations in America. They faced three choices. They could ignore the blacks who were, or would eventually become, free. They could work to help ameliorate the conditions of free blacks. Or they could fight to remove them. Most chose to take on the added task of protecting the legal rights of the freed while pushing to "uplift" their new neighbors socially. Just a few months before he died, Benezet persuaded fellow Quakers to revive the abolition society, naming it the Society for the Relief of Free Negroes. They quickly reached out to like-minded non-Quakers, opening the society up to larger membership. In 1787 they renamed the organization the Pennsylvania Society for Promoting the Abolition of Slavery, the Relief of Free Negroes Unlawfully Held in Bondage, and for Improving the Condition of the African Race.

The reorganization of this group stemmed from Benezet's successful defense of a group of kidnapped free blacks and illustrates the gradualist tendency to push for attainable goals rather than employ radical means that would alienate whites. Just before the American Revolution, the English abolitionist Granville Sharp had suggested that since divine law was an accepted part of English common law, it would not be illegal to help escaped slaves. He went further in 1793 by calling on American abolitionists to disobey the newly passed Fugitive Slave Law (the nation's first law dealing with the issue on the national level). American gradualists, however, were not yet ready to take such drastic actions. When Benezet consulted Benjamin Rush, a fellow Philadelphia abolitionist, about Sharp's recommendation for civil disobedience, Rush answered, *"They would knock us in the head if we did."* Finding Rush's advice more sage than Sharp's in this case, Benezet determined that helping those free under recognized law would have to serve as a starting point. He pushed for the reorganization of the PAS in hopes that it would do just that. The issue of civil disobedience was left for the next generation of abolitionists to embrace.[21]

After the abolition society was reorganized, Benjamin Franklin was elected president, and Benjamin Rush and Tenche Cox were made secretaries. Franklin's affiliation brought the group much-needed prestige and legitimacy, but James Pemberton, a Quaker, remained in charge behind the scenes. Putting the more prestigious name out front and hiding the extent of Quaker involvement, in an era in which Friends were still seen as disloyal because of their pacifism during the war, proved a successful tactic. Within a decade PAS enthusiasm had spread. A number of states founded similar societies to protest slavery and fight on behalf of the freed. In 1794, delegates from these different groups came together in Philadelphia for the first national convention of antislavery societies.[22]

Meanwhile the PAS immediately went to work overseeing the black community and trying to condition them for productive citizenship. Given their history of supervising the morals of fellow Friends, these reformers were on familiar ground. They were optimistic and reported to London Quakers that the freed were behaving "*more* orderly" than poor whites. Still concerned with those in bondage as well as those who had gained freedom, they continued to push for revision of the abolition law. The legislature responded by providing that enslaved families could not be separated by more than ten miles, and that those guilty of kidnapping free blacks and selling them into slavery in other states would be punished. They also made it harder to cheat the original law by sending children out of state before they reached the age at which they should be freed. With this revision, abolitionists had forced the state to add protection of blacks to their agenda.[23]

Emancipation in the North occurred during an era filled with the spirit of general reform. Around 1800 an evangelical zeal emerged throughout the region, spurring the Second Great Awakening and fueling the growth of benevolent societies and voluntary associations which sought to educate the poor, provide for the needy, and elevate the morals of all. Concerned all along with the effect of enslavement on human character, and feeling a patriarchal responsibility for the formerly enslaved, abolitionists joined these crusades. Having achieved the original aim of abolishing slavery in the state, the society directed its attention "to the moral culture and mental elevation" of free blacks. Appointing themselves moral guardians of the black community, they presented their advice in black churches, mutual aid societies, and even homes.[24]

Educating the former slaves played a central role in the crusade to uplift free blacks. This stemmed from a belief shared by many of Pennsylvania's white intellectuals and PAS members, most notably Benezet and Rush, that educating the children of the poor, regardless of their color, would help reduce crime. In 1787 Rush warned the citizens of Philadelphia that the "ignorance and vices" of poor children "contaminated" the children of "the higher ranks of society" and that the trend could be stopped only through education. This attitude went hand in hand with the PAS agenda of keeping the freed in line in order to preserve the social order and protect both blacks and whites. Most subscribed to environmentalist theories that the races were inherently equal but that the condition of enslavement had held blacks back. They argued that since "the unhappy man who has long been treated as a brute animal, too frequently sinks beneath the common standard of the human species" and "the galling chains that bind his body, do also fetter his intellectual faculties, and impair the social affections of his heart," education and social conditioning would be crucial.[25]

Benezet's works offer insight into understanding the importance of social conditioning to the gradual abolitionist movement. Like most intellectuals of the time he was an environmentalist, and he insisted that slave owners made up the idea of black inferiority to justify slavery. In truth, "the negroes are generally a sensible, humane, and sociable people, and . . . their capacity is as good and as capable of improvement as that of the whites." If blacks seemed inferior, it was because of the conditions they lived under. After all, they faced a language barrier and a hostile master class that had no desire to help them improve. Those who were freed gained incentive and, in many cases, outdid white former servants.[26]

The solution was simple. Educate blacks and provide them the incentive to succeed in this new environment. To secure this end, Benezet founded a school for blacks in Philadelphia in 1759. In 1770, the Quakers opened a similar school, and Benezet used his experience to run it, serving as headmaster. He also continued to solicit funds and contribute his own money and time until his death, upon which he left most of his estate to the institution. At the urging of Benezet and his friend Rush, the Quakers and the PAS expanded these efforts, opening additional facilities in later years.[27]

Of course, Benezet's crusade to educate the freed was also an attempt to control them, but his worldview was one in which the morally enlightened and educated hoped to control the lower order, regardless of color.

As a devout Quaker, Benezet took great care to live a simple, moral life, free of laziness, greed, or ostentation. Outside of abolitionist circles he was known for rebuking young people for dressing inappropriately and for behaving in any manner that would "render [them] less useful than they might otherwise be." Like any good father figure, he was not above offering advice to all youth in the community. In one case his "long connection" with a young woman's father, as well as his "earnest desire" for her "true welfare" prompted him to take the liberty of appealing to her "good inclinations . . . and good sense" to encourage her to resist "giving any countenance to the vain and corrupting dissipation which are proposed to be soon entered upon in this city, in which thou wilt doubtless be pressingly invited to join in." He told her that fellow Friends "much desire that thou wouldst let us have thy company at our religious meetings," and he expressed a sincere desire to help her "break through the tinsel scene of vanity and folly that surrounds us." He reminded another young woman of "the apostle's injunction 'that christian women ought to be arrayed in *modest* apparel, *not costly*, but with *sobriety* and shamefacedness.'"[28]

The term "patriarchal" has gained negative connotations in today's individualistic world, but it meant something quite different in Benezet's day. Roberts Vaux, a Pennsylvania reformer himself, chronicled Benezet's life within a generation after the reformer's death and celebrated his "patriarchal mode of living" which "bore testimony to the consistency of his practice." Again in language that would carry less positive meaning today, Vaux described his subject favorably as "remarkable for his kind and condescending manner." Thus, although it would be easy to see Benezet's efforts to control the freed as arrogant and intrusive, Quaker patriarchalism actually began as an effort to guide fellow Friends to live lives that accorded with the church's ideas. They simply applied their existing social conditioning ideas to their work with the black community. Most opposed general emancipation in favor of private manumission, which would follow a period of social conditioning. Gradualists were on a mission to prove to whites that free blacks would not destroy society, and they used familiar techniques to secure that end.[29]

Feeling a sense of duty to both the freed and the white society, the PAS amended its original plan in 1789. Admitting that a lack of education may have left many unprepared for freedom, it promised to look after the newly freed. In the decade after the group had helped secure emancipation, it had come to believe that "slavery is such an atrocious debasement of human nature, that its very extirpation, if not performed with solicitous care, may sometimes open a source of serious evils." Clearly influenced by the growing unrest of the times, the PAS believed that abolition's ultimate success depended on convincing whites not to fear free blacks. But this would not be easy. The organization admitted that without proper guidance the ex-slave's freedom could become "a misfortune to himself, and prejudicial to society." Feeling a special duty because of its role in pushing for black freedom, the PAS expressed a hope that "attention to emancipated black people . . . will [some day] become a branch of our national police," but it offered to fulfill the role of guardian in the meantime.

To keep this promise the group created four committees to oversee its charges. The committee of inspection had the broad power of superintending "the morals, general conduct, and ordinary situation of the Free Negroes," offering them "advice and instruction; protection from wrongs; and other friendly offices." More ominously, the committee of guardians promised to supervise a system of apprenticeship in which free black children would be bound out like apprentices, "partly by a persuasive influence on parents" and "partly by co-operating with the laws which are, or may be enacted for this and similar purposes." The committee of education agreed to "superintend the school-instruction of the children" and keep vital statistics such as marriage, birth, and manumission records. Finally, the committee of employ would help blacks find jobs, even if it meant "prevailing upon them to bind themselves" out as indentured servants.[30]

This revamping of the PAS reveals an undercurrent of unease that existed even among antislavery people, and changes in Pennsylvania's black population heightened this tension in the next decades. At almost the exact moment the PAS was developing its agenda to manage free blacks, free blacks were developing their own leadership. Richard Newman demonstrates this best in his biography of black leader Richard Allen, describing his crucial role as "the forerunner of modern civil rights activists." He began by working as a liaison between the PAS and the black community, taking recently freed blacks as apprentices in his chimney-sweep business and hiring people of color. Strongly supporting the PAS uplift agenda, he added to it a self-help element, insisting that freed blacks learn useful crafts and work hard to support themselves and their community while remaining humble and pious. Central to this self-help agenda was his work in founding an important black mutual aid society, the Free African Society, in 1787 and clearing the path for independent black religious leadership by founding Mother Bethel

Church at roughly the same time and the African American Episcopal denomination in 1816.[31]

Even as the black leadership class was becoming a force, conditions for free blacks were deteriorating in many ways. Employment opportunities for free blacks were even more limited in the North than in the South, and the PAS, consciously or not, fostered discrimination by encouraging blacks to take a limited number of low-paying jobs rather than fighting for better opportunities. It continued to believe that the structure of American society degraded African Americans by leaving them no incentive, yet it perpetuated the relegation of blacks to the lowest rungs of society.[32] The PAS focused on ameliorating the conditions of blacks, hoping that the small population in Pennsylvania could be trained to serve useful functions in the community or at least be kept under close supervision.

Even as the PAS sought to ameliorate conditions, others continued the struggle to limit the black population in the state, focusing on controlling the number of free blacks. Between 1790 and 1800 the slave population of Philadelphia dwindled considerably, but the free black population increased by 2,661. This meant a total black population of 4,265 in a city of 41,220. Just as the enslaved of Pennsylvania began to complete their indentures, blacks from other states, freed either by their masters or by their own initiative, continued to seek asylum in the state known for philanthropy and a relatively low level of racial intolerance. Because of its proximity to the South, along with its reputation for black freedom, Pennsylvania drew fugitives and immigrants from many parts of the country, particularly from neighboring Virginia. On five different occasions between 1805 and 1814 the legislature considered banning immigration of blacks into Pennsylvania or taxing the state's free blacks to provide for the care of indigents. Though the effort failed, it signaled an era of growing discontent as the black population started to increase.[33]

This demographic change came at an unfortunate time. Particularly in Philadelphia, the second largest city in the country after 1810, general growth began to disrupt the traditional social order. A city undergoing industrialization earlier than many, it attracted a number of immigrants, including whites from throughout the world, free blacks, and fugitive slaves. During periods of economic slump, these migrants competed in a shrinking job pool. Urban growth led to changes in residential boundaries and fostered a large amount of migration within the city, leading Philadelphia to lose its walking-city quality before many others. Because the black population in Philadelphia had been generally smaller and more stable than those in other major cities in the eighteenth century, the growth between 1800 and 1850, though still lagging behind the rate of white population increase, alarmed many observers.[34] This growing population, many with lifestyles and customs foreign to white northerners, caused a panic. Even many whites who had worked to help native blacks establish themselves began to lose confidence in their efforts at uplift.

Despite the success of many of Pennsylvania's freedpeople, the influx of newcomers caused whites to fear a growing public dole, increasing crime statistics, and the possibility of racial mixing or black violence. Although the black population in the almshouse did rise during this period, white immigrants made up the highest share proportionately. Still, most whites thought in terms of numbers rather than proportions. Crime rates were a similar story. Though convictions among blacks had been low in the 1790s, they grew after the turn of the century. By 1810, 45 percent of the prisoners in the Walnut Street Prison were black, and contemporary observers became "convinced that the black population . . . was peculiarly given to gambling, drunkenness, and prostitution." Of course, most black criminals had been convicted of petty theft and other small crimes, and their presence in jail is evidence of the limited opportunities available in an increasingly racist society and the resulting economic desperation rather than inherent black criminality. Contemporary observers, however, did not see it that way. Even abolitionists chose to blame the newcomers. Most whites, however, failed to make even that small distinction and began assuming that "black" meant "poor" at best and "criminal" at worst.[35]

Despite the growing tension, the PAS and black leaders such as Allen were able to promote fairly smooth race relations early on through their work in uplifting the black community. Both black and white leaders continued to focus on encouraging free blacks to behave in a manner that would "convince the world that emancipation was indeed a blessing," rather than combating white racism. Hoping to help blacks gain civil equality by learning to blend into American society, the PAS prescribed a detailed system of conduct in 1800, calling on free blacks to "manifest a suitable sense of gratitude" by attending church and avoiding "idleness, dissipation, frolicking, drunkenness, theft, cheating or any other vice." It also asked the newly freed to "carefully avoid law-suits" and allow a PAS committee of inspection to give them "advice and assistance" so they would not cause "animosity" and "unnecessary expense." The petition also warned free blacks to "observe simplicity" in "dress and furniture,

and frugality in the expenses of [their] families." Calling on them to remain carefully in their places, the PAS asked free blacks to encourage
those still in bondage to remain submissive and obedient. It concluded
the address by praising those who served as "good examples to [their]
brethren" and encouraging them to keep up the good work. This advice
may sound condescending, but, as Newman has shown, white reformers
were not the only ones who "enshrined moral behavior as the corner-
stone of the American republic." Black leaders also worked to control the
masses through such groups as the African Society for the Suppression
of Vice and Immorality, founded in 1809. Leaders of this group visited
the "more dissipated parts of Philadelphia" to preach moral uplift and
"offer advice, instruction, and persuasive measures."[36]

Even so, black and white leaders were unable to stem the tide of growing racial animosity. The situation grew increasingly worse as blacks
continued to seek refuge in the state. By 1805, Philadelphia saw its first
segregated July Fourth celebration and the beginning of a strong effort
to pass discriminatory legislation against free blacks. Between 1805 and
1814 the legislature moved from trying to keep slaves out to attempting to exclude free black migration or at least tax black Pennsylvania
householders for the support of black indigents. The increase in the poor
black population, fueled by immigrants from the South, played a role in
the growing tension, as did fear of black rebellions. Finally, socioeco-
nomic factors figured into the equation, with upper-class whites fearing
violence and racial mixing and lower-class whites resenting job competition. In this climate, black achievement, whether through the formation
of independent churches or through economic success, invited white
resentment.[37]

At the same time, a growing number of successful blacks were ignor-
ing PAS injunctions to live as meekly as possible. Tired of hiding in the
background, and refusing to see their freedom as a gift from whites,
most were living according to their economic means and challenging
the existing order. What unfolded was a tragic cycle in which white animosity played a larger role than black indigence, and black success led to
white jealousy and resentment.[38]

* * *

Colonization ideas did not immediately gain wide acceptance in Pennsylvania, however, as the diligent work of the PAS and free black leaders counterbalanced the growing racial tension. Yet a seed of discontent

was germinating, as both the gradualists and black leaders such as Allen began to reconsider whether racial uplift and self-help could effectively convince whites to make room for blacks in the new republic. The PAS, which exists to this day, trudged onward with the daily tasks of protecting free blacks from kidnapping and other infringements of their personal liberty, fighting against the remaining vestiges of slavery, and trying to oversee their acculturation. Black leaders also continued to work as intermediaries, pushing the masses to remain sober and strive for success while seeking to prove to whites their legitimacy as moral and virtuous leaders of their own racial community.[39]

But by the time the ACS emerged, abolitionists had their own problems to face. To begin with, by 1805, twenty-five years had elapsed since the gradual abolition law had passed, and many of those who played prominent roles in that crusade had either died or retired. The new generation of abolitionists was less energetic. They basically gave up on abolition in the South, focusing on consolidating their gains in Pennsylvania. The Yearly Meeting revised its Discipline in 1806, leaving out the provisions adopted in 1754 against slave trading and slave owning. The Friends kept only a short clause about their refusal to own slaves and a reminder to help all blacks. They began meeting less frequently and sometimes lacked a quorum to convene.[40]

In some ways, the PAS was becoming a victim of its own success. Not only did many whites see the work of antislavery as complete once the gradual abolition law passed, others resented the end of slavery and its concomitant growth in the free black population in their state. In pushing for an end to slavery, the gradualists had turned their state into a "beacon of liberty," inadvertently encouraging blacks from other states to take their destiny into their own hands. The PAS's continuing work on behalf of the freed continued to entice black immigrants, and no matter how hard-working the newcomers were, this situation turned much of public opinion against the abolitionists. Thus, Edward Needles, a Quaker who served as PAS president in 1848, attributed the society's apparent confusion between 1804 and 1817 to "the inveterate malice by which they were assailed at all points."[41]

A statement issued by the PAS to the American Convention of Abolitionists in 1809 supports this claim. The Pennsylvania delegates, including Benezet's biographer and later colonizationist Roberts Vaux, told fellow abolitionists assembled for the Twelfth Annual Convention of American Abolitionists that "hitherto, the approving voice of the community, and the liberal interpretation of the laws, have smoothed the path of duty, and promoted a satisfactory issue to our humane exertions." Now, however, something was going horribly wrong. "Prudence has become necessary to our security, and persuasion to our success." The group attributed "this change of opinion, so injurious to the cause we have espoused . . . to the success, rather than to the misconduct of the Society." Their antislavery crusade had "awakened the attention, and secured the approbation of a large portion of our fellow citizens." After all, the group assembled was there partly to celebrate a federal ban on the slave trade. But at the same time, they faced a new set of hurdles. "The oppressed became emboldened by success," and as the news of abolitionist achievement spread, "hundreds of our fellow beings in the neighbouring states, who bore with patience the galling yoke of slavery, availed themselves of every opportunity which circumstances might furnish, to claim the protection of our statutes." Even free blacks had sought asylum in Philadelphia, hoping for assistance from the celebrated "friends of the Negro," but "as the burthen increased," the PAS's reputation "diminished" among previously uncommitted whites.

This posed an additional challenge for the abolitionists. Sounding sadly like their less humanitarian neighbors, the PAS blamed these immigrants for the growth in public hostility. "Freed from the shackles, but not from the vices of slavery, those victims of inhumanity thronged our streets in search of employment—but too many . . . serve only to swell the list of our criminals, and augment the catalogue of our paupers." It would have been easy to give up, but instead the PAS continued to push for black assimilation while trying to convince others to disavow slavery. It successfully resisted efforts of the city government and citizens of Philadelphia to prohibit free black immigration and curtail the rights of free blacks.[42] But it could stave off the colonizationist message only for so long. Indeed, the colonizationist message began to make inroads even into the black community as white racism grew.

Resettlement was not a new idea among the antislavery community. Shortly before joining the PAS in the late 1790s, Benjamin Rush toyed with the idea of resurrecting Benezet's efforts to provide free blacks with land and offer them opportunities to be something other than "servants and sailors." He drafted a letter to the PAS president, pointing out that most of the black emigrants to the state were farmers. Thus he offered to donate 5,200 acres of land in Bedford County for the abolitionists to distribute among them and help them "obtain employment . . . more congenial to their knowledge and former habits." He suggested creating a settlement much like the one proposed by Benezet before the American

Revolution, and he even suggested naming it after the "worthy and indefatigable advocate of the freedom of the blacks." It is unclear whether Rush actually mailed the letter, but its existence shows that this celebrated abolitionist grappled with the role of colonization in the antislavery movement. Like Benezet, however, he simply advocated providing blacks land, which would give them opportunities for independence and self-sufficiency without taking them away from white society.[43]

Others took the idea further by calling for removal to lands more distant from white settlement. At least one Philadelphian, the physician Jesse Torrey Jr., had proposed an African settlement, but the Louisiana Purchase lands provided a more popular scenario. John Parrish, a Philadelphia Quaker, saw this territory as prime land for colonization. He suggested that the federal government grant homesteads in the area to black families, believing that such a program would encourage southerners to emancipate their slaves by offering them somewhere to send those they freed.[44]

Black leaders had also considered resettlement at different points throughout the 1790s and early 1800s. William Thornton, a Quaker physician from Britain, first reached out to black Philadelphians in 1786 to support an African colony for both former slaves and free blacks. He sought the support of Richard Allen and the Free African Society but was rejected because, as Richard Newman has pointed out, he "gave up on American racial redemption far too soon." Even so, as racial conditions deteriorated, Philadelphia's black leaders continued to debate the idea of resettlement and still had not decided on the matter when a black ship captain named Paul Cuffee arrived in the city seeking support for the British colony of Sierra Leone. According to Newman, "the 'pull' of African redemption and the 'push' of American racial oppression" led leaders such as Allen, Absalom Jones, and James Forten to join Cuffee's movement and found a Philadelphia chapter of the African Institution. Believing that hardening racial relations would prevent African Americans from achieving the level of success many of his generation had managed to reach, Allen started to question the uplift and self-help agenda he had long pushed, and as a bishop in the AME church, he relished the thought of spreading his religious mission to Africa.[45]

In 1816, a year before the ACS founding, the Abolition Convention itself began to flirt with resettlement. Delegates at the convention that year met to discuss a number of pressing issues such as black education, the domestic slave trade, and the kidnapping and selling of free blacks as slaves. After dealing with these matters, they read "several letters addressed to the Pennsylvania Abolition Society ... from individuals residing in the southern and south-western states, who are desirous to emancipate their slaves, but are prevented by the existing laws of their respective states." The committee that was assigned the difficult task of finding a solution to this matter concluded that they could not "at present, propose any specific plan" to help these benevolent masters. "But feeling the importance of the subject, and being impressed with the weight of the responsibility which the advocates of the rights of persons of colour have assumed," they chose not "to be discouraged by the magnitude of the task," proposing that the convention draft a memorial to Congress.[46]

The memorial began by describing the problems of kidnapping and illegal slave trading before turning to the state laws that restricted and discouraged manumission. The committee admitted that Congress had no jurisdiction over such local matters. But they pointed out that "no legislative enactment can stop the progress of individual sentiment," and "experience has shewn that the gradual amelioration of feeling in the slave-holding states, towards the people of colour is constantly evincing itself in the liberation of their persons from bondage by individual owners." They insisted that many more slave owners would follow suit in the "humane design" of emancipation but for "the difficulty of finding an asylum for the persons proposed to be emancipated." Thus, they asked that Congress "consider how far it may comport with the interests of humanity, and public policy, to set apart a portion of the ... extended territory owned by the United States, for the colonization of legally emancipated blacks." If colonization was not an option, they asked that Congress do something else "to prevent the injury of the mixture of too large a proportion of such persons amongst the white people of our country." Concerned with both blacks and whites, they insisted that any plan adopted provide a "suitable government" which would oversee "the civilization, improvement and happiness of [the slaves] and their posterity." Proper intervention "would redound no less to the honour than to the security and welfare of the community." The delegates then voted to open a dialogue with English colonizationists to further investigate the issue.[47]

By the time the Abolition Convention convened for their next meeting in 1817 the American Colonization Society had formed, and the issue had become much more complicated. The abolitionists did not rule out the ACS plan, but an investigative committee expressed the "unqualified wish" that no plan of removal "be permitted to go into effect, without an immutable pledge from the slave holding states of a just and wise system of gradual emancipation." The abolitionists ultimately resolved that "the gradual and total emancipation of all persons of colour, and their literary and moral education, should precede their colonization." Though the Abolition Convention did not take a clear stand for or against the new African venture, the delegates made clear their reluctance to trust the new group, especially since many of its leaders owned slaves and free blacks resisted it strongly.[48]

The black resistance that factored into the Abolition Convention's decision had an interesting history of its own. Although black leaders such as Richard Allen, James Forten, and John Gloucester had embraced the plan put forth by Cuffee, the free black community in general resisted colonization from the beginning and forced its leaders to respect its position. In a famous 1817 confrontation at Bethel church, written about by abolition scholars for generations but best described by Newman, the grassroots black community took the leaders by surprise when over three thousand voices shouted "no" when asked to vote on colonization. Black leaders learned at that point that they could not automatically speak for the masses and that the masses had no desire to remove to Africa or anywhere else. At this point, black leaders publicly took an anticolonization stance, yet they continued to meet with white colonizationists to discuss resettlement plans, including the one put forth by the American Colonization Society. According to Newman, the dichotomy of opinion resulted from key differences in perspective among the black community. Leaders such as Allen felt the need "to consider the merits of every plan aimed at racial justice, including ACS schemes," but most blacks were more suspicious of white leaders, believing "that colonization entailed forcible removal of African-descended people, something reminiscent of the slave trade." They also realized that, unlike men such as Allen, Forten, or Cuffee, they would not have the resources to return to the United States if things did not work out in Africa. Taking their cue from the community, black leaders wrote an anticolonization pamphlet and presented it to the Abolition Convention. They expressed their community's apprehension toward colonization and renounced the ACS, and they vowed to continue fighting slavery in the United States.[49]

By 1818 colonization and the illicit slave trade had become so pressing that two member societies appealed to the president of the Abolition Convention to convene and discuss both matters. The Pennsylvania Abolition Society took the lead in placing special emphasis on the former. Its delegation began by immediately warning that "the period had arrived, when a serious investigation of the probable result of this measure, ought to be no longer avoided," and the members pleaded for the convention's "solemn attention to the inquiry, whether such colonization will subserve the interests of humanity, or whether it will have the effect to perpetuate slavery in the United States." They also asked their fellow abolitionists to consider the proposals being circulated for Haitian immigration.[50]

Beginning its report with a disclaimer that its members had not been afforded the proper amount of time to examine such a weighty issue, the committee in charge attributed the idea to Thomas Jefferson and his fellow Virginians, and they saw the ACS as an outgrowth of southern sentiment. Quoting the deliberations at the organization's inaugural meeting, the committee showed that many of the founders hoped to use colonization to strengthen slavery. The committee ultimately deemed the project unfriendly to the abolitionist agenda. Furthermore, it declared the plan "impracticable," and added that "if it is practicable . . . it will be attended with fatal consequences" and "its effects upon the condition of the free people of colour, and on the slave population of the United States . . . may become greatly injurious." The committee members were not worried, though, because they believed that colonization was doomed owing to free black resistance and phenomenal expense. Thus, the Abolition Convention concluded by reaffirming their resolution of 1817, insisting that complete emancipation and "literary and moral education" precede any plan of removal.[51]

The gradualists tried one last time to put the matter to rest at their 1819 convention. After discussing the ACS scheme in more depth they determined that they simply could not trust it. Seeing ambiguity in the society's efforts to reach both supporters and opponents of slavery, they were weary. "To those who are opposed to the continuance of slavery, colonization abroad is presented as a scheme strongly conducive to gradual emancipation; to the slave-holder it is affirmed that the removal of the free blacks will render their slaves 'more obedient, faithful, honest and useful.'" Not sure which argument to believe, the committee remained unwilling to take the chance that the ACS agenda would have "even a remote tendency to rivet the unhallowed fetters of the slave," so they refused to embrace it.

Willing to at least consider the idea of black resettlement under proper conditions, however, they discussed a plan that combined Anthony Benezet's focus on reparations with a colonization plan to remove former slaves to the territories acquired through the Louisiana Purchase. First and foremost, they insisted that all colonists would be willing participants in any resettlement plan and would be protected by "a ter-ritorial or provincial form of government, calculated for the protection of property and personal right." They would be given land "without cost, and without power of alienation to white persons," and "all involuntary servitude except on convictions for crimes" would be "for ever prohib-ited." "Agriculture and domestic manufactures" would be "made the principal objects of attention," and, at least in the beginning, the colony would enjoy the protection of the United States government. Aware of possible objections from whites, the committee that offered this alterna-tive promised that any such colony would never become a haven for fugi-tive slaves, and that "careful and specific regulations [would] be adopted to prevent the introduction of improper persons." To make sure, they suggested that the site of any such colony would be "as much secluded as possible from water communication."

Unlike an African settlement, such a colony would benefit both the black settlers and the United States. Although slaves lived in conditions that made them natural enemies to the nation, black freeholders in an independent, adjacent nation would be friendly and could perhaps help civilize the Native Americans. With freedom and incentive to succeed on their own, a growing black population would no longer be a threat. "Such increase, under a wise and judicious organization, among them-selves, and with good conduct on our part, will only increase the number of our friends and auxiliaries." Still close enough to benefit from white Christian moral guidance, they could even impart the benefits of the gospel to the Indians and "in time form a strong and useful barrier to the progress and effect of their hostile inclinations."

The committee, which included second generation PAS members William Rawle and Richard Peters Jr., as well as future colonizationist George Boyd, ultimately chose to table the matter of resettlement. They decided to continue their focus on educating free blacks and protect-ing them from unscrupulous whites while trying to urge slaveholders to educate their slaves and treat them kindly to avoid "driving this hapless race to desperation." "Our first duty is to provide that their peace and happiness, their moral system, their political rights, and their adhesion to our religion, should be enforced and secured." By the next conven-tion the abolitionists had ruled tentatively against colonization, either in Africa or western North America.[52]

* * *

The Abolition Convention may have been prepared to act the issue to rest at that point, but it was not that simple. Many white and black Pennsylvanians initially viewed the ACS with skepticism, agreeing that a dominance of southern leaders and a focus on removing free blacks served as evidence that the ACS was a proslavery group that actually wanted to strengthen the institution. Indeed, many contemporaries and historians have faulted the ACS for deliberately trying to trick benevolent northerners into supporting its work by hiding its scheme under a veil of philanthropy.[53] Other contemporaries, however, saw early on that a handful of important humanitarians such as Robert Finley, a celebrated Presbyterian minister from New Jersey, and Leonard Bacon, a student at Andover Seminary who extolled the missionary prospects of African colonization, played a crucial role in the group's founding, and they thus saw a humanitarian side to the project. They believed that colonization had a great deal of antislavery potential because a large number of upper South slaveholders had come to question the system and simply needed a way out of what they saw as an inherited conundrum. As the letters the PAS presented to the Abolition Convention had shown, many slaveholders were weary of the system yet desperately afraid of the consequences of releasing those they held in bondage. Seen in this light, some argued that the Abolition Convention and the black masses made the wrong decision by rejecting the ACS outright because colonization would encourage such masters to free their slaves, offering them a way to do it safely by sending the slaves to a distant land.[54] This group gained a number of converts in the 1820s and 1830s, and they eventually played a role in forming a strong auxiliary to the American Colonization Society—the Pennsylvania Colonization Society (PCS).

2 / "A certain simple grandeur . . . which awakens the benevolent heart": The American Colonization Society's Effective Marketing in Pennsylvania

As late as the 1820s the gradualists held the loyalty of most of Pennsylvania's humanitarians, but within a decade the colonizationists managed to find their own niche in Pennsylvania abolition. By 1829 the American Colonization Society would develop the perfect marketing scheme to entice a broad range of Pennsylvania's white citizens into considering its plan. In desperate need of national support, it saw a chance to capitalize on the conflicting emotions in this border state, which celebrated its antislavery heritage even as it grappled with the tensions created by a growing black immigrant population. Playing on the fears of most whites of the increasing free black community but also reaching out to free blacks, Pennsylvania Abolition Society members, and other humanitarians by continuing to stress colonization's possible use as a vehicle toward emancipation, ACS leaders found a way to reach both friends and enemies of the state's black population. By 1830 their work paid off, and the Pennsylvania Colonization Society became a strong force in the nation's antislavery movement.

The PAS decision to try to help free blacks fit into white American society reflected a belief that humankind had potential for improvement. This attitude was quite common in the first decades of the nineteenth century, and it comported well with the state's reform legacy. Efforts to perfect society by suppressing vice, reforming the prisons, training the poor, and offering assistance to the indigent were all movements that appealed to Quakers and abolitionists. Perhaps the most optimistic

FIGURE 4. "A view of Bassa Cove (in Liberia)." Philadelphia: Lehman & Duval Lithographers, ca. 1836. (Courtesy of the Library Company of Philadelphia.)

crusade—the use of prisons to reform rather than merely punish—began early in the colony's history when founder William Penn sought to introduce hard labor as a substitute for capital punishment. Benjamin Rush pursued this effort in the late 1780s, arguing that the government had no right to take life, even as punishment. By the 1830s, Pennsylvania prisons relied on a combination of solitary confinement and hard labor to teach inmates the error of their ways. This went hand in hand with Pennsylvania reformers' efforts at educating and controlling the poor of both races. Philadelphia's House of Refuge played an important role in this effort. Funded by state aid, money from the county, subscriptions from the public, "legacies of the benevolent," and "the labour of the inmates," this organization sought "the employment of the idle, instruction of the ignorant, reformation of the depraved—a general diffusion of good morals, enlargement of virtuous society, and the protection of life and property."[1]

This reform spirit and the organizations it spawned spread throughout not just Pennsylvania but the rest of the United States and England as well. Most historians see it as part of a larger evangelical movement. Following the Great Awakening many Americans began to actively try to make the world a better place, and one of the main vehicles was the voluntary association. These groups were staffed by a new professional class of secretaries, media propagandists, and traveling agents, and the state auxiliary played an important part in their efforts to spread their various messages throughout the nation. Religious groups, such as Bible and Sunday school societies and missionary associations, were some of the first to employ these new energetic reform tactics. Their goal was to help usher in the millennium, a time of reformation in which humanity would accept God's moral agenda and forgo vices such as greed, violence, all forms of crime and dishonesty, and, by extension, slavery. Of course, this reform agenda was always permeated by fear of, and a desire to control, the lower orders.[2]

Pennsylvania reformers had faith in this agenda and tried to fit abolition into it, but some began to question this effort once the state's black population grew beyond reformers' ability to control it. The problem actually stemmed from a growing number of poor newcomers in general, but though the number of white immigrants far outweighed the number of blacks, and both groups shared the vices that alarmed middle-class onlookers, the blacks drew more attention. Because most whites, including abolitionists and government officials, had seen a small black population as desirable all along, black immigration scared whites from all walks of life. While the blatantly racist pushed for legislation to exclude blacks, most PAS members continued the struggle to serve as patriarchs of the growing African American community, and black leaders continued to work in partnership with the PAS to prove that, if educated and treated with respect, freed slaves could become valuable citizens.[3]

In many ways efforts to guide free blacks, whether led by the PAS, the ACS, or black leaders, resembled the movement to reform the poor in general. Within a decade, however, many reformers lost their optimism, and even some gradualists began to reconsider their efforts at uplift. Many who opposed slavery, both black and white, began to agree that the attitude of most white Americans ensured that blacks, no matter how well educated or financially secure, would be forever relegated to a permanent lower class. Seeing the growing racial tension around them, a few important emancipationists, and some black leaders, started to listen to ACS speakers as they toured the state. For most humanitarians, however, the jump to supporting the removal of free blacks remained just too far.[4]

* * *

Attempts to gain Pennsylvania support for colonization began as soon as the ACS formed in 1816. That year Robert Finley, a minister from New Jersey, concluded that the meliorative efforts of gradualists were not working and that as the number of northern free blacks grew so too did their "wretchedness." He began to travel throughout the nation, including Philadelphia, speaking to members of Bible societies and supporters of black education in an effort to enlist possible members for a society dedicated to sending free blacks to Africa. He gained the interest of Richard Allen, a black leader, and succeeded in convincing Samuel J. Mills, a traveling agent and cofounder of the American Bible Society, Francis Scott Key, a lawyer from the District of Columbia, and Elias Boudinot Caldwell, a Supreme Court clerk, to help him lobby for political support for his endeavor. Believing that the success of African colonization depended on federal assistance, these men reached out to congressmen, senators, and other wealthy members of D.C. society. A number of well-known political and religious leaders, most notably Daniel Webster and Henry Clay, joined them at a meeting in the capital in December that year, and by the time they adjourned they had formed the American Society for Colonizing the Free People of Color in the United States. Of the original thirteen vice presidents chosen a few days later, Robert Ralston and Richard Rush were celebrated reformers from Pennsylvania. The PAS's Bishop William White would join this list by 1819.[5]

Supporters began to publicize their new society immediately and to canvass the nation to gather financial support to fund a "mission of inquiry" to Africa. Mills used the experience he gained as an agent for missionary and Bible societies to travel throughout the Northeast and plant ACS auxiliaries in cities such as Philadelphia, New York, and Baltimore. In Philadelphia Bishop White, Presbyterian minister Jacob Jones Janeway, and Baptist educator and pastor William Staughton helped him form an auxiliary that attracted the support of wealthy citizens such as William Meredith, a bank president; Samuel Archer, an importer; Robert Ralston, director of the Bank of the United States; Richard Dale, a retired naval officer; and Horace Binney, leader of the Philadelphia Bar.[6] The money gained from this first attempt at national organization went to fund a fact-finding mission to Africa. Two years later Pennsylvania's Samuel Bacon joined another expedition as a representative of the federal government.

Although this group of wealthy and influential Philadelphians pledged their support in 1817, colonization activity in the state remained lukewarm throughout the first decade, partly because once the immediate need for funds was met, ACS agents backed off. This lack of sustained pressure from the parent organization hurt in the long run by letting the topic of colonization lapse until new funding needs arose. The parent society continued to rely on the support of states from both the North and the South, however, for a number of reasons. Most obviously, the ACS needed money to fund further explorations of Africa as well as to transport and support colonists. Just as crucially, because of increasing monetary demands, the society hoped to convince the federal government to take over the project once it got started. To succeed in this endeavor, colonizationists would have to use pressure from all regions to lobby the government. They would eventually learn the value of a sustained publicity campaign.

Although southern states, particularly Virginia, had shown enthusiasm for the movement early on, the northern and middle states offered only token support. Nevertheless, General Robert Goodloe Harper, a vice president of the American Colonization Society, shared the belief that middle state support would prove essential to the group's success. Perhaps realizing that a small black population and large-scale white European immigration had been essential to the gradualist agenda all along, he maintained that "the evils of slavery are most sensibly felt, the desire of getting rid of the slaves is already strong, and a greater facility exists of supplying their place by white cultivators," in these states. He and other leaders enjoyed a brief hope of enlisting emancipationists from this part of the country in their endeavor by emphasizing their scheme's usefulness as a tool in the fight to suppress the slave trade and thus help manage the size of the nation's black population.

Though this line of argument helped to convince the federal government to offer limited support and funds through the Slave Trade Act of 1819, it failed to garner as much gradualist support as ACS managers had hoped for. That year colonizationist leaders tried to resurrect Mills's old auxiliaries to raise funds to send a group of recaptives, currently in state custody in Georgia, back to Africa. The ACS secretary, Elias B. Caldwell, reported success in his tour of Philadelphia and New York, but his report was overly optimistic. The society's annual reports show that the Philadelphia chapter continued to contribute small amounts but had not sent the parent society a list of officers as late as 1822. The York, Pennsylvania, society had contributed a list of officers by then, but there were no donations listed for that chapter. Apparently this situation prevailed among northern chapters, because the society decided to adopt the new voluntary system of organization so popular with Bible and Sunday school societies. This system included employing traveling agents in a renewed push for support in 1823. Most of them realized that linking colonization to the PAS's reputation for philanthropy and humanitarianism would boost their efforts throughout the North.[7]

The renewed drive for federal aid in 1824 led the ACS to seek the support of all state governments. It immediately won over the Ohio, Connecticut, New Jersey, and Delaware legislatures, and voiced optimism that support from Pennsylvania would be forthcoming. Once again, the ACS's confidence was premature, because a representative of Haiti was in Philadelphia promoting an emigration scheme that was capturing much more attention than African colonization at the time. General Charles Fenton Mercer was much more realistic when he spoke at the seventh annual meeting that same year, warning fellow colonizationists that "the plan itself is imperfectly known or understood; in those parts of the Union remote from the slave holding states, we have few auxiliary societies, and the subject is little addressed." A year later, agents who toured the middle states reported that they had to dispel the impression that "the Colonization Society was an expedient devised by the holders of slaves to get rid of the free black population." In doing so, they emphasized the New Jersey origins of ACS founder Robert Finley and insisted that the society was in no way proslavery.[8]

This tour was important because it revealed the need for a change in tactics. Although the first annual report had cited the ultimate goal of gradual abolition and the society initiated a campaign against the slave trade the next year, colonizationists had remained reluctant to stress these points too loudly for fear of losing southern support. Ralph Gurley, a known northern humanitarian, became the society's secretary in 1825 and immediately began taking steps to push the antislavery aspect of the movement. He hoped to appeal to northern humanitarians and enlist their support in an 1824–25 drive to get the federal government to use the Slave Trade Act to justify funneling money to the colony. Trying to appeal to northerners who wanted to end slavery but feared the "radical" rhetoric and action of the abolitionists, he focused on the colonization movements' role in suppressing the trade and returning the victims of illicit merchants to Africa. He also hoped to use nationalism by challenging northerners to "save" southerners. Finally, he focused on colonization's potential as a vehicle for missionary work in Africa.[9]

* * *

Gurley was not alone in his desire to stress the humanitarian side of the movement. Earlier in 1824, a writer for the *Christian Spectator* offered a plan to gain support for colonization. Stressing the need for a grand object and effective publicity, the author pointed to the Bible and missionary societies as good examples. The former built upon a "simple grandeur ... which ... awakens the benevolent heart," and the latter seized "on the attention and affections of the public, by the charm which is thrown over all its proceedings" by issuing progress reports that inspired its supporters to share in "a higher joy and a livelier interest." The concluding recommendation that the ACS employ similar tactics caught the attention of colonizationists, and they reprinted the article in their seventh annual report that year. Gurley followed up on the suggestion for better publicity early the next year by founding and editing the *African Repository*, a monthly journal dedicated to reporting on the society's efforts and progress.[10]

Throughout 1825 and 1826, arguments for the benevolent motives of the ACS grew. The Reverend Leonard Bacon explained the benefits to Africa, and Francis Scott Key gained the support of Pennsylvania philanthropist Roberts Vaux, who had initially spoken out against the group, by insisting that colonization promoted manumission. Key's reputation as a defender of blacks no doubt added validity to his claims. Though

Philadelphia Friends protested the scheme at first because they resented the intrusion on their efforts to uplift free blacks, Key's appeals paid off, and he managed to entice to the cause such Quaker humanitarians as William Short, a diplomat; John Elliott, a merchant; Joseph Hemphill, a congressman; and Sarah M. Grimke, a reformer. Gurley found the new Quaker support quite encouraging and hoped it would provide an inroad into Philadelphia's humanitarian inner circle. In accord with PAS traditions of working through the legal system, many of these new followers immediately suggested sending petitions and memorials to Congress to gain support for the society.[11]

Quakers and philanthropists were not the only ones paying attention to ACS speakers. At the same time that Key focused on antislavery aspects of colonization, other speakers and writers cited the removal of a volatile and dangerous population as chief among their goals. Most who addressed the issue of what they saw as the degraded nature of African Americans blamed the conditions on American society, chiefly the denial of incentive for betterment, which arose from the prejudice most whites felt toward blacks. Unlike later immediatists, however, they argued that this impediment could not be overcome, because they saw no end to racial prejudice. Rather than addressing contemporary assumptions about blacks, some found it easy to capitalize on prejudice in pushing for support for their project. Because their emphasis on philanthropic motives alienated some southern supporters and was gaining only minimal converts in the North, they also played on racial fears and antiblack sentiment to build a bridge between whites in both regions. They used arguments that would convince northern whites they faced the same dangers as their southern counterparts. They emphasized the growing numbers of black indigents and the rising black populations in the jails and prisons and stressed the dangers of racial mixing and the possibility of blacks seeking retribution for past wrongs.[12]

* * *

Leaders had been discussing the detrimental effects of the growing black population from the beginning of the society's founding. Charles Fenton Mercer, one of the society's vice presidents, pointed out that the nation's free black population had grown from fifteen thousand to thirty thousand in the decade between 1818 and 1828. He claimed that this growth "impaired the value of all the private property in a large section of our country." In 1829 the third report of the society expanded on this theme, taking care to reveal that this "large section" included the middle states. According to the author, laws requiring emancipated slaves to leave their home states had turned Pennsylvania and Ohio into the "nearest asylums" for large numbers of blacks. In one case, the states acquired five hundred of Virginia's outcasts. This theme permeated colonizationist writings by the end of the 1820s, when an article in the *African Repository* warned that these immigrants were not assets to the community: "It is impossible, in the nature of things, that a population, just emerged from slavery, distinguished by the peculiarity of its colour, and cut off by unavoidable necessity, from the most powerful incentives to individual exertion, and to moral elevation, should constitute a valuable portion of any community, on which it may be cast. It can add neither to its wealth, its character, nor its strength."[13]

Not only would they not add to the community, many argued that they would drain it of its resources. Insisting that colonization would benefit the North as well as the South, the *Christian Spectator* asked what the "thousands of blacks in New England" contributed "to the good order and happiness of society." Arguing that southerners made great sacrifices not only in giving up valuable property but also by contributing money for the removal of that property to Africa, the article challenged northerners to provide for the transportation of a group that adds "more to the poor rates of the parishes in which they reside than they do to the income of the government." According to the *African Repository*, only colonization could remedy the situation. Since blacks had been excluded by law and by custom from the benefits of American society, "we are urged by self-love, by justice and charity . . . to restore them to the country of their ancestors," where they could presumably become productive members of society. Mercer applied this argument directly to Philadelphia in his 1829 address to the twelfth annual meeting of the ACS, arguing that although Philadelphia remained "the pride and ornament" of the country, he had witnessed "squalid and hopeless misery—such as he had never witnessed in any part of the globe" among the blacks of that city.[14]

The number of blacks in almshouses alarmed many whites, but the numbers in jails and prisons received even more attention. A contemporary study of Philadelphia argued that one in sixty-five of the city's free blacks had been convicted of some form of criminal activity, a statistic that led the author, and certainly many of his readers, "to a very unfavourable estimate of the moral character of the coloured inhabitants of Pennsylvania." The *African Repository* capitalized briefly on this theme in February 1826 by including a one-sentence article on the last page that claimed that "when the white population of Pennsylvania amounted to 800,000 and the people of colour to 30,000, one half of the convicts in the state Penitentiary were of the latter class." They followed up on this argument by claiming that one thirty-fourth of the general population but one third of the prison population in the state was black. Although the vast majority of prisoners had been convicted of larceny, most likely due to the discriminatory nature of society and the resulting desperation among citizens who faced the dual challenge of being both poor and black, this line of argument took hold.[15] Some colonizationists conceded that the biases inherent in American society encouraged this situation, but they refused to try to change white attitudes.

Colonizationists argued that their scheme would allow for the removal of a lazy and criminal population, but they also emphasized that it would save the entire white race by preventing racial mixing and black retribution. At the first annual meeting in 1818, Vice President Robert Goodloe Harper had told listeners that though he respected Paul Cuffee, a black leader and early emigrationist, he could not imagine allowing his children and Cuffee's to marry. Harper was not alone, and the fear of racial mixing grew throughout the next decade. An 1829 report on colonization warned that blacks who did manage to transcend the racism and discrimination in America enough to gain any degree of success faced an additional challenge because, while they no longer fit in with other blacks, even "the warmest friend of the cause of abolition would shrink with disgust from the idea of a matrimonial connexion between his children and this unfortunate people."[16]

Not only did intermarriage disturb many, it was illegal in several states. Although the law preventing such unions in Pennsylvania had been repealed in 1780, complaints of the "commonness" of intermarriage and the claim that black men were seducing white women led to an unsuccessful petition asking for new laws in the 1820s against intermarriage. Legal or not, mixed marriages "came to be considered increasingly odious" throughout the 1820s and 1830s, and the issue led to rioting in Pennsylvania. This particular issue would linger for decades, even causing disruption at the constitutional convention in Philadelphia in 1837.[17]

Pennsylvania whites, like those throughout the country, had also been grappling with the specter of retribution at the hands of blacks for over a century. In addition to the high import duties imposed to keep the number of slaves low, officials struggled to prevent any unruly behavior on the part of the bound laborers. In 1737 a Philadelphia judge called for a "strict hand to be kept over" the enslaved because of "insolent Behavior ... in and about the city, which has of late been so much taken notice of." Forty years later a resident of Bucks County requested the local committee of safety to dispatch ammunition "in order to quiet ... people ... who have been somewhat alarmed with fears about Negroes and disaffected people injuring their families." In addition, a series of arson attempts by enraged blacks in York in 1803 led the governor to call out the militia. An influx of slaves from Haiti during the Haitian Revolution increased the alarm, as their owners spread tales of black brutality and wanton destruction. Even after slavery ended in Pennsylvania, residents thought they remained in imminent danger of revolts because of the proximity of slave states. Gabriel Prosser's uprising in Virginia in 1800 caused alarm in many adjacent areas.[18]

But slaves were not the only danger to white safety. In 1822 a prosperous carpenter in Charleston who had bought his freedom with a winning lottery ticket twenty-two years earlier was arrested for plotting against his white neighbors. Sixty years old at the time, Denmark Vesey was liked and even trusted by many whites who saw his strong connections to the African Methodist Episcopal Church as reassuring. The discovery of slave conspiracies always strengthened the hand of colonizationists, but this incident had to be especially alarming to a state with many respected free black citizens with similar affiliations. Abolitionists had argued for over a century that slaves were dangerous because they would some day grow angry enough to revolt, but the Vesey plot turned the focus on free blacks, even those who had seemed harmless. This development soured more people to the gradualist agenda. Even a professed Christian newspaper concluded that "the public safety forbids either the emancipation or the general instruction of the slaves," since a need for vengeance could continue to smolder after emancipation, causing men like Vesey to "stand forth in the might and dignity of manhood." Thus, "the danger is not so much that we have a million and a half of slaves, as that we have within our borders nearly two millions of men who are necessarily any thing rather than loyal citizens—nearly two millions of ignorant and miserable beings who are banded together by the very same circumstances by which they are so widely separated in character and in intent from all the citizens of our great republic."[19]

Colonizationists used this terror of revenge to their advantage. Once again drawing on the *Christian Spectator*, the ACS warned that slaves were learning of their own power and that "a general insurrection in the southern states, might indeed" cause destruction and desolation.

Though confident that whites could rally together in such an instance and ultimately save the county, the author added that it would be better to come together in an effort to send blacks to Africa before such drastic measures could occur. At least two authors used a metaphor of a volcano to explain the impending danger. Enoch Lewis, the abolitionist editor of the *African Observer*, agreed with the colonizationists on this point and warned that, even when slaves appear content, their "dormant passions are not extinct. The tranquility which prevails may be suddenly disturbed—for the slumbering volcano retains its fires, and those who occupy its smoking verge," slaveholders or not, "may themselves become the victims of the devouring element." At the ninth annual ACS convention, William Fitzhugh told the audience that this situation could be averted and that the cost of removing this threat would be much less than people realized. The ACS plan would both save white Americans from ruin, "possibly by slow decay, probably by sudden violence," and bestow the "richest benefits" upon a "suffering and degraded people."[20]

* * *

The ACS's strategy of emphasizing both higher motives and white self-interest paid off. By 1826 Pennsylvanians were showing interest and asking for more information. Men such as the Reverend W. Paxton could celebrate the society "as calculated not only to break the chains of slavery but also to introduce civilization and the light of the gospel into the rude and dark region of Africa." Yet even as they and their followers gave money to help free slaves and send missionaries to Liberia, others gave money to a cause they saw as the savior of white republican society. The demographic and social issues and the fears of racial mixing and black retribution had finally provided the grounds on which two varying strains of colonizationists could begin to "understand each other." The State Colonization Society of Pennsylvania formed in that year, and auxiliary societies in Pittsburgh, York, Washington County, Meadville, Brownsville, Bridgeport, Waynesburg, and Connelsville soon followed. Within a year, a man from West Chester wrote to the ACS to tell of the auxiliary recently formed in his community. He explained that his group had "tried an abolition society, and given it up" because "from our local situation, we experience the evil of a free coloured population, in its fullest extent."[21]

Although more than twenty state and local societies formed throughout the country the same year as the Pennsylvania State Society, the

African Repository especially celebrated ACS success in Pennsylvania, immediately conferring upon the auxiliary "a distinguished place." "The place of its location, . . . the character of its members, and the zeal and success with which it has commenced operation" made this particular society a crown jewel and lent the endeavor a humanitarian angle. A member of the Crawford County, Pennsylvania, auxiliary agreed: "As *Pennsylvanians*, we cannot but approve the grand design, as it is perfectly in accordance with the policy of the state, and the feelings of the citizens."[22]

Indeed, the Pennsylvania Colonization Society's first annual report revealed an enthusiasm that gave the parent society cause to celebrate. Clearly influenced by both their state's antislavery legacy and colonizationist rhetoric, PCS members began by voicing hope that the African colony would serve as a useful tool in combating the slave trade but soon turned to the argument that the nation's racial climate left blacks "doomed to hereditary degradation." Lamenting the failure of efforts to keep the black population small from the beginning, the report pointed out that although measures had been taken against further importation of slaves, "their increase was every year becoming more alarming, and a dreadful convulsion in the South seemed likely to be the catastrophe." They hoped the colony would secure "the removal of immediate danger to the peace of the country and ultimately the total extirpation of slavery throughout the nation, without any invasion of the constitutional rights of the slave-holders." They thought colonization would lead to abolition, since "in proportion as the number of white inhabitants increases relatively to the slave population, the inducements to emancipation are multiplied and manumissions are rendered safer and easier." Importantly, they saw "the great exertions" being made in the South "to promote emancipation" as evidence for their optimism.[23]

Thus, the Pennsylvania auxiliary, like the parent society, supported the endeavor from a complex mixture of selfish and humanitarian reasons. John Peaco, a white colonizationist recently back from a sojourn in Africa, and Charles Fenton Mercer, a national ACS leader from Virginia, both spoke at the meeting that would lead to the founding of the PCS and promised that the colony would help combat the illicit slave trade. Describing a thriving settlement with a "civil constitution," an "efficient government," several "societies for religious worship," a school that offered education to both settlers and natives, a well-stocked library, and a town fortified against "hostile attacks," Peaco maintained that "a firm foundation had been laid" and the good works could commence.

The report concluded that the colony's prospects were "pleasing," and "the cause of Liberty in our own country is constantly gaining ground," leaving "the success of the colonization plan . . . encouraging." African colonization had won out over western colonization because of its promise to stop the slave trade and introduce Christianity and civilization to the "dark continent," and by 1827 eight of the ACS's eighty auxiliaries were in Pennsylvania. For many the matter was settled. African colonization had become "the only certain means that can be employed for the extinction of the slave trade, as tending to meliorate the condition and elevate the character of a race long oppressed and degraded," while "introducing civilization, peace and true religion into an extensive and populous region."[24]

Many church leaders agreed. The Philadelphia Yearly Meeting appropriated money to resettle more than three hundred slaves in Liberia, and Gerard Ralston, an officer in the revived PCS who assumed the task of overseeing the society's growth, reported this "favorable change in . . . sentiments" to Gurley. The ACS had gained favor with North Carolina Friends by offering an asylum for slaves left under their care, and Ralston congratulated the parent society for this prudent move, "as this gives you a hold on the whole sect." He pointed out that Quakers were "extremely clannish," and "if you can influence their leaders you will be able to move the whole mass and when they move in a body their power is immensely great in the middle states." The Lutheran Synod also offered support by voicing approval of the colonization society and "most earnestly" recommending all churches under its care to offer support and patronage.[25]

Pastors of various denominations did just that, many collecting Fourth of July contributions each year to send to the society. An Adams Country minister told Gurley that his congregation contributed because they saw the society as both an antislavery force in the United States and a civilizing force in Africa. Just how deep their appreciation went, however, is unclear because the same note included both an apology for such a small donation and a plea for further information as to the "objects and progress" of the society. Indeed, many July Fourth contributions included similar apologies. Adam Miller of Susquehanna County sent the $6 he raised and attributed the low amount to a small black population in the area and insufficient information about the colonization society.[26]

According to an ACS agent sent to collect money in western Pennsylvania, pastors there were joining the movement, but their flocks were often slow to follow. Frustrated at his limited success, he reported to Gurley that these "curious Christians . . . would send off tomorrow a *bible* and a *tract* to every *heathen* in Africa, printed in *English or German*—whether the poor Africans might *read them* or *understand* them is their own look out." He added that the Germans were reluctant to part with money "for *any* benevolent purpose, save *to build* churches." Nevertheless, the pastor of the Moravian Church in Bethlehem refused to give up and even went so far as to appeal to his congregation in both English and German. The discouraged agent also maintained a degree of optimism, reporting that two Methodist ministers had pledged their support, and a Catholic priest had promised to collect money. Whether he saw the humor or not, he told Gurley that the latter contribution would come only after the congregation finished paying for their new church. Even if the average person was slow to gain interest, the PCS had at least succeeded in initiating a top-down approach.[27]

William B. Davidson, who was secretary of the PCS, offered an optimistic assessment of the situation, prematurely claiming success among secular humanitarians as well as church leaders. He wrote to Gurley that he "heard it hinted" that the gradualists planned to discuss "the expediency of their furnishing pecuniary aid to persons willing to emancipate" at an upcoming meeting. He quickly added, though, that any PAS money would be used "not to pay the value of the slaves but to defray the expense of their transportation to free countries out of the bounds of the US." As it turned out, no PAS funds would be used for any purpose related to African colonization. At this meeting, which was held on September 27, 1827, the emancipationists adopted a resolution offered by President Thomas Shipley and seconded by Secretary Joseph Parker, that colonization was "wholly unconnected" with the objects of the abolitionist society and that the PAS "will take no part in the measures of the Colonization Society." It did offer its wishes for "full success to every truly benevolent and disinterested scheme for the improvement of the condition of the African Race" and voiced support for Quaker and Free Produce supporter Enoch Lewis's new Philadelphia newspaper, the *African Observer*. This paper, like its PAS and Quakers supporters, devoted most of its attention to fighting kidnappers of free blacks, supporting black education, celebrating the accomplishments of outstanding African Americans, and calling for amelioration of the conditions of all blacks, both slave and free.[28]

Despite this rejection, donation records provide evidence that some people were listening to the colonizationists and liking what they heard. In 1820, Pennsylvanian colonizationists donated $275 and pledged $283 over a five-year period. This sum was quite paltry compared to Mary-land's donation of over $3,000 and pledges of $134 annually and $705 over the next twenty-five years. Virginia, though only donating $308 outright, pledged to donate $755 per year in addition to contributing more than $6,000 over the next five years. Washington, D.C., donated over $1,500 and pledged a yearly contribution of $418. Two years later the parent society took in only $800 total, but by 1824 things were looking up and donations totaled $4,700. The amount grew to $10,000 in 1825 and $15,000 in 1826 and 1827. Pennsylvania supporters contributed to this rise. In 1827, the new PCS immediately gave $600 at its inaugural meeting to help relocate emigrants. Individual donations also increased, with the *Repository* reporting more than $900 over the next two years.[29]

Pennsylvania colonization chapters did more than collect money. In 1827, the state society began to prepare memorials to send to the state legislature in hopes of gaining government support for the cause. Soon after, several local auxiliaries followed suit. Though "not sanguine of success with the assembly of Pennsylvania," the society stated "some strong facts," which, they hoped, "may have a good effect." The PCS then presented a memorial to the state legislature in 1828, relaying the claim that 117 of the state's 296 convicts were black even though the black population was roughly one fifth of the white. According to the report, "Had the number of coloured convicts been proportional to the coloured population of the state, there would have been but 6 instead of 117." This argument eventually worked, and by 1829 the legislature had set aside $2,000 to send the state's blacks to Liberia.[30]

* * *

In an 1828 speech celebrating the reinvigorated movement in Pennsylvania, Francis Scott Key explained that the ACS had always expected the northern cities to embrace the "scheme of patriotism and Christian charity" it had offered for over a decade. He admitted that although the ACS "looked with confidence to Philadelphia, in particular, knowing that many of her citizens were zealous in the cause of the abolition of slavery," ACS members "were disappointed" at the lukewarm reception in the state early on. Now, however, Key proudly pointed out that abolition, which had taken up so much of Pennsylvania's time, had failed. Only colonization, he insisted, could remove abolition's main obstacle by providing "on the shores of Africa, a refuge for her outcast children" and opening "an outlet for our greatest evil." With apparent satisfaction, he said that racial uplift had proven ineffective even in the state that many thought offered the best prospect for freedom and equality in the new nation. Claiming that "even among you, where every thing that benevolence could do, has been done, to make the freedom . . . of the colored population beneficial to them," he found proof that "they cannot be adequately protected in their personal, much less in the exercise of . . . civil rights." "Even here," he concluded, "they have but the name of liberty." The emphasis on the "degraded condition" of free blacks was paying off.[31]

More whites in Pennsylvania were beginning to accept colonization. The PCS set out to correct the "misconceptions" most Philadelphians harbored about the ACS, and it reported happily that "a great and auspicious change has taken and is taking place towards our cause, in the opinions and feelings of the people of Philadelphia." Indeed, even some Quakers had joined the movement. Though the PAS had rejected colonization, many gradualists were beginning to see it as a logical outgrowth of their agenda. Hoping to convince even more that their shared concerns should unite them with colonizationists in their goals, Key once again offered a solution.[32]

In his 1828 speech Key had begun his campaign to gain antislavery support by pointing to the emancipatory aspect of colonization. He told his listeners that so many southerners had offered their slaves for removal to Liberia that the society was unable to keep up with the transportation demand. In October 1829 he pursued this line of argument to deliver what he hoped would be the finishing touch to the ACS drive for support in the state known for its philanthropic legacy. Speaking at a public meeting at the Hall of the Franklin Institute, he pled for Pennsylvania's support, explaining that the group was out of money and, tragically, six hundred slaves waited eagerly for the group to provide transportation funds so their master would release them. He told listeners that most southern states "discourage the manumission of slaves, unless they are removed from the state," leaving "benevolent persons who may wish to liberate their slaves" the task of finding them new homes. Since those benevolent owners "who . . . offer to liberate their slaves, deprive themselves, by so doing, of a large portion of their property," they "deserve every assistance in executing their benevolent intentions." He also added that colonization benefited whites and blacks in all sections of the country since the cruelties of sudden and unqualified emancipation would throw the former slave "upon his own resources" and make him a burden to society. If masters were unwilling to adopt abolitionists' plans for amelioration, surely a colony closely supervised by fellow humanitarians would offer a viable alternative.[33]

Key's speech invigorated those present. The picture of six hundred souls waiting to be rescued from bondage brought the project alive for many Pennsylvania philanthropists, who vowed to work for "the liberation of the slaves referred to." Gerard Ralston wrote to Gurley a week later, sending him over $400, collected mostly from Episcopal and Presbyterian donors. He celebrated Key's visit and the "favorable impression" it made and called for further action immediately to avoid letting the excitement "pass over without taking advantage of it." Other participants at the meeting shared his enthusiasm and immediately set to work raising money to free the waiting slaves. They renewed their support and vowed to work with the PCS managers to form a committee and raise funds "on condition that they be applied exclusively to the outfit and transportation of slaves, who, being willing to join the colony, can be liberated only with a view to their emigration." Wasting no time, the committee published a circular appealing especially to abolitionists to help them send the conditionally liberated captives to "the well-established, and prosperous colony of Liberia." Not only would they be helping the slaves, they would also be helping to "ultimately put an end to the odious foreign traffic in human flesh." Furthermore, their support would "contribute more effectually to promote, and ensure the abolition of the institution of slavery in the United States, than any plan that has hitherto been devised." Anyone interested in participating in this grand scheme was asked to leave money, agricultural and mechanical implements, clothing, books and supplies for the school, and other provisions with Dr. James, Gerard Ralston, Elliott Cresson, the Reverend G. Boyd, or the Reverend C. M. Duprey. By March 1830, the committee had raised $2,290 and obtained subscriptions of $1,000 and $300 to be paid in ten yearly installments, and by the end of the year it had raised $3999.50.[34]

In the light of the committee's success, the ACS asked the PCS to use the money to oversee an expedition to take the slaves to Africa. By the end of December the auxiliary decided to give it a try, but only after reiterating that any voyage it funded would be to send slaves liberated under the condition of transportation. Free blacks could go, but only if they paid their own way. The PCS chartered the newly built *Liberia* to travel to Norfolk, Virginia, and pick up the conditionally freed emigrants, agreeing to pay $25 per passenger over twelve years of age and $12.50 for each passenger age two to twelve. Those under two could accompany their families for free. Though the PCS prepared to fund passage for one hundred emigrants, the parent society managed to deliver only fifty-eight, of whom only forty-nine were liberated slaves, to Norfolk. Unfortunately, thirty liberated slaves walked six hundred miles from Georgia, only to arrive at the port just after the *Liberia* had sailed. The PCS learned of their fate and fitted another voyage that April to send these and forty other emigrants on the *Montgomery*. All told, the PCS spent $3,214.22 to send 128 colonists.[35]

The PCS issued an exuberant third annual report in 1830. Calling colonization "the best mode of promoting the cause of abolition, a cause deservedly cherished by the philanthropists of Pennsylvania," it projected that "by this means hundreds may be emancipated, and placed in a situation to enjoy all the blessings of liberty, at a comparatively small expense." If the PCS could send only one voyage a year, "the colony would soon be in a condition to render foreign support unnecessary." After all, *Liberia* captain W. E. Sherman, as well as many U.S. naval captains, had sent back glowing reports of the colony.[36]

* * *

By 1830, the ACS and the PCS were optimistic that their campaign to reach out to Pennsylvania abolitionists seemed well-founded. At least thirty-one PAS members had either joined one of the two organizations or contributed money to the fund drive to send emigrants to the colony. Of the one hundred donors listed by name in the West Chester Colonization Society's ledger, fifteen were clearly, and eight were likely, affiliated with the abolition society. Abolitionists who joined the colonizationists included the Reverend George Boyd, who helped recruit for the PCS in 1823 and 1824; John B. Davis and the Reverend John H. Hopkins, who officially joined the PCS in 1826; William H. Dillingham, who was appointed a delegate to represent the Chester County auxiliary at the ACS convention in 1828; and the Reverend William White, who pledged support during the 1829 fund drive. Richard Rush, a well-known PAS member, was one of the thirteen original vice presidents of the ACS, and John Todd, another Pennsylvania abolitionist, became a vice president of the PCS in 1827. The Reverend James Wilson of Philadelphia's First Presbyterian Church joined the movement as well, and Philip Garret became a PCS manager in 1827. Of the four men from Pennsylvania who joined the Gerrit Smith plan, pledging ten annual payments of $100, two—Mathew Carey and Elliott Cresson—were members of the PAS.[37]

Mathew Carey and Elliott Cresson would give much more than $1,000 to the cause by the time their subscriptions expired. Actually, these re-cruits became two of the most vocal and strongest supporters of coloni-zation in Pennsylvania, each coming to personify one of the two sides of the movement. Both saw colonization as an antislavery movement, but Carey's greatest hopes revolved around benefits to the republic and its white citizens. A well-known publisher, he would carry forward the idea that colonization offered the best hope for ensuring the country's future economic prosperity. Cresson was an energetic Quaker abolitionist and advocate of black education, who had become thoroughly convinced of colonization's benefits to both American blacks and Africa. He resigned from the PAS on November 26, 1829, and began to work tirelessly to prove that Liberia was a valuable vehicle for uplift of the race on both continents. Throughout the next decade he fought to ensure that the PCS, if not the ACS, would live up to his humanitarian standards.[38]

3 / "Calculated to remove the evils, and increase the happiness of society": Mathew Carey and the Political and Economic Side of African Colonization

By the end of 1828, the American Colonization Society's propaganda had caught Mathew Carey's attention. A noted humanitarian, Carey had devoted considerable energy before and after his retirement from the publishing business to encouraging economic, political, and cultural unity, and his rather sudden embrace of colonization apparently came as a result of reading the Tenth Annual ACS Report (1828), which linked colonization to his own agenda of establishing a modern industrial nation. In addition to emphasizing the unifying aspect of the scheme, the report focused on black population growth, presenting arguments that resonated with this author and publisher, known for his own use of statistics and numerical data.

After reading the report and perhaps attending some of the society's presentations in Philadelphia, Carey grew intrigued by the predictions that the nation would contain ten million African Americans within his own lifetime, and he started to consider the implications of a biracial society. He had long supported the rights of immigrants but only under the condition that they assimilate fully into American society. Black skin could complicate this agenda. At the current rate of population increase, by 1882 his children and grandchildren would be living alongside fifteen million blacks. Deciding that removing blacks would be easier than helping them find a place in the new republic, he wrote to the society's journal, the *African Repository*, to pledge his support. No expense would be "too great to avert the horrible consequences" of such an increase in this

FIGURE 5. "Mathew Carey," 1825 by John Neagle. (Courtesy of the Library Company of Philadelphia.)

degraded and demoralized caste. He had once considered African colonization a "utopian scheme," but the report taught him that it involved much less capital outlay than he had assumed—$20 for the transport and initial support of each colonist rather than the $100–$150 he had calculated. In his newfound enthusiasm for what he once had considered "one of the wildest projects ever patronized by a body of enlightened men," he managed to convince himself that the reports of high mortality rates from the ACS colony of Liberia "have been greatly exaggerated" and "sink into insignificance, when compared with what took place in the early settlement of Virginia." After promising to send ten yearly payments of $100 through the Gerrit Smith plan, he set out to help convert others to the cause. More than a humanitarian endeavor, African colonization had become for Carey an important means of preserving and strengthening the nation.[1]

The colonization society gained an influential spokesman when Mathew Carey joined the movement. Referred to by one historian as "the high priest of American Nationalism," Carey had already devoted more than forty years and countless pages to promoting a national culture and independent identity for the new country. Through his magazines and numerous pamphlets, he had helped foster the creation of an independent American literature and contributed greatly to the forging of the economic ideology that would gain political expression in Henry Clay's American System. This system, an outgrowth of Alexander Hamilton's economic agenda, consisted of four main goals. To begin with, it called for using the protective tariff to build up American industry. To facilitate the transportation of the goods produced, internal improvements such as roads and canals would be built at the national government's expense. Sale of public lands would provide the funds. Finally, the Bank of the United States played a key role by providing a stable and uniform currency. One historian described Carey as "a staunch and effective supporter" of this system, but another went so far as to argue that Carey deserves credit as a cofounder. Carey and Clay both hoped industrial development "would serve as a source of national wealth and as a constant nourishment for an urban population that, in turn, would furnish a steady and reliable home market for the nation's agriculture." According to Edward Carter, Carey's most thorough biographer, "When Clay rose to speak in the Senate in favor of the Bank of the United States, internal improvements, or the tariff, the chances were good that his factual data was drawn from the writings of Carey."[2]

The story of American politics in the Early Republic and the role of

African colonization in it centers largely on the work of these two men. Historian David Brion Davis was perhaps the first to place abolition in this context. He argued that the abolition societies in both Philadelphia and New York were "parts of an interlocking network of public and private organizations designed to give order and direction to municipal life," adding that leading abolitionists in both places also served in internal improvement organizations. Douglas Egerton and Daniel Walker Howe both applied this test to the colonization movement by demonstrating that many border-state colonizationists such as Clay were National Republicans or Whig nationalists who shared a vision of an industrialized society based on a free labor economy of both factory and farm. Seen this way, ACS efforts to send free blacks to the colony were just the first steps toward emancipation. Thus, Clay and Carey saw colonization as a way of ridding the nation of an outdated system of production. It would also encourage cultural uniformity and solidify the bonds of interest between farmers, merchants, and manufacturers. Carey's writings offer a clear picture of the America he envisioned and the role of colonization in it. His efforts are less well known than Clay's, who served as ACS president from 1836 to 1849, since in the colonization movement, as in politics, he chose to fight from behind the printing press rather than seek public office. Even so, examining his roles both in fighting for American political and economic nationalism and in the colonization movement reveals how closely the two agendas were linked in the minds of men such as Clay and Carey.[3]

* * *

Ironically, the man who would provide the strongest support for American economic nationalism spent the first twenty-five years of his life in Ireland. Mathew Carey was born in Dublin in 1760 to a Catholic family who had to endure daily the religious persecution of the Penal Laws. Even so, Christopher and Mary Sherridan Carey provided comfortably for their five sons, three of whom earned entries in the *Dictionary of National Biography*. Carey, a baker who made a "handsome fortune" selling bread to the British Navy, managed to provide an education for his sons and establish each in his chosen profession. This posed a particular challenge when it came to Mathew, who insisted on becoming a printer and bookseller despite the Penal Codes, which forbade Catholics to enter this profession.[4]

Growing up in an environment that relegated his family to second-class citizenship made a lasting impression on Carey, whose situation should sound familiar to any student of American race relations in the late eighteenth and early nineteenth centuries. Like American free blacks, the Careys "must have found it frustrating to have been excluded legally from the rights of citizenship while they acquired culture, remained loyal to the [government], and increasingly bore heavier taxes." Even though the religious restrictions gradually loosened throughout the eighteenth century, Catholics were still denied the rights of citizenship.[5] Carey's parents remained reluctant to challenge this situation, but Carey adopted a more radical stance that led first to a brief exile in France and then to a permanent relocation to America.

Much of Christopher Carey's reluctance to allow his son to become a printer stemmed from his familiarity with Mathew's temperament and political ideas. He realized that neither would mix well with the printing profession in such a volatile climate. He was right. Mathew had been reading oppositional literature since 1775, and his apprenticeship only added to his controversial politics. His master, Thomas McDonnell, and his partner, Michael Mills, printed the *Hibernian Journal*, one of the two most radical newspapers at the time. Strong supporters of the rebelling colonies, these men linked the Irish and American struggles, warning that if the Americans were subdued the Irish would be next. After the war, McDonnell, who would later join the United Irishmen, pushed for the relief of Catholics while Mills focused on the importance of an independent Irish parliament. As he worked in what Carter referred to as this "center of liberal thought in Dublin," the young apprentice took in the conversations and read the pamphlets and newspaper articles, becoming increasingly radical himself. As a writer, Carey immediately revealed these influences and displayed the temperament his father feared. Amid a "rising storm of Irish patriotism" in 1779 he decided to ride the coattails of a growing movement for political independence and "strike a blow on behalf of his fellow Catholics who continued to labor under many legal disabilities."[6]

Though his resulting pamphlet, *The Urgent Necessity of an Immediate Repeal of the Whole Penal Code against the Roman Catholics*, was printed anonymously and was little more than a mild rehashing of arguments that had already appeared in print, Carey's marketing of the work stirred controversy before it was even published. In hopes of enticing the public to buy the pamphlet, he sent its title page along with an *Advertisement to the Roman Catholics of Ireland*, to a number of Dublin papers. He also printed handbills, which he distributed throughout the city. Unfortunately for Carey, the *Appeal*, though never finished, "was highly seditious" and appeared to call for revolt. This move proved disastrous for the Catholic community since the Irish parliament was currently debating reforms in the Penal Laws. These reforms had been introduced by the British ministry as an attempt to gain the loyalty of Irish Catholics. Carey's seditious advertisement, however, strengthened the enemies of Catholic relief and led to the defeat of the penal reform measures. Catholic community leaders deeply resented this destruction of their years of hard work at the hands of an unknown agitator. To show their loyalty and perhaps regain the lost concessions, they pledged to identify and punish the author.[7]

When Christopher Carey learned that his son had written the seditious material, he took measures to have the pages that had been printed suppressed and offered to burn the work if the prosecution would be abandoned in return. His offer rejected, he sent his son to France in 1781. This exile put Carey in contact with Benjamin Franklin and the marquis de Lafayette, two men who would help him during a second exile five years later, this time to America. The final removal came after he called the Irish legislature a "den of thieves" and "a Gomorrah of iniquity" while appearing to call for the assassination of John Foster, the chancellor. A heated campaign to relieve Irish cloth manufacturers with protective tariffs against English cloth prompted this attack. The Irish artisans had been basically driven from business by a market flooded with English goods and, deprived of both American and European markets by the English, had been made so destitute that they were talking of revolution. Carey suggested the tariff as the remedy for their plight, and much of the public had grown to support the measure. When radical members of Parliament introduced such a bill, however, Foster pushed it aside. Public response was riotous, and Carey's articles in the *Volunteer's Journal* only added fuel to the mix. As a result, the Crown told Foster to deal swiftly with the rebellious press, and the end result was Carey's emigration to America.[8]

By the time the twenty-five-year-old embarked for Philadelphia in September 1784 he had formed a clear political and economic ideology. Carter describes Carey at this point as "a defender of the downtrodden" who believed in "universal toleration." Politically he was a radical republican owing to his study of liberal seventeenth-century English political writers, eighteenth-century Commonwealth theorists, and leaders of the French Enlightenment. His political ideas had been tested by the American Revolution and the Irish Volunteer movement, and "his own personal experience had made him a strong Irish nationalist, an ardent if somewhat naive admirer of America, and an implacable opponent of England." Economically, he supported "a rather crude form of protectionism," which Carter sees as "a natural outgrowth of his intense nationalism."[9] Each of these factors would play an important role in shaping Carey's American agenda.

Carey arrived in Philadelphia in November 1784 and through the patronage of General Lafayette was able to establish the *Pennsylvania Evening Herald* in January 1785. The articles he wrote or printed in this paper, like those in his *Columbian Magazine* and *American Museum*, show that he entered Pennsylvania politics promoting a specific agenda, one which called for internal improvements, encouragement of domestic manufactures, and unity under a strong central government. The creation of an American cultural identity would be a crucial step in fostering this program.[10]

* * *

Knowing firsthand how constant discrimination and second-class status fostered resentment and rebellion, one of Carey's first projects was to encourage a cultural identity for the new nation that would allow toleration while celebrating American liberty. His ideas about the role of immigration fit well into this aspect of his agenda. When a Boston politician proposed a thousand-pound fee as a condition of naturalization in 1785, Carey grew horrified, insisting that "the very novice who has not gone through his political horn-book, must have heard, and must be convinced, that people constitute the real wealth of a country." Even European nations had learned this lesson and taken measures to guard against a further drain of their populations. "Perhaps, then, instead of discouraging naturalization, the time is not too remote, when so liberal a plan will prevail, as to hold out substantial advantages to encourage it." To do so, he recommended purchasing "necessary utensils for poor emigrants." To make sure only the most useful settlers could take advantage of this plan he suggested requiring "a certificate of their sobriety, industry and integrity, from the pastor to whose flock they belonged in their native country." A period of "probation" in the United States before granting the suggested inducements could further protect against fraud.[11]

Of course, the last thing Carey wanted was a hodgepodge of different cultures causing disunity in the new nation, so he insisted that assimilation accompany immigration. In August 1785 he applauded

the founding of a Baltimore society devoted to helping German immi
grants. According to Carey, newcomers faced uncertain circumstances
upon their arrival, and the natural tendency was to react by entering
into "hastily-formed connections," which created "a sort of bar between
the old settlers, and the new comers." It also left newcomers easy prey
to political demagogues. For the past year, this society had sought to
prevent this by meeting German settlers as they disembarked, ascertain-
ing their circumstances, protecting them from fraud, and helping them
learn American ways. The group also helped their charges make contacts in their new home and find employment. Aware of nativist sentiment, the group's president warned members that because the "character
and reputation" of the entire German nation was "in danger of being
tarnished by the base conduct of some traitors and dissolute vagabond
runaways, it is . . . incumbent on us, to make it appear that our institution is not . . . designed to screen such miscreants; but merely to succour
the necessitous of our nation, whose conduct shall render them worthy
of protection." Carey knew what was at stake and lauded the thinly dis-
guised effort to make sure new arrivals were speedily brought in line.
Indeed, he called on "settlers here from other nations, particularly the
Irish and Scotch," to form similar societies.[12]

Education also played a crucial role in assimilation, and Carey applauded efforts in that field. He reprinted an address from a German-
language newspaper in Pennsylvania calling for an academy for German youth. The author pointed out that though Germans constituted
"one third part of the inhabitants of this commonwealth, . . . contribute
their quota of taxes for the support of government," and have "freely
shed their blood in the acquisition of American independence," their
offspring were largely excluded from the "liberal professions" of church,
bar, or faculty. They also "frequently, through ignorance of the laws of
the land, lose their property, in sales and purchases, and in making testa-
ments." This despite a "temperate, peaceable, and indefatigable" nature
that "renders them better calculated for liberal studies, and constitutes
them the best members of a republican government." To objectors, such
an academy would preserve German language and encourage isolation.
The writer argued, however, that the school would allow students to learn
in German but that "their improvement in their own language, would be
the means of their earlier acquiring a perfect knowledge of the English."
"Besides," he added, once Germans realized that fluency in English "was
indispensably necessary in acquiring reputation at the bar, and arriving
at honour, as well in the assembly of this commonwealth, and in the

congress of the United States, it would be unnecessary to spur them on to learn to speak and write it with propriety and elegance." Further, he assured any doubters, the first teacher hired for the academy would be an English instructor. Finally, "an academy for the Germans would, by enlightening their minds, pave the way for their close union with their British and Irish brethren, and render them whole, what every honest man must wish, ONE PEOPLE."[13]

Carey urged his readers to take heed. He argued in an introductory paragraph that the essay "certainly involves, and in no very remote degree, the welfare of the whole community." Given the need of an informed citizenry in a strong republic, "to have so numerous a body of people unprovided with proper means of cultivation, must be a very alarming consideration" since "history points out, that ignorance has in every part of the world, been a most successful engine in the hands of those scourges of mankind, the ambitious, and the tyrannic, as well civil as religious, who find no difficulty in rendering an uninformed people subservient to their purpose." Carey shared these fears of corrupt leaders and a malleable populace with most of his contemporaries. "Experience has fully evinced, that the more enlightened nations are, the more amenable they are to the laws, to order, and to police; and the less frequently do they perpetrate those species of violence . . . which reduce humanity to a level with the brute creation."[14]

Though he supported immigration, Carey sought to provide a realistic assessment of life in America, and he urged prospective immigrants to consider their options carefully. He did so out of concern for people who would seek prosperity in the new nation, but he was at least equally interested in ensuring that only those who could truly contribute to the young republic would join it. Through the *Columbian Magazine* he offered prospective immigrants information about the various regions of the nation and advice as to which occupations they could most successfully pursue. "Industrious, sober, and attentive farmers" faced a hopeful situation, and manufacturers of iron products, especially those which "bear relations to husbandry" were needed. America could also use people skilled in construction trades and manufacturers of coarse clothing products. However, makers of luxury products "will find no employment." Forty years later he issued similar reports, this time trying to discourage professionals, farmers, cotton and tobacco planters, and most manufacturers while encouraging "mechanics and laborers," two groups especially needed to assist with internal improvement projects. In all cases, he stressed that "it is indispensably requisite to success, that the omigrant bo activo and industrious," and he repeated his suggestion to require "proper recommendations" from clergy and magistrates, attesting to prospective immigrants' "sobriety, industry, and honesty."[15]

Carey insisted that the newcomers, once assimilated, deserved the full rights of citizenship. In this vein, he served as secretary of the Lately Adopted Sons, and in 1790, helped found the Hibernian Society. The goal of the latter group, which performed the same functions as the Baltimore society, was to make the public see the Irish community as patriotic Americans eager to assimilate with the broader American society as smoothly as possible. As an added measure, Hibernians forged strong ties with noted American leaders by inviting them to dinner regularly, where they would be asked to speak on patriotic themes. Thus, to keep his fellow Irish in the good graces of the general community, Carey had developed a program to protect and educate them, fostering their "Americanization."[16]

Optimistic that as long as immigrants found a way to contribute and fit into American society, all would work out, and nativists could be defeated, Carey even held hopes that such an Americanization program would allow Catholics to gain a place in the strong and unified nation he envisioned. Free black leaders held similar dreams for their community, but sadly white supporters of the industrial agenda limited their view of citizenship to those who shared their skin color. Both groups believed that survival of the new nation depended on frugal, hard-working, temperate citizens, but white proponents of the American System also felt the community had to be homogenous so members could share economic opportunity. This rough equality, they hoped, would help prevent the jealousy and bickering that had destroyed former republics.[17]

* * *

Carey realized early on that the American racial climate would complicate his quest for a unified population. The first step to rectifying this situation would be to stop further importation of blacks. He included an article in a supplement to the *Columbian Magazine* in 1787 that protested the slave trade. Sounding much like Anthony Benezet, the author described the horrible means Europeans employed in procuring their human merchandise, arguing that Europeans often encouraged wars among African nations by supplying guns in hopes of a large return in captives. Also, since the beginning of the slave trade, enslavement had become the means of punishing African criminals, and the number of punishable crimes had been expanded to accommodate the demands for supply. Even worse, Africans were kidnapped as they worked in their fields or sought water at the local stream. Once they entered the market, captives faced extremely high levels of mortality along the journey to the African coast, in the Middle Passage, and during the initial years in the New World.

The article then examined the probable consequences of the abolition of the slave trade. To begin with, removing the supply of new slaves would force planters to treat the ones they already had more humanely to encourage longevity and reproduction. Furthermore, stopping the trade would protect white society by lessening the threat of insurrection. The end of the trade would also decrease the number of suicides, increase the land under cultivation, greatly improve revenue, and lay a foundation for "a general emancipation." Carey's inclusion of this article in his supplement next to pieces about such pressing matters as the American government, education, and the encouragement of manufactures shows the importance he assigned the matter. Two years later he depicted the horrors of the Middle Passage in graphic detail by publishing a drawing of a cross section of a slave ship.[18]

Through articles in the *Pennsylvania Evening Herald* and the *Columbian Magazine* from 1785 to 1787, Carey revealed at least a passing interest in slavery beyond the trade. He mentioned efforts to stem imports and to create a manumission society in New York in his "Postscript" column in the *Herald*. More important, in the light of his later embrace of colonization, he reprinted observations by a French traveler about the nature of slavery in Virginia and the prospects of a biracial society. The observer maintained that slavery in Virginia was milder than in the sugar colonies and that because the slaves in this state were native-born they were "generally less depraved" than those on the islands. The white Virginians "treat their negroes with great humanity" and "seem afflicted to have any slavery, and are constantly talking of abolishing it." Of course, this sentiment was based on a number of factors from moral and philosophical to economic, but the writer found it "fortunate that different motives concur in disgusting men with that tyranny which they exercise upon their fellow creatures."[19]

Abolition in the United States, however, would be no easy endeavor. Offering insight which pertained to Carey's assimilation plan and hopes of a culturally unified society, the author pointed out that American slavery posed an unprecedented challenge. "Sufficient attention has not been paid to the difference between slavery, such as it exists in our colonies, and the slavery which was generally established among the ancients." That difference was race. "A white slave had no other cause of humiliation, than his actual state; on being freed, he mixed immediately with free men, and became their equal." In a situation that paralleled Carey's hope for immigrants, the ancient slaves could become accepted members of society and enfranchised "without danger." This allowed for a degree of incentive among the freed to work hard and attain respectable stations in society, an incentive that would forever be denied free people of color. In America, "it is not only the slave that is beneath his master, but the negro who is beneath the white man," and "no act of enfranchisement" could rectify this situation. Carey's program of education and Americanization could not transcend this barrier. The gradualist agenda of racial improvement and assimilation was simply unattainable.[20]

The solution, according to the observer, was removal and planned amalgamation. He proposed sending black men away and encouraging white men to marry black women. He suggested repealing laws that passed slavery from mother to child and offering freedom to black women who married white men. "Such a law, aided by the illicit, but already well established commerce between the white men and negresses, could not fail of giving birth to a race of mulattoes," which with each generation would grow progressively lighter until "the colour should be totally effaced."[21]

Although Carey did not officially embrace colonization until 1828, he began to consider the idea around this time. In one of the first articles in his new *Columbian Magazine* he mentioned a prophetic dream he had about the year 1850. Employing the journalistic tactic he often used in the *Pennsylvania Herald*, he included short news blurbs from throughout the United States, describing the economic and political progress at this point in the future. In a paragraph labeled "Charleston, April 15," he reported that in two years 10,000 blacks had been sent from South Carolina and Virginia to an African settlement. "Very few blacks remain in this country now; and we sincerely hope that in a few years every vestige of the infamous traffic, carried on by our ancestors in the human species will be done away."[22] Though this mention of the issue is short, sketchy, and couched within a fictitious framework, it shows he had colonization on his mind long before the ACS won his support.

＊ ＊ ＊

Carey joined the colonization society during what biographers call his humanitarian phase, but this project, like the other reforms he pursued, actually fits into his nationalistic agenda. The tendency to separate his career into a distinct humanitarian phase probably results from an April 1829 letter Carey sent to the Philadelphia papers promising to devote the rest of his career "to render my time and my slender talents as extensively useful as possible." Already having devoted much time and "at least $400 per annum" to promoting the public good through his economic agenda, he now pledged to concern himself more deeply with prison discipline, infant schools, and the plight of the poor, especially underpaid women. Although he did produce a great number of essays on these topics from 1829 on, he clearly did not abandon his push for economic nationalism, and these causes, along with colonization, fit into his industrial agenda.[23]

Carey saw many of the reforms he supported as important to an orderly society. Prisons had been transformed "in some degree" from "colleges of vice" to "schools of reformation." Similarly, infant schools had saved many children "from the contamination of an education in the streets" and provided parents free time to "pursue their avocations without the hindrance and molestation arising from attention to their children." At the same time, education helped instill "habits of docility and order." Attributing the success to the Quakers, he called on them to extend these benefits to black families. Though these essays all appeared in reprint collections after 1826, Carey's support of education actually began in 1790 when he joined efforts with the Protestant Episcopal Bishop White and the Universalist Benjamin Rush to establish free schools, which they promised would avoid "party, religious bigotry, intolerance, and superstition." This endeavor, like his other reform projects, further reveals his nationalistic desire for a population who shared relatively equal opportunities to earn a competence.[24]

Carey's extensive efforts on behalf of the poor further reveal this nationalistic side to his reform program. Between 1828 and 1830 he produced at least five essays on the topic of underpaid seamstresses, arguing that destitution could turn even the most virtuous to a life of crime. Pointing out that many widowed or abandoned women were left to raise children on a mere fraction of male wages, he argued that they often became desperate enough to send their children out to beg. After their pleas went unheeded they ended up stealing, entering a cycle of "wickedness" that led to the penitentiary. As this occurred, society became further divided along class lines because those who turned to crime gained much more attention than "the thousands and tens of thousands, who are industriously employed, early and late, to make a sorry subsistence, at a miserable pittance" but "pass wholly unnoticed."[25] For Carey, who chaired the Committee of Superintendence, or Committee of the Poor Fund, charity helped people through such lean times. He tried repeatedly to garner support for the city's benevolent organizations and to convince doubters that charity organizations prevented crime rather than encouraged laziness. Even William Lloyd Garrison, who was in favor of immediate abolition, admired this aspect of his agenda, reprinting a couple of his admonitions in the *Liberator*.[26]

Carey's assessment of the plight of the poor also applied to the black community, but the belief he shared with other republican thinkers in the need for cultural uniformity presented a conundrum. The republican worldview posited the need for a rough equality of economic opportunity, but many adherents believed that the American racial climate would forever exclude blacks. This situation in turn caused racial inequality by leaving free blacks a permanent dependent class. Colonizationists realized that class and race intertwined. Carey equated his crusade for poor women with his support of colonization, trying to enlist the sympathy of the ACS's Ralph Gurley. The colonizationist Charles Fenton Mercer made an even clearer connection after traveling to England, witnessing the social conditions brought on by industrialization and becoming "obsessed" with the idea of class warfare. He even compared British removal of paupers to locations in the New World to African colonization. This was not unique. Historian David J. Rothman has placed the colonization society itself within a broader movement to reform penitentiaries, insane asylums, almshouses, orphanages, and reformatories. According to Lawrence Friedman, founders of all of these groups, including the ACS, "were out to restore community cohesion and social balance in a nation that desperately needed both."[27]

The issue of whether Carey and his contemporaries could be labeled "racist" by modern terms is complicated. Carey faced criticism from Richard Allen and Absalom Jones, both free blacks, for his negative portrayal of black nurses during the 1793 yellow fever epidemic. In one of the few pamphlets that generated a profit, Carey chronicled the events in Philadelphia during the calamity and mentioned that some who attended the sick charged high fees for their services and others pilfered. The problem was that he criticized blacks who did so in the body of his essay while hiding his censure of whites in a footnote. In other sections, however, Carey praised black efforts and likely saw himself as an unbiased reporter of a tragic time that brought out both good and bad in many people. The problem, as Jones and Allen pointed out, was that, whether he meant to or not, Carey provided ammunition to whites who resented free blacks. "We have many unprovoked enemies, who begrudge us the liberty we enjoy, and are glad to hear of any complaint against our colour, be it just or unjust." Though his comments hurt free blacks, Carey likely meant no harm. His remarks, however, did reveal at least a subconscious bias. As the historian Phillip Lapsansky has shown, Carey not only criticized blacks, he also dismissed their efforts and downplayed their sacrifice by arguing that they were less susceptible to the fever than whites. More thoughtless than racist, these comments hurt men such as Jones and Allen, who had directly contributed more than Carey to aiding fever victims.[28] To these men, such dismissal and censure indeed felt like racism.

So-called scientific racism and theories of inherent black inferiority, however, did not gain popularity until the second half of the nineteenth century. Instead, most of Carey's contemporaries believed in what historians have termed the "depraved condition" argument. A form of environmentalist theory, this line of thought argued that slavery left blacks with underdeveloped moral faculties and resentment toward whites. Combined with the republican emphasis on racial homogeneity and an environment that excluded almost all blacks from any real opportunity, this created what many saw as a dangerous situation. Northern whites monitored the progress of free blacks, viewing their behavior as evidence either in favor of or against general emancipation, and many concluded that free blacks posed a threat to the country. Even though humanitarians attributed the situation to environmental factors, their conclusions unwittingly provided fuel to those who opposed further emancipation and encouraged the idea that "freed blacks would run up against barriers to equality which would inevitably make them a dangerous and degraded pariah class."[29]

* * *

Political and economic unity of interests was as crucial as cultural homogeneity to Carey's plan for a well-ordered society, and the American racial situation factored in here as well. On this front, Carey became one of Pennsylvania's chief advocates for internal improvements. His earliest foray into the subject of internal improvements called for the very simple measure of using a small tax to fund the numbering of houses and clarification of street addresses. He soon progressed to more sophisticated projects such as canals, railways, and roads to facilitate travel and communication throughout the nation. Carey seems to have realized this need as he traveled across the country seeking subscriptions for his periodical, the *American Museum*. After journeying as much as 1,300 miles on horseback on some trips, he became convinced that the government had a responsibility to direct projects that would make travel easier. During his campaign for such improvements, he gave a speech in 1824 that led to the formation of the Pennsylvania Society for the Promotion of Internal Improvement. Chosen as a vice president of the group, he also served on the acting committee. According to Carey, the construction of a "navigable communication between the Atlantic States and those to the westward" figured prominently in the society's agenda, and after much wrangling and party politics the Union Canal was completed in May 1827. The Chesapeake and Delaware Canal followed in 1829. Carter credits Carey with playing a key role in the success of this project.[30]

After the project was complete Carey defended internal improvements as worth the cost in taxes. He maintained that such projects provided employment opportunities, increased the value of land, and enabled productive citizens to get their goods to market. The canals also lowered freight charges on merchandise and agricultural products, thereby increasing their value. Finally, once canals and railroads had generated enough revenue to pay for themselves, they would continue to bring in money and "afford a fund for the support of government, and ample provision for public schools." Most important, connecting the state's major waterways would unite the people of Pennsylvania "in one indissoluble bond of prosperity and sentiment, to make all *parts* of the commonwealth one flourishing and inseparable *Whole*."[31]

The greatest resistance to internal improvements came from the slaveholders of the South who resented the taxes required to fund such projects. By the time of the nullification crisis, Carey was quite familiar with the danger tax unrest posed to the union. The War of 1812 had provided the first clue. Federalists cited the war as evidence of French influence on the Republicans, and, already irritated at what they perceived as Jefferson's economic bias toward the South, had initiated a "peace movement" that encouraged sectionalism and almost led to disunion. Carey responded with his most famous work, *The Olive Branch*. Attempting to encourage national unity over sectional and party loyalties, he exposed the hysteria generated by both groups. "Violent and impassioned"

Federalist leaders, in their "lust of office and power," had enlisted the help of sympathetic journalists and managed to convince New England merchants that "natural and inevitable hostility" existed between their section and the South because one was commercial and the other was agricultural. They also argued that slavery gave hostile southerners an advantage in Congress, which had allowed them to dictate a program calculated to destroy the Eastern commercial states.[32]

These faulty assertions "by dint of incessant repetition" had turned Boston into a "seat of discontent, complaint, and turbulence." In turn, the city had "thwarted, harassed, and embarrassed the general government" and "spread restlessness and uneasiness in every direction." Emphasizing his own impartiality, Carey provided statistics to show that not only were the Eastern states fairly represented but that, led by a small number of merchants, Boston, not the slave south, had "acquired a degree of influence beyond all proportion greater than her due share . . . a degree of influence which has been exercised in such a manner as to become dangerous to public and private prosperity and happiness, and to the peace and permanence of the Union." The nation now "approached the banks of the Rubicon," and the only way to prevent "anarchy and civil war" was to ignore "the intrigues and management of demagogues," eschew party politics, and compromise.[33]

Later, when southern leaders began calling for "nullification," Carey immediately noted parallels between the two crises. In both cases, a logical measure had been portrayed as evil by partisan leaders, and the press stepped in to blow the situation out of proportion. This time southern agrarians were calling the tariff an unconstitutional "direct robbery perpetrated by the Eastern states on the South" that allowed manufacturers to inflate prices. Carey attacked both arguments. First, he argued that the very men who wrote the Constitution supported the tariff. Furthermore, tariffs led to lower, rather than higher, prices. He then insisted that cotton and tobacco planters had enjoyed protection but now hoped to deny it to manufacturers. Economic stress in the South, he maintained, resulted from overproduction rather than the tariff, and European claims to allow the United States free trade were exaggerated.[34]

Again trying to prevent a split in the union, Carey tried to appeal to moderate southerners this time, calling on them to use reason and ignore their power-hungry leaders. He warned that the nation once again faced civil war, but this time the troublesome states were in an even greater danger from their own folly. Again, separation would clearly lead to war, but if this occurred, southerners would face the wrath of both the northern states and the enslaved. They would be easy prey because of the "disparity of white population, . . . the disaffection of the slaves," and "the naval power belonging to the middle confederacy." Though he had cried out for a strong union of mutual interest for thirty-five years, Carey finally grew tired of southern resistance to economic development, as well as their antiquated labor system. He even went so far as to admit that his section's best interest would be to simply let the South go. After all, this backward section stalled the progress of the rest of the nation by denying economic retaliation against British tariffs. He attributed southern distress to slavery, which led to overproduction, and glutted markets. This in turn caused southern leaders to attack protection, a major aspect of his economic agenda.[35]

Carey wanted the South to participate willingly in the strong domestic economy he envisioned, but they would have to learn to put the nation's interest first by abandoning their decadent lifestyle and accepting the tariff. Pointing out that Britain rose to greatness through trade protection, he argued that "self-preservation" dictated that "every article which can be manufactured here" be protected. Foreign manufactures hurt the young nation by robbing Americans of jobs, and had "drained away the specie of the land." It had also encouraged "a pernicious taste for luxury," threatening the moral fiber of the new country and hastening its drive toward decadence and decay.

The southern lifestyle served as evidence of this decline. In 1785 Carey had noted a "spirit of party" in Charleston and attributed it to speculation in slaves and "a greater degree of luxury and profusion than elsewhere." A year later he included a letter to the editor of the *Columbian Magazine* which pursued this idea by describing the various "manias" that afflicted man. The first, "Negro Mania," had led to greed, luxury, and laziness among the inhabitants of the Carolinas and Georgia. If the owners of the land in these states "cultivated their lands with their own hands, they would not be able to roll in coaches, or to squander thousands of pounds yearly in visiting all the cities of Europe, but they would enjoy more health and happiness in a competency acquired without violating the laws of nature and religion." Thus, slavery fostered luxury among whites and led to factiousness that threatened the republic. Tariffs would help rectify this situation by removing the temptation of foreign goods and reverence for decadent European lifestyles. This neomercantilistic attitude permeated Carey's early work, and his prodding eventually led to the organization of the Philadelphia Society for the Promotion of National Industry.[36]

Throughout the rest of his career, Carey continued to advocate for American industry and its protection by tariffs. His embitterment toward the British and desire to see the United States surpass his old oppressor likely played a role, but his agenda was more visionary than reactionary. He believed the general lack of balance in the American economy held the country back. Economic development and protection of industry would lead to "general prosperity, class harmony and a salutary increase in the nation's population and power." Without manufactures, he warned again in 1831, the United States would allow itself to remain on the losing end of a colonial relationship with Europe. Slavery encouraged just such a relationship, with the South exporting raw cotton and buying expensive finished goods from Britain.[37]

Carey hoped that southerners would realize that protecting manufactures would benefit all sectors of the economy, including agriculture. If the manufacturing sector prospered, farmers and merchants would prosper as well. The tariff would create higher wages, lower the cost of living, keep in the country specie which would otherwise be sent abroad and thus make money more plentiful. In turn, agriculture would gain a steady home market. In short, cooperation would create a strong interstate exchange network that would link the areas together in a system of mutual reciprocity and dependence. Ultimately this scenario would also promote peace by removing the need to deal with foreign nations and by unifying the agricultural and commercial regions of the nation.[38]

Prosperity depended on a strong central government actively coordinating all of these interests and promoting unity between the different sections of the nation, something that would never occur as long as slavery continued to foster division in the nation. Carey first revealed this belief in his push for a revision and strengthening of the Articles of Confederation. At that time he warned that withholding "those powers, that are necessary to render the federal government efficient, and to unite the various interests of the several states," left the country "weak and defenseless." Under the Articles, "each state is induced to arrogate to itself, individually, that portion of sovereignty, which it ought only to exercise, in conjunction with the others, as a part of one Commonwealth." Coming of age in a nation torn by religious, economic, and social division gave Carey "a fetish" for unity. Excited over the prospect of central power, he printed the new constitution in its entirety in *The Columbian Magazine* immediately upon its completion, and once the Constitution was ratified, Carey continued the fight for cohesion. He relished the possibilities he saw in the new experiment in democracy and republicanism.

"The government proposed for America," he insisted "will, upon cool enquiry, be found the most perfect system of government ever contrived for the preservation of liberty, the advancement of arts and sciences, and the happiness of the individual." Of course, this all hinged on its success, and unity would play a key role in the outcome. The reasoned should avoid affiliation with "ignorant partisans," since "among the impediments to the progress of truth, there is scarcely any more formidable than the spirit of party."[39]

By this point, however, party formation was well under way, jeopardizing Carey's dream of America as a democratic beacon to the rest of the world. Though Carey never pledged unqualified allegiance to any party, he initially favored the nationalistic side of the Federalist agenda, staunchly supporting Alexander Hamilton's programs. Like many others, however, he drifted from Hamilton's camp in the 1790s and joined Jefferson's Republican followers once the Federalists began to deny artisans protective tariffs and to tax their products. Letters from Ireland also encouraged Carey's tendency to side with the Jeffersonians on foreign policy, since by aiding the English in any way, the Federalists were hindering Ireland's chances for independence. Closer to home, the party joined a growing nativist attack on Irish immigrants. Finally, during the War of 1812 the issue of slavery led New England Federalists to threaten national unity. As Matthew Mason has shown, their efforts to fight "slave representation" by pushing for a repeal of the Three Fifths Clause was a major factor in the secessionist sentiment that was embodied in the Hartford Convention. Angered that the clause gave southern states an unfair share of power in Congress by allowing them to count each slave as three-fifths of a person, "a majority of articulate New England Federalists" began to repudiate the Constitution, and one even went so far as to use inflammatory language more often associated with later immediatist William Lloyd Garrison by comparing it to "a covenant with death." As Mason points out, this tense rhetoric was what led Carey to write his most famous work, *The Olive Branch*. It also likely informed his attitude toward slavery and colonization by showing just how inflammatory the issue could be and revealing its potential to threaten the union.[40]

Though he changed party affiliation, philosophically Carey remained in the middle of the two camps. Andrew Shankman's book on Pennsylvania Jeffersonians sheds new light on this by dissecting the party and revealing two very different groups: the radical "Philadelphia Democrats" and the more conservative "Quids." The latter, supported by Carey and Tenche Coxe, who organized the Pennsylvania Society for the Encouragement of Manufactures and the Useful Arts, continued to promote internal improvements, protective tariffs, and the Bank of the United States. Support for the tariff provided the main difference between this group and the Federalists. The Quids' direct assistance to craftsmen provided "a Jeffersonian version of economic diversification and expansion." Unlike many Democrats, however, they feared "ungovernable passions," which could "discredit the American political experiment," so they "struggled to describe a more sober and responsible method of democratic politics." Taking ideas from both parties, they linked democracy and capitalism through a system of economic development "based on the internal economy and expected social mobility." They believed that abundant productive resources made material independence attainable for all, and they hoped such opportunity would lessen political conflict. Though Carey agreed on these aspects, he eventually parted with the Jeffersonians over the bank recharter issue, again choosing issue over party.[41]

* * *

While Carey left the realm of political affiliation, most of his friends, including Clay, went on to form the Whigs in 1834. Their platform sounded much like the agenda Carey had always supported, and colonization fit into it quite well. It called for consciously directed improvements, emphasized a unity of interests across class, regional, and productive sectors, and focused on morality or duty over equality or rights. Specifically, it called for federal intervention through tariffs to protect American industry, internal improvement subsidies, and support for the Bank of the United States, all programs that relied on centralized direction. Like Carey, Whigs saw a need for a distinct American cultural identity and believed that the "diversified, capitalistic social order they wanted required a population that was literate, ambitious, and disciplined." They also drew their political philosophy from the same commonwealth ideas Carey had, and they shared his classical concern for luxury and decay and disdain for violence, traits many of them associated with the slave South. In general, Whigs, and later Republicans, also opposed slavery for political and economic reasons and supported colonization.[42]

Like Clay and other Whigs, Carey saw both slavery and unqualified emancipation as incompatible with the industrial agenda. Hoping to compromise, however, most of these men, unlike New England Federalists at the Hartford Convention, remained reluctant to attack slavery.

Carey went even further than most Whigs in seeking to conciliate the South. He briefly supported a project proposed in the upper South to move slaves from the farm to the factory. Arguing that such a move could restore southern prosperity and lessen the region's reliance on imports, he even developed a mathematical formula to show that slave labor would be more profitable than free in manufacturing coarse cotton cloth. It would also relieve the glutted raw cotton market. Most important, it would remove "the jealousies and heart-burnings that prevail on the subject of the protecting system" and "will, therefore, tend to knit more closely the bonds of union between the different sections of the country." Even this offer of peace was ignored as tension over the tariff increased.[43] Carey's determination to forward his nationalist agenda severely clouded his judgment in this case, but his proslavery career was short-lived.

Within a month he found a more palatable solution in colonization, a movement that bridged the gap by offering something to both Carey the reformer and Carey the nationalist. It provided the only solution that accorded well with his opposition to slavery and his role as peacemaker. Though he opposed slavery, Carey could not join the abolitionists because he feared their "imprudent zeal" would "produce more substantial injury than the animosity of decided enemies." At the same time, he and a growing number of northern border-state residents resented slaveholders' insistence that the federal government help not only to protect their human property but also to ensure their rights to take slaves with them when they traveled throughout the free states. These two situations, along with southern resistance to the tariff, were gravely threatening the union.[44]

Providing four possible emancipation scenarios, however, Carey painted a gloomy picture. He argued that slaveholders could develop a sense of guilt and free their bondspersons, but he deemed this unlikely. Indeed, gradual abolition like the policy that Pennsylvania had adopted was no longer feasible in most of the South due to the large black population. On the other hand, the nonslaveholding states could "coerce" the slave states to free their workers, but this idea was "too absurd to be discussed for a moment." Likewise, the federal government could fund compensated emancipation, but that would cost too much. Finally, the slaves could revolt and emancipate themselves, and this scenario was growing more likely as abolitionist tactics were leaving slaves "sullen, discontented, unhappy, and refractory." Carey saw revolt as likely and offered population statistics to show just how disastrous it could be. To prevent this he called for amelioration of the slaves' conditions and possible removal to Liberia.[45] A year later he pledged unequivocal support for colonization after the ACS also began to stress population growth.

More important than providing sheer numbers, the report that caught Carey's attention placed colonization clearly into the American System. Unsurprisingly, much of the report came from Henry Clay himself, and historian David M. Streifford, like Carey, noticed the connection. Clay's focus on black population growth resulted from his republican ideology and its focus on a homogenous population. Colonization would solve this dilemma. Clay argued that the scheme both respected states' rights and promised to reduce the black population by colonizing the annual increase of free blacks. He argued that all the society would have to do is transport six thousand free blacks annually to achieve this goal. At $20 per person, this would cost only $120,000 annually. Of course, the scheme ultimately offered much more, and as it became more successful, states would see it in their best interests to contribute by expanding the scope to include slaves and thus "ultimately rid themselves of an universally acknowledged curse." He provided detailed population statistics to show how these two sides of the plan would work together to eventually remove both segments of the black population, and he called on both federal and state governments to help. The society would concentrate on removing free blacks. "Collateral consequences, we are not responsible for." All that was needed was a way to convey to the public the beauty of this plan and thus gain the support of both federal and state governments.[46]

Carey took it on himself to fulfill this role. He adopted the movement as his own and used his publishing skills to help the cause reach a broad audience. Beginning in 1830, he produced three major colonization pamphlets that went through several editions each, most of which he printed at his own expense. Unable to understand why only $125,000 had been donated to the colonization society during its twelve-year existence, Carey compared the scheme to great movements of the past that had faced serious opposition, such as the abolition of the British slave trade, Catholic emancipation, and the building of the Erie and Hudson canals. He hoped to win the support of the two groups who resisted colonization most strongly yet, in his view, stood to benefit the greatest from its success—free blacks and South Carolinians.[47]

Using his common pseudonym "Hamilton," Carey described the society's objectives in a way that he hoped would appeal to both groups' self-interest. Colonization would rescue free blacks from degradation by providing them a place where they could enjoy the "benefits of free government," while also helping to spread civilization, morals, and religion throughout Africa, a continent that had once been great but now was "sunk in the lowest and most hideous state of barbarism." It would encourage emancipation by giving guilt-ridden slaveholders somewhere to send freed slaves, and by providing such an asylum would "avert the dangers of a dreadful collision at a future day of the two castes, which must inevitably be objects of mutual jealousy to each other." In this sense, it would also further the industrial agenda by providing the chance to end slavery without creating a biracial society. This would save the union by allowing the various regions to forge the ties Carey had been calling for while also protecting all whites from black retribution. Because it promised so much to so many, the scheme, like internal improvements and economic development, deserved government support, and with such support the plan could succeed.[48]

Half of Carey's objective in writing his colonization pamphlets was to gain black support by showing that they, unlike European immigrants, could never assimilate in American society, and that Liberia offered much better prospects. Waiving "all inquiry whether this be right or wrong," he argued that conditions for most free blacks were "more unfavourable than [those] of many of the slaves." Relegated to low-paying jobs and laboring under "oppressive disadvantages," they shouldered "all the burdens, cares, and responsibilities of freedom," but enjoyed "few or none of its substantial benefits." With very rare exceptions, "no merit, no service, no talents can ever elevate them to a level with the whites." He lamented the forced removal of free blacks from Ohio as well as recent efforts to prevent free blacks from settling in Louisiana. Even states that did not exclude free blacks outright severely restricted their residency by requiring them to post hefty bonds to ensure good behavior. Carey cited as an example a recent North Carolina law that called for enslavement of free blacks who could not pay a $500 "fine." According to Carey, this was no idle threat, as a free black had recently been made a slave under this law. "Intended as security from danger," such laws nevertheless caused "cruelty and hardship" and had only become more common after "the Southampton massacre." Indeed, Georgia recently decided to quarantine "all vessels having free coloured persons on board" for forty days, outlaw incendiary pamphlets, and penalize anyone for teaching free blacks to read or write. Likewise, Maryland's lawmakers called for the removal of all blacks manumitted after a set date.[49]

Further, white prejudice hampered black efforts to assimilate in other ways. "A coloured individual, of great talents, merits, and wealth, may emerge from the crowd," but "cases of this kind, are to the last degree, rare" due to legal and social discrimination. When blacks tried to assimilate through education, they faced serious barriers. "The strong opposition to the establishment of a negro college in Newhaven, speaks in a language not to be mistaken . . . and there is no reason to expect, that the lapse of centuries will make any change in this respect." Even industrious blacks could never truly contribute to national prosperity since "in some of the states, they are actually doomed to idleness, because, however skillful they may be, in any branch of manufactures, white operatives cannot generally be induced to work with them."[50]

Conditions in Liberia were different. Unlike the forced removal that sent blacks from state to state, emigration to this African colony was voluntary. Opponents had discouraged blacks from going with accounts of poor climate and high mortality, but Carey used stock colonizationist arguments to contend that conditions were actually no worse than white settlers had faced in Massachusetts, Virginia, and North Carolina. Liberian soil was good and fertile, and commerce there was "respectable and increasing annually." The nearly two thousand colonists were moral and temperate and thriving, exporting goods and making money to support themselves. Carey urged doubters among the black community to assemble a committee to go to the colony, investigate the situation, and report back to the free black community. He was certain they would find that "all the difficulties have been surmounted, and the colonists enjoy all the comforts of independence and consideration in an equal degree with their former masters." Though degraded in America, in Liberia they "will be lords of the soil, and have every inducement and every opportunity to cultivate their minds." Most important, "they will not be borne down by that sense of inferiority, from whose goadings they cannot escape here, and which is enough to depress minds the most highly gifted." With hard work, they could even aspire to the bar, the bench, and the medical profession.[51]

Free blacks would not be the only beneficiaries of a successful African colony. According to Carey, colonization had arrested the slave trade by encouraging African chiefs to choose legitimate commerce while also offering a place for the government to return victims of the illegal slave trade. Carey cited examples from Virginia, Maryland, and North Carolina in which "entire families have been blest with their freedom," in some cases at the owners' expense. Finally, colonization promised to help "regenerate" the continent. Again using popular ACS arguments, Carey insisted that "Africa, though brutalized by wars, the invasions of barbarians, and the most grinding despotism, was once . . . as proud an eminence in point of civilization as any part of Europe." Indeed, "Christianity and civilization were early introduced" there. The slave trade, through its exploitation of Africa's human resources, had temporarily destroyed this progress, but colonization could make it right again.[52]

Colonization also offered a great deal to white America. It would hasten the South's progress toward modernization by freeing it from a now unprofitable labor system that "retards improvement" and hurts manufacturing efforts, leaving for whites "no diversity of occupations, no incentive to enterprise." At the same time, it would strengthen the union by removing friction over interstate travel with slaves and leave extremists on both sides without a cause. Finally, the ACS agenda would prevent an otherwise inevitable race war.[53]

Even though his colonization writings focused on the benefits blacks would gain from colonization, Carey admitted in private correspondence that fear of insurrection prompted much of his effort. Drawing once again on standard colonizationist rhetoric, he lamented the failure of early efforts to keep the black population small from the beginning and blamed first the British government, and, later, constitutional legitimation, for the current volatile situation. The resulting "heterogeneous" caste system left the entire country vulnerable to "the danger of an explosion such as took place in St. Domingo." He warned that "although the vigilance employed in the southern states has hitherto, and may for a long time to come, avert this calamity; yet vigilance is oftentimes relaxed, and in a moment of relaxation, a favourable opportunity of trying to shake off the yoke, may arrive—a convulsion take place—and, though the attempt would probably be suppressed, the country be devastated in the struggle." Thus, it was in the best interest of all whites to support the colonization endeavor.[54]

To win South Carolinians over, Carey relied on a tactic that had played a key role in his own conversion to the movement—statistical analysis of white and black population figures. He traced a progression in the population "east of the Blue Ridge" from a white majority of 25,098 in 1790 to a black majority of 81,078 in 1830. He also pointed out that in the "five original slave states," from 1790 to 1830 the white population had increased 79 percent while slave numbers grew by 112 percent, the same rate of white increase in the "middle and Eastern states." This created a situation "pregnant with alarming consequences, likely to explode

sooner or later." Assuming that such growth disparity would only continue or increase, Carey, who overlooked the importance of these laborers to the southern economy, asked "Who can reflect on this probable
state of things without horror, and without lamenting over the infatua-
tion which leads our southern fellow citizens not only not to strain every
nerve in aid of the colonization scheme, but strenuously to endeavor to
prevent its success!"[55]

Consistent with his lifelong belief in centralized direction, Carey insisted that success hinged on government support at both the state and
federal level. To convince the public to allow the government to fund
the plan, he repeated Clay's figures on the cost of transporting colonists.
He added that it would become even less expensive "when the situation
of the colony becomes better known, and the prejudices which have
been industriously created against it, are done away," because free emigrants, once convinced of the colony's merits, will pay their own way,
and masters will pay to send manumitted slaves once they come around
and support the movement. Once in Africa, settlers will be able to support themselves because a scarcity of labor makes jobs readily available.
Transport costs for preventing an increase in the black population would
total $1,500,000, but the nation had managed to raise $100,000,000 in
just a year and a half to fund a war. Furthermore, the government's annual revenue was $20,000,000 to $25,000,000, and the national debt was
nearly paid off.[56]

Carey saw the combined efforts of the government and the ACS to
return recaptives as a sign of even greater possibilities. Optimistically,
he suggested a constitutional amendment to strengthen this relationship
by providing funding. Carey made this part of his agenda a sectional
issue, however, by assuming that nonslaveholding states, along with
Maryland, Virginia, and North Carolina, could override any objections
from the southernmost states in securing this amendment. In support
of a funding plan offered by Henry Clay, he also included excerpts from
John Marshall and James Madison suggesting that money from the sale
of western lands be applied to the endeavor. Clay, who had become the
ACS's most influential political advocate by 1825, believed that congressional emancipation would be unconstitutional, so he linked colonization to internal improvements and drafted several bills to use western
land sale revenue to fund both objects. Southerners saw right through
his plan, and by 1828 colonization had become a partisan issue. James
Hamilton Jr., governor of South Carolina, and John C. Calhoun tied colonization to the tariff agenda during the nullification crisis of 1832–33.

The version of the bill Clay proposed in 1832 passed the Senate but ultimately caused a tremendous backlash when Andrew Jackson vetoed it after winning the presidency that year. From that point on, colonization became a partisan issue in the popular mind, and Democrats opposed it as too much government interference. Jackson's veto pretty well ended the colonizationists' hope for federal aid. Some supporters, including Carey, had warned against tying the movement so closely to one party, but to no avail. Indeed, P. J. Staudenraus, the leading expert on the colonization society, has shown that many Jacksonians privately supported the movement but could not support it publicly in the election year for fear of losing political followers.[57]

It is ironic that partisan politics helped kill one of Mathew Carey's pet projects, especially since the ideologies of the two parties were not very different in his state. Shankman has shown that "the political mainstream in Pennsylvania between 1828 and 1840 belonged to the procapitalist Jacksonians," a group that supported such Whig measures as a high tariff and the Bank of the United States. In 1824, however, Pennsylvania was "the only significant northern state to vote for Jackson," and the state continued to support him in 1832. Pessen attributed this state of affairs to "identification with the Old Hero and masterful demagogy." At any rate, Pennsylvania colonizationists such as John H. Kennedy knew the climate of their state and begged the ACS to wait until more propitious times to push for state aid. He warned Ralph Gurley, who was the secretary of the ACS, that their organization was "viewed as a political engine in some parts of the country, particularly this state," since Clay "advocated it totally" while Jackson opposed it. Since the Pennsylvania delegation was Jacksonian, Kennedy asked the society to wait until after the election to press the issue, at which point "the most prominent representatives from this state will vote in our favor." For now, however, "we must not entangle ourselves needlessly."[58]

Carey's role in trying to gain support for the group was underappreciated. He often distributed his colonization pamphlets gratuitously and lost a great deal of money in the endeavor despite repeatedly asking Gurley for help in distributing them and raising enough contributions from ACS chapters to break even. When he did charge, it was a fee of $5 for 100 copies, "the cheapest publication ever offered for sale in the United States."

The ACS reprinted eight pages of one of his pamphlets in its fifteenth annual report and ordered copies of his pamphlets to distribute at meetings, but Carey clearly took the initiative to publish new editions of each work, without the aid of the society. Not only did Carey end up paying for most of the printing, but the editorial assistance he sought was late in coming, when he got any response at all. When he offered to debate Thomas Dew during the latter's 1832 campaign against the Virginia legislature's consideration to fund colonization, the society chose someone else. Carey died in 1839, and the 1840 ACS report did not even mention it. Carey profited on only a couple of his pamphlets, neither of which were his works on colonization. Indeed, in this endeavor he lost money. Even so, a year before his death, he looked back on his career with pride that "I have never written a line of which I have reason to be ashamed." He had presented the nation a coherent plan for economic development, a plan which showed respect for all sectors and interests of the white community. The one sad blot on his legacy, however, was that he never overcame the tendency to put his nationalism above all else, and that he turned the idea of cultural homogeneity into one of racial sameness. This left him unable to see black Americans as anything more than numbers to be put into neat little formulas and subtracted from the broader picture of his unified nation.[59]

* * *

This political strand of antislavery had evolved from the Federalist Hamiltonian camp and progressed through the Whig and Republican agendas. Both antislavery and antiblack at the same time, it included ideologies of Free Soil and Manifest Destiny. Free Soilers, many of whom were former colonizationists like James G. Birney, would eventually ignore Carey's frequent calls for peace and abandon the colonizationists' attempts to maintain friendship with the South. They would choose, instead, to cry out forcefully against the efforts to protect and expand slavery, coining the term "Slave Power" to describe southern leaders' dictatorial and tyrannical behavior. Carey had fought against such sectional resentment in several versions of *The Olive Branch*, but as tensions grew throughout the antebellum years, his moderation was no longer viable.[60]

Free Soil arguments nourished northern antislavery sentiment, and the Republicans took Carey's critique of the effects of slavery on southern society even further, using this argument to help build their political antislavery movement in the decade before the Civil War. They brought Carey's overall economic agenda into their ideology, primarily by relying heavily on the free labor doctrines of his son, Henry Charles Carey. The younger Carey echoed and expanded on his father's argument for economic development and a unity of interests across economic classes. His theories strongly influenced the Republican free labor agenda, and in turn fueled their opposition to slavery. Unfortunately free soil and free labor opposition to slavery featured the same antiblack ideas that influenced much of the colonization movement. At the same time, the immediatist abolitionists that Carey feared as divisive to the union also sought to expand opposition to bound labor, but their brand of opposition included a call for racial justice and equality of opportunity for blacks in the United States. In the end the self-interested type of antislavery sentiment ultimately won out, but war still resulted.[61] Carey's vision of colonization as the means to preventing this scenario failed.

There were many problems with the political strand of colonization. For one thing, the focus on central control prevented politically minded colonizationists from appreciating the voluntary system that most philanthropic organizations had come to employ by this period. Indeed, when Carey issued a plea for support of Pennsylvania's public charities in December of 1828, the state's colonization society had sixteen annual subscribers and thirty-four life subscribers. The group's total receipts for the previous year were $482, barely more than half of what the abolition society took in. At the same time, the quest for federal aid and direction never materialized. This was one area in which Whigs and Democrats held significantly different ideas. Once Jackson took office, he and his supporters, suspicious of federal involvement in slavery, effectively ended hopes for government involvement in the scheme. The idea lived on in the political arena even into the Civil War, but by that point, as we will see when we discuss Martin R. Delany's story, black Americans had become even more determined to resist removal. Instead, they chose to seize the opportunities provided by political expediency to win their own freedom and prove their worthiness as American citizens. Before we return to this theme, however, we must explore the other strain of the movement by becoming acquainted with humanitarian colonizationists' crusade to end slavery. As we will see, Elliott Cresson, though often overzealous, did manage to find a place for grassroots organizing in the colonization movement by focusing on the antislavery dimensions and using a specific case tactic that allowed individual whites to feel that their efforts were helping to achieve black freedom in a concrete way.[62]

4 / "We *here* mean literally what we say": Elliott Cresson and the Pennsylvania Colonization Society's Humanitarian Agenda

The October 17, 1835, *Colonization Herald* reads like an obituary. Articles celebrating the progress of education and internal improvements in the colony of Liberia are surrounded on all sides by reports of death and destruction. Trusted natives had attacked Bassa Cove on the night of June 10, 1835, and killed about twenty unarmed settlers. A dispatch from nearby Edina begged for assistance from the Liberian capital: "We are at present in a state of war" with only one barrel of powder. As soon as their appeal reached the capital, the Monrovians provided the needed assistance, and together the Liberians laid waste to native villages, exacting revenge for the slaughter. According to one of the missionaries, this "lamentable catastrophe" furnished sufficient proof of just how "visionary it is to think of erecting a settlement of civilized men among savages, without having in possession ample means of self-defense."[1]

This lesson in the dark side of human nature should not have shocked the settlement's founders. Consciously or not they had long admitted the inherently ugly side of the human psyche by arguing that white Americans could never accept free blacks on terms of equality in the United States. Even so, they expressed complete shock. Supported mostly by Quakers, the Young Men's Colonization Society of Pennsylvania had joined with the New York City Colonization Society to found this settlement on principles of temperance and peace. They had been careful to purchase the land fairly and secure the acceptance of the nearby kings. As a sign of good faith, one of the kings had even sent his son back with

FIGURE 6. "Elliott Cresson," ca. 1838 by John Sartain. (Courtesy of the Library Company of Philadelphia.)

the Americans to be educated in the United States. Excited about the prospect of their new town, they had already sent a second expedition of settlers and were preparing a third when the "disastrous news" reached the United States and "clothed the friends of Africa in mourning." Refusing to give up, though, they immediately began collecting money to rebuild and fortify their part of the colony.[2]

Bassa Cove was an independent venture born out of years of bickering and dissent among supporters of the American Colonization Society. Whereas men such as Mathew Carey and Henry Clay had hoped that colonization of blacks to distant lands would save white Americans and their republican experiment, another group of colonizationists, including Philadelphia's Roberts Vaux, Gerard Ralston, and Elliott Cresson, focused on the movement's value as an agent to secure the end of slavery and the uplift of blacks throughout the world. This group of supporters looked to missionaries Robert S. Finley and Samuel J. Mills as the most important founders of the movement and tied their efforts to a larger reform agenda that included antislavery and temperance as well as the spreading of Christianity and education. For these men, the colonization movement was the logical extension of gradualist efforts and fit comfortably into Pennsylvania's Quaker reform legacy. The ACS won their support by promising to free slaves and civilize Africa, and they determined in turn to force the organization to live up to that promise.

Indeed, for Cresson, keeping the colonization movement in line became an obsession. He began working for the ACS diligently in 1829 and continued his efforts until he died in 1854, but the high point of his involvement came in the 1830s. At the beginning of this decade he joined the movement full of hope, but he soon grew disenchanted with the parent organization's efforts to maintain its southern support. Contrasting Cresson's efforts with Carey's reveals the dual nature of the colonization movement within the state and offers a better understanding of the forces that split the movement nationally. Such a comparison must look at the humanitarian agenda of some of the movement's founders and the efforts of men such as Cresson to keep the movement true to the promise of antislavery and black uplift.

Colonizationists of Cresson's persuasion joined the movement because they saw the scheme as the only realistic way to end slavery in the United States. Many were current or former members of the Pennsylvania Abolition Society, as well as the Society of Friends. The ACS had long coveted their support and finally managed to earn it completely when Francis Scott Key toured the Keystone State in late 1829 to plead

the case of six hundred slaves waiting to be freed once funds were secured for their transportation to Liberia. The image of fellow human beings waiting in chains and groaning under the lash galvanized Cresson
and his colleagues into action, and this group of philanthropists became
Pennsylvania's most diehard colonizationists. Thanks to their efforts the
ACS went from sending mostly free blacks to Liberia to sending mainly
manumitted slaves.[3] This change was due largely to Elliott Cresson's determination that colonization was founded on the humanitarian principles of antislavery and black uplift.

* * *

Cresson represented the seventh generation of a Quaker family that pre-
ceded William Penn to the new world. Born on March 2, 1796, in Philadelphia to Mary and John Elliott Cresson, Elliott apprenticed under his
merchant uncle Caleb Cresson and succeeded him as partner in Cresson
and Wistar in 1818. According to one biographer, he made a fortune as
a merchant "but is better known for how he gave it away." Paramount
among his philanthropic interests, according to another biographer, was
"the betterment of the condition of Negroes." Cresson inherited this
concern from his Quaker family, which included a great uncle who went
to England with John Woolman in 1772 to plead for the emancipation of
slaves. Cresson's Quaker heritage influenced his work, and he once told
an associate that his admiration for William Penn inspired him to work
for the human race. A lifelong bachelor, Cresson lived with his mother
on Sansom Street until he died of gangrene at the age of 58 in February of
1854. Historian Richard Blackett, who focused on his work in England,
found it "difficult to determine whether Cresson's antislavery posture
was genuine or a mere ruse to win support for colonization," but viewing
his efforts over the nearly three decades he devoted to the cause reveals
his sincerity.[4]

Like most whites of his time, Cresson shared a deep ambivalence about
the race he struggled to help liberate, but his work with the colonization
movement demonstrates his determination to end slavery. The movement caught his attention by 1826, when he was county director of Negro
schools and a member of the Pennsylvania Abolition Society. He offered
tepid support in 1828, intrigued by the scheme but disgusted that the
colonization society's president, "instead of sending his own people to
Liberia, chose rather to *sell them*," creating hostility among abolitionists
and free blacks. Cresson had been pitching the plan to both groups, but

many were now convinced that any society under such leadership "can not have in view any other than sinister and selfish ends." At least one writer in *Poulson's American Daily Advertiser* had already accused the society of seeking the "perpetuation" rather than the "extermination" of slavery, and in such a charged climate Cresson had not been able to make "one solitary convert." He suggested that Ralph Gurley, known also for his humanitarian bent, attend the Abolition Convention in Baltimore to repair the situation and "convince them of the importance of cooperating heartily with us." He remained hopeful that they could enlist abolitionists' pecuniary aid since both groups "are labouring to attain the same end." Though a life subscriber at this point, Cresson feared that Pennsylvania's antislavery and free black communities were "not ripe for the scheme yet," and he still harbored reservations, which left him unable to "prove my own zeal by becoming one of the $1,000 members."[5]

The idea of helping free slaves proved a strong inducement. First, North Carolina slaveholders offered "more than 2000" slaves to their state's Yearly Meeting "on condition of their transporting them" to Africa in 1828. Since the Quakers lacked the resources to achieve this end, Cresson pledged that "no stone be left unturned to obtain aid either from individuals, states, or the general government." Soon afterward, Francis Scott Key issued his plea, and Cresson was chosen secretary of the committee to raise money for the expeditions. According to historian Kurt Kocher, at that point "the history of Pennsylvania colonization . . . entered a new phase," becoming "virtually a 'one-man show'" starring Elliott Cresson. Julie Winch agrees, calling Cresson "the most influential supporter of the ACS in Philadelphia." Once the Pennsylvania Abolition Society finally rejected colonization, Cresson resigned from that group to work full time for the ACS, but his support was contingent on the scheme fostering emancipation.[6]

Many Pennsylvanians shared Cresson's outlook. Public meetings convened in Philadelphia in October 1829 and January 1830 resolved to raise funds for the cause "on condition that they be applied exclusively to the outfit, transportation, and subsequent support, of slaves, who being wiling to join the colony can be liberated only with a view to their emigration." This resolution resulted from the belief that "several hundred persons, now held as slaves in the Southern States, may be gratuitously liberated" once the ACS could send them to the colony, "and that the emancipation of such slaves cannot be effected by any other arrangement." Appealing across the Atlantic, the Pennsylvania group convinced the Female Anti-Slavery Society of London to send £50 to be applied specifically to this purpose. Additional contributions totaling £100 came from England "with the clear understanding that [the money] goes to the distinct fund for the release of slaves from bondage." The Reverend George Boyd, who served with Cresson on the committee to raise funds for the *Liberia* and *Montgomery* expeditions, wrote to Gurley that a member of his congregation had offered to contribute $20 annually "so long as he would be enabled to do so, if that sum may secure the transportation" of a liberated slave.[7]

Even as the parent society struggled to maintain support in both the North and the South, the Pennsylvania auxiliaries remained open about their antislavery stance. In 1831 Cresson issued a public statement outlining his view of the ACS's agenda and progress. He blamed England for introducing slavery to the Americas and hampering colonial efforts at abolition by striking down import taxes. He then described revolutionary antislavery sentiment and support for colonization but added that both the Articles of Confederation and the Constitution left the issue of slavery under state jurisdiction. Optimistic, however, he added that "the number of slaves offered gratuitously by benevolent owners, exceed ten-fold the present means of the society to receive and convey them to Africa," and that only South Carolina showed hostility to the scheme. That state's resistance, he added, only afforded "the most incontestable evidence" that colonization deserved support, since they "ground their opposition upon the *inevitable tendency* of colonization *to eradicate slave-holding*, and thereby deprive them of their *property*."[8]

Many of his Pennsylvania coworkers agreed. Whereas the ACS professed one goal—colonization of free blacks in Africa—the Pennsylvania Colonization Society's constitution listed emancipation as one of its goals. This stemmed partly from a desire to enlist the support of black Pennsylvanians, but given the number in this auxiliary who came from the abolitionist ranks, it is also a reflection of a sincere desire to end slavery in a gradual, legal manner that respected the limitations of the Constitution. According to historian Eric Burin, "manumission dominated PCS leaders' thinking and rhetoric," and the promise to apply funds specifically to transport freed slaves and help them get settled in their new environment made benevolent members of the overall community feel that they got something concrete in return for their contributions. Thus, when the *African Repository* reprinted details about the passengers on the *Liberia*, those who had contributed could follow with personal interest the story of George Erskine, the black Presbyterian minister who embarked for Africa to find a new home for his family after purchasing the freedom of each member himself. Readers were likely touched even more by the picture of his eighty-year-old mother returning to her homeland after a hard life of relentless toil. The image of a seventy-year-old patriarch named Cook ushering his family of thirty to a life without the fear of forced separation likely drew equal interest. Cresson realized the value of such anecdotes and rarely passed up a chance to remind listeners and readers that every $25 helped free a slave. Even better, for every $50 spent since the society's "commencement, we have not only a settler to show, but an ample and fertile territory in reserve, where our future emigrants may sit under their own vines and fig trees with none to make them afraid."[9]

Though minuscule in the broader view of population statistics, the roughly 500 emigrants from other states sent to Africa by the PCS were significant to those who helped secure their liberty. According to Burin, colonizationists helped about 560 slaveholders send approximately 6,000 manumitted slaves to Liberia between 1820 and 1860. For those such as Cresson who adhered to the gradualist agenda and strongly believed Congress lacked the power to intervene in slavery, reaching out to southerners to build a cooperative antislavery movement was the only option. Unlike the ACS, however, Pennsylvania colonizationists insisted on stating clearly, publicly, and repeatedly their antislavery agenda.

* * *

Linking colonization to the social utility reform ideology of "disinterested benevolence," humanitarian colonizationists saw themselves as the protectors of the movement's true aim. According to historian P. J. Staudenraus, there was much in the history of the movement that would support this view. Quakers such as John Parrish and William Thornton suggested colonization before the ACS was founded, and Staudenraus compares Thornton, an English Quaker, with Pennsylvania founder William Penn.

The ACS was one of many "evangelical-inspired" voluntary societies. Through these societies, Robert S. Finley, a Presbyterian minister and educator in a country academy at Basking Ridge, New Jersey, began his reform career by trying to distribute Bibles and religious tracts to free blacks. Eventually abandoning such efforts, Finley began to consider African colonization and turned to Samuel J. Mills, an agent for the New York and New Jersey Presbyterian Synod's African Education Society. Mills and four of his classmates at Andover Seminary had founded

America's first missionary society and had played a role in establishing the American Bible Society in 1816. His classmates were some of the first American missionaries to visit India, Ceylon, and Burma, but his concern rested mostly with America's urban poor and free blacks. After offering to pitch Finley's scheme during his fundraising ventures for the African Education Society, Mills learned that his collections were larger when he stressed the connection between the two groups.[10]

Together Finley and Mills proposed the colonization society. They introduced most of the ideas that would endure as the movement solidified, including the need for federal aid, the role of melioration, the belief in racial equality under the right circumstances, and the belief that colonization would save white society while also uplifting Africa. Their associate Ebenezer Burgess, who went with Mills on a mission of inquiry to Africa in 1818, added the argument that colonization would combat the slave trade. Their political allies, including Henry Clay, urged them to tone down their antislavery stance, but it was exactly that stance that attracted some of colonization's most able supporters, including Cresson, who specifically expressed his admiration for Finley. In general, historians have placed the work of these founders and their staunchest followers within the benevolent reform movement. According to Andrew E. Murray, "Colonization held out the millennial vision of a regenerated Negro race, of suppressing the hated slave trade, and of transforming the African continent into an earthly Eden."[11]

Humanitarian colonizationists believed that the ACS scheme would attack slavery on two fronts. First, they were convinced that slaveholders were trapped in a system they genuinely wanted out of, and an African asylum would allow them to release their bondspersons without fear of reprisal or racial mixing. Second, colonizationists believed that a successful colony would showcase black potential and convince all whites that slavery was wrong. Those who subscribed to this belief often added Paul Cuffee to the list of important early colonizationists, and those such as Cresson who had experience working with the black community were most likely to embrace this aspect of the agenda. A letter from Pennsylvania printed in the *African Repository* described colonization as a "great experiment" that, if successful, would remove "the strongest, the only apology for slavery." Professing himself an abolitionist but adding that state sovereignty made colonization the only way to achieve this end, the author added that "nations are becoming better acquainted with each other, and if it shall be made certain that the African race are competent to self-government, slavery cannot long withstand the reprobation of mankind." Others modified the plan by focusing on missionary work and the introduction of Christianity. Either way, the goal was uplift, first in Africa and then in the United States.[12]

Though ACS efforts have drawn deserved criticism for choosing to remove the black population rather than improve the lot of blacks in the United States, the humanitarian colonizationists thought their work would give Africans and African Americans better conditions under which to live. The most obvious way the scheme would improve Africa, in their view, was by directly combating the slave trade. Their hope was that the presence of the colonies would discourage local chiefs from selling human beings. At the fourteenth annual ACS convention Cresson announced that in the nine years since the first colonists had landed, two kings had "thrown down their crowns at the feet of the infant republic," seeking an alliance "for the holy purpose of exchanging the guilty traffic in human flesh and blood for legitimate commerce." Just as important, the trade had been outlawed in the United States and Europe, so officials in American and British settlements such as Sierra Leone could keep a watch for illicit activity and provide a local policing force to "recapture" human cargo. In 1831 Cresson claimed that in the eight years of the colony's existence they had gained ten thousand "aborigines" as settlers. He and many others saw each new group of recaptives brought to Liberia and Sierra Leone as proof of their success as a humanitarian endeavor, and Cresson urged both the American and British governments to pursue slavers aggressively. He even proposed reaching out to Mexican and Colombian officials to combat Spanish slavers. Indeed, his disgust for the slave trade outweighed his Quaker ethics of nonviolence enough that he protested when a settler "detected with a slave for the purpose of sale" was flogged. "Certainly if ever hanging is allowable," this was the time.[13]

In addition to fighting the slave trade, the humanitarians also sincerely, if naively, believed African colonization would improve the daily lives of Africans. In the same speech at the fourteenth annual convention, Cresson claimed that the African chiefs sought "equal laws, civilization and religion." They also "ask for schools—factories—churches." The society used the *Repository* and annual reports to disseminate stories of success in the colony and harmonious relations with the neighboring Africans. They made especially good use of any positive reports or letters they could get from settlers and employed settler Francis Devany's 1830 visit to the United States to great advantage. Cresson even took the opportunity to tour with him and establish auxiliary societies. After John B. Russwurm, a settler sent to superintend the schools in 1829, started the colonial newspaper, the *Liberia Herald* in 1831, they borrowed from it extensively. In addition to reprinting items in their own newspapers, journals, reports, and tracts, they sent clippings to sympathetic newspapers throughout the country. Humanitarian colonizationists refused to see how overstated many of the positive reports were. They deluded themselves into believing that Liberia was helping them make up to Africa for the crimes committed by kidnappers and slave traders. When critics pointed to problems in the colony, they always found a way to explain them away.[14]

* * *

Another way humanitarians tried to make amends was by educating American blacks before and after sending them to the colony. Abolitionists, including Britain's Charles Stuart, criticized the ACS because the group's emphasis on state's rights left them unwilling to challenge southern laws forbidding the education of slaves. They also asserted that colonizationists led the opposition to educating northern free blacks. Although the ACS as a group deserves such criticism for insisting on state sovereignty in such matters, and some individuals who claimed to support colonization did a great deal to hamper black education, humanitarians such as Cresson, Leonard Bacon, and Theodore Frelinghuysen saw education as a vital part of their uplift agenda.[15]

Less concerned with constitutional matters of state authority than many colonizationists, Cresson wrote to Gurley on several occasions about the importance of educating blacks, whether they wished to go to Liberia or remain in the United States. Property or not, he saw slaves as human beings who deserved proper moral guidance. He pointed to the hypocrisy of "those professing religion and yet permitting these poor creatures for the crime of a black skin, to perish like the beasts of the field." Communication with slaveholders had shown him that many masters held slaves to a lower moral standard and assumed that all slaves were natural thieves who held low regard for family and matrimonial ties. Cresson, who saw such faults as a product of the system, expressed dismay at such ignorance among whites. "Are we *really* the most pious and enlightened nation on earth?" he asked. "When will Christian missions be established to teach the moral doctrines that negroes have souls !!! and that owners, especially *religious* ones, are responsible for the errors [their slaves] commit for want of knowledge?" Whites had a duty to provide moral guidance to those who had been forced to live under such an amoral system for far too long. "I am serious. . . . If we have torn them from their country and reduced them to slavery, they surely claim our sympathies." Even if assisting in black uplift "does not absolve us from the sin of holding our brother man in chains, it will at least palliate it."[16]

Whether Gurley expressed sympathy for Cresson's views or not, the ACS as an organization did little to heed his warning. "It is time for us to Reform," Cresson wrote a few months later as English officials debated the fate of slavery in their colonies. "I not only hang my head with shame for some of our laws, but when I feel convinced that slavery will soon be destroyed by England—I tremble for the fate of those who act as we are doing." Considering the possibility that English emancipation would encourage American slaves to rise up, he warned Gurley that "we . . . must pay a bloody recompence, unless we are brought to repeal some of our atrocious acts—to permit the introduction of religious instruction and enable them to read their bibles—and to institute marriages among them instead of the intercourse now permitted and even encouraged." Not only did the current state of affairs jeopardize black and white morals and put all Americans in danger, it also hurt the colonization cause throughout the Atlantic world.[17]

Cresson also strongly believed that free blacks deserved education. His work as an agent for black schools shaped his agenda in the colonization movement, and he soon decided that the two goals went together nicely. Thanks to the efforts of both black and white advocates of education in Pennsylvania, "the means of both religious and literacy instruction are open to all of them, so that from the rising generation much may reasonably be expected." To help entice members of this generation, he encouraged Gurley to send free copies of the *African Repository* to the Clarkson School. Reporting proudly in 1828 that two new schools had been built, he bragged that Philadelphia's black schools were equal to "any white schools among us." These schools were preparing blacks for productive citizenship, and once enlightened, perhaps even reluctant blacks would grasp the value of the asylum offered to them. If not, at least they would be better prepared to be good citizens in the United States.[18]

A number of Cresson's associates shared his concern for black education. Historian Hugh Davis describes an influential group of northern colonizationists who worked diligently "both to assist free blacks in their communities and to remove them from American society." He lists Cresson, Gurley, Gerrit Smith, Lyman Beecher, and Theodore Frelinghuysen but focuses his study on Leonard Bacon. These colonizationists saw the establishment of an African seminary in the United States as an important part of their plan. On the way back from his mission of inquiry, Samuel J. Mills had contracted a fever and died, and Davis argues that this absolutely convinced Bacon and his associates that "whites could not survive in the African climate." Cresson agreed heartily with this view and tried repeatedly to dissuade the ACS from sending white missionaries. Since their version of the colonization plan required teachers and missionaries for Africa, however, these men realized that to fulfill these objects they would have to trust well-trained blacks, whom they mistakenly thought naturally able to deal with the African climate. Training these future leaders became a crucial component of their overall agenda.[19]

In this sense, environmentalist ideology influenced their work in two ways. Their belief that whites could not physically withstand the African climate, combined with their certainty that blacks were inherently equal to whites, encouraged their efforts at black education. Many colonizationists, such as Henry Clay, believed that humankind consisted of a number of distinct races and that those races should not mix, but that did not necessarily mean that under perfect circumstances the races could not be equal. Although many of the most famous and most studied colonizationists are known for venomous antiblack vituperations, others portrayed blacks favorably, both in the United States and in Liberia, and many northern and southern members agreed on at least some level that blacks had a capacity for moral and intellectual development.[20]

John P. Carter, a Pennsylvanian in favor of black education, warned against any assumption of black inferiority. "What opinion concerning the Saxon race would be formed, by an instructor of their youth, who has lived long enough to observe the result of his training, in their common want of energy, vacillating purpose, and frequent shocking antipathy to high and sustained intellectual effort?" Though incorrect and unfair, "an inference in disparagement of the whole Saxon intellect would be as legitimate" as the idea of general black inferiority. Whereas "the blighting, crushing influence of their condition, accumulated for two hundred years, has been to develope the animal, and to stultify and extinguish the intellectual and spiritual . . . a careful and candid estimate" would admit that "they are capable of very great improvement."[21]

The way to prove this assertion was to educate African Americans and send them to Africa to "demonstrate THE EQUALITY OF THE RACES as members of the human family." According to Joseph Ingersoll, another colonizationist who was a proponent of uplift, African Americans were already "colonized . . . in the heart of the land of their birth." This left them without incentive, making them at least "degraded" if not "vicious and corrupt." Once removed from the stifling effects of racial prejudice, however, they could achieve moral uplift, and their innate ability would be easy to demonstrate. This belief explains why so many humanitarian colonizationists were so eager to ignore problems in Liberia and believe that everything was progressing smoothly in Africa. In their view, African Americans had a special divine mission to spread republican government, Protestant religion, and the English language to the "dark continent," and it was their role to help prepare them for this task.[22]

Unfortunately, in the hands of the overly optimistic, this argument could sound much like a justification for slavery. Cortlandt Van Rensselaer, another member of this group, developed in great detail a portrait of providence's plan for Africa. Slavery brought Africans into contact with Christianity and the other key components of civilization. Unlike the Native Americans, Africans survived the experience. Also, despite assumptions that climate would determine skin color, they had maintained distinctly African physical characteristics that left them uniquely qualified to return "home" and share what they had learned with the rest of the continent. Only providence could have made this all work so smoothly. According to Van Rensselaer, God had even thought to prevent black retribution against whites so they could fulfill their roles as teachers. As ridiculous as this scenario may sound, it is but an extreme version of the ideology shared by humanitarian colonizationists.[23]

Focus on this "degraded condition" argument forced colonizationists into a self-imposed paradox. In order to gain support for black uplift they felt compelled to make both blacks and whites aware of just how stifling conditions were in the United States. "Painfully sensible of the indifference which so generally exists towards the colored people, and the ignorance and misapprehension so widely prevalent in relation to the cause of colonization," editors of Pennsylvania's *Colonization Herald* tried to arouse public sympathy by disseminating as much information on the degraded condition of American blacks as they could gather. The problem was that this effort could easily backfire and increase the very fear and prejudice that kept blacks down in the first place. Even humanitarian colonizationists failed to notice this paradox, and when immediatists pointed it out, rivalry between the two groups forced colonizationists into a defensive posture.[24]

Despite the faults in their logic, proponents of African civilization worked to encourage black uplift, and they founded a number of organizations to further their preparatory agenda. Bacon helped establish the

African Improvement Society in 1825, and he, Gurley, and Frelinghuysen, among others, organized the Society for the Education of African
Youth a year later. When the latter failed, Cresson, Gerrit Smith, Arthur Tappan, Francis Scott Key, Charles Fenton Mercer, and a few others joined the effort and helped found the African Education Society in
1829. According to Davis, the goal was to gain national support "for a
school that would teach 'sober and industrious habits' to twenty or thirty
black males each year."[25]

An enthusiastic vice president of the African Education Society, Cresson sought repeatedly to enlist the ACS in its work. Emphasizing the
"intimate connection" between colonization and education, "and the
necessity of the latter to secure the important objects of the former,"
he constantly badgered Gurley to keep in mind the need to pursue this
agenda. He also tried to enlist ministers, including the bishop of Roch-
ester in England, to aid in educating blacks. He even developed a grand
plan to convince London's African Institution to spend £10,000 to found
an African Education Institution. He wrote to Gurley to ask if he could
"obtain an equal sum for the purpose at home" and asked what Smith,
Freylinghuysen, and Tappan would think of the plan. He eventually
gained an admission from Gurley that "more efficient means must be
adopted to enlighten the minds of our coloured people." Hoping to turn
this concession into action, he added that "some of the most intelligent
free people complain that you take no pains to do so." Despite Cresson's
best efforts, however, the African Education Society never gained tan-
gible support from the ACS, and it never acquired sufficient funding to
open its proposed seminary. Even some of the more sympathetic colonizationists doubted the school's feasibility and remained reluctant to encourage public hostility by pushing so vigorously for black education.[26]

* * *

The second part of the abolitionist accusation, that colonizationists led
the drive against northern free black education, also needs qualification.
When William Jay made this assertion, he offered two examples to but-
tress his claim. In the first case, members of the 1831 Philadelphia convention of free blacks and their immediatist allies had resolved to build
a manual labor school in New Haven, Connecticut. A number of cler-
gymen, including Bishops White and Onderdonk, publicly denounced
the idea, and their disapprobation drew the attention of the mayor of
New Haven, who called a town meeting to consider the plans. The mayor,

aldermen, common council, and a number of citizens of New Haven re solved "by every lawful means" to resist the school, which they connected to the immediatist movement. The secretary of the New Haven Committee of Correspondence of the ACS supported the resolution. According to Jay, the colonizationists could have spoken up against the suppression of the school, but instead "their influence was exerted not for, but *against* the improvement and elevation of their colored brethren."[27]

Colonizationists deserved criticism for their silence, but abolitionists exaggerated their level of involvement. Jay identified one of the protestors as an actual member of the society, and some of the protestors from Philadelphia were also colonizationists. The men associated with the humanitarian strain of the movement, however, neither participated in nor sanctioned the opposition to the school. As to why they failed to protest, one likely explanation is that the school was indeed associated with the immediatist movement and even the most humanitarian colonizationists would have shied away from supporting any immediatist endeavor.

The second event Jay described also involved an attempt to educate blacks in Connecticut. In this case, Prudence Crandall, who operated a boarding school for girls in Canterbury, agreed to admit a black student. The locals became outraged, but their anger only prompted Crandall to close her existing school and open a school exclusively for black girls. Opposition intensified. Led by Andrew Judson, who expressed colonizationist sentiment during the battle and afterward became an agent of the society, the locals had Crandall arrested under a law that forbade teaching blacks who did not reside in the community. Her first trial ended in a hung jury, but she was later convicted. She was eventually exonerated on a technicality.[28]

The Crandall affair was even more a product of hostility between immediatists and colonizationists than was the New Haven incident. To begin with, Crandall approached William Lloyd Garrison for support before announcing her intention to open the black school. She also enlisted the aid of most of the country's leading immediatists, and according to historian Bruce Rosen, they in turn used the affair as "an attempt to goad the citizens of Canterbury who were associated with the American Colonization Society to more and more provocative activities." Cresson was in England at the time of the battle, but Bacon condemned the persecution. The matter quickly became a power struggle, however, and when Judson and his followers sent a petition to the ACS describing the struggle in Canterbury, they focused on the actions of the immediatists rather than Crandall.

For the immediatists, events in Canterbury provided a perfect media opportunity. As Rosen points out, the picture of "hard-hearted attacks on a single woman trying to run a school for Negro girls would have melted the hearts of the most adamant men in Canterbury itself had the school been located, and the events occurred, anywhere than in their community." Fortunately for the immediatists, most who heard about the events were not from Canterbury.[29]

The parent society infuriated Cresson by embracing Judson after the affair. By the time Cresson got news of the events in England, it was already a publicity battle rather than a struggle for black education. Realizing the significance of the matter, he warned Gurley, "You must disown the *Crandall Persecution*. . . . [I]t has done us infinite harm." Again dismayed at the parent society's failure to live up to his standards, he accused it of "judicial madness" after learning that "the chief conspirator has *since* been appointed one of our agents!!!"[30]

Though the matter had escalated into an organizational battle, that the initial opponents tended to invoke colonization and that the parent group was willing to admit them to the fold serve as reminders of the complicated nature of the movement. Too often men such as Cresson, though responsible for gaining the humanitarian portion of the movement's following, were marginalized by the parent society, intentionally or not. ACS leaders worked hard to avoid alienating possible supporters, some of whom were slaveholders. In this case, speaking up for Crandall would have allied them with the "modern abolitionists," a step that they were not ready to take.

* * *

Organizationally as well as ideologically, humanitarian colonizationists filled a unique space in the American reform movement. They shared a great deal in common with the PAS and other early abolitionist groups. To begin with, their ideology focused on the evil of slavery but the need for a gradual solution. They also drew their leaders from society's elite ranks, turning primarily to doctors, lawyers, ministers of high rank, and wealthy merchants to fill the important offices in their auxiliary societies. Colonizationists shared with emancipationists an elitist attitude toward free blacks and working-class whites, but this subset of colonizationists began the process of appealing to the broader public for support. They reached out to pastors of all ranks to take up collections for the society and held public meetings to foster a wide following.

Like immediatists they also employed the press in a number of ways to introduce their movement to as many people as possible. Tracts such as Mathew Carey's went through several editions, and publishers offered discounts to auxiliary societies that purchased a large number for distribution. Both the parent society and some of the larger auxiliaries also published annual reports and sent them to subscribers, especially ministers, and friendly newspaper editors, hoping they would then share the contents with potential followers through sermons or republication. One agent wrote to Gurley expressing the determination "that there shall be scarcely a press west of the mountains not pressed into our service." In addition, several periodicals existed specifically to share the colonizationist agenda. The parent society's monthly journal, the *African Repository and Colonial Journal*, is the most well known, but some of the larger local groups also supported their own newspapers, such as Philadelphia's *Colonization Herald*. Finally, they appealed to a wide range of donors and encouraged contributions of any size or form, including books, clothing, medical supplies, and agricultural implements. Following Cresson's lead, they also urged the formation of youth auxiliaries.[31]

Antislavery colonizationists also reached out to two specific populations ignored by previous abolitionists. They realized that for their movement to succeed they needed the support of African Americans, so they tried to reach out to that community. They remained convinced that their scheme offered a great deal to all blacks, and they tried to enlist leaders of that community in their efforts. Attracting Russwurm, America's first black newspaper publisher, was perhaps their most noted success in this field, and Cresson tried repeatedly to gain James Forten's support. He urged the ACS to try harder in this endeavor in early 1828. "Forten is a man of both *wealth* & *respectability*," whose "coming into the measure would do great good in our city." Forten's opinion "has great weight with our coloured population, many of whom are affluent and intelligent"—just the type of people needed for the colony.[32]

The ACS paid little attention to Cresson's prodding, though, and its lack of enthusiasm about this goal hurt the humanitarians' efforts. As in other matters, the parent board ignored warnings like Cresson's that "your entire carelessness of the approbation of the free blacks and shewing no disposition to receive their co-operation has wounded their self-love and convinced them that the object of the Society was to 'get rid of them.'" Even the humanitarians fell short in this area, however, falling between emancipationists, who responded when blacks sought their aid, and immediatists, who tried to work with blacks to create a biracial movement. Antislavery colonizationists tried to reach out to blacks but never overcame an arrogant vision of themselves as the leaders and blacks of all ranks as junior partners. Cresson himself fell into this trap, expressing willingness to use *"flattery"* on Forten if necessary.[33]

They envisioned a similar role for women. Perhaps the Quaker connection played a role, since women of that denomination had established the first female charity society in the United States and created a number of organizations to educate black women and poor children. Aware of this or not, Cresson continually expressed pride in the women of both England and the United States, mentioning the work of "the ladies" in most of his dispatches. He was not alone in his admiration. ACS agents wrote of women joining local auxiliaries and even forming their own groups to support the cause. The Fredericksburg and Falmouth Female Colonization Society, founded in early 1829, had collected $500 in a little over a year. They sent much of it to the parent society as a general contribution but used $120 specifically to buy life memberships for the pastors of the Presbyterian, Episcopal, Methodist, and Baptist churches in their area. This idea caught on and became one of the main activities of women's auxiliaries. Other popular activities included buying or making clothes for the emigrants and holding fairs. Finally, the women of Philadelphia, led by Beulah Sansom, set an important example in creating an auxiliary devoted specifically to raising funds for education in Liberia. This group, the Ladies' Liberia Association, drew repeated praise from Cresson, and others soon followed their lead.[34]

Colonizationists' record with women, however, like that with blacks, has its limits. To begin with, Bruce Dorsey has shown that although men founded two hundred auxiliaries between 1817 and 1831, women organized only nine. Even so, a number of reports and letters from traveling agents celebrate the women's efforts. John H. B. Latrobe, a leader with the Maryland Colonization Society and benefactor of part of the $2,500 raised by the ladies' fair, praised their work at the thirteenth annual ACS meeting in 1830. "The moral influence of female zeal, exerted in a cause like this, can scarcely . . . be too highly appreciated." Noting similar work throughout the country, he added that "in many other places is the hand of beauty and refinement seen holding out its generous offerings to a cause which appeals irresistibly to the pure and lively sensibilities of the female mind."[35]

Cresson appreciated women's efforts so much that he competed with immediatists for their support. Like many men from his state, he particularly valued their assistance in founding, funding, and supplying the school. He also sought their participation as teachers.[36]

The men felt comfortable with the women's efforts because the women, though active in the cause, remained within their traditional place, auxiliary to the men. In cases where representatives of both sexes met together, men represented the female societies. At an annual meeting of the Male and Female Colonization Societies of Greene County, Ohio, both groups met together at first, but a man read the women's report, and the groups then adjourned to work separately. Representatives sent to the annual ACS meetings by women's groups were male.[37]

Female colonizationists shared a generally conservative outlook with their male counterparts and appear content with remaining in their "contracted sphere." According to the women who had formed one of the first female auxiliaries, by focusing on activities that left them "perfectly within the sphere which christianity describes," they had set an important example both to women throughout the union and to the future generation. Espousing sentiments of "Republican Motherhood," they hoped that through their examples "our sons and daughters will be brought up to feel a tender and compassionate interest in those whom providence has subjected to them—and that the principles of the nursery in this matter, as we know they do in other things, may exert an expanded influence upon society." For conservative reformers, colonization was a better fit for women because they could focus on the religious and evangelical aspects of the plan. By finding room for women in their movement, colonizationists formed yet another bridge between "traditional" and "modern" abolitionists.[38]

* * *

The humanitarian group's insistence on remaining part of the antislavery and reform community caused a crisis for the parent society in the 1830s. The first signs of trouble surfaced in 1830, as the PCS worked to send conditionally freed slaves to Liberia. Immediately after Key's visit the PCS raised $2,000 and sent 59 emigrants out on the *Liberia*. Following this voyage it raised $3,200 more and sent 70 out on the *Montgomery*. It then sponsored two more expeditions, the *Carolinian*, which took 107 in October 1830, and the *Valador*, which took 82 a few weeks later. The parent society praised the Pennsylvanians for their "liberality" and offered special thanks to Cresson "for the energy and perseverance with which he has engaged in efforts to increase the funds and promote the interests of the Society."[39]

Under the friendly facade, trouble lurked. Thanks to the parent society's slow movement, much of the PCS's money was wasted on empty berths, and the Pennsylvania group soon learned that transporting emigrants involved much more than picking up waiting passengers. Also, tension erupted between the parent group's agenda of sending free blacks and the PCS's desire to send only the conditionally manumitted.

Whereas the PCS raised the money immediately, the ACS took months to gather emigrants, and the number gathered generally fell short of the PCS's lofty expectations. John Hanson, the captain of the *Liberia*, was ready to sail on December 7, 1829, but it took numerous letters from him, Ralston, and Cresson to get the voyage under way. Cresson warned Gurley in November that prompt action would ensure future success in the state, and J. W. Bayard, secretary pro tem of the PCS, wrote in early December to let Gurley know that the PCS had arranged for one hundred emigrants. He asked Gurley to have them at Norfolk and Savannah ready to embark. Hanson wrote on December 7 and 19 to try to get the ACS moving with the passengers, and Ralston started getting nervous by the end of the month. He wrote to inform Gurley that if the ship was detained past January 10, it would cost $25 a day and the ACS would be responsible for the added expense. This should not happen, though, because "we have always understood from you and Mr. Key that you had the names of 600 slaves, who would be liberated as soon as funds could be furnished to convey them to Monrovia, and you will of course, we presume, have as many ready as we have engaged to pay for . . . since we have given you more than a month's notice."[40]

Even with the prodding, the ACS managed to collect only forty-nine liberated slaves and ten free blacks, as noted earlier. When this news reached Ralston, he wrote Gurley expressing surprise and warning him that the PCS would pay only for the liberated. He also argued that the Pennsylvania group had agreed to pay only for transporting the manumitted, not for their support once they arrived. Since the PCS had promised donors that every $30 would secure the freedom of a slave, it had to spend the contributions accordingly. Also, it would be "bad policy" for the PCS to pay for two of the items on the list of supplies—gunpowder and muskets. These would offend their donors, many of whom were Quakers. Cresson seconded Ralston's complaints. Pennsylvania donors would not contribute money to support colonists beyond the seasoning period of six months since they were going to such a fertile country.

"They must be permitted to give in their own way, or not at all." Despite the problems, the PCS offered to fund a second voyage if the ACS would buy the supplies. "The abolitionists will assist liberally" in helping to secure freedom of slaves, but "they will not give a cent" to buy supplies.[41]

The second voyage also required much prodding from PCS leaders to get under way. In early February Cresson urged Gurley to get moving before the public learned of the tardiness and paltry size of the first voyage. The PCS offered to pay to send one hundred liberated slaves but added that free blacks could join the expedition only if they would pay their own passage. The ACS did not respond, and by mid-February Cresson was "almost tempted to give up the Colonization Society as a bad job," since the ACS board had been "too apathetic to form a committee" to consider the PCS offer. By March he was "between grief and indignation" at ACS lethargy. The ACS had promised the public that six hundred slaves and sixteen hundred free applicants awaited, yet it had sent only sixty after three and a half months' notice. "Nearly all our Board are quite disgusted with the course things have taken," Cresson wrote to Gurley, "if the money so hardly won, is to be again paid *without value received*, we dare never again have the assurance to ask for another dollar." He and Ralston both urged Gurley to find free blacks who could pay their own way to fill the empty berths. Cresson pointed out that they had thrown away more than $1,000 on the first two voyages by failing to meet minimum passenger requirements. Gurley tried to find the passengers, but even slaves were averse to going if given the choice.[42]

This state of affairs prevailed throughout the early 1830s. Cresson continued to push for frequent voyages and to insist on large expeditions. When the third voyage failed to launch in what he considered a timely manner and carried fewer passengers than he had hoped, Cresson took the failure as "cruel towards *me* and absurd in itself." "I presume your board will not think it worth a second thought—But remember! You played the same game with both the *Liberia* and *Montgomery*, and a few more such tricks and no one will be found to submit to a repetition." Tempted to take the advice of his physician and retire to the country to recuperate, Cresson offered an ultimatum. Before "I forever wash my hands of this concern," he said, "you pledged yourselves to send one hundred on the first of October—Do you, I ask, intend to redeem that pledge?" Apparently not, because this third failure left two hundred potential colonists "disappointed." "If your board continues to act thus they will destroy all faith and confidence," he warned at that point. "Depend upon it," he added six months later, "if you intend to carry on this great work in a style commensurate with the *hopes* and *demands* of the public voice, you must *wake up* and cease to procrastinate." The only way to "ensure patronage" is to "*shew fruits*."[43]

Cresson's lofty aspirations were not limited to the frequency of voyages. After consulting men familiar with conditions in Liberia, he determined that the colony could easily receive 500 emigrants at a time. Gurley disagreed, insisting that 250 at a time were too many. Isaac Orr, an ACS traveling agent, appealed to Gurley to indulge Cresson on this matter, warning that "he has the patronage of Philadelphia under his thumb, to a greater extent than I should tell *him*." He had arrived at this conclusion through his own observations and added that Cresson likely had no idea of his own power, but "woe to the day when that commanding influence shall in *any way* be broken or thrown aside." Neither man realized that the issue of how many emigrants could be accommodated was irrelevant when so few could be enticed to go, so bickering over the issue continued. Undaunted, Cresson wrote in early 1833 to ask if the ACS could "from all sources send 2800 this year instead of 800" if the PCS could raise the money.[44]

Disagreement over the allocation of funds also continued. Cresson remained adamant that colonists need not be supported in a fertile land and should be encouraged to provide for themselves immediately, but he apparently compromised on the gun issue. After expressing reservations, he even agreed to include whiskey, but he held stubbornly to his insistence that free blacks must pay their own passages. First, he insisted, "the benevolence of the North . . . will be called forth toward *slaves* when it would remain dormant if free emigrants were to be paid for," since sending slaves gave them "*two* good acts by *one* payment." Furthermore, the colony had plenty of "merchants and pedlars," as most free blacks were, and needed more "*field hands*," since "we want agriculture *much* more cherished than it is." Sadly, however, Cresson's argument degenerated into a racist tirade against mulattoes, since he feared many of the free blacks would be of this class, which he saw as "more violent and difficult to govern." All "waiters, or barbers, or hucksters," he added, "not one of them will work hard." He offered a compromise, however, by suggesting that free emigrants unable to pay their own way be allowed up to three years to pay the society back. He also took the liberty, after consulting with a doctor, of changing the bill of rations for the voyage to save money.[45]

Cresson offered two solutions. First, he and Latrobe suggested a "packet day scheme" whereby specific days would be chosen, perhaps years in advance, to launch ships of emigrants. He suggested July 4 and

January 4. Slaves "could be received at all times and maintained and partly prepared with an outfit by adopting some measures . . . to employ them on the Canal—ad interim." This would ensure that passengers were ready on time and also prevent "the shameless manner in which heirs often refuse to grant the freedom conferred on slaves by will" by allowing the ACS to "secure them as soon as possible after a proffer is made." It would also pay for many of their passages.[46]

In addition to systematizing emigrant collection, Cresson wanted to streamline the purchasing and distribution of goods in the colony. He suggested repeatedly that the ACS buy as many supplies as they could in the states, using cash to secure discounts. When cash could not be had, he suggested they buy in the states on credit. He realized that Hanson had secured a virtual monopoly over colonial trade by sending his own supply ships and conveniently running out of room for ACS supplies on commissioned voyages. Claiming at times to offer the provisions at cost, he was actually charging a premium for them, and by offering credit at the colony he had trapped the society into a vicious cycle. When asked to help fit out a voyage, Cresson used his own money as security and took great pains to combat Hanson's practice of sweeping the market of colonial goods. In one case he managed to get most of a certain type of bead popular with Africans before Hanson could buy them. He pleaded for Gurley to stop "the ruinous system of purchasing at Liberia, by making judicious Investments here at perhaps *one fourth* the outlay of *cash* and frequently too with the benefit of 6, 9, and 12 months credit." He reported proudly to Gurley when Russwurm confirmed his efforts by letting him know the goods he had purchased for resale in the colony "sold at 100 to 600 percent profit."[47]

Perhaps taking Cresson's cue, Dr. Joseph Mechlin, the colonial governor, soon expressed a desire for a coppered schooner to facilitate colonial trade. Within a couple of weeks Cresson had obliged by convincing the PCS to fund the project, and in five months the colony had such a ship, the *Margaret Mercer*, named after a cousin of the evangelical colonizationist Charles Fenton Mercer. Despite Cresson's efforts, however, the board failed to heed his warning and Mechlin informed him that Hanson continued his practices.[48]

* * *

Hoping to capitalize on Cresson's enthusiasm and fundraising ability while seeking a reprieve from his constant prodding, the board sent him to England in 1831. Cresson had first offered to go two years earlier after his correspondents in Britain had sent contributions to the ACS through him. Crossing the Atlantic to seek assistance for what he saw as an anti-slavery cause, he found himself following the footsteps of his great-uncle who had traveled with Benezet to promote abolition in England.[49]

Cresson initially met with success in England. He secured endorsements from abolitionists George Thompson, William Wilberforce, and Thomas Clarkson, but Dr. Thomas Hodgkin became his strongest supporter. Clarkson and Hodgkin both qualified their endorsements, the former insisting that emancipation not require emigration and that the society educate settlers before sending them to Africa, and the latter calling on the ACS to speak out unequivocally against both slavery and mass expulsion. Rather than conflicting with Cresson's vision, each of these requirements would, if met, only force the ACS further along the path he had sought from the beginning. Portraying the scheme as he saw it, Cresson convinced Clarkson that it fostered voluntary uncompensated emancipation and had the support of a growing number of planters. As a result, Clarkson issued a public endorsement of the ACS, and by the end of his first year Cresson had collected $4,000 and had enlisted the support of a number of English periodicals. He had hoped to achieve even more, but, as he pointed out to Gurley, the timing of his trip forced him to compete with West Indian Emancipation and the Great Reform Bill for public interest.[50]

Cresson soon found himself competing with English abolitionists as well. As in the United States, the argument for immediate versus gradual emancipation had begun to gain support, but when Cresson first arrived, some abolitionists, especially Quakers, were willing to consider the scheme. Pamphlets sent to England by American abolitionists had gained attention, but Cresson found that "in most cases. . . a patient elucidation of our peculiar circumstances and the character of the blacks, has had its weight in dispelling prejudice." Calling attention to "what we owe to and may now perform for Africa (*Africa* and not *America*)" also helped. He realized he would have "to do this extensively . . . previous to making any attempt to reap the fruits." His English friends agreed that such a course would prevent economic jealousy and an all-out attack by abolitionists. Cresson even went so far as to turn down contributions from William Wilberforce and the bishop of Quebec to show his higher intentions.[51]

Even so, the attack he feared came in early 1832 when British immediatist Charles Stuart issued a reply to Clarkson's endorsement. Using the

African Repository and the parent society's annual reports, he argued that the organization was proslavery, appealed to racist sentiment for support, and was impractical. At first, Cresson tried to convince the antislavery society to hear his side of the story, but by April of 1832 British abolitionists were breaking up his meetings, and one launched a vicious verbal attack upon him in the street.[52]

That same month he tried to answer a number of their complaints in a letter to the editor of the *Albion*. Reiterating that the ACS sought ultimately "the final and entire abolition of slavery," he argued that critics took quotes from "mutilated portions of the speeches of individuals" to attack the colonization movement. To refute these accusations he set out to show what the society had actually accomplished. According to Cresson the slave trade, which had formerly exported ten thousand "fellow-creatures" a year had been eradicated, and four slave factories destroyed. Africans who once participated in the trade were now enjoying "the Christian example and uniform kindness" of their new emancipated neighbors. The colonists, likewise, enjoyed living under an "independent government of their own, administered by officers of their own selection and colour." Only the governor and colonial doctors were white, and Cresson hoped to soon change that by finding qualified black physicians. Indeed, "many thousands of their brethren, both bond and free, are panting to follow," and the ACS was diligently working to raise the money to accommodate them. Finally, colonists benefited from both common and Sabbath schools, chapels, churches, a newspaper, and an established export trade to the United States worth $150,000 the previous year.[53]

Cresson also tried to draw a careful distinction between the ACS's plan and the Sierra Leone Company, whose mismanagement and expenses had jaded the British public. The ACS, he claimed, neither held nor sought political or economic power over this independent colony. Despite rumors to the contrary, the colony was developing nicely, and he invited doubters to go and see for themselves. The support offered by state governments, he insisted, was a product of the local governments' drive to end slavery within their jurisdictions.[54]

Even if some had started to believe Cresson's claims, his trouble intensified when Nathaniel Paul, a black American abolitionist, arrived around that time to seek British support for his own Canadian colonization scheme, the Wilberforce Settlement. According to Blackett, Paul's color "made him the 'representative' of black Americans and gave him entry to abolitionist circles." Cresson, who had already tried to get the

ACS to reach out to educated free blacks, now more than ever saw the need for such an able representative of its own. He suggested that the society send Russwurm to entice supporters for Liberia but was ignored. By November he reported, "I could, with a black skin, do you infinitely more service."[55]

Paul's visit basically sealed Cresson's fate, but the summer of 1833 brought even more trouble. William Lloyd Garrison learned that despite his low-key tactics, Cresson "has procured funds to a considerable amount," and he set out to give a lie to claims that the ACS was an anti-slavery organization. Gurley wrote Cresson in June to warn him, but the letter arrived the same day as Garrison. Ostensibly there to raise money for the black school in New York, Garrison opened an immediate assault on Cresson by saying he was an "imposter" not actually endorsed by the ACS. At the same time he sought to portray the colonization cause as dead by arguing that members of the board were deserting and even taking signs down at headquarters. Together Paul and Garrison managed to convert a number of Cresson's former supporters, including Quaker William Allen. After taking Garrison's advice and reading ACS documents, Allen wrote that he could not believe his North American friends had failed to inform him of "the real principles of the said Society." He was even more surprised that "Elliott Cresson, knowing as he must have known, the abominable sentiments it has printed and published, should have condescended to become its agent." Perhaps most important, Garrison managed to secure a number of important signatures on a "transatlantic protest" against the ACS. The most notable of these signatures, that of William Wilberforce, ignited controversy, since the venerated abolitionist signed it on his deathbed, leaving abolitionists and colonizationists to debate the soundness of his faculties at the time.[56]

Despite his constant battle with the abolitionists Cresson did gain some support in England, mostly by relying on his old tactics of appealing to broad audiences and raising money for specific uses. Some of the uses were quite noble. For example, the London Female Society gave £50 to help a family and asked in return for information about the members and their progress. Two other women gave specifically "to be considered as paying for Betsey Johnson," a black teacher, and initiated correspondence directly with her. Many others gave money to free a specific number of people and hoped to develop lasting contact with those they helped. Some even planned to offer future aid to the same people. On a grander scale, a committee in Scotland gave £100 and pledged £800 more to found a settlement of one hundred people "to be called Edina."

Other specific causes that gained support included missionary work and education.[57]

In his zeal to gain support, Cresson found himself endorsing some ridiculous pet projects. Robert Graham of Glasgow offered to support a colonist with his "continued regard" but only under the condition that the chosen colonist take the surname Scotland. Failing to realize the offensive nature of this request, Cresson urged repeatedly that Gurley find "a proper person" for this request "as soon as possible." Two years after presenting the request, Cresson noted with irritation at Gurley that Graham, feeling neglected, had withdrawn the offer. Cresson saw this as another case of the parent society's neglect rather than a degrading and self-serving offer. This serves as a sad example of Cresson's inability to see things from the perspective of those he fought to help.[58]

Cresson's anger at Gurley and the ACS in general for failing to respond to Graham's request was silly, but his anger at their overall neglect of his mission was quite valid. Indeed, the mission began on an ominous note when he asked for letters of reference but got no assistance. He wrote in July 1831 to ask Gurley why he had received no communication in three and a half months, and in October complained that all he had in six months was a letter from Governor Mechlin and a "meager note" from Gurley. "How can I fight (for fight I must) if I have neither weapons or ammunition? Must I like the Spider spin them out of my unaided self?" He was there well over six months and had sent twenty letters to Gurley before getting a second reply. By the end of 1831 he turned to Ralston, also in England at the time, to goad Gurley into action. He needed fresh information on ACS activity in America and conditions in the colony. Sending a copy of Stuart's latest attack, he asked Gurley to "shew this to your managers and ask them if it is fair that I be left to combat such enemies without one solitary fact, document or paper for many months together." He added, "If I am to be treated with utter neglect I cannot hold out much longer." He finally got a letter from Gurley in September 1832, but instead of new information it brought only questions about Cresson's statistics on the number of slaves sent to the colony and the number of friendly natives near Liberia. In reply, Cresson maintained that any errors in his figures resulted from being forced to extrapolate and guess since Gurley failed to send him precise data. Cresson correctly predicted that the situation would be *ruinous to the interests* of the cause," as one historian has shown that Garrison "won this battle for Britain by making Cresson truly appear cowardly" when he refused to answer the call for a debate. Given his lack of "weapons" and Garrison's full arsenal, he had little choice.[59]

Personal neglect was bad enough, but the ACS also failed to make sustained contact with the committees and auxiliaries Cresson managed to establish. Cresson took care to tell Gurley, in great detail, how to reach each new group, and he begged the secretary to forward reports and numbers of the *Repository*. "If they *work* for us," he warned, "they must have tools." For Cresson, these groups would play a crucial role in keeping colonization in the public eye and helping establish new settlements to combat the slave trade and provide an asylum for American blacks, so he begged Gurley not to "starve" them.[60]

He also urged Gurley to pay closer attention to the messages the parent society's publications were sending. First, he wanted the ACS to speak out clearly against slavery and make more sincere efforts to befriend free blacks. He had been urging Gurley to speak out and emphasize the emancipatory promise of the scheme, but Gurley must have told him an unequivocal statement would be impolitic. At first Cresson tried to follow the board's direction, and when he published an antislavery statement of Mechlin's while abroad, he justified himself by arguing that "as it is intended only for England, the full expression of the belief in entire cure, will I hope be deemed advisable."[61]

Cresson grew increasingly disgusted, however, that though the ACS took such pains to mute antislavery arguments, it published much that offended him and those whose support he sought. At first he distributed what the society gave him despite his personal qualms about such "suicidal expressions." As the parent society continued to publish, and the American press continued to reprint, comments made by the society's slaveholders and those less friendly to free blacks, his irritation grew. "If we abide faithful to correct principles we shall be hailed by all good men the world over as the purest philanthropists" and raise enough money to aid the cause for a century and protect "the future interests of unborn millions." The society would simply have to stop printing the sentiments of those who embraced the cause for the wrong reasons and instead publish "documentary evidence" of its good deeds to disprove "A.S.S. slanders." Letters recounting success in the colony "from both blacks and whites, going more into *details* and giving graphic sketches" would help. Cresson managed to keep Clarkson's support by keeping "the *orthodoxy* of our *acts* constantly before his mind's eye" despite "the reckless *heterodoxy* of sentiment I have so often and so vainly expostulated with you about," but if Gurley continued to publish such material "our *insertion* will be deemed *our approval*."[62]

Despite speeches and tracts to the contrary, Cresson continued to see the ACS as an antislavery organization dedicated to black uplift, and the society's insistence on printing objectionable material baffled him. After finally receiving a copy of the fifteenth annual report, he accused Gurley of feeding into the notion of a proslavery agenda, "while *I* have striven in public and private to prove it one of the noblest efforts ever made to destroy the whole system" of slavery. "If I really believed that I was thus cajoled to pander to the avarice of southern tyrants, I should indignantly wash my hands of so vile an empire of oppression." Even so, he remained convinced that he and the parent organization shared emancipationist goals. After he heard in 1833 that Gurley had conceded in the *Repository* that some colonizationists supported continuing slavery, he once again expressed dismay but was "still determined to work for Africa and incidentally for you."[63]

By this point Cresson had begun to realize the difference between colonization as a movement and the ACS as an organization. He began working to form an independent "*British* Colonization Society" that he hoped would rely on the United States for colonists. He also hoped that this society would be immune to "the strong prejudices widely spread against us, growing, I am sorry to say, as much from your own imprudent publications, as from the violence of our enemies." By late 1833, however, he had determined that the views of too many ACS supporters "are much at variance with my ideas of the genius of the A.C.S." Though he had "represented it as an institution which had *equally* at heart the *welfare of Africa* as the good of *our own* negroes," he was beginning to see that many others saw it differently. Some of his colleagues had arrived at the same conclusion, and Bacon, feeling "driven to get up one or more periodicals in keeping with the tone of the society's best friends," founded the *Journal of Freedom* to focus on the humanitarian agenda.[64]

Cresson realized the importance of southern cooperation, but his patience had limits. An English associate mentioned concern that "we were lending ourselves to aid the states of Maryland and Virginia to banish the free blacks by means of enactments so severe as to drive them off." He argued against such measures, even after West Indies emancipation caused him to fear a greater chance of slave revolt in the United States. He urged the society not to "give any encouragement to the South" to institute the oppressive measures "they will be but too ready to adopt." To support coercion would make colonizationists "an auxiliary to tyranny."[65]

Making conditions more favorable in the colony, especially by reducing the mortality rate, would entice even free blacks and make coercion unnecessary. Cresson consulted colonial officials and a "Government

Physician of great celebrity" who had been at the colony as he sought to develop a plan to save settlers' lives. He concluded that employing the natives to clear brush and providing more appropriate clothing would solve much of the problem. He also expressed continued concern about the state of the colony's schools and agriculture, suggesting a tax to fund the former and a colonial farm to raise plantains, sugar, or coffee to help encourage the latter. He also pushed for the development of a timber industry and the erection of a sawmill after hearing of success in this field in Sierra Leone. Finally, he urged the society to secure a neutral and independent status for Liberia to protect the colony in case of hostility between the United States and Britain.[66]

As Cresson offered new ideas and found the same cold results from the parent society, he began to feel more and more insulted, and his wounded ego played a role in his eventual decision to work independently of the parent group. He had long objected to the society's choice of officers, board members, and agents, calling for the board to stop trying to "dazzle by *mere* names" and choose "respectable persons of less *pretensions*, but possessed of *zeal*." Accordingly, he repeatedly suggested Roberts Vaux be made a vice president. Apparently unaware that he had no power to make such important decisions on his own, he went so far as to offer vice presidencies to the duke of Sussex, Lord Brougham, and Lord Bexley while in England and became quite angry when the society failed to honor his appointments. Similarly, he took the liberty of interfering with the society's choice of agents. Outdoing Isaac Orr became almost an obsession, and he criticized him repeatedly in letters to Gurley. Unhappy with Orr's appointees, he took it upon himself to choose agents of his own and even to adjust salaries. Gurley had offered one agent $800, but Cresson raised it to $1,500 plus expenses because of the candidate's large family. After making the offer, he wrote to Gurley for approval.[67]

When Cresson did not get his way, he often insulted others. He called Orr "unfit," and he delighted in pointing out when he managed to raise more money than Orr. Dunn, the publisher of the annual reports and *Repository*, was "incorrigible" for refusing to accept his unsolicited advice. When Gurley included excerpts from Carey's pamphlet in the annual report, even though the figures refuted some of Cresson's claims, he accused the secretary of siding with "that prating Paddy Carey." Likewise, when competition with Paul escalated in England, Cresson grew irritated and called him a "lying mulatto preacher," and when the colonial governor failed to live up to his standards he called for "that traitor Dailey" to be banished from the colony.[68]

Most of all, Cresson blamed Gurley for the failure of his English appeal and believed that he could do Gurley's job better himself. He had long voiced concern that the society expected too much of Gurley. "Really, dear Gurley," he wrote in 1833, "I have felt *very* unhappy at seeing thee in such precarious health and must *order* thee to be more careful, if not for *thy own sake*, for thy *little ones*, and that of *thy estimable wife*." After returning from England, he expressed regret that Gurley's "whole soul was not thrown into *one* channel," especially since "much good would be effected by thy pen being always ready to meet each exigency." Pointing out that "this is ... the age of 'division of labours,'" he suggested that "each concern had expanded so widely that each Department needs a separate head." The tone of his letters revealed a desire for one of those positions, and by April 1834 Gurley figured out what was going on. Though Cresson never expressed outright his desire for an ACS general agency, "the general tenor of his conversation and the course of his conduct" had finally betrayed him. Deeming Cresson "ardent, enthusiastic, active, persevering, and bold," by confidential letter, Gurley warned headquarters that Cresson "greatly lacks discretion." Zealous humanitarians, both he and Finley "are eccentric and erratic but will not fail to stir the elements in their course."[69]

Once he returned from England Cresson became increasingly determined to do just that. Summing up his feelings on his return, he wrote to the board that "I much regret that a stern sense of duty and a love for the sacred cause, which has more than once brought me nigh unto death in consequence of over exertion and anxiety so frequently compel me to tell unpalatable truths." One such truth was that the colony was in a state of shambles. After speaking with a former colonist he learned that the problems stemmed not from climate but from poor management and "the utter disregard manifested by the present physician and late governor, together with the grinding oppression and heartlessness of the host of salaried officers." The public stores were empty, and "a few purse proud colonists" were exploiting the others. At the same time, the financial state of the society itself fared no better. Debts exceeded $40,000, and monthly income was at an all-time low.[70]

On a more personal level, the society had completely botched the effort, begun in 1830, to relocate North Carolina Quakers' slaves. This project had gained much of the support he managed to enlist in Britain, and the PCS had sent out about ninety of these emigrants while Cresson was overseas. By 1833, however, Quakers had been "much offended" by bad reports from these colonists. Ralston reported that someone, presumably a Quaker, had issued "a severe attack on the warlike propensities of the colonists" in *Poulson's Daily Advertiser*. "I fear it is impossible to get the cordial co-operation of the Quakers," Ralston reported. "They are a peculiar people, and like to manage matters in their own way." Appropriately, he asked about Cresson in his next sentence.[71]

* * *

Much of the parent society's neglect stemmed from the pressure it felt at home. By late 1832 it faced opposition on two fronts. In September a forceful southern defense of slavery as a "positive good" appeared in the *American Quarterly Review*. This argument was not necessarily new, because proslavery arguments had been around since at least 1790, when South Carolina and Georgia used them to object to Pennsylvania's antislavery petitions to Congress. Even so, this essay, which was the response of Thomas R. Dew, a professor at the College of William and Mary, to the debates on slavery in the Virginia legislature, spurred renewed debate. The legislative concern with the fate of slavery at this juncture was a response to Nat Turner's slave revolt in Southampton County—the bloodiest in American history. Some, including colonizationist Thomas Marshall, presented arguments similar to those Clay and Carey often made, that slavery hampered industry and progress. A number of members agreed and supported a bill for gradual emancipation. On the other side, colonizationist William H. Broadnax characterized slavery in a similar vein but argued against interfering with private property. He introduced a bill for appropriating $100,000 to colonization in hopes of ending slavery while respecting property rights. The bill failed, but the debate prompted Dew to attack emancipation as dangerous and colonization as infeasible. The black population grew much faster than colonizationists could remove them, and removing slaves would deny Virginia an essential labor force and destroy the state's economy.[72]

Robert Walsh, the editor of the *American Quarterly Review*, immediately asked Gurley for a response. John Crosby, the ACS agent for Pennsylvania, asked who would write it. "[Dew's] views of slavery, considered morally or politically, are behind the spirit of the age," and "the majority of the people of this land would veto them." Rather than concern, Bacon expressed a sense of relief, claiming that once the apologists began actively defending slavery, they broke a seal and made the issue of slavery fair game for colonizationists to attack. Though Gurley shared Bacon's and Crosby's views on slavery, he realized that the matter was not so simple. No matter how much his antislavery cohorts wanted him to, he could not dismiss southern support, so he chose Jesse Burton Harrison of Virginia to answer Dew with the same arguments Marshall had used in the legislative debates. To further smooth things over, he added that colonization had nothing to do with abolition. Even after Dew, few important colonizationists abandoned the movement because of the proslavery critique.[73]

The continued abolitionist assault, however, cost the movement dearly. Garrison intensified the campaign he began in his newspaper the *Liberator* with his *Thoughts on African Colonization*, published within a month of Dew's essay. Intentionally or not, this pamphlet hurt the cause in the South by leading many to equate any plan of emancipation with a radical attack on southern life. More important, Garrison had portrayed northern colonizationists as well-meaning dupes of slaveholders and vowed to "change their admiration into abhorrence; to convince them that their well-meant exertions have been misdirected, and productive of greater evil than good; and to induce them to abandon an institution to which they now fondly cling." In many cases he delivered on this promise. Historian James Brewer Stewart has shown how men such as Lewis and Arthur Tappan, Joshua Leavitt, James G. Birney, Simeon S. Jocelyn, Amos Phelps, and Samuel J. May, all former colonizationists, joined with Garrison in renouncing gradualism and focusing their energies against the very society that introduced them to the evils of slavery and the techniques for organization.[74]

Arthur Tappan took this step in 1833, criticizing the ACS for failing to insist on temperance in the colony. Cresson had voiced a similar objection while helping supply the voyages in 1830. Apparently asked to buy liquor, he replied that neither he nor Ralston could "*conscientiously* buy your *liquid poison* to demoralize either colonists or natives." He also pointed out that such an action would alienate humanitarian supporters. To his dismay he learned from Hanson that five hogsheads per cargo had gone to the colony, and 3,540 gallons had been sold there the previous year. "Blushing" over the incident, he asked Gurley to prohibit importation. Roberts Vaux made the same request two years later on behalf of the Temperance Society of Pennsylvania. He got the same answer Cresson did, that prohibition would be impossible but that ardent spirits were "subject . . . to a heavy duty, and the expense of a license to retail is such as to amount to a prohibition." Also, the society used "the best moral means" to encourage temperance. Furthermore, prohibiting spirits altogether would alienate locals and push them into trading with local slavers.[75]

Tappan had played a leading role in forming the New York City Colonization Society in 1829, but the temperance issue began to bother him by 1830. Cresson wrote to Gurley in November that he had labored unsuccessfully for two hours to enlist Tappan's support for the ACS and African Education Society but "found that your *rum* and *whiskey* had so *poisoned* his mind that I could do nothing." By 1833, when an Andover student wrote to ask him if the ACS was "worthy of the patronage of the Christian public," Tappan had decided in the negative. In a response printed in the *Liberator* he claimed that the society sold fourteen hundred barrels of "liquid poison" in one year, as well as tobacco, powder, and balls. After reading Garrison's arguments he deemed colonization a scheme to get rid of free blacks and secure slavery. The society responded that the claim of such extensive trade in liquor came from faulty thirdhand accounts; the society sent spirits for medicinal purposes only, and prohibition would just send locals elsewhere, especially to slavers, to get alcohol. Most important, the *Repository* pointed to the huge leap in logic from concerns with temperance, tobacco, and weapons to accusations of supporting slavery. By 1835 Tappan was president of the immediatist American Anti-Slavery Society.[76]

The society sustained an even more powerful loss when Gerrit Smith joined the immediatists in 1835. One of the society's greatest financial supporters, in 1827 he had offered to contribute $100 a year if one hundred men would match the offer. A vice president of the New York State Colonization Society, he asked Gurley in 1831 to be more public about the emancipation aspect of their plans. Though he unwittingly undermined the colonization cause by providing abolitionists with powerful quotes on the degraded condition of blacks, he shared enough concern for black uplift to help found the African Education Society. When many of his friends began leaving the colonization society in 1833 he warned the ACS not to attack the abolitionists. He chided men such as Tappan for insisting on prohibition in Liberia when no American government had adopted this measure. At the seventeenth annual ACS convention in 1834 he called for members to renew their financial commitment and give half of their estates to the society. He offered a plan to raise $100,000 for the ACS in ten years by getting one hundred subscribers at $100 a year. The effort failed, but he honored his commitment of $5,000. At the same meeting he challenged those present to "greatly increase our love to the people for whom we have undertaken to provide a home." He missed the next year's meeting but sent a letter expressing his "warm attachment" and including $1,000. At this point immediatists were already trying to entice him to their camp, and they won once mobs dispersed the state antislavery convention in Utica, New York. The final straw for Smith was an attack on white civil liberties.[77]

Though William Jay wrote in 1835 that colonizationists were "almost daily . . . awakening as from a dream" and discovering "the delusion into which they had fallen," some reform-minded members chose to stay and lead the ACS back to its humanitarian roots. Leonard Bacon warned that "at the present crisis, there may be some danger of forgetting that our Institution is primarily and preeminently benevolent." In justifying the myriad "ulterior results and complicated bearings of the work," the society must not "overlook the immediate and grand design of doing good to the wretched, elevating a degraded race and rescuing Africa from 'deep darkness.'" It must also stop alienating free blacks. "The people of colour are not ignorant" of the speeches and articles that portray them "as a nuisance to be got rid of," and such a negative portrayal forces them to "prove themselves men . . . of like passions with us, but resenting it." Hoping to reclaim colonization as Finley and Mills intended, he pointed out that Garrison's goal was to make people feel that by supporting colonization they were endorsing all the "opinions and principles" expressed by any other members. "The opinions, speeches, essays, and professions of colonizationists are one thing; and colonization itself, is another thing." Optimistically, he added that the abolitionist attack might bring some colonizationists back to the society's true antislavery aim and force more prudence on the group's management.[78]

Gurley tried to do just that. At the sixteenth annual meeting in 1833 he barely failed in an effort to weight the society's power toward his antislavery colleagues. He quietly and routinely presented a list of nominees for the board of managers, hoping nobody would pay enough attention to notice that he had removed five slaveholders, including Francis Scott Key, from the list. He moved three of the names, including Key's, to the list of vice presidents to create a smaller, more powerful board made up mostly of northerners, since the North had more auxiliary societies and contributed more money. This almost worked, but once the delegates realized what was really going on, it took four long, "boisterous" meetings to resolve the matter and reinstate the deposed managers by a vote of 63 to 57. Though he lost in his bid at reorganization, Gurley had finally come out vocally and unequivocally on the side of emancipation. Feeling a sense of release from his previous need to appease everyone, his speeches and letters after that point grew increasingly antislavery, but he did continue to argue the value of cooperation with antislavery southerners. He pointed out that Garrison's tactics only caused masters to tighten their hold on slaves and jeopardized the nation's unity.[79]

The attempt to remodel the parent society continued at the next annual meeting. After four meetings and much debate, those present, including Gurley, Cresson, Frelinghuysen, Bacon, and Smith, helped rewrite the ACS constitution. Instead of one secretary, article 4 now called for "one or more" full-time salaried secretaries and a salaried treasurer. The board of managers, previously consisting of all officers plus "12 other members of the society," now included only the secretaries, the treasurer, the recorder, and nine other members. The board, once elected by life members present at the yearly conventions, would now be elected by delegates from auxiliary societies, and life members and would be required to present a detailed statement of operations at the yearly meetings. Auxiliary societies would now be responsible for arrangements for transporting and temporarily supporting emigrants. Gurley tried unsuccessfully to whittle the board even further to seven managers.[80]

Cresson had been calling for a smaller executive board since 1830, but by this point he wanted more. By 1834 he and Finley were both trying to reclaim the movement for the humanitarians. Both listed the society's problems as a lack of organization and energy, failure to send out timely expeditions as advertised, failure to protect emigrants' health, and failure of officials to reply in a timely manner to those who offered money or slaves or sought information. As usual, Cresson saw increased vigor in sending out expeditions as the cure to the society's ills, but the parent groups did not agree. Instead, they decided to focus on repaying current debts.[81]

In turn, Cresson and some of his associates decided to take colonization into their own hands. The Baltimore, Maryland, society, founded largely thanks to Cresson's and Finley's exertions, was the first to take independent action. In 1831 the pair had convinced the auxiliary to revive by promising independence in "applying their own funds." Tension surfaced immediately, and the group founded its own colony by 1833, leaving Gurley certain that "the tendency of that society is to destroy the Parent Institution." After the 1834 reorganization of the ACS, the New York City auxiliary, disappointed in the limited reform, began to plan an independent settlement of its own that would promote agriculture and temperance. The settlement would also include an organized system of education for both colonists and nearby natives. The group also took the opportunity to unreservedly come out in favor of emancipation and black improvement. Soon after, the PCS resolved to raise $10,000 in Pennsylvania to have the ACS managers form a settlement in Africa called "Pennsylvania." The board approved the New York group's plans but not the Pennsylvanians', and Cresson became jealous. "I should feel much obliged by this new mark of their condescension," he wrote to Gurley, "did I not know how *peculiarly prompt* they are in acting on my suggestions." Soon afterward Gurley expressed a fear that "our Institution will be broken into fragments. . . . If the state societies take colonization into their hands, we are a nullity."[82]

The Pennsylvania state auxiliary agreed with Gurley and refused to press the matter, so Cresson led a coup and formed the Young Men's Colonization Society of Pennsylvania in 1834. By this point he was insisting that he could not raise any money for the parent group because people no longer trusted it. Openly embracing emancipation, the new auxiliary stated as its objects the civilization and christianization of Africa through black emigrants from the United States and the promotion "by all legal and constitutional means, the intellectual and moral improvement of the African race." The group, supported generously by Cresson and Gerrit Smith, also set out to found its own colony based on temperance, emancipation, and peace. By the end of the year the Pennsylvania and New York groups had joined forces and founded Bassa Cove. They envisioned a partnership with old school abolitionists, whom they hoped would assist in preparing blacks for productive citizenship in Liberia. They also pledged continued support to the ACS once their colony was up and running. Cresson, the driving force behind this movement, had earned a vice presidency by 1838.[83]

* * *

In the broader scheme of antislavery, Cresson and his colleagues fall between the nationalist colonizationists and the advocates of immediate emancipation. Their concern for settlers' welfare in the colony, their efforts to establish schools in the United States and Africa, and their emphasis on sending slaves rather than free blacks reveal their humanitarian agenda. They failed horribly as philanthropists, however, by continuing to insist that free blacks could never gain acceptance in the United States. They never realized that the greater favor to blacks would be to combat white prejudice rather than black "degradations." Indeed, in enlisting aid for black uplift and colonization, they overemphasized the degraded condition argument, and they arrogantly assumed they knew what was best for African Americans.

When immediatists began to take that leap after forming close friendships with blacks on a personal level, antislavery colonizationists became too conservative for the northern reform community even though their antislavery stance made them too radical for the South. They shared the immediatists' ultimate goal and had pioneered many of the tactics modern abolitionists would later use, yet they adhered to the PAS's gradual agenda, respect for property rights and reluctance to attack slave owners. To make matters worse they labored under a patriarchal worldview even stronger than that of most gradualists.

The humanitarian colonizationist agenda also suffered from two inherent defects. First, they had a more concrete goal than the immediatists, and concrete goals require funding. Acquiring funding required both reaching out to as broad a base as possible but also appealing to the more steady aid of those with substantial assets. Whereas Cresson leaned more toward the former, Gurley saw the need for the latter, but this left him too reluctant to alienate any possible support, no matter the agenda behind it.

Second, Cresson's insistence on focusing on the conditionally emancipated left the movement open to the charge of sending unqualified colonists. In 1831 Francis Taylor, a Philadelphia merchant, who had explored Africa himself and seen the colony, wrote to Gurley from Philadelphia to warn him that the society needed to send fewer recently freed slaves and more "of the respectable class of free colored people" to better "answer the purposes of colonization and civilization." Urging the ACS to develop the colony's commercial potential, he used English control of India as an example. He argued that the English would not send paupers to settle in India because there were already plenty there. What was needed in both cases were able farmers and professionals such as administrators and teachers. The parent group continued to point this out to Cresson, but he insisted that PCS money be applied only to the manumitted. His tunnel vision left him impervious to such warnings and to later abolitionist criticism along the same lines. He and his compatriots' antislavery stance, mixed with their certainty that black freedom in the United States would mean racial discord, forced them into stubborn adherence to the agenda, even as both slaveholders and immediatists pointed to its impracticality.[84]

For Cresson personally, pride and stubbornness played a large role in keeping him in the colonizationist camp. By the time Garrison attacked the cause, reformers such as Cresson and Bacon had already made their marks as spokesmen for the ACS. In Cresson's Pennsylvania, as in

Bacon's Connecticut, much of the clergy, press, and business community had responded to their urging and embraced colonization. To abandon the cause and take cover with the immediatists would have violated their own nonradical reform principles. Even when men such as Tappan and Smith left, men such as Cresson chose to stay and fight. Once he promised that colonization would foster emancipation he never gave up trying to make it do so. Realizing it or not, he offered insight into his own adherence to the cause when he told Gurley that "if I can enlist them warmly on our side, the very pride of opinion will keep them straight."

* * *

One group Cresson was never able to enlist in his cause was the free black community. As we saw earlier, black leaders initially viewed African colonization with a guarded optimism, but grassroots opposition from the black community caused them to change their stance. Cresson and those of his viewpoint continually tried to change the minds of black leaders, especially James Forten. We will now turn to a case study of Forten to examine the relationship not only between black leaders and colonizationists but also between black leaders and white immediatists such as Garrison, who, after taking a cue from blacks, transformed the antislavery movement.

5 / "They will never become a people until they come out from amongst the white people": James Forten and African American Ambivalence to African Colonization

As white abolitionists sought to help but also to control Pennsylvania's black population, and colonizationists sought to gain the support of black leaders, the black community continued to blossom in the years leading up to the Civil War, despite a number of challenges. As we saw before, leaders such as Richard Allen, Absalom Jones, and James Forten shared a number of the biases of the gradualist generation, and by the 1830s, they too found themselves trying to control the growing free black population. At the same time, they were the first antislavery reformers to have to grapple with the implications of the emerging colonizationist movement. Their ultimate rejection of the American Colonization Society gained the attention of a new breed of white abolitionists, a group willing to move beyond gradualist efforts to win over slaveholders and instead label them as "sinners." As a leader of this community in 1817, an associate of many white gradualists, the man whose support was most strongly sought by Elliott Cresson and other colonizationists, and the man best known for influencing radical antislavery whites such as William Lloyd Garrison, Forten provides the best case study for a closer look at the early black abolition movement and its relationship with gradualism, colonization, and immediatism.

James Forten was a fourth-generation American. Born in the same Philadelphia neighborhood, neither James nor his father had ever been owned by another, and both were literate, skilled sailmakers and dedicated Anglicans. By all accounts, the Forten family enjoyed the respect of their Philadelphia neighbors and counted among their friends Anthony

Benezet, who served as executor of at least one Forten estate and over-saw James's education after his father died. Among the property Benezet helped disperse in this legacy was a slave and a great deal of wealth pos-sibly acquired from involvement in the slave trade. But for their skin color, the Fortens would have been counted among Philadelphia's elite.[1]

James Forten himself added to his family's social and material suc-cess. At the age of fourteen he joined the Revolutionary cause, serving on a privateer vessel. Though optimistic of the Revolution's promise, and of his right to share what America offered, the limitations and prejudices he faced on a daily basis would eventually cause him to grapple with the idea of racial separation. Throughout most of his adult life, Forten considered whether emigration to Africa or Haiti would provide suc-cessful free blacks like himself a much-deserved chance for true freedom and self-rule. For Forten, any such move would have to be self-directed under black leadership, so despite their best efforts white colonization-ists never succeeded in gaining his trust. Indeed, once African coloniza-tion became a white man's initiative under the American Colonization Society, Forten followed the lead of his black neighbors in resisting the scheme, and he played a crucial role in formulating the organized resis-tance that would grow into the immediate abolition movement in the 1830s. Forten's interest in black emigration and his resistance to white-led colonization adds another dimension to the story of Pennsylvania's, and the nation's, abolition and colonization movements. After all, Afri-can Americans were never passive onlookers, and the beliefs and opin-ions of men such as James Forten and his friends were ultimately the most important in shaping the destiny of both African colonization and a biracial America.

* * *

As a free black man in the first state to legalize gradual abolition, James Forten lived in an environment filled with both hope and uncertainty. He was thirteen years old when lawmakers described abolition as a debt they owed to God for delivering them from British oppression and passed the gradual abolition law of 1780. They also alluded to racial equality by admitting that, though of different colors, all men were created by the same "Almighty Hand." Such words offered the state's black residents hope. According to Forten biographer Julie Winch, "What the quality of citizenship might be for a black Patriot he would have to wait and

FIGURE 7. "James Forten." Leon Gardiner Collection. (Courtesy of the Historical Society of Pennsylvania.)

see, but the abolition law, with its statements about justice and an end to prejudice" convinced Forten "that society was being reordered, and that merit, rather than complexion or condition, would be rewarded in the new republic."[2]

Eager to serve the country that offered him so much, Forten joined the crew of a privateering vessel and set sail three months before he turned fifteen. During his second cruise, however, his ship was captured, and he found himself a prisoner of the British. Being of African descent, he faced enslavement but instead was offered a chance to live freely in England. He refused that opportunity as well as a chance to escape, instead choosing loyalty to the new country, at least part of which had just offered freedom for blacks. Throughout his life he would expect that country to honor his loyalty and wartime service by making good on the promise that he would enjoy the same rights as white Americans.[3]

After the war Forten joined the crew of a merchant vessel and traveled to England where he spent a few months. The British antislavery crusade had just begun, and a year after he left, abolitionists there began discussing the possibility of an African colony. Although Forten may have heard rumors of the possible colony, the plans did not truly take shape until after he left, so he would have heard limited details.[4]

Back in the United States, Forten apprenticed under Robert Bridges, a white sailmaker who later became his partner. In 1792 Bridges financed a two-story brick house in Southwark for him, just a few blocks from the sail loft. Six years later Bridges retired and left Forten in charge of the business, making him the employer of about two dozen workers. By 1805 Forten had twenty-five apprentices, most of whom were white, and he played a patriarchal role, enforcing his own strict rules on alcohol and sexual propriety. He also encouraged education, even helping to establish a school. Like other black entrepreneurs and craftsmen, Forten supported his family comfortably while helping to build churches, schools, and mutual aid societies to foster black community. His hard work and efforts at self and community improvement revealed an overall optimism.[5]

This optimism, however, competed with fear and frustration. Forten's city also saw the birth of the federal Constitution in 1787. It offered a great deal of promise in general, but this same Constitution deemed slaves worth merely three-fifths as much as their owners. This ran counter to the state legislature's declaration of equality. Forten soon learned that even in Pennsylvania, freedom would not automatically mean citizenship for blacks.[6]

Not yet aware of this reality, blacks throughout the country continued to see the home of the most active and vibrant abolition society as a beacon of liberty, but their hopes for a new life in the state only intensified a growing racial tension. Many whites grew increasingly nervous, especially with the arrival in the late 1780s of black refugees who had been exposed to the fervor of the French Revolution. They feared these Haitian blacks, who were familiar with atrocity stories of revolutionary excesses and retribution. The immigrants also brought yellow fever, sending the city into turmoil in the summer of 1793.[7] Though many members of Philadelphia's black community toiled selflessly to help both black and white victims of the fever, as we saw before, publisher Mathew Carey downplayed their role, instead citing the few cases in which black nurses accepted high fees for their services. Insulted, Absalom Jones and Richard Allen issued a pamphlet that detailed the events from the black perspective and described the many sacrifices blacks made to help whites. Despite their able refutation of Carey's charges, the insult permanently harmed the image of the black community.[8]

That same year Forten and his community were further insulted and terrorized when the federal government passed a new Fugitive Slave Law. Trying to make it easier to catch fugitives, this law enabled kidnappers to abduct free blacks with little effort. All white claimants had to do was swear in court that a black was a runaway and the defendant was "returned" to slavery. Of course, the Pennsylvania Abolition Society and black leaders protested, but the law stood.[9]

In 1799 a group of African Americans from Philadelphia responded with a Petition of the People of Colour, Freemen within the City and Suburbs of Philadelphia. The group asked first that Congress do something about the kidnapping. Then it pointed out that the only sure way to do this was to remove the temptation by outlawing slavery. Sounding much like their white colleagues in the PAS, however, the African Americans called for gradual, rather than immediate, emancipation so that the enslaved could be prepared for productive free lives. Robert Waln, a representative from Pennsylvania, introduced the petition, but ultimately the only legislator willing to consider it was George Thacher of Massachusetts.[10]

Forten followed the debate closely and when it was over sent a letter to Thacher. He thanked the congressman for defending "Africans and descendants of that unhappy race," expressing fear that even though he enjoyed his freedom, under current laws he could end up in bondage at any time. Forten promised that Philadelphia blacks would not rise up in violent protest, like those in Haiti had, because men like Thacher gave them faith that the government would eventually correct the situation. They were more interested in gaining education and earning a place of equality in the new nation. Though a "deep gloom" pervaded the black community, they held out hope since at least one lawmaker had shown sympathy.[11]

That same month, black leaders found themselves at odds with their most important white allies, the PAS. They offered a plan to the Pennsylvania legislature to tax free blacks to help fund a general compensated emancipation. Members of the House drafted and passed a bill providing for this scheme, but the Senate rejected it. Though the bill would have freed all remaining slaves in the state, the PAS opposed it. The group's lawyers focused on legal and abstract principle rather than expediency. They insisted that the plan called for buying the slaves and thus amounted to participation in the system. Any participation, regardless of motive, would acknowledge the legitimacy of bondage. They added that slave owners should not be awarded compensation and that it would be discriminatory to tax only one group of the population. They preferred to stick to the plan to have slavery declared unconstitutional.[12]

The PAS may have objected, but half of the plan appealed to less friendly whites. At the end of 1804, Delaware and Chester county residents asked the state legislature to tax all free blacks to fund the support of black indigents. Although this attempt failed, it was only the beginning. The argument spread throughout the state, including Philadelphia, that blacks tended to be lazy and were prone to criminal behavior. As a result, the legislature saw more and more calls for stricter punishment of black criminals and vagrants, and many began to ask for restrictions on black migration into Pennsylvania. Forten and other leaders continued their drive for racial uplift, hoping that if more blacks behaved respectably, whites would see the overall community as orderly and worthy of fair treatment. They founded more churches, schools, and mutual aid societies as well as self-improvement clubs such as the Society for the Suppression of Vice and Immorality.[13]

* * *

Despite black efforts at self-help and community uplift, racial hostility grew. In the decade between 1790 and 1800 Philadelphia's racial climate changed drastically, and conditions only worsened from there. Economic tensions coincided with a rising black population made up mainly of southern fugitives who had no resources and often relied on public relief. Others became beggars or, in the worst cases, resorted to criminal behavior. Already alarmed over the influx of blacks and the apparent rise in crime, Pennsylvania whites were also aware of revolts and unrest in slaveholding areas. The year 1805 marked the beginning of a sustained attempt at legal discrimination against free blacks. In the ensuing decade the legislature dealt with five different bills to prevent black migration or tax African American householders to support poor blacks. Between 1805 and 1807, three such bills passed one branch of the legislature, though none met ultimate approval. This campaign gained popularity in 1813, however, as Jacob Mitchell, a Republican and a merchant in Philadelphia, irritated at the large population of runaway slaves, sought to end the state's reputation as a haven for such migrants. Many southern states required former slaves to leave once freed, and many of these former slaves went to Philadelphia in search of opportunity.[14]

Mitchell wanted to stem the growth of this population by prohibiting blacks from settling in Pennsylvania. Though he did not include plans to remove those who were already there, he did suggest a number of measures to keep them under tight control. He wanted the legislature to require every black resident to register or face the possibility of enslavement or imprisonment. His bill also proposed that black criminals be sold and the revenue used to pay restitution to their victims. Like others before, it also included the provision to tax black householders to support black indigents. Even worse, this bill, unlike earlier ones, was backed up by petitions from Philadelphia's mayor and aldermen. The PAS and the black community united in protest against these measures.[15]

Forten issued one of the most famous protests, "Letters from a Man of Colour." Addressed to the legislature, these letters employed the rhetoric of the American Revolution to point out the injustice of Mitchell's plan. The "self-evident" truth "that God created all men equal" should apply to all men, and representatives of "the only state in the Union wherein the African race have justly boasted of rational liberty and the protection of laws" should not now join in their oppression. Not all blacks were poor refugees. "Many of us are men of property, for the security of which we have hitherto looked to the laws of our blessed state, but should this become a law, our property is jeopardized, since the same power which can expose to sale an unfortunate fellow creature, can wrest from him those estates, which years of honest industry have accumulated." Of course, guilty men of all colors should be punished, but the state already had sufficient laws for this purpose. Forten pointed out a number of problems with the proposed registration system, showing that it, like the Fugitive Slave Law, would result in many innocent free blacks being enslaved. As for closing the state's borders to migrants of color, "Where shall he go?"[16]

Forten tried to make whites recognize that most blacks contributed to the community. "If there are worthless men, there are also men of merit among the African race, who are useful members of Society." He cited as evidence their benevolent institutions and the numbers they had clothed and fed through independent initiative. "Punish the guilty man of colour to the utmost limit of the laws, but sell him not to slavery! If he is in danger of becoming a publick charge prevent him!"[17]

This bill, however, threatened to undo years of black self-help efforts. "It is in vain that we are forming societies of different kinds to ameliorate the condition of our unfortunate brethren, to correct their morals and render them not only honest but useful members to society" since the bill left all blacks "doomed to feel the lash of oppression." Forten argued that whites who supported the proposed measurers may as well outlaw the Gospel and use "all endeavours . . . to cut us off from happiness here-after as well as here!" In short, the bill would "destroy the morals it is intended to produce."[18]

The institutions Forten cited as examples of black initiative did indeed play a crucial role in Philadelphia's black community. For one thing, they allowed the African American community to forge a unique sense of identity. Historian Patrick Rael has argued that independent black churches "served as a training ground for black public leaders and as a forum for black clerics to set forth a vision of racial unity through public speech." As this sense of community grew, leaders conducted parades and public celebrations that, deliberately or not, served as public expressions of racial unity.[19] Of course this process was double-edged because contemporary whites also noticed and grew alarmed at this developing sense of racial community and its attempts at independence.

Whites began to resent, rather than appreciate, black efforts at racial uplift. Economic tensions may have fueled the growing racism among poorer whites, but ironically, successful black churches, schools, and self-help societies also irritated middle-class white intellectual and political leaders. Absorbing new "scientific" theories about race distinction and black biological inferiority, they resented African American attempts to enter the middle and upper class. They especially feared that "uppity" black men would try to increase their social status by marrying white women. Wealthy men such as Forten especially irritated less prosperous whites. Emma Lapsansky-Werner studied race riots that occurred in the mid-1830s and found that rioters specifically targeted wealthy blacks, one of whom was Forten's son. She maintains that in this case whites who rented houses from the Fortens resented their landlord's material success. Examining the victims of the riots, she concludes that "individuals, groups, and property which represented economic and social 'success' and 'respectability' were prime targets for rioters' resentments." Racist caricatures depicted blacks who dared to dress in finery, ride in carriages, and adopt other middle-class habits as further evidence for this class resentment.[20]

Caught in a vicious cycle, black leaders responded with typical self-help arguments, which served only to further irritate their white neighbors. "Though these leaders understood that they were the scapegoats of American society," Lapsansky-Werner contends, "still they continued to pursue the only strategy they could conceive: to convince that society of the Afro-American's respectability." Proud of their independence and personal restraint, they stressed how well they took care of their community and how few blacks were in the almshouse. She concludes that "while the white mobs were expressing their frustration at their own social immobility, black people, for their part, were concerned with publicly exhibiting the proof of their progress toward the 'respectable' life. This set of dynamics proved mutually antagonistic."[21]

By emphasizing self-help and uplift of their community, black leaders were employing tactics introduced by the PAS and encouraged further by the American Convention of Abolitionists. This latter group, which remained largely in the hands of Pennsylvania and New York abolitionists throughout its existence, carried on the PAS mission of encouraging industry, morality, and sobriety among the freed. Hoping to use clear evidence of improvement in the free black community, the convention wrote a prescription that future abolitionists, including immediatists of both hues, would standardize. The freed should regularly attend public worship and read the Bible. They should seek education and teach their children "virtuous trades" while always working hard themselves. They should remain honest in all dealings and "acquire habits of industry, sobriety, and frugality" while avoiding "dissipation and vice" and practicing temperance and faithful monogamy. They should also avoid lawsuits, "expensive and idle amusements, and noisy and disorderly conduct on the Sabbath." If he followed these injunctions while also conducting himself "in a civil and respectable manner," the free black was told he "could effectively refute the objections which had been raised against him as an inferior being and at the same time justify the cause of abolition everywhere." Without realizing it, gradualists were giving advice that only compounded the problem.[22]

Unfortunately at this point black leaders saw little other choice than to trust their old friends. When they did try to strike out on their own and fight independently, they met resistance even from those who claimed to represent their interests.[23] Seen as drains on society, they worked tirelessly to prove otherwise, yet their efforts only drew increased resentment. Stereotyped as dependent, they tried to fulfill leadership positions within their community, but even friendly whites failed to acknowledge their independence. Little wonder, then, that Forten paid attention when another black leader with ties to the maritime community approached him with plans for a scheme that appeared to offer a significant chance for black leaders to participate in the redemption of Africa and the push for racial equality in America.

* * *

Paul Cuffee, a wealthy black Quaker entrepreneur, ship owner, and captain from Westport, Massachusetts, came to Philadelphia in 1807 after hearing about a British settlement in Africa. First settled in 1781, this colony had been governed by the Sierra Leone Company until the Crown took it over in 1806. British abolitionists had played a role in the colony from the beginning, helping to recruit settlers and offering advice to the colonial government. In 1807 some of these same philanthropists who had fought to end the slave trade had founded the African Institution. Though the government controlled the colony at this point, members of the institution hoped to carry on the philanthropic aspect by overseeing settlers' morals, protecting them from African and European dishonesty, and using the colony to combat the slave trade. Cuffee turned to Philadelphia Quaker and PAS president James Pemberton for more information.[24]

After contacting Zachary Macaulay, former governor of the colony and member of the institution, Pemberton learned that the group, familiar with Cuffee's reputation, desperately wanted the black captain's support. By this time he was one of the most successful blacks in the United States. He and his family and other business partners owned at least two ships, a shipyard, a two-hundred-acre farm, a windmill, and a gristmill. A well-known and respected member of the Westport Weekly meeting, he was also known for his efforts at black education. Sierra Leone needed settlers with important agricultural and mechanical skills, and the directors of the institution wanted free blacks to fill these roles. Not only did Cuffee fit the description, they also hoped he could recruit more men like himself. Once enlisted, Cuffee in turn appealed to influential free blacks in Philadelphia and New York, seeking especially to win the support of Philadelphia's James Forten, Absalom Jones, and Richard Allen.[25]

The plan Cuffee presented to Forten and other prospective supporters involved using the colony to foster economic development that would replace the slave trade while also providing a civilizing force that would lead Africans to a respectable place in the Atlantic world. American blacks would emigrate temporarily and help Africans build the necessary agricultural and economic infrastructures, but, at least initially, Cuffee did not promote mass exodus. Though deeply connected with the Quakers, Cuffee's first goal was to promote commerce. Once the process of civilization began, Christianity could be introduced, but he agreed with institution members William Allen and Thomas Clarkson that this was not primarily a religious endeavor. Even so, the quality of the settlers would determine success or failure, so Cuffee screened applicants very carefully. He wanted only those with skills useful to the colony, and he insisted on letters of reference to ensure their moral caliber and sound work ethic.[26]

A crucial part of Cuffee's plan for transatlantic trade and racial uplift involved a network of black and white philanthropists and leaders on three continents working together to make the colony successful. This process was set in motion when African Institution members Macauley, William Roscoe, William Wilberforce, and William Allen deemed Cuffee "most unquestionably . . . a desirable accession to the population of Sierra Leone" and began to court him. Their encouragement, along with the group's emphasis on the colony's importance in combating the slave trade, convinced Cuffee to sail to Sierra Leone in 1810. While Cuffee was in Africa, the institution convinced Britain's Privy Council to concede the American merchant a six-month trading license to carry goods between England and Sierra Leone. On leaving Africa, Cuffee traveled to England to meet with these men and discuss this partnership further. In the process he forged a lasting friendship with Allen, staying at his home and bonding with his family.[27]

While nurturing this connection with the English group, Cuffee founded the Friendly Society of Sierra Leone to serve as the second point of contact in his transatlantic network. This mutual aid society, founded in 1812, concentrated on commercial concerns in the colony, seeking to protect the interests of black merchants. John Kizell, a native of Sherbro Island who had spent much of his life as a slave in South Carolina, served as president. Kizell came to Sierra Leone with other blacks who had remained loyal to the British during the American War for Independence. This group of settlers had originally been granted land in Nova Scotia by the British government but found conditions there unsatisfactory. Their main complaint was that the British government had promised free land to more loyalists, black and white, than they were prepared to serve and had given whites priority in land grant assignments. The blacks appealed to the government for land and a chance for independence elsewhere in the empire. They turned to Granville Sharp, a well-known British philanthropist and influential figure in Sierra Leone's founding, for assistance. Sharp managed to convince the government to pay for their transportation and help them get settled in the colony.[28]

A few of these settlers, like Kizell, actually were returning to their native land, but Ellen Gibson Wilson has shown that most of these black loyalists brought with them uniquely American ideas of independence and democracy, as well as an attitude of superiority that led them to look down on the majority of settlers who were "recaptives," or native Africans rescued from slave traders. These settlers felt qualified to fulfill the colony's black leadership roles, and Cuffee agreed. He placed his hopes for Sierra Leone's commercial success with the Nova Scotians. However, as a wealthy merchant and well-known captain, he in turn saw himself as one step above the former Americans and an important intermediary between them and white leaders in England and America.[29]

The network of African Institution Auxiliary societies Cuffee established in Philadelphia, New York, and Boston constituted the final point in his trade triangle. Though he began a correspondence with white Friends and free blacks in Philadelphia in 1807, it was not until his return from Africa in 1812 that he called on a gathering of Philadelphia's free black merchants and clerics to join his effort by forming the auxiliary. During this visit, he met with Absalom Jones and James Forten, as well as the white abolitionist and acquaintance Benjamin Rush. After hearing the details of his select emigration plan, free black leaders agreed to form the society, with Forten acting as president and his associate Russel Parrott, the well-known assistant to Absalom Jones, serving as secretary. The group began seeking recruits to settle in Sierra Leone, and in 1815 they recommended the families of Anthony Survance and Samuel Wilson to the Friendly Society "as persons of good moral character." By this time Cuffee had applied to Congress for assistance with his plan, and

Forten and Parrot came forth to offer a public endorsement in *Poulson's American Daily Advertiser,* telling readers of Cuffee's hope of "aiding in the civilization and improvement of Africa," they described his plan "to take with him a few sober, industrious families" to aid in this endeavor.[30]

Like Cuffee, the Philadelphia group screened applicants carefully to ensure they were "of good report, united with a knowledge of cultivation of produce familiar to the African climate, or those useful branches of the mechanic arts." Both of the settlers they sent knew the African climate quite well. A native of Senegal, Survance had been a slave in Haiti until the Revolution, at which point he gained his freedom and sailed to the United States, eventually settling in Philadelphia, where he acquired property and achieved a degree of success. One of the most determined settlers, the self-educated Survance insisted on paying his own passage and refused "assistance from any quarter." Wilson, a Congo native, was also eager for a new start in Africa. For both of these men, Cuffee's project truly offered a chance to "return home."[31]

Cuffee managed to establish African Institution branches in New York and Boston as well, but he placed most of his hopes on Forten's Philadelphia group. Although the Boston chapter provided thirty-two of his thirty-eight passengers, Forten's group offered their support first, and Cuffee hoped this chapter would carry forth his plan "should I not Live to see the object carried into effect." Perhaps he expected the group to eventually recruit a larger number of settlers because he wrote on several occasions about the large free black population in the city. He also apparently placed a great deal of faith in Forten's abilities. In 1815 Cuffee tried to enlist him to convince black subscribers to make contributions of hundreds of dollars each "so as to come into Common Stock and Build a Vessell of about 200 tons for an African trader in order to keep up and open an intercourse between the united states [and] africa." He believed such a project "could be done with profit and mutual advantage" if directed by the Philadelphia African Institution. Later that year he proposed that the group buy half of his own ship *Alpha,* which was currently for sale, for this purpose, but the co-op plan never took shape.[32]

Enthusiasm for the endeavor began to wane in Philadelphia by 1816. Though prospective settlers continued to inquire about Sierra Leone, someone was spreading "many unfavourable reports" about the mission among the free black community. As Philadelphia support slackened, however, support from the South grew. Andover Theological Seminary's Samuel Aiken reported that antislavery sentiment was growing in Tennessee and Virginia. This news came after Cuffee had been corresponding with and advising members of the school's antislavery community for two years. Samuel J. Mills, an evangelical pastor who had played a leading role in forming the first foreign missionary society in the United States, the American Board of Commissioners for Foreign Missions, and was a cofounder of the American Bible Society, had approached the captain in 1814 after hearing about his work with the institution, and Nathan Lord had asked for further information in April 1815. These men offered Cuffee their support for what they mistakenly viewed as an effort to introduce Christianity to Africa. They hoped to use colonization to combat slavery in a more direct way than Cuffee envisioned. Cuffee remained certain that black achievement in the United States and Africa would end slavery by awakening whites to black equality. The Andover group, however, keenly aware of laws that prohibited manumission and social customs that discouraged it, hoped colonization would encourage slaveholders to free their chattel by giving them a place to send them. Nevertheless, their interest offered Cuffee hope for the same interracial cooperation he enjoyed with William Allen and the African Institution in Britain.[33]

Despite Forten and Cuffee's high hopes, it was not quite so simple, and Cuffee began to understand the limitations of black leadership opportunity during his first trip to the colony. He saw that white settlers, though less than 1 percent of the population, controlled 60 percent of the property. Furthermore, the colonists told him that white merchants sought to restrict black business efforts by dictating trade terms.[34]

The tension between the black quest for independence and white leadership was never resolved. By the summer of 1816, revolts throughout the slaveholding areas and the brutal repression whites used to suppress them were beginning to convince Cuffee of the merits of the Andover group's use of colonization to directly foster emancipation, but his heyday in the British colonization scheme had passed. By the time he came to advocate mass migration over select emigration, he was in communication with men who would soon form the American Colonization Society and had arrived at the sad conclusion that American slaves faced death or perpetual servitude on the one hand and freedom qualified by racial separation on the other.[35]

Had Cuffee and Forten known more about the history of British colonization in Africa they might have been more skeptical of white leaders' ability to accept blacks in truly powerful positions. One black leader in the Atlantic abolitionist crusade, Olaudah Equiano, had joined the venture as part of the war against slavery. Encouraged when the government asked him to serve as commissary of stores for the expedition, he showed interest and at least guarded enthusiasm because he saw the endeavor as a possible chance for black independence and self-sufficiency. During his four months as commissary of stores, however, he uncovered corruption and witnessed the "most wretched" conditions of the settlers as they waited on board for the ships to set sail for the colony. He tried to correct the situation by reporting the abuses to the Navy and quickly found himself dismissed from his post. In the light of Equiano's treatment, another black abolitionist in Britain, Ottobah Cugoano, initiated a public campaign to keep colonization out of the abolition movement. Under such scrutiny, white-initiated colonization grew increasingly suspect.[36]

* * *

American blacks shared similar suspicions when presented with the idea of African colonization, especially once the American Colonization Society took the leading role in the cause. What white colonizationists, first in the Andover group and later the ACS, failed to realize was that blacks might have been interested in settlements founded and operated under black leadership. The last thing they wanted, however, was to be dragged back across the Atlantic by whites who had exploited black labor for centuries but now deemed those laborers and their descendants unfit for citizenship in the nation they had helped forge. Patrick Rael has argued that nationalism was a developing ideology throughout the world at this time and that in the United States two very different strains were beginning to emerge. According to his model, Cuffee's attempt to create a Pan-African model of black agency stemmed from an emerging black nationalism, while white-initiated colonization derived from the belief that blacks could not participate fully in a white nation.[37]

What is easily overlooked, however, is that Cuffee's initial plan called for select and temporary immigration, not full-scale exodus and was thus a variant on the self-help and racial uplift agenda. Like the Puritans who settled in his part of the country almost two centuries before, he wanted to create a model society to serve as a beacon to the world. Instead of showcasing religious piety, he hoped to demonstrate black equality. This could be achieved only under genuine black initiative and leadership.

Likewise, Forten supported African colonization when he thought it offered a chance for blacks to control their own destiny, but he learned to question white supporters' motives, especially after humanitarians such as the Reverends Robert Finley and Samuel J. Mills joined with slaveholders from Virginia and other upper South states to create the American Colonization Society. The humanitarian element, represented by Finley and Mills, did consult Paul Cuffee, who in turn recommended they meet with Forten, but their motives seemed suspect. Though Finley told Cuffee he agreed that blacks should leave only "with their own consent," his *Thought on the Colonization of Free Blacks* told a different story, recommending that slaves be freed "on condition" of colonization. Thus, though Forten wrote to assure Cuffee in 1817 that "my opinion is that they will never become a people until they come out from amongst the white people," he had to warn his friend of a growing resistance and vocal opposition. Free blacks had begun to see colonization as another white attempt to dictate their choices, so Forten had to report that, "the majority is decidedly against me." For now, "I am determined to remain silent, except as to my opinion which I freely give when asked."[38]

Regardless of his personal feelings and awareness of the difference between Cuffee's plan and that offered by the ACS, Forten felt a duty as a leader of the black community to respect the general climate. He and Parrott, once the leading forces behind Philadelphia's African Institution, took the lead in the movement against the ACS. Though more and more Philadelphia blacks were coming to believe the society had forced removal in mind, Forten did not initially share their concern. He did realize, however, that colonization and select emigration were two very different ideas.

Resistance reached a crescendo when the colonization society brought the scheme closer to home by forming a Philadelphia auxiliary, and once again Forten found himself presiding over a protest meeting. After this meeting at a schoolhouse in Green's Court, he and Parrott issued *An Address to the humane and benevolent Inhabitants of the city and county of Philadelphia*, in which they resolved that "we have no wish to separate from our present homes, for any purpose whatever." They pleaded with the city's abolitionists not to be fooled by the scheme. The ACS plan was "not asked for by us; nor will it be required by any circumstances, in our present or future condition; as long as we shall be permitted to share the protection of the excellent laws, and just government which we now enjoy, in common with every individual of the community."[39]

At this point, Forten and Parrott renounced and disclaimed all connection to the ACS scheme, pointing out that colonization had no role in the abolition movement. Thanks to Philadelphia's antislavery community, "the ultimate and final abolition of slavery in the United States, is, under the guidance and protection of a just God, progressing." More blacks gained freedom each year through gradual emancipation and were able to seek "instruction and improvement" in the United States. "But if the emancipation of our kindred shall, when the plan of colonization shall go into effect, be attended with transportation to a distant land, and shall be granted on no other condition," the freed would not be prepared to accept it. "The consolation for our past sufferings and those of our colour, who are in slavery . . . will cease for ever." This statement is perhaps too conciliatory, but it would have appealed to those PAS members who dedicated themselves to uplifting and educating free blacks, as well as opposing slavery. Perhaps Forten and Parrott really believed that those in bondage needed to be made ready for freedom and thus found gradual emancipation justified. Whatever they believed, they hoped that the idea of southern slaves emancipated on condition of emigrating, left unprepared to fend for themselves in a foreign land, much less to pursue higher levels of improvement such as education and religion, would pull at the heartstrings of Philadelphia reformers. At the same time, they likely feared that unprepared settlers "without arts" or "habits of industry, and unaccustomed to provide by their own exertions and foresight for their wants," would destroy the dream of a successful black settlement by turning any colony into "the abode of every vice and the home of every misery."[40]

Furthermore, if slaveholders were allowed to free only the slaves of their choice, they would destroy families and strengthen the system of slavery at the same time. Forced migration would bring back "all the heart-rending agonies which were endured by our forefathers when they were dragged into bondage from Africa." The ACS scheme also offered slaveholders a chance to orchestrate a select emigration of their own, but instead of sending the most talented, ablest settlers, they would surely send the most troublesome slaves, thus eliminating those who challenged their authority and retaining those who were most timid and least likely to resist bondage.

Forten and Parrott begged Philadelphia's white philanthropists to join them in opposition to this dangerous scheme. "*We humbly*, respectfully, and fervently intreat and beseech your disapprobation of the plan of colonization now offered by 'the American society for colonizing the free people of colour of the United States.'" The PAS may have had its limits, but most blacks appreciated the group's work and counted on it to be there in times of need. Now more than ever, they needed their old friends to help fend off this new group that presumed to speak for them. Forten and Parrott made this clear by emphatically declaring at the end of the address that the ACS did not speak for blacks and actually threatened the abolition movement.[41]

On December 10, 1818, the PAS and gradualists from other states responded to the black leaders by calling a special meeting of the American Convention of Abolition societies. Since "those who are engaged in the same cause, should act in concert," the gradualists decided to investigate the new society and its agenda. After "much and serious deliberation," they concluded that the ACS plan "ought not to receive the support of the friends of universal emancipation," primarily because free blacks opposed the plan and would not participate "unless by force." They cited Forten and Parrott's *Address* and argued that the sentiments expressed likely "prevail very universally." They agreed with the Philadelphia protestors that the freed were better off in a place where "all the benefits bestowed upon our nation by science and the arts, are to a certain extent necessarily communicated to them." They pointed to problems in Sierra Leone and argued that "on the whole Atlantic coast of Africa, south of the great Desert, no place can be found in a healthy climate, unembarrassed by European claims, in which there is a tract of land, fit for cultivation and lying in one body, sufficiently extensive to support a colony numerous enough to defend its own independence." Even if a site could be secured, the problems of transportation would be insurmountable. Also, there was the question of whether the colony would be a permanent dependency of the United States, an independent state, or a free nation. As to the fear of colonization being used to secure slavery in the United States, "our object being gradually to abolish this kind of property, we do not perceive the expediency of our supporting a measure, the tendency of which, is admitted by some of its most distinguished friends, to be hostile to the purpose which we are labouring to effect."

Finally, they agreed with Forten and Parrott that colonization threatened abolition. "Should it receive the approbation of Congress or of the legislatures of the slave states, so as to induce an expectation in those parts of the Union that it will be executed, it is highly probable that the question of emancipation will become connected with it." If this should happen, "every attempt to procure a gradual abolition of slavery will be resisted, on the ground that measures for that purpose cannot conveniently be taken, until a colony shall be established, to which the liberated slaves may be transported." Since the colonization plan was "impracticable," no site would ever be ready, so emancipation would be delayed indefinitely. Thus, the gradualists repeated a previous resolution that "the gradual and total emancipation of all persons of colour, and their literary and moral education, should precede their colonization." They had also been approached about an emigration scheme to Haiti and considered it as well. On that matter, they concluded that they needed more information before rendering an opinion.[42]

Although most African Americans avoided white-initiated colonization, some agreed to give it a try. Twenty-two Philadelphia free blacks left on the ACS's first voyage to the colony of Liberia, and twelve more joined them the next year. These settlers expected to be treated with respect and given independence once in the colony. Floyd J. Miller has argued that even though they applied to the ACS for passage to Africa and land grants, the emigrants who went under the society's auspices "assumed they would be sovereign in all territorial and political matters" once in Liberia. No sooner had they departed, however, than it became clear that white agents were, and would remain, in authority. Not surprisingly, the tension began immediately, and as word of such discontent made its way to the United States, fewer and fewer blacks agreed to go. Lott Cary, an emigrant from Virginia who went to Liberia on the second settlement voyage in 1821, worked hard to ensure a degree of black self-determination, but to little avail. Marie Tyler McGraw's study of black settlers revealed that between 1817 and 1832, "free blacks who had once been willing to consider emigration to Africa" started to see colonization as "less an opportunity presented to them than a judgment placed upon them."[43]

Forten began to feel this way as ACS agents continued to try to badger him into joining their movement and accepting their outwardly imposed national identity. In 1827 a Pennsylvania colonization leader wrote to ACS headquarters that Forten had decided "that the people of colour in this country are by birth entitled to all the rights of freemen" and should be allowed to enjoy full citizenship. By this point Forten had also concluded that the ACS's work tended "to excite apprehensions in the mind of the southern planters," causing them to increase "the rigour of their laws relating to the blacks." Finally, he had decided that "Africa is a land of destruction where the sword will cut off the few wretched beings whom the *climate* spared."[44]

* * *

Forten believed that the white movement to send blacks to Africa fostered hatred and discord, but he became intrigued by another emigration scheme closer to home. It began in 1816 when Prince Saunders, a highly educated free black from Connecticut who had shown interest in Cuffee's plan, approached the American Convention of Abolitionists to gain their approval for a project to settle American free blacks in Haiti. Organized and supported by people of color, this scheme seemed in many ways to fulfill the dream of black self-rule. Formerly a French colony, Haiti had gained independence during the upheavals of the French Revolution. It became the first black republic in 1804, following a revolutionary war led by Toussaint L'Ouverture.[45]

Acting as an agent of the Haitian government, Saunders told the abolitionists that, unlike the ACS plan, Haitian emigration was feasible. Though currently laboring under civil unrest, which, he was certain, would be cleared up in a matter of time, the black republic was already independent. He assured his listeners that neither the Spanish nor the French would try to retake the territory, and he promised that "in this great island there seems to be some foundation for the hopes of those who are to emigrate to rest upon." The governments were established, and though "they may be arbitrary, and somewhat allied to military despotism in their present features and character," they were "still susceptible of being improved, whenever a tranquilized state of society, and their stability and independence as a nation, shall authorize it." Saunders, who had met and worked with most of Cuffee's English contacts, assured the American abolitionists that "there are many hundreds of the free people in the New England and middle states, who would be glad to repair there immediately to settle." Furthermore, "the recent proceedings in several of the slave states towards the free population of colour in those states, seem to render it highly probable, that, that oppressed class of the community will soon be obliged to flee to the free states for protection." Why not help them settle in Haiti instead? Saunders compared his Haitian plan to British work in Sierra Leone, and he called on the American abolitionists to support his plan for black settlement.[46]

Though the abolitionists made no commitment, Forten supported the plan. This new scheme seemed a fitting tribute to Cuffee's work. After all, the new nation was founded as a result of the only successful slave revolt in the New World and was now an independent republic governed by blacks. If this government succeeded, it would offer proof that blacks could govern themselves. Forten had noticed this potential early on, researching the country by reading and interviewing people who had been there, including Anthony Survance, the Sierra Leone settler. Other American blacks shared his interest, and Saunders found a receptive audience.[47]

By 1824 the Haitian project changed hands, but Philadelphia blacks continued to pay attention. At this point, Jean-Pierre Boyer had assumed leadership in Haiti, and he welcomed American black emigration, promising free passage, free land, and several months' provisions for sober, hard-working settlers willing to work unimproved land. Boyer sent a representative to Philadelphia to sell the scheme and managed to enlist the support of Mathew Carey, Nicholas Biddle, president of the Bank of the United States, and Stephen Girard, a wealthy merchant. Eighteen black leaders pledged support by forming the Haytien Emigration Society of Philadelphia. Richard Allen served as president, and James Forten was on the board of managers. They began recruiting efforts immediately.[48]

Between eight thousand and thirteen thousand settlers joined the resulting exodus, but it is impossible to determine how many were from Pennsylvania. What is clear is that though Forten continued to resist the ACS, he wholeheartedly endorsed the Haitian scheme. Five of his close associates, including three of his apprentices and one fellow Haytien Emigration Society manager, went to Haiti. Perhaps more important, Forten's wife's brother, Charles Vandine went and stayed. Nevertheless, things in Haiti did not conclude on a positive note. Settlers found a land destroyed by warfare and a highly stratified caste society that valued light skin and at least some degree of European heritage. The Americans did not find the equal opportunity they sought and were even denied participation in the political process.[49]

Haitian settlement faced a number of obstacles. First, American emigrants to Haiti took with them unrealistic expectations and found conditions in their new home unacceptable. James and Lois Horton argue that the ACS contributed greatly to this by sending "plants" into the black community to exaggerate Haiti's potential just to heighten expectations and make disappointment even greater when the colony could not live up to the expectations. The black oral tradition fed into this problem, because potential settlers listened to these "plants" rather than reading the details in the literature distributed by Haitian representatives. As to the incompatibility between American blacks and Haitians, Catholicism played a large role, and a language barrier and unfamiliar customs compounded the tension. The final problem was that the settlers were not interested in cultivating the farms given them by the government, choosing instead to sell or rent the land out and move to the cities.[50]

Forten abandoned his support of mass black migration to the republic but remained interested in the country and continued to consult his contacts there for firsthand knowledge. Though disappointed with events in Haiti, he simply could not abandon his hope for a successful independent black republic. He decided that black Americans should stay at home, but he continued to hope that a successful black nation would emerge and prove racial equality.

* * *

Meanwhile, white colonizationists continued to try to enlist Forten in their cause, but even as he flirted with Haitian emigration, he became increasingly determined to resist white efforts to control black destiny. Like other black leaders throughout the North, he respected his PAS allies, but he realized that more direct action had to be taken to deal with race riots and concerted efforts to exclude free blacks from every state in the union. And he realized that colonizationist efforts were only making these problems worse. By the end of the 1820s the society had become the boogeyman behind every instance of racial oppression and discord in the nation, and most free blacks throughout the state shared the opinion that slaveholders wanted to use the ACS to strengthen slavery. Forten blamed the group for the strict enforcement of Ohio's Black Codes beginning in 1829. These laws required blacks in the state to post sizable good behavior bonds, and local whites took the opportunity to harass blacks and attack their homes and businesses. Two years later, following the Virginia slave rebellion led by Nat Turner, a group of Pennsylvania whites again proposed similar measures for their state.[51]

Blaming free blacks from the northern and eastern states for the current slave unrest, a group of men met at Upton's on Dock Street on November 23, 1831, to profess their support for colonization. Of the men listed in the meeting's report, however, none had served as officers or appeared on the contribution list of the Pennsylvania Colonization Society's reports for the preceding years. Although two of them, John White and J. Washington Tyson, shared surnames with known colonizationists, neither appears to have been actively involved in the state's organized colonization movement. At any rate, the Southampton events caused them to call for forced removal of "all negroes within the boundaries of the United States." Historians and many contemporary observers have exonerated free blacks in the Turner affair, but these contemporary whites feared the connection, just as many free blacks feared the idea of forced removal. Though it is highly unlikely that these men read abolitionist papers, it is worth noting that two days before the Turner plot was put into motion, "A Colored Philadelphian," most likely James

Forten, warned readers of the *Liberator* that blacks would eventually "Fight for liberty, or die in the attempt." Of course there was no connection, but in a climate of hysteria any such coincidence could add to fears of conspiracy.[52]

Resentful of southern and midwestern states' efforts to expel free blacks and inadvertently send them seeking asylum in states such as Pennsylvania that had no such laws of their own, nervous whites called on their state legislature to do something. They wanted lawmakers not only to end the Keystone State's tenure as an asylum for black refugees but also to make provisions to remove blacks already in the state. Their requests often went beyond the goals of the organized colonization movement. Though the *United States Gazette*, the newspaper that reprinted the minutes from the meeting, professed support for the ACS, it defended free blacks from the charges of stirring unrest and argued against forced removal.

Nevertheless, proposals for exclusionary legislation continued to reach the legislature. One example was House Bill 446, which called for any black entering the state to post a bond of $500. All black residents, established or new, would have to register in their home counties and could not move at will. Employers would be fined for hiring unregistered blacks, and the federal fugitive slave law, not the milder state one, would be followed. In a letter worded much like Forten's address to the PAS, one black writer noted the connection between exclusionary measures in Virginia and a recent rise in the number of Liberian emigrants from the region. Taking issue with ACS claims that eighty recent emigrants in Southampton were manumitted slaves, he voiced suspicion that "most of them" were likely free blacks driven from their homes after the Turner plot.[53]

Hoping to prevent a similar expulsion in Pennsylvania, Forten, William Whipper, and Robert Purvis issued an appeal on behalf of "the people of color of the city of Philadelphia and its vicinity," begging the legislature not to restrict black migration and to continue to protect fugitives. They called on the state to uphold its antislavery legacy, and they repeated arguments they and the PAS had presented before. Many blacks were productive citizens, and, despite popular stereotypes, they were no more prone to criminal behavior than whites. Consequently the state should "remove *barriers* that stand in the way of our present *elevation*." Furthermore, whites had gone too far in "presuming to legislate for a respectable body of their fellow citizens, possessing rights as sacred and dear as theirs, *without making them a part in the legislation*, and in opposition to their *often* expressed views and interests." The bill was lost in committee, but similar calls for curbs on migration and support for the ACS continued to surface.[54]

Many free blacks from New York and Philadelphia responded to the hostile climate by calling the first of a series of black conventions in 1830, and some gathered in Philadelphia in 1831 to consider Canadian emigration. Forten, however, was beginning to consider a different tactic. His PAS allies continued to fight through the legal system to defend victims of human bondage on a case-by-case basis, and to push for free black uplift in the North with their schools. Forten appreciated the effort, but he began to see gradualism as "a dangerous doctrine," the continued reliance upon which would serve only to prevent any real progress. Furthermore, he was painfully aware that, though they professed to guard the interests of the black community, PAS leaders had never invited any African Americans to join their ranks and had yet to come out unequivocally against colonization.

* * *

Tired of gradualist timidity, Forten wanted a vibrant biracial movement to combat the colonizationists while taking the struggle beyond the PAS agenda. Already able to rely on friends such as James and Lucretia Mott, Sarah and Angelina Grimké, and Benjamin Lundy, he also forged a number of important new alliances with former colonizationists such as Arthur Tappan, Gerrit Smith, and William Lloyd Garrison.[55]

These former colonizationists had joined the ACS in hopes of fighting slavery but left looking for a better solution. Smith had been the single largest financial contributor to the colonization society, and Tappan had lent his organizational skills. Garrison had offered tepid support for the ACS until he met and consulted with black leaders, including Forten and his son-in-law, Robert Purvis. Perhaps Forten explained to him the difference between African American settlement plans and white efforts to further manipulate black destiny. At any rate, the energetic young editor changed his mind and joined Forten's crusade, assuming the role as the leading white opponent of colonization.[56]

Those who opposed both slavery and colonization built a much more radical movement than their predecessors. They reignited a theoretical framework articulated first by eighteenth-century English radicals such as Richard Price, Joseph Priestly, Granville Sharp, and John Cartwright. This "Dissenting" framework found its way into American politics through Thomas Paine's revoluationary-era propaganda and Thomas Jefferson's Declaration of Independence.[57]

The connection with Sharp is of particular interest in terms of the antislavery movement. Whereas Anthony Benezet and Benjamin Rush rejected Sharp's civil disobedience tactics as dangers, immediatists would accept them as important innovations in their efforts to awaken the American people to the evils of slavery. Also, while gradualists focused on ending slavery through political and legal means, some of the most radical abolitionists would reject voting altogether and refuse to pay taxes, and they would draw on this radical tradition, which, as Staughton Lynd has shown, stressed the inalienable rights of free speech and liberty of conscience and action over the right of property. According to Lynd, this was a crucial step in transforming the antislavery movement. "What mattered about the abolitionist questioning of private property was that it weakened respect for the state power by which that property was protected." In short, they concluded that laws "varied from time to place," so man "was not bound to obey national law if it conflicted with allegiance to God." In coming to this conclusion, immediatists made a major leap that gradualists and colonizationists had refused to consider.[58]

Whereas the radical ideas of the Dissenting tradition may not have been paramount to many PAS members, Lynd has shown that they did affect the beliefs of some Quaker abolitionists, such as John Parrish, Elias Hicks, and Benjamin Lundy. This makes sense in light of the Hicksite schism that split Quakers in 1827. It is also significant that Lynd included Lundy in this list because he was Garrison's mentor and had established an antislavery newspaper in the basement of Pennsylvania Hall, moving his press in just days before the mobbing.[59]

After joining forces with Forten, Garrison's first instinct was to follow Lundy's example by creating a newspaper of his own. By this time the print media had gained a tremendous importance in the American reform movement, and Garrison had plans to establish a newspaper specifically dedicated to immediate abolition. Quakers had been editing similar papers since 1817, but they had developed no clear consensus on how exactly to end slavery, advocating a range of options from gradualism to colonization to immediatism. Garrison's paper, however, would call forcefully and unequivocally for uncompensated, immediate abolition without removal. As one of the most successful businessmen in the United States, Forten was in a position to contribute financially, and he did. He also offered Garrison material for publication. Through his pieces in the *Liberator*, Forten attacked colonization relentlessly, denounced slavery forcefully, and described in great detail the racial prejudice that haunted free blacks like himself on a daily basis.[60]

Forten, who often signed his pieces "A Colored Philadelphian," was one of Garrison's most loyal correspondents. Among other things, he relayed accounts shared by a friend in Liberia of the death rate among settlers, challenging the popular assumption that blacks could handle the deadly climate because of natural immunity. He also offered Garrison and his readers a firsthand look into black America and helped them understand slavery and abolition in a way that few gradualists had. He cited his own service in the revolutionary war to claim America as his home, and he called on philanthropists to contribute their money and efforts toward assisting in the drive to uplift American blacks rather than wasting money on "conveying some of the superannuated slaves to Africa." Forten argued repeatedly that money would be better spent on educating and training black youth to be productive members of American society, and he asked whites to overcome their racial biases and employ blacks as apprentices. He reiterated some of his favorite themes to the *Liberator*'s audience, arguing that many blacks were taxpaying assets to the community, that the number of black criminals and paupers was smaller than many whites believed, and that blacks took care of their own through mutual aid organizations. Though Garrison and other white immediatists never completely overcame the paternalism that hampered the earlier struggle, working with men such as Forten helped them come close. Indeed, the paternalism with which they addressed the black masses was similar to that which pervaded the writings and speeches of wealthy free blacks such as Forten.[61]

Forten also helped Garrison compile information for his 1832 pamphlet *Thoughts on Colonization*. The ACS distributed procolonization literature through its own newspaper, the *African Repository*, and its published annual reports. The ACS propaganda machine was further fed by supporters such as Mathew Carey, who issued tracts extolling the merits of African settlement. By 1832 Forten and Garrison had had enough. With the help of an inside source, the Liberian colonist Joseph R. Dailey, Forten was able to supply Garrison with information about oppressive and unhealthy conditions in the colony. He gathered further intelligence from his shipping contacts, specifically Captain William Abels. The ACS had hired Abels to sail its ship, the *Margaret Mercer*, on several voyages to Africa. On one of these trips the black crew members contracted "Africa fever," and almost all of them died. This sad episode provided concrete evidence against the often-cited ACS argument that blacks were immune to African diseases. Forten relayed all of this information to Garrison, who promptly included it in his pamphlet.[62]

Unfortunately, not all of the information Forten provided Garrison was completely true. Forten used *Thoughts on Colonization* to erase his past, conveniently forgetting his earlier support of colonization and supplying Garrison only with evidence of resistance. With the other members of Philadelphia's African Institution dead, Forten was able to revise history and portray himself as the foremost opponent of colonization from the outset.[63]

Garrison's pamphlet energized the emerging immediatist movement, and within a year the new generation of abolitionists decided to meet in Philadelphia to form a national society to further their goals. Forten's son-in-law, Robert Purvis, served as a delegate at the founding meeting of the American Anti-Slavery Society in 1833, while Forten likely sat in and looked on in approval as the delegates rejected gradual emancipation and compensation for slaveholders. Purvis and Forten both held offices in the new society throughout the 1830s, and Forten helped establish a local auxiliary, the Philadelphia Anti-Slavery Society in 1836. Purvis, along with Forten's sons James Jr. and Robert, helped form the Young Men's Anti-Slavery Society of Philadelphia, and Forten's wife, daughters, and daughter-in-law helped found the Philadelphia Female Anti-Slavery Society. Finally, Forten played a crucial role in pushing for the state auxiliary, the Pennsylvania State Anti-Slavery Society, which was founded in 1837. At the age of seventy-three, he traveled one hundred miles to attend the inaugural meeting in Harrisburg. All of these societies were interracial, though even Forten was excluded from truly contributing to policy formation.[64]

Despite the new immediatist support network, the black community suffered further indignity in the late 1830s, and Forten continued to see the hands of the ACS at work. In 1837 the state legislature held a Reform Convention to change the state constitution. They met to consider abolishing property qualifications for voting rights but in the process opened Pandora's Box when some delegates realized that such a move would qualify blacks to vote as well, unless otherwise specified. Vague wording had left a loophole in the original constitution, and propertied men such as Forten sometimes used it to vote, though Winch suggests that most, including Forten, respected custom and did not assert this right. At the convention a number of delegates spoke up in favor of propertied and educated blacks, but ultimately the group voted 77 to 45 to qualify the franchise by including the word "white" in the constitution.[65]

Whether they voted before or not, Forten and his colleagues saw this blatant exclusion as a larger attack on their rights as citizens. Importantly, they believed their citizenship "would never have been denied, had it not been for the scheme of expatriation" offered by the ACS. They expressed "abhorrence" of this "darling project . . . which comes in the guise of Christian benevolence." Vowing to "cling to . . . our native country, much as it has wronged us," they begged their white neighbors not to ratify the proposed constitution. "We are PENNSYLVANIANS, and we hope to see the day when Pennsylvania will have reason to be proud of us, as we believe she has now none to be ashamed."[66]

The PAS tried to intervene and assist in the appeal to white voters by proving that blacks were hard-working and virtuous and thus worthy of the franchise. To bolster their claims, it conducted a detailed census of Philadelphia's African American community. It found that "the colored population of Philadelphia and its suburbs" amounted to 18,768 people who shared a total of $1,350,000 in real and personal estate and paid $3,252.83 in taxes the previous year. Appreciative of the assistance from its longtime allies, the black community used the gradualists' findings in their appeal to white voters. They also incorporated an 1830 report of the Guardians of the Poor of Philadelphia to argue that only 4 percent of those receiving relief were black, "while the ratio of our population to that of the city and suburbs exceeds 8 1/4 percent." Further, black paupers in the almshouse "did not exceed four percent of the whole." The appeal then went on to argue that the black community was taking care of itself through mutual aid societies, churches, schools, and libraries, and argued that loyalty and service in past wars qualified blacks to enjoy fully the rights of American citizenship, regardless of what colonizationists thought.[67]

As this drama played out, Pennsylvania gradualists and immediatists joined forces to raise money to build Pennsylvania Hall. Stating all along that their building was first and foremost to serve as a "temple" of free speech and thus protect both white and black liberty, the managers of the Pennsylvania Hall Association asked David Paul Brown, the respected Philadelphia lawyer and abolitionist, to deliver the opening address. In that address Brown spoke out forcefully against the recent disenfranchisement of black Pennsylvanians, and he implored both gradual and immediate abolitionists to join together and protect their black neighbors from such abuse. Not happy with what he saw as gradualist timidity (despite the fact that Brown was an officer in both the PAS and PASS), Garrison rose to challenge Brown and speak out against colonization. As we have seen, the results were disastrous for Philadelphia's blacks as well as for the antislavery community. Even so, Garrison had a valid point. Neither James Forten, nor Robert Purvis, nor any other black leader had been asked to speak at the dedication ceremony. Thanks to Forten's outreach, Garrison and his white immediatist friends had become quite conscious of such slights.

*　*　*

It would be easy to see Forten's attempts to build this biracial antislavery movement as a compromise on his nationalist dream, but this is not the case. Forten's consideration of emigration is complicated. Rael has argued that Forten and Cuffee developed an "urban bourgeois-looking" variety of black nationalism that catered to the "black intelligentsia." He claimed that these "self-appointed representatives of the marginalized" existed in a strange world between slaves and mainstream American society. Though "highly restricted in public life by law and mob rule," they were "technically free to organize and march." They were educated, but generally in segregated schools. "Sufficiently literate to form a community of writers, publishers, and readers who could sustain a flow of nationalist ideas in print" yet "marginally though inextricably linked to an urban economy and its values," people of this class "were enough *of* the bourgeois social order to be steeped in its ethos and armed with its resources." Yet they were "sufficiently alienated from it to resent its exclusion." Thus they "crafted (by both necessity and choice) an identity distinct from it." He also argues that Forten, Cuffee, and their associates "forged a potent sense of *racial* identity . . . that held greater promise than the class-encumbered values of elevation and respectability for uniting African-descended people across a wide spectrum of potential differences." [68]

In reality, however, Forten did not have the luxury of choosing between race and class identity. He was both black and wealthy. His skin color left him affiliated with blacks of all classes, and his circumstances made him obligated to do something to help the less educated and less well-off. In an attempt to fulfill this duty and with no truly viable alternative, Forten and most other black leaders of his generation and the next continued to hold firmly to the self-help and racial elevation agenda. Even their forays into black nationalism were really attempts to prove black equality and gain acceptance in the United States. In 1835, Forten even tried to co-opt the black convention movement by founding the biracial American

Moral Reform Society in one final attempt to prove black worthiness. These ideas continued to figure prominently in the black abolitionist movement that developed throughout the antebellum years, and even the immediatists remained unable to solve the conundrum of black elevation and white resentment.

The new abolitionists of both colors, like their gradualist counterparts, kept pouring their energies into schools, libraries, literary societies, churches, and mutual aid societies, and African American leaders continued to try to take care of their racial community by providing poor relief and education. Black relief societies provided a privately operated poor relief system in Philadelphia. The number of societies increased from more than fifty in 1832 to nearly one hundred in 1837, with about 80 percent of Philadelphia's black adults participating, collecting nearly $18,000 annually in dues. Clearly, the black population of the city was not depending on white tax dollars for support but was instead taking care of their own community. Forten shared such information with the *Liberator* to prove that many "industrious and exemplary" blacks had managed to elevate their condition and lay "the foundations for their . . . families to become useful, respectable and pious citizens." His words show that even future immediatists had taken PAS and Abolitionist Convention advice quite seriously and incorporated the self-help agenda in their own crusade. Forten never necessarily abandoned small-scale, black-initiated, select emigration, but he insisted on using immediate abolition as a way of reserving the right for himself and others to choose whether they wanted to stay or go.[69]

Finally, the sustained efforts most black leaders put into racial uplift and programs such as those supported by the PAS and the American Convention of Abolitionists shows a reluctance to part with their identity as Americans. Indeed, they worked out of hopes that they would be accepted as legitimate members of society in the United States. That is why white-directed mass exodus had to be defeated. Successful black republics with black leaders could help their cause, by showcasing black capability, but large-scale removal to a distant land where they would remain under the control of white leaders did nothing for their cause, which was to prove racial equality and gain acceptance for blacks in the United States. They appreciated PAS support, but self-help was also important to their cause. Though racial uplift could result from emigration, if blacks were allowed to dictate their own terms for leaving and in setting up the new colony, removal to a white-controlled colony would do nothing to secure black independence and equality.

* * *

The movement Forten helped create became an important component in what can best be described as a three-pronged antislavery drive that included the PAS's gradualist campaign, the ACS's colonization movement, and the American Antislavery Society's push for an immediate end to human bondage without the qualifying provision of removal. These three groups and ideas would continue to compete for the leadership of Pennsylvania antislavery and black racial uplift until the Civil War. Whereas the immediatist movement developed out of black resistance to colonization, the relationship between the first two groups was not always so clear-cut, as we will now see through the antislavery career of Benjamin Coates, another white Quaker.

6 / "A thorough abolitionist could not be such without being a colonizationist": Benjamin Coates and Black Uplift in the United States and Africa

Even with the rise of the immediatist movement, antislavery colonizationists did not give up easily. From the mid 1830s to the late 1850s the Pennsylvania group continued to use the cause as a vehicle for emancipation. Only in 1857, a year that saw the Supreme Court rule that blacks were not citizens of the United States, did they shift their focus to sending free black Pennsylvanians to Liberia. The fallout from the Dred Scott case affected all sectors of the antislavery movement. In many ways, the worsening racial climate brought new emphasis to the vision of colonization as a means of saving the union. On the one hand, this brand of colonization grew in popularity as northerners who held tightly to the political agenda of the founders of the American Colonization Society joined the strange mix of political abolitionists and blatant racists in forming the Free Soil and Republican parties. On the other hand, it led to sectional division within the movement itself as some members of the Pennsylvania Colonization Society continued to focus on the humanitarian agenda of black education and uplift.

A young Quaker emerged to take the lead in this endeavor, creating another bridge between abolition and colonization. For Benjamin Coates, who shared the immediatist view of slavery as a sin and wanted civil rights as much as freedom for blacks, the Pennsylvania Abolition Society and the ACS collectively offered a reform outlet that he could take part in without facing censure from his orthodox Quaker community. Believing deeply in an uplift agenda that he thought depended equally on both causes, he worked to foster what he saw as a natural

FIGURE 8. "Benjamin Coates," ca. 1834 by John Huston Mifflin. (Haverford College Library, Haverford, PA, Special Collections, Fine Arts Collection.)

union. His vision is best understood after examining the changes in the colonization movement in the antebellum years, the continued efforts of gradualists to help free blacks prove their equality, and efforts to combine the moral imperatives of Free Produce with the search for alternative sources of cotton, as the nation, and the world, began to anticipate the disruptions of Civil War.[1]

Throughout most of the antebellum years, the ACS struggled to balance the PCS's insistence on emancipation with the society's material needs, which relied on a broad base of support. Ralph Gurley, the secretary of the ACS, continued to reach out to northern supporters, especially those in Pennsylvania and New York. Even as these groups began their cooperative effort at Bassa Cove, he called for unity of all colonizationists based on the principle of benevolence. Success of the endeavor as a whole depended on cooperation. It also depended on state and federal aid, and he and other antislavery colonizationists remained insistent about this, so much so that they began to alienate a number of southern supporters. Though one Virginia man at the twenty-first annual meeting in 1837 ultimately decided not to abandon the society, he expressed regret that he and Henry Clay were the only two southerners at the meeting. He also responded to a resolution in which Gurley called for congressional aid with a dissenting statement defending private property interests. He wanted the society to stick to its original goal of sending away free blacks and not to become abettors of the "fanatical crusaders" who had initiated "warfare upon the institutions and domestic rights of the South."[2]

This exchange at the twenty-first meeting serves as a stark reminder of the fine line colonizationists walked in their quest for government aid. For supporters of both stripes, this goal was crucial to the movement's overall success. Political colonizationists such as Clay and Mathew Carey tried many times to tie their scheme to the federal agenda, and humanitarians such as Gurley and Elliott Cresson also shared the hope of government support. Outraged by a Spanish attack on a colonial schooner off the coast of Africa in June 1831, Cresson called for President Andrew Jackson to take active measures to protect both the colony and the African trade. He even took the liberty of meeting with the President and came away furious that colonizationists closer to Old Hickory had allowed him "to remain so wretchedly ignorant of the true condition of Liberia." Unsure whether he had enlightened Jackson enough during his visit, he urged Gurley to increase the pressure. "Tell him that if the protection of our own Government is withheld, I shall feel it my duty as a fellow creature and a Christian . . . to ask that protection from the

British Government which is so cruelly . . . withheld by our own." While in England Cresson saw Secretary of State Martin Van Buren and sent the same warning through him as well, arguing that the possibility of a lucrative trade in African oak made the colony worth defending. Prepared to follow through on his threat, he worked diligently to gain the British government's interest in and support of the colony, encouraging them to send a consul to Liberia.[3]

Had Clay succeeded in his bid for the presidency, he would likely have tried to use his skills of compromise to find a way for the government to fulfill the vision of the ACS founders by taking over once Liberia was up and running. The Jacksonian leaders of the time, however, shared little interest in the scheme. Even those who may have sympathized personally remained much more concerned with the issues of property rights and state sovereignty. Southerners in general became increasingly alienated from this part of the agenda as they came to see immediatism, and by extension all forms of antislavery, as a direct attack on their personal interests.

Though more and more southerners had come to fear the interventionist aspect of the colonization agenda, even the most ardent supporters of government involvement maintained respect for states' rights. They argued that colonization was the only way to save the union. Even as the "positive good" defense of slavery replaced the reluctant participant picture offered by slaveholders of the Revolutionary era, Pennsylvania colonizationists clung tight to the idea that most southerners were growing weary of holding the "wolf by the ears." Colonization was their contribution to southern freedom—white and black.

Letters such as one from "A Southern Abolitionist" to the *Colonization Herald* only reinforced their determination. Promising that his neighbors wanted to end slavery but feared such a large number of unrestrained blacks, the author criticized the hypocrisy of northern efforts to prevent black migration. "How can the northern people expect that the South will submit to have a free coloured population of about two millions among three millions of whites, when five millions in the North are so opposed to an increase of their coloured population . . . that if forty or fifty were to emigrate in a body to any part of the Northern States, it would probably occasion considerable excitement?" Colonization would solve both problems, and focusing on removing those in bondage in the South first showed northern good will. Thus, as abolitionist insults to the South intensified, northern colonizationists tried to offer understanding and friendship in hopes of keeping southern antislavery sentiment alive.

Increasingly the PCS and the ACS offered colonization as a plan to preserve the nation, and they naively believed that most southerners agreed
with their correspondent.[4]

The Pennsylvania group and the parent organization shared a desire
to preserve the national union, but to varying degrees, and tensions
between the two groups continued to grow until the New York and
Pennsylvania groups managed to lead what Early Lee Fox described as
a northern coup in 1838. Much of the tension involved debate about the
colonization movement's role in the broader reform agenda. Humanitarian leaders insisted on emphasizing antislavery, black uplift, and temperance, but those who were more eager to avoid the taint of immediatism
and to court southern support wanted them to mute the moral reform
aspect of their agenda and focus more on preserving the union and removing free blacks.

On a material level, tension also developed over fund allocation because the state societies with their own colonies kept more and more of
the money they collected, hurting the ACS's already dwindling coffers.
The Maryland society pronounced the parent group's functions "at an
end," moving for complete independence in 1838. They argued that "the
discordant views" of colonizationists throughout the country prevented
any "unity of sentiment and action." The money they collected would
thus be applied only to the colony of Maryland in Liberia. The Pennsylvania and New York groups never took separate action that far, but
the parent society did accuse them of withholding much-needed funds.
The Young Men's Colonization Society of Pennsylvania (YMCSP) responded by insisting that donors gave them money specifically because
they trusted them to apply it as promised, whereas they feared the parent
group would squander it, especially since the ACS's financial problems
were public knowledge. The *Repository* responded in turn that the parent
group's financial problems resulted from being pushed "by friends whose
zeal was little tempered by prudence" to send more emigrants than the
society could support. Insisting on saving as many slaves as they could,
Cresson and his colleagues had paid little regard to age, gender, occupation, and other key issues of "quality." Despite ACS warnings, they had
sent "unprepared" and unskilled colonists in large numbers.

Now that events were justifying the "excessive caution" the parent board had been "reproached" for, the zealous supporters who had
pushed to overextend the society's resources were blaming the board for
the embarrassment and had abandoned the original project. The founders of Bassa Cove had promised that their support of the new colony

would not distract from their efforts for Liberia and the ACS, but "would add greatly to its resources, and . . . increase its strength." Instead they had appealed for money in their states by promising that they would better apply funds than had the parent group. According to the *Repository*, "they destroyed public confidence to a great extent, in the General Society," and essentially bullied the ACS into allowing them to form a new colony even while Liberia itself needed support. Fox agrees with this view of the New York and Pennsylvania groups' actions in creating Bassa. He described their efforts as "a policy calculated either to kill the older organization or to force it to submit" and to completely deprive the South of any influence.[5]

By 1838 the humanitarian colonizationists had indeed forced an overhaul of the American Colonization Society, and PCS members did play a large role. The YMCSP had merged back into the PCS in 1837 and soon afterward the consolidated group decided to ask the ACS board to call a convention in Philadelphia to discuss "remodeling the parent society." The result was a new constitution and "Plan of Federal Government for the Colonies of Liberia."[6]

The new constitution completely reorganized the society, turning it into a federation of state auxiliaries. The board of managers was disbanded, and Gurley was demoted from his position as secretary and made answerable to a new board dominated by representatives from New York and Pennsylvania. Of the ten men elected to the new board, three were from New York, three from Pennsylvania, two from Virginia, and two from Washington, D.C. Samuel Wilkeson, a New York judge, was first named general agent, then president of the board of directors. Whatever his title, he wielded the true power. Respected for his financial management skills, he contributed much toward restoring the ACS's credit and finances. Under his leadership the Pennsylvania and New York societies returned to their auxiliary status, and Bassa Cove joined all other settlements except Maryland in Liberia in forming the Commonwealth of Liberia. Thomas Buchanan, a Pennsylvanian, was appointed the first governor.[7]

Given the historiographical emphasis on the society's finances as the catalyst for the split, it would be easy to see the reunion as evidence of faith in Wilkeson's financial abilities. Kocher has also suggested that by this point the Pennsylvania group had entered a period of decline and needed the parent society's monetary support. Perhaps, but that is only part of the story. As the lead figure behind the Pennsylvania group, Cresson played a large role in the reorganization, and Fox has thoroughly documented this. Part of his determination probably resulted from lingering anger at Gurley over the failure of the English trip. More important, however, the coup left the society's affairs in the hands of northerners who would further the humanitarian agenda. He had been begging the board to stop appointing slaveholders to key posts, and now that problem was solved. Wilkeson, the new leader, embraced both the black uplift agenda and a commercial scheme that accorded well with Cresson's suggestions. He had shown this in 1837 by proposing a Liberia packet scheme. He wanted to buy ships and sell them to black men willing to use them to transport goods and colonists.[8]

Wilkeson believed in black potential and saw colonization as a way to prove racial equality. He had traveled throughout the southern and southwestern states and, becoming acquainted with enslaved and free blacks, gained respect for their abilities as skilled workers. "I am satisfied that the colored man is as capable of acquiring trades as the white man," he wrote to the ACS just before the reorganization. The "difficulties and discouragements incident to his condition" were all that relegated free blacks to low-status jobs, and the racial climate of the United States offered no hope. "My project offers present relief, opens a field to him in which talents, education, and skill can be successfully employed." It would give the "good colored seamen," who "are now numerous" a chance to own their own ships by offering extended repayment terms.[9]

In addition, the reorganized society chose Buchanan, a Pennsylvanian known for his opposition to slavery and the slave trade, to govern the new commonwealth. Buchanan's reputation for fighting slavers reinvigorated antislavery colonizationists. Cresson, appointed an agent by Wilkeson, embarked on a self-funded trip through New England, New York, and New Jersey in 1839 to raise money and awaken "the old friends of the cause to new resolutions and efforts." The twenty-second ACS report boasted that the "great acceptance" he met with, and the $25,000 he raised in cash and pledges, revealed "the practicability of reviving the colonization spirit even where apathy has long prevailed."[10]

At the same time, Gurley and Calvin Colton, an associate from Pennsylvania, used an essay by Sir Thomas Fowell Buxton, a British abolitionist, as evidence that the colonization cause was finally defeating the immediatist agenda. A "sober" abolitionist and known friend of the venerated William Wilberforce, Buxton investigated the African slave trade and determined that "instead of being on the wane," it was "expanding with wider malignity, and blacker horror than ever." Tired of waiting on European and American governments to more strictly enforce the laws which had declared the slave trade piracy, he suggested "civilizing" Africa and introducing Christianity—two of the goals humanitarian colonizationists, according to the delighted *Repository*, had "been aiming at for the last twenty years." According to the journal, Buxton's conclusion embodied the same ideas "daily defended by the eloquence of Gurley." Gurley also saw the parallel and applauded the increase in awareness that colonization offered the only realistic means of combating the slave trade, and he offered Buxton's work as a reiteration of ACS principles.[11]

Colton also emphasized Governor Buchanan's assault on the slave trade and insisted that the reorganization had "given new life" to both the ACS and the colony. He expressed hope that southern abolitionists who left the ACS after the immediatist onslaught would return to the fold and help the movement return to the flourishing state it enjoyed in the late 1820s. He clung to the idea that human nature in general was too ugly to allow for racial uplift in the United States, but he hoped that as soon as blacks saw how different things were in Liberia, they would be eager to go. Once they gave the issue sober consideration, they would see the magnitude of the opportunity to civilize and Christianize Africa while fighting the slave trade.[12]

Genuinely convincing themselves that the future looked increasingly bright, both men tried to reach out to former supporters. They applauded southern efforts by stressing repeatedly the value of the liberated slaves. This served two functions. First, it showed those who "donated" their slaves that their contributions were as valued as the monetary gifts from the North. Just as important, it allowed them to play up southern support in their own minds and thus reinforce the idea that the cause was growing. A contribution of one slave here and there may look paltry, but once translated into cash value, it looked much more impressive.

Gurley also tried to enlist two groups Cresson had once reached out to—the PAS and the English public. In late 1839 he appealed for the gradualists' help in sustaining Governor Buchanan "in his resolute and effectual measures against the slave trade." Five years earlier, PAS president David Paul Brown, while eulogizing William Wilberforce, had declared colonization an impractical plan for abolition but admitted that the scheme "originated in the desire to improve the condition of this afflicted race." The ACS neither supported slavery nor impeded abolition. It was simply impractical as a means of freeing American blacks. At the same time, however, it was "beautiful and beneficial, so far as it related to the introduction of civilization, commerce and Christianity into Liberia, and so far as it conduces to check the slave trade." This last clause gave

Gurley hope that he could use Buxton's figures on the slave trade and Buchanan's reputation for fighting it to finally earn PAS support.[13]

The Pennsylvania group shared the optimism of Buxton's pamphlet. Consequently, in 1839 it handed its remaining interests in Bassa Cove back to the parent society. The ACS assumed PCS debts, and in return the PCS promised to give all collections, minus its operating expenses, to the ACS, provided the money be spent on active operations rather than "contingent expenses." Two months later it pledged to raise $4,000 to help Governor Buchanan meet colonial expenses, if the New York group would match the contribution.[14]

* * *

Even more important than Brown's half-hearted nod was the full-fledged support of Benjamin Coates, who joined the PAS and ACS at roughly the same time, soon after Brown's speech. At a quick glance, Coates, even more so than Cresson, would have made the ideal immediatist. He grew up a block away from the family of Robert Douglass, a prominent black hairdresser and community leader, and was roughly the same age as Douglass's children Sarah and Robert Jr. In fact, the Coates and Douglass families both attended the Arch Street Meeting, though there is no record that they ever interacted in the early years. As an adult, however, Coates's interest in black education brought him to know Sarah, by then a teacher at the Institute of Colored Youth, and he shared an interest in colonization with Robert Jr. Regardless of whom he played with as a child, Coates took Cresson's efforts to reach out to black leaders to a more personal level, developing friendships with Henry Highland Garnet, an abolitionist and emigrationist, and Joseph Jenkins Roberts, president of Liberia.

Coates also sometimes worked with and supported the antislavery efforts of Hicksite Quakers who joined immediatist organizations despite warnings by his orthodox community to withdraw from such worldly and political matters. His sympathy for their cause, however, was not strong enough to lead him to join the Hicksites or the immediatists, and he remained Orthodox and in favor of the PAS and PCS. As historian Ryan Jordan has shown, this was not unusual, given the disdain many Quakers felt for immediatist militancy. Whereas Garrisonians valued agitation "as the necessary moral earthquake to crack apart the chains of oppression," many Friends saw such rhetoric as responsible for provoking angry riots and as a genuine threat to the union. Thus Coates, like other colonizationists and many Quakers, avoided extremes and maintained a middle course.[15]

A dry goods merchant who sold, among other things, cotton textiles, Coates shared much in common with Cresson. Besides the Quaker connection, both men never married and lived with either their sisters or their mothers throughout their lives. Both became involved with benevolent associations early in life, working for Philadelphia's poor as well as for the specific cause of black education, both with and independent of the colonization society. Coates began his philanthropic career by joining the Union Benevolent Association, an organization of businessmen in the city founded in 1831 to give food, fuel, and clothing to the poor of both races while educating them to become self-supporting.[16]

Coates entered the world of Pennsylvania antislavery the year of Brown's speech when he joined the YMCSP, drawn in by the emphasis on black education. In 1837 Philadelphia Quakers opened the Institute for Colored Youth, and he became active in that group in 1839. By 1842 he was a member of the advisory board; by 1854 he was on the board of managers; and he remained active in the organization until the late 1870s. Through this organization he met Robert Campbell, a native of the West Indies who, like Sarah Douglass, was a teacher. Campbell, like the Douglass men, had developed an interest in emigration to Africa. The elder Douglass was originally chosen by Martin R. Delany, a black abolitionist and emigrationist, to explore the western coast of Africa in 1859, and when he could not join the mission, he was replaced by Campbell, who would eventually turn to the ACS, through Coates, to secure funding.

In 1842 Coates also joined the PAS, again as part of his interest in black education. The Clarkson School drew him to the gradualist organization, and he was elected to that group's education committee right away. By the time he wrote his famous colonization pamphlet in 1858, he was vice president of the PAS.[17]

Though he remained committed to colonization throughout his life, Coates distanced himself from the PCS in 1837, choosing instead to work directly with the parent society. He had joined the YMCSP out of admiration for Cresson's "young man's zeal," but he was soon put off by Cresson's domineering personality and efforts to control the organization. Even so, he continued to maintain his relationship with the parent society and, ironically, like Cresson, remained vigilant that the ACS not alienate black supporters.[18]

Indeed, for Coates colonization would be a useless endeavor without black support because it was a movement for freedom and racial uplift. For this reason he shared Cresson's irritation with the ACS for its refusal to stand firmly against slavery and its reluctance to alienate southern members. Also, just as Cresson tried to reach out to Forten, Coates tried to enlist the support of Frederick Douglass, the most famous black abolitionist of his generation. Trying to win him over to the colonizationist camp, he told Douglass that antislavery colonizationists had led resistance to the 1838 effort to add the word "white" to the Pennsylvania constitution, and he pointed out that in many cases northern colonizationists were the very same men the free black community turned to so often for assistance. Though he never won Douglass over, some blacks, namely Henry Garnet, Delany, and Mary Ann Shadd Cary, saw Coates's colonization as well-meaning, regardless of how they felt about the ACS.[19]

Perhaps blacks arrived at a more positive assessment of Coates because he seemed to realize the clear need for black leadership in a colony that was supposed to showcase black equality. To begin with, he was clear that if Liberia was to serve as evidence of black success, the colonists sent must be prepared to excel. From the late 1830s onward, even as Cresson was trying to send as many colonists as funds would allow, Coates was seeking to recruit colonists with useful skills and talents. He tried to encourage Wilkeson to fund passage for an experienced black shipper, and he tried to recruit skilled laborers such as millwrights. He even offered to fund a round-trip passage to Liberia for a group of conditionally manumitted skilled slaves; he hoped that once they arrived in Liberia they would find conditions acceptable and not need the return passage. His hope was that the skilled emigrants would start successful enterprises and send for their skilled friends to join them, building up a population of brickmakers, tanners, soap makers, and other professionals. Obviously for Coates, mass exodus was not the goal: "I would prefer seeing a half dozen such [skilled] men going to build up a colony to as many shiploads of common, ignorant, lazy emigrants."[20]

Importantly, however, he did not envision blacks simply as skilled laborers but also as leaders. At a time when the PAS was only beginning to accept black members, such as Forten's son-in-law Robert Purvis, who joined at the same time as Coates, this acceptance of black leadership was quite progressive.[21] His appreciation and respect for black leadership is perhaps best illustrated by his friendship with Joseph Jenkins Roberts, the first president of independent Liberia.

Since federal assistance never materialized, ACS directors pushed the

Liberians to proclaim independence in 1846. By 1848 they had created a republican government with a chief executive modeled after the American System. Great Britain, France, and other European nations diplomatically recognized the new nation immediately, though the United States waited until 1862. Perhaps American recalcitrance stemmed from the fact that this new republic had a black president, a touch that was sure to raise the ire of slaveholders.

A successful republic administered by a black leader would undermine proslavery claims of black inferiority while bolstering the colonization cause as a vehicle for black independence and self-governance. Coates was well aware of this and began corresponding with Roberts. Whether he intended to or not, he created a friendship that would last until Roberts died in 1876. Emma Lapsansky-Werner and Margaret Hope Bacon describe this friendship as "warm," and they point out that when the Roberts family visited the United States they often stayed in the Coates home, a level of interracial intimacy that was quite rare at the time, even among immediatists. The closeness extended beyond the two men to their families, as Roberts's wife and Coates's siblings also developed close friendships.[22]

Coates's correspondence, not only with Roberts, but with other white colonizationists, also clearly reveals that he admired the president's leadership skills; Coates respected him both personally and professionally. Importantly, Coates and Roberts shared a vision of Liberia as the one place where African Americans had a genuine chance to thrive economically. Both men were merchants who valued international trade and the possibilities brought through profitable business ventures, and perhaps they dreamed of creating an exchange network by which they could both profit. Even so, Lapsansky-Werner and Bacon point out the irony that this close interracial friendship, admirable on so many levels, "was predicated on their mutual agreement about the economic value of racial segregation."[23]

Despite, or perhaps because of, Liberian independence, the colonization cause throughout the United States had lost much of its zeal by the 1840s. Liberia contained more than three thousand residents who were increasingly dissatisfied with colonial laws, relations with their indigenous neighbors, and confusion over political authority and jurisdictions. Factional fighting ensued almost immediately after the governorship was created, and despite grand hopes of a self-governing republic supported and defended by the United States, Liberia became more and more "a dead weight" on the finances of a struggling and increasingly unpopular society.[24]

Once the ACS freed itself of governing and supporting the colony, it basically became an emigration agency throughout much of the United States, but not necessarily in Pennsylvania. Despite Coates's call to limit their efforts to skilled laborers and self-sufficient settlers, Pennsylvanians continued to try to send as many emancipated slaves as they could rescue. In 1848 Cresson, by now a vice president, was stubbornly still traveling and lecturing on colonization's importance in the battle against slavery. In 1851 he returned to England and continued to seek support there. From 1848 to 1854, the ACS chartered forty-one ships and sent nearly four thousand settlers to Liberia, and, according to Eric Burin, "more slaveholders sent more bondpersons to Liberia between 1848 and 1860 than in the previous thirty years combined."[25]

Of course, the increase in these conditional manumissions resulted more from the nation's worsening racial climate than colonizationists' efforts. During the twenty years before the Civil War, southern states began requiring that the freed leave their borders. At the same time northern states fought to exclude black migrants. Increasingly, then, slaveholders who wanted to free their laborers saw no alternative but colonization, and many of these masters applied to the ACS for assistance in relocating their former slaves. The PCS continued to raise money for that purpose and to employ Cresson's specific case tactic. It argued that state laws in both sections showed that most whites did not want free black neighbors, regardless of how they felt about slavery. Whether they agreed with the prevailing sentiments or not, Pennsylvania colonizationists thought that through their scheme both races would "be allowed to work out their destinies apart, and undisturbed by, and undisturbing each other."[26]

* * *

Even as it continued to follow Cresson's lead in raising money to help southerners liberate slaves, the PCS began to pay more attention to Coates's suggestions and to reconsider its policy of sending newly freed emigrants. The PCS sent the editor of the *Colonization Herald* to Liberia in late 1854 to investigate conditions there. Then, when a Georgia master asked for help in sending seventy slaves to Liberia, William Coppinger, a PCS officer, expressed doubts about sending destitute bondspersons. In the 1830s the YMCSP had tried to enlist state aid in Harrisburg because the number of slaves offered for conditional manumission greatly exceeded "the limits of private benefaction." It finally gained the state legislature's support in 1853, when lawmakers appropriated $2,000 to help fund passage of free blacks from Pennsylvania. However, these funds were available "for those *only* who are actual residents of, and depart from" the Keystone State.[27]

Although this stipulation would have irritated Cresson and his compatriots, the new generation of PCS leaders approved for a number of reasons. On the one hand, some agreed with Coates on the importance of black success and had come to see colonization as the means to black independence. On the other hand, some, perhaps most, had come to see things more as the political colonizationists such as Carey had. Both strains of thought existed side by side throughout the life of the movement, and both appeals to the state legislature had included elements of humanitarianism and self-interest. The YMCSP's 1836 appeal, after asking for money to help facilitate emancipation, added that if something was not done to remove those slaves to Liberia they would eventually end up in Pennsylvania.[28]

The 1852 appeal, delivered by William Pettit and John Durbin, included a similar ambivalence and an even stronger focus on self-interest. After listing the objects of the colonization society as to remove free blacks of the United States "from their political and social disadvantages," to "place them in a country where they can enjoy the benefit of a free government," to "afford slaveholders who may wish to liberate their slaves, an asylum for their reception," to "arrest and destroy the African slave trade," and "to spread civilization, sound morals, and true religion over the whole continent," Pettit admitted that many friends of the cause also acted from the "belief that it would be the most effectual means for saving ourselves and our posterity from those dangers which are apprehended from the presence of two separate and distinct races in our land." "Nothing is more surely written in the book of fate, than that these people are to be free," he added, "nor is it less certain that the two races, equally free, cannot live in the same government." He warned the legislators that they were still in a position to "direct the process of emancipation and deportation peacefully." However, if "it is left to force itself on, human nature must shudder at the prospect held up." The result would surpass the evil of the Spanish "deportation or deletion" of the Moors.[29]

Pettit argued that colonization was more important than ever, as southerners felt a "strong disposition to emancipate" yet were "jealous of the presence of free blacks." Southerners who freed slaves tried to expel them from their home states, but northern states, not eager to become the refugees' destination, were creating laws to exclude them. Free blacks already in the North suffered from a flooded labor market that forced them to be "driven from one occupation to another, until his field is limited and circumscribed to those that remunerate the least." Thus many become "vagabonds and outcasts, and [are] impelled by despair to violence and crime." The most recent census had found fifty-three thousand blacks in Pennsylvania, and rumor had it that a "large proportion of them" crowded the state's prisons, almshouses, and houses of refuge. This situation would only increase if the employment situation grew worse. "We propose then, both as a measure of public policy, as well as of justice to them, that the State make some provision under the peculiar circumstances of their case, for the removal of such of these people from our own State as may desire to go to the land of their fathers." Removal would "be for their good, and for the peace and safety of our common country."[30]

The PCS as a body was unsure which side to take. It tried to gain support for the cause by focusing on the growth of the slave population and included articles in the *Herald* that emphasized the detrimental effects of a growing black population. According to one article, blacks created half of the "expenses of our criminal business and our paupers" even though they made up less than one thirtieth of the population. Three-fourths of Harrisburg's blacks, it continued, received public or private charity or supported themselves through theft. Blacks even went so far as to sue each other just to earn the stipends given to witnesses. The black population, though only contributing probably less than $150 in tax revenue, had cost the city $4,000 last year, according to "A Tax-Payer."[31]

The *Colonization Herald*'s editor, though reprinting this excerpt from the *Keystone*, must not have bought the argument completely because three months later the paper printed a report which sounded much like a PAS census. According to the statistics presented, Philadelphia had a population of about twenty-five thousand free blacks, and their real estate value amounted to $850,000. The city's free blacks had fifteen churches, thirty-five clergymen, twenty-one schools, twenty-seven Sunday schools, sixty-four benevolent societies, and four temperance societies.[32]

While the Pennsylvania colonizationists wavered, the general population grew increasingly certain that both their black neighbors and their state would be better off if the former would go away. The assault on black liberties endured by James Forten intensified for the next generation, and Pennsylvania colonizationists argued that the "mutual prejudices of the two races" were greater in the 1850s than ever before. By the time Forten died in 1842, blacks had been made to feel like pariahs in their home state, attacked repeatedly by rioters and denied basic rights like the franchise. They were excluded from much of the opportunity offered to whites who sought a fresh start in the new western states, and those still enslaved faced tighter restrictions as whites' fear of retribution grew.[33]

* * *

Racial conditions grew worse throughout the remainder of the antebellum years, and the national government, in an effort to keep peace between the sections, contributed greatly to black oppression. Two examples include the Compromise of 1850's Fugitive Slave Law and the 1857 Dred Scott decision. The first replaced an often disobeyed 1793 fugitive slave law that required state officials to help masters apprehend slaves once they had proven the fugitive's identity. Because state officials were often disinclined to provide such assistance, the 1850 law called on federal marshals to assist in apprehension. It also threatened the security of all northern free blacks by placing the burden of proof with the accused and denying him the right to trial by jury. It even created a bounty system that rewarded commissioners $10 for each slave returned to his master, but only $5 for each case in which the accused was found innocent. Realizing the danger to the union if the law was not respected, most northerners reluctantly accepted the new law and their role in its application. It did, however, increase the fear that white civil liberties were gradually falling victim to a southern "slave power," which was forcing the entire nation to accept and defend slavery. The compromise of which it was a part had been drafted to appease slave interests by allowing settlers in new territories to vote on whether or not to allow slavery. Of the territories taken after the Mexican war, California was declared a free state, but the others would have popular sovereignty, and the fugitive law was thrown in to further calm proslavery interests. The Dred Scott decision was a similar victory for slaveholders, pronouncing that neither free blacks nor slaves could be considered citizens of the United States.[34]

The status of new territories affected the antislavery climate throughout the 1850s. Abolitionist or not, most northern whites became determined to keep bondage confined to the states in which it already existed. Southerners, in contrast, were equally determined that their labor system and way of life should spread. Most everyone believed that confining bondage to the South would lead to the demise of slavery, and abolitionists wanted slavery excluded from the new states as a victory in their fight to end human bondage in general. Abolitionists and colonizationists both believed that without room to grow slavery would die out and that if masters could no longer sell surplus slaves the system would lose profitability. Also, every new state meant more congressional members, and each side wanted to claim those seats. Although the two sides were locked in a battle to protect white political interests, the status and rights of all blacks hung in the balance.[35]

Many who had not considered the moral implications of slavery, and others who had led all-out assaults on radical abolitionists in the early 1830s, eventually embraced this exclusionary aspect of the antislavery agenda. In 1848 this desire to end slavery by surrounding it with free states reached fruition in the political arena first in the Free Soil Party. It also figured prominently in the formation of the Republican Party. For those attracted to Free Soil, it was a matter of white rights to land ownership, and most were primarily concerned with protecting northern civil liberties from greedy slaveholders. For many abolitionists, the union with the Free Soil party was an uncomfortable one, but a majority of political immediatists who had formed the Liberty Party in 1840 reluctantly migrated to the Free Soil camp out of expediency.[36]

For colonizationists in general the fit was more comfortable. This strange mix of abolitionists, politicians, and what Leonard Richards called "negrophobes," actually looked much like the colonization society had from the beginning. Richards argues that "the ground upon which one might hold antislavery views was tremendously broadened" in this period, but what actually broadened was the range of people receptive to antislavery arguments that had existed within the colonization movement all along. Political antislavery and Free Soil clearly followed in the tradition of the political colonization movement. Even the immediatists who refused to join the political agitation made use of white self-interest by emphasizing the Fugitive Slave Law and the attempt to spread slavery as an attack on white freedom.[37]

In this high-tension climate, the PCS appointed a committee of six in 1857 to evaluate its efforts to that point. It realized that its focus on manumission had diverged from the stated ACS goal of sending free blacks to the colony. More important, the PCS worried that sending large numbers of unprepared emigrants may actually have hurt Liberia in the long run. The parent organization had warned against the policy before, and abolitionists had argued for years that Liberia served as nothing more than a dumping ground for cast-off slaves too old or feeble to work profitably for their masters. The truth was not so cut-and-dried. Tom Schick analyzed the census of immigrants from 1820 to 1843 and found that this was not the case. Looking at age and sex ratios he found a pattern of family migration with the "prospect of steady population growth." Burin agrees and adds that most manumissions were made in good faith.[38] Nevertheless, by 1857 the focus shifted from slaves to free blacks from Pennsylvania.

The significance of the Dred Scott case in influencing this change cannot be overstated. Kenneth Stampp has argued that the decision marked the point of no return for the North and South, making the Civil War inevitable. Burin added that it played a similar role for the colonization movement, leaving northern colonizationists no longer able to convince themselves that their project could keep peace between the sections. Also, it showed the futility of their gradual abolition plan by finally laying to rest the myth of latent southern abolitionism. The case was important also in helping create a climate that forced free blacks to reconsider the ACS's offer, even as men such as Coates, who became vice president of the Abolition Society that year, continued to push for black uplift. In the two years after this decision, 110 black Pennsylvanians accepted the offer and moved to Liberia. This was almost as many as had gone in the previous twenty years together. According to Burin, the "decision to concentrate on removing the state's black residents," bolstered by the Dred Scott decision, "proved successful beyond the organization's means," and it had to turn to the parent society for money. Their success continued, with 107 Pennsylvania blacks joining the colony from 1859 to 1861. In 1861, the PCS collected $5,344.66.[39] This grim success was fueled by the general despair brought on by the disinheriting of black Americans.

Even in this climate, antislavery reaction to the Dred Scott ruling was swift on all fronts. By this time, the membership rolls of the gradualist PAS and the immediatist Pennsylvania Anti-Slavery Society (PASS) overlapped in many ways. Pennsylvania immediatism began in the early 1830s with the founding of the Clarkson Association of Lancaster and Chester Counties, the second immediatist organization in the United States. Two years later came the Philadelphia convention which witnessed the founding of the American Anti-Slavery Society, the first national immediatist organization. The PASS followed in 1836, attracting most Pennsylvania abolitionists, black and white. This was the group that publicly weathered the growing hostility of the 1840s and 1850s. While the PAS worked through the courts to secure such victories as the 1847 personal liberty law passed to fight fugitive slave catchers, the PASS fought in the court of public opinion against slavery and for black civil rights. It was the PASS that took the initiative of speaking out in the wake of the Scott decision to assure Pennsylvanians that their state remained at the forefront of the antislavery movement.

Pointing out that opponents of slavery had met resistance from the beginning, the PASS predicted a "glorious triumph" for the abolition cause despite the disheartening events of the preceding two decades. Though Pennsylvania had not yet been "converted to antislavery doctrines," the state was on the way to "returning to her original position as the declared friend of impartial and universal freedom." Contemporary antagonists were citing the dangers of emancipation, crying out that it would lead to violence, racial mixing, and destruction of the union, but so had those who had opposed the PAS a generation before. Indeed, that generation had the daunting task of calling for social reform in an era of growing conservatism brought on by the perceived excesses of the French and Haitian Revolutions. "French Jacobinism was in no better repute, or regarded with no more favor in those days, than is Garrisonian abolitionism at the present," explained the PASS at its twenty-first annual meeting. Yet the PAS had managed to secure the passage of the gradual abolition act, and the immediatists would not rest until their goal of unconditional emancipation had been met. In the very language that prevented men such as Coates from joining their crusade, the PASS vowed never to "assent to, or be parties under, a compact which, like that of the Federal Constitution, binds Pennsylvania and the other free States to aid the South in retaining her slaves; requiring them to deliver up the fugitive, to strike down the insurgent, and to concede to the slaveholder an extra proportion of political power." In true Garrisonian fashion, it went on to denounce the Constitution as "an iniquitous bargain, an unholy covenant, a league with oppressors, unworthy of respect and fit only to be broken." Members of the PASS also expressed willingness to serve as martyrs for the cause.[40]

* * *

Of course, an Orthodox Quaker such as Coates could not take this stance. To these Friends, such heated rhetoric only invited violence, and as pacifists they were quite unwilling to put themselves in positions that might require self-defense and result in violation of their basic principles. They also dreaded the mob violence that could likely, and often did, result, and they feared that such unrest could lead to a revolution over slavery that would destroy the nation. The also made a clear distinction between the moral realm of the meetinghouse and the political jurisdiction of lawmakers, and they did not think the two should cross.[41]

Even so, Coates felt compelled to respond to the growing tensions of the times. The same year the PASS renewed its vow of "No Union with Slaveholders," Coates took the lead in furthering the humanitarian agenda of the colonization movement through his pamphlet *Cultivation of Cotton in Africa, in Reference to the Abolition of Slavery in the United States*. A longtime member of both the Pennsylvania Abolition Society and the American Colonization Society, he combined Forten and Cuffee's commercial emphasis on the African venture with ideas popular among humanitarian colonizationists. In addition to describing colonization as important to African evangelization, this pamphlet, more importantly, followed the lead of British abolitionists in combining colonization with Free Produce, a movement described by immediatist William Lloyd Garrison's son, W. P. Garrison, and historian Carol Faulkner as the most morally radical of all antislavery endeavors.[42]

Coates's *Cotton Cultivation in Africa* reintroduced plans presented by British abolitionist Sir Thomas Fowell Buxton in his 1840 tract, *The Remedy*, to use African colonization as a vehicle for Free Produce and black uplift. Buxton had proposed a string of agricultural settlements to be led by select West Indians capable of teaching Africans farming techniques and Christianity. To promote this idea he had founded the African Education and Civilization Society, not to take control of African resources, but to "teach its natives their use and value." Rather than serving as an outlet for an unwanted population, Buxton envisioned colonization as a way to "show Africa the folly as well as the crime of exporting her own children." Instead of mass deportation, the goal was to use a select few to serve as "a leaven" for taking Christianity and commerce to Africa. This is similar to the vision Coates had for Liberia. Buxton and Coates were also both careful to stress that colonization must be voluntary on the part of the colonized.[43]

Coates began his pamphlet by trying to assure readers that, if carried out properly, emancipation could "be commenced immediately" and "eventuate, at no distant period" in a general freedom "without violence of any kind, and without any collision with the laws of the land." Since slavery originated and is sustained "in the spirit of gain," he proposed to "make use of the same agency to accomplish its overthrow." The trick was to make slavery unprofitable, and the answer was free labor. Using research conducted by the Cotton Supply Association of Manchester, England, he then set out to show that African soil was more fertile than that in the American South and that it was "particularly adapted to the growth of cotton." All of the best varieties currently cultivated in the

United States could be raised more cheaply in western and central Africa, and as a bonus, there were also a number of indigenous types of "superior quality" that were already popular in the English market. Also, cotton grew naturally in much of Africa and was perennial, whereas it had to be planted annually in the United States.[44]

As for labor, it too was superior in Africa. According to Coates, "the free sons of Africa" could exceed the output of U.S. cotton annually "in their native land, at less than one-half of its present cost." Importantly, this could be done "while amply compensating the laborer, and, at the same time, greatly improving his condition in other respects." The beauty of the plan was that success with African free laborers would not only produce a superior crop more than sufficient to exceed the current demand, it would also benefit that laborer by introducing him to Christianity and respectable commerce. Perhaps even better, it would put a stop to the slave trade and liberate American slaves by making their labor obsolete. Once slavery was replaced with a more profitable system, "all the Bible arguments of southern theologians, or the patriotic appeals of pro-slavery politicians, will not avail to sustain an institution that occasions a clear loss to every individual connected with it." At that point, all of the laws and behavior that sustained slavery, such as the Fugitive Slave Law, would crumble under the dead weight of the obsolete system and leave "the master running away from the slave."[45]

True to his longtime support of black uplift and independence, Coates insisted, however, that African cotton cultivation must not redound to the benefit of capitalists in England or America. Africans would be trusted with the business of collecting the cotton, cleaning it, pressing it, and exporting it, and no whites, not even abolitionists, would be allowed to profit. The only Americans who would be allowed even to oversee the process were "enterprising colored men from the United States, properly educated, so as to be qualified for the work, and who are capable of appreciating the immense benefits to the world that must result from their labors." Furthermore, his black settlements would help prevent European imperialism from spreading throughout Africa, as it had through China and India. It would ensure that Africa would remain "possessed and controlled" by blacks rather than whites.[46]

Finally, Coates's colonization plan would allow him to further his support of black uplift, both in the United States and Africa. First, prospective settlers could be educated in the United States in a more positive atmosphere than had prevailed before. They would be studying with the awareness that they would be going to a place where they could use their skills and education unfettered by white racism, and their new confidence would, in turn, help combat that very racism. Coates saw his plan as a way of creating a cycle in which "the success of these pioneers, in the great work of civilization, will give encouragement and strength to their brethren in America, who will thus acquire greater confidence in their own powers to work for the elevation of their race in America, as their friends are doing in Africa." After all, "No one knows of how much he is capable, until there is something to call forth his energies. It is great occasions that make great men." Also, much could be done to further education in the settlements themselves by establishing schools for both men and women throughout Africa.[47]

Though he had supported Liberia for decades, his pamphlet was referring to something larger. What he was envisioning at this point resembled Buxton's chain of settlements. Instead of West Indians, however, Coates wanted to put these colonies under the direction of black Americans. Furthermore, he stated unequivocally that this would be no mass exodus. Instead, he wanted only fifty thousand "of the intelligent and educated" to settle within the next decade. "This number, distributed in some eight or ten different settlements along the coast, would form the nucleus of probably as many independent States, hereafter to form a confederacy similar to our own" and introduce the republican system to Africa. Like white settlers to California and Australia at the time, these black settlers would be motivated by the prospect of gain, in addition to the hope of escaping persecution. Even if his settlements were to be independent, they would be modeled after Liberia, which he claimed had already "fully established the capacity of the African race for self-government and the highest degree of civilization."[48]

Perhaps to avoid the proslavery taint that hampered ACS efforts among the black community, Coates argued that the measures he proposed "do not come within the prescribed duties of any existing organization." He clearly wanted to avoid sectionalism, calling for "a union of all the friends of freedom in America, whose sympathy for the oppressed is not limited by geographical boundaries or national sovereignty," to unite with British philanthropists in the founding of a new African Civilization Society. This new organization would "occupy a different field of labor from any other anti-slavery association, and thus be free from the objection of many, whose exertions have been limited to mere partial measures," most notably members of the Society of Friends, "who deeply feel the wrongs of slavery, and who would gladly avail themselves of an opportunity of more extended usefulness, but who have not deemed it their duty to take an active part in the political conflict that the slavery question has engendered." Thus, this new colonization endeavor would offer a "quiet and peaceful, yet most effective mode of overcoming the principal obstacle to our national prosperity." All that was needed was for the right type of African American leaders to join his endeavor.[49]

One black American who responded favorably to Coates's plan was Henry Highland Garnet. After reading *Cotton Cultivation in Africa*, this New York minister was inspired to help publicize the African Civilization Society and gain support for the settlement scheme. He appealed to the public by explaining that, though blacks had resisted colonization for the most part, they now "perceive their duty as well as privilege" to "be the agents, in God's providence, to introduce the Gospel and a true Christian civilization into Africa." A growth in African exploration had "opened a new field of Christian enterprise, as well as commercial activity," and American Christians, especially black ones, had a duty to aid in the spread of Christianity and the redemption of the continent. "The idea that they can aid in destroying the inhuman Slave-trade, as well as introduce pure Christianity to their 'fatherland,' besides directly elevating all branches of the great African family of nations, has deeply moved the hearts of multitudes of noble-minded Christians of African descent," who wanted to help establish "Christian industrial settlements" in West Africa. He issued a flyer that paraphrased Coates's pamphlet and explained the Free Produce plan, showing how legitimate commerce would end the slave trade. He ended with a call for donations to begin the glorious work. Coates welcomed the support of Garnet, who became the society's first president and principal spokesman, and hoped that together they could create an organization that would appeal to blacks and whites alike.[50]

* * *

After dedicating most of his adult life to the reform efforts of both the ACS and PAS, Coates thought his new organization would bridge the gap between these groups. It also brought a new dimension to the struggle with its focus on free blacks over conditionally freed slaves. Men such as Garnet would be qualified to help rectify a number of the problems ACS critics had cited and use colonization to create just the type of free black nation envisioned by earlier emigrationists Paul Cuffee and James Forten. In that sense, it would contribute to the immediatist efforts at securing racial equality as well as freedom. With this added dimension,

Coates insisted, the African Civilization plan would "combine within it-self the best features and missionary spirit of the colonization enterprise, with the philanthropic spirit of the various anti-slavery associations" and "supersede them all." Blacks such as Garnet and Martin R. Delany must have seen some merit in Coates's new direction. Delany found the economic and Free Produce aspects of the plan particularly appealing, as we will now see in our final case study.

"Our elevation must be the result of *self-efforts*, and work of our *own hands*": Martin R. Delany and the Role of Self-Help and Emigration in Black Uplift

Just as the racial climate of the 1850s helped convince white Pennsylvania colonizationists to focus their efforts on gaining free black settlers, it also led a number of free blacks to consider emigration on their own terms. James Forten had died in 1842, but a handful of men from his children's generation, including Pittsburgh's Martin R. Delany, began to advocate a black-led back-to-Africa movement much like the one proposed first by Forten and Paul Cuffee and then developed by Benjamin Coates. Like his predecessors, Delany hoped that a successful colony under black leadership would create the conditions for both self-rule and economic independence, proving black equality while combating both slavery and racism. Like Forten, he was convinced that this could be achieved only under genuine black leadership. Though historians have disagreed as to whether Delany's emigrationist vision was the first real stirring of a true black nationalism or the product of defeat and despair, it was actually an extension of the self-help and racial uplift agenda created by the gradualists and Forten. Based on the premise of select emigration, it can best be described as a "City on a Hill"—an intended showcase of black self-sufficiency and achievement. It was part of, rather than a departure from, his lifelong efforts to gain a legitimate place for blacks in American society.[1]

As we have already seen, the American Colonization Society scheme was extremely complicated, ambiguous, and often contradictory. So was Delany's. Just as historians have read a number of meanings into colonizationists' writings, scholars have emphasized different aspects of

FIGURE 9. "Martin R. Delany," by William J. Simmons. (Courtesy of the Library Company of Philadelphia.)

Delany's plan to arrive at varying conclusions. On the one hand, some have described him as the "Father of Black Nationalism," America's first true pan-Africanist. On the other hand, some have pointed out that Delany shared the same Eurocentric biases of white Americans, and they argue that his interest in Africa was self-serving. This debate makes Delany one of the most controversial figures in this study.[2]

The problem lies in the higher expectations that can easily result based on Delany's skin color. Black intellectuals such as Delany saw themselves as uniquely qualified to lead Africa back to its past greatness based on two assumptions. First, their ancestors were Africans and they shared the physical characteristics that would allow them to fit in and relate to the people in Africa. At the same time, however, as Americans they were more "civilized" and could take their cultural refinement with them and share it with Africans. White colonizationists shared these ideas, hence much of their effort to enlist the support of black leaders such as Forten. By the same token, it has been easy for historians, consciously or not, to see black nationalists as somehow less intrusive or threatening than colonizationists because of the expectation that they could relate more to Africans. This racially essentialist argument could make it easier to admire black nationalist efforts to "uplift" Africa. Viewed through the eyes of African specialists such as Basil Davidson and Tunde Adeleke, however, the admiration can easily turn to disappointment of failed expectation. As these historians have both shown, blacks who had imbibed Western, and particularly American, culture were little more capable of seeing the complexities of African cultures and appreciating them for their own merits than were white colonizationists. Even so, while admitting their limitations, we must not fall into the trap of heightened expectations and thus heightened criticism.

Delany felt a greater sense of urgency than did white colonizationists such as Mathew Carey, Elliott Cresson, or even Coates. Successful African colonization for Delany would have meant so much more than an end to slavery. It could have led, in his vision at least, to black respect and equality in the United States. Coates, and to an extent Cresson, had made a similar argument, but because Delany was black the idea was brought to the forefront of his agenda. It meant that he was fighting not only for the freedom of slaves but for his own freedom. In that sense, his emigration plan was the ultimate extension of the self-help agenda nourished by the previous generation of black leaders.

The only way to truly understand the sophisticated and multidimensional, but always assimilationist, Delany is to examine the specifics of his emigration plan, which was typical of its time in many ways. Like Forten and Cuffee, he wanted only industrious settlers to participate, so he did not seek mass emigration. Instead, he infused the Puritan concept of the "city on a hill" with the middle-class values of his own time, seeking to create a black-led colony that would prove black equality, generate self-confidence among the larger black community, and beat whites at their own economic game.

This idea makes sense only when it is placed within the context of the antebellum abolition crusade, a movement influenced by both optimism and despair. Despite times of great disappointment, abolitionists of both races continued to rely on the belief shared by Forten's generation and the gradualists that if African Americans worked hard, remained upstanding citizens, and earned their own keep, they would eventually prove their worth and be accepted in their native land. Even as he called for emigration, Delany maintained this hope.

* * *

Martin Robison Delany was born May 6, 1812, in Charles Town, Virginia, to Patti Peace, a free black woman, and her husband, Samuel Delany. Samuel Delany was a skilled slave who was allowed to work for wages in his free time, and, with his wife's help, bought his freedom when Martin was eleven years old. According to Delany's biographers, both parents claimed royal African ancestry, and his grandfather and father were both known for refusing to allow whites to punish them. His mother, referred to by her neighbors as an "uppity negress," also set an example of defiance by teaching her children to read and write despite Virginia laws against black literacy. Caught in this act of defiance when her sons allowed their ability to be discovered, she had to flee with her children to Chambersburg, Pennsylvania, where Samuel Delany joined them after securing his freedom. [3]

Thus, at age eleven Martin Delany found himself in a stable, two-parent family in a black neighborhood in the North. Though they had to worry about the slave catchers ubiquitous in southern Pennsylvania, the Delanys enjoyed at least limited rights as well as the stabilizing influence of the broader community of thirty-five to forty black families in the Chambersburg neighborhood known as Kerrstown. These families worked together and set up their own Methodist Episcopal congregation, which included a Sabbath school as well as a regular school for the children, funded by a self-imposed "occupation tax" paid in addition to state taxes, which were given to the white schools. This financial sacrifice left Martin able to attend school at an age when many children already worked. [4]

In 1831, at the age of nineteen, Delany moved to Pittsburgh to further his education. This move came one year after black leaders called the first in a series of "black conventions." The immediate abolition movement was beginning, and Delany arrived just after local black leaders met formally to pledge resistance to the growth of the local branch of the American Colonization Society by issuing a vehement denunciation of colonization, whether to Africa, Canada, or Haiti.[5]

Though he arrived too late to participate in the meeting, Delany became friends with the chair, John B. Vashon, a veteran of the War of 1812 and a successful barber. Vashon's career resembled Forten's in many ways. Both men had achieved not only success but wealth. Both veterans of American wars, each led his town's black community, often serving as the middleman between his black and white neighbors. Both also worked to educate and train the next generation of abolitionists. Forten mentored men such as Garrison and Robert Purvis, and Vashon mentored Delany.

Between Vashon and another local black leader, the Reverend Lewis Woodson, Delany would be groomed to play his own role in the antebellum freedom struggle. He began by founding the Theban Literary Society in 1832 and the Young Men's Moral Reform Society of Pittsburgh in 1834. He also served as an officer in the Philanthropic Society, a group that helped fugitive slaves find safety in Pittsburgh. His work with this group earned him the position of Vashon's successor as diplomat between the black and white communities.[6]

Delany's diplomatic role gave him a degree of authority in the community and led the white mayor to turn to him on at least one occasion. Pittsburgh, like Philadelphia, suffered from an epidemic of antiblack riots in the 1830s, and by 1839 Vashon and the members of the Philanthropic Society had had enough. In April a fight between a white and two or three blacks led the white and his friends to plan an attack on the black neighborhood of Hayti, a common target for such activity. That night, however, Vashon gave guns to a number of the society's members and told them to fight back. Delany took a delegation of the members to a local judge and warned him that they were going to defend themselves this time since they had learned from experience not to count on the police for protection. The mayor, Dr. Jonas R. McClintock, responded by asking Delany for a list of black men who would be willing to serve in a special police force. He then used his emergency powers to pair black and white men to patrol, protect the black community, and prevent the riot. As a result, the April 27, 1839, riot was, according to Delany's biographer, Victor Ullman, the last of its kind in Pittsburgh, though slave raids continued.[7]

Delany's life illustrates what some whites knew but most chose to overlook—that the black community was complex and contained different economic and intellectual classes. More than material wealth, these classes reflected people's occupations and levels of education. Despite what any white thought, "black" did not mean "slave" or even "servant," and Delany, who, like Forten, had never been either, wanted all whites to realize it. Like Forten, Delany felt the weight of an outwardly imposed racial unity forced on all blacks by whites who refused to appreciate differences within the community.[8]

* * *

Delany left a clear record of the dilemma he faced as a member of the black upper class. Many of his writings express an admiration for Africa and a pride in pure African ancestry that have led some historians to refer to him as the "Father of Black Nationalism." Just as important, however, they also serve as a plea for white acceptance. An early adherent to an Ethiopianist view of world history, which stressed the fact that Ethiopia was one of the oldest continuous civilizations and had a glorious past, he wrote a great deal about the superiority of ancient Africa and the dependence of whites on African skills. He argued that America had a unique system of servitude because the difference in skin color between the oppressors and the oppressed made the subservient class easily identifiable.

Like the gradualists and the first generation of black leaders who mentored them, antebellum black leaders believed that prejudice was based on inequality of condition rather than skin color. Although many white members of their own northern communities disregarded the intellectual and economic accomplishments of African Americans, black leaders continued to argue that moral and economic uplift would lead to equality. Even as free blacks lost what limited rights they once enjoyed, many black leaders held firm to their moral suasionist ideas.[9]

Indeed, self-help remained the primary goal of most black leaders, even as a growing number of white Americans began to subscribe to ideas then known as "scientific racism." Through the 1830s, most scholars and the general public had shared the idea that, despite different physical characteristics, all humans had descended from one set of original parents—Adam and Eve. Another popular belief was that environment shaped both the appearance and intellectual development of humans. These ideas of monogenesis and environmentalism, best supported by the work of Samuel Stanhope Smith, who published *Essay on the Causes of the Variety of Complexion and Figure in the Human Species* in 1787 and 1810, encouraged the idea that Africans, and African Americans, could overcome the obstacles they faced and eventually become equal to whites. Some even followed the logic of environmentalism so far as to assume that, given enough time in the new climate, those of African descent would eventually lighten and essentially become white.[10]

In the 1830s, however, these theories came under question in scientific circles, and by the 1840s much of the public had begun to question environmentalism and accept the idea of polygenesis. According to this theory, each race was created separately and thus constituted a separate species of human. Introduced to the scientific community and, eventually the public, through such works as Charles Caldwell's *Thoughts on the Original Unity of the Human Race* (1830), it led to attacks on abolitionism in general—both gradualists and immediatists. It also helped support a new "American school of ethnology" introduced by Samuel George Morton, a Philadelphia physician, in *Crania Americana* (1839). Morton collected and studied human skulls, concluding that clear differences existed among the skulls of each "species" of humans and that these differences persisted from ancient times. In other words, blacks, whites, and Native Americans were different in appearance and custom in the 1830s, just as their ancestors had been all along, and no amount of environmental modification would make any one species more like another. This idea was very popular among proslavery ideologues as well as scientists, gaining its most famous convert when Louis Agassiz, the famous Swiss biologist, emigrated to the United States to teach at Harvard in the late 1840s. Thus, as men such as Delany struggled to prove their equality, more and more white Americans were beginning to believe that science had proven that racial characteristics were permanent and indicative of distinct species rather than varieties of one species. Doctors and researchers from the University of Pennsylvania and College of Physicians of Philadelphia contributed much to this new field, and Isaac Hays, M.D, a fellow of the Philadelphia College of Physicians and a member of the American Philosophical Society and the Academy of Natural Sciences of Philadelphia, printed many reviews and articles of craniological topics in his *American Journal of the Medical Sciences*.[11]

Even as it developed, however, Delany and many other black leaders underestimated the depths of scientific racism and followed their predecessors in focusing on racial uplift, or what Delany called "self-elevation," to overcome what they still insisted was conditional inequality. Sharing Jacksonian optimism and a reverence for Western culture, they urged other African Americans to adopt the Protestant work ethic and strive to become productive members of American society. Indeed, here was the beginning of Delany's "city on a hill." According to Ullman, "His concept was the creation of a distinct minority group, so changing itself as to become a pattern for the majority society around it." This would require education, exemplary living habits, and "an individual and collective commitment" among blacks "to strive for all that white America preached and failed to achieve." At the same time, economic self-sufficiency would be crucial, and Delany shared Cuffee's hope that creating a successful merchant class would prove racial equality and encourage the abolition of slavery. William C. Nell, a colleague of Delany's and one of the nation's first black historians, expressed a common sentiment of the day when he insisted that "any person of ordinary capacity, must know that, to become elevated, he must cultivate and practice the same traits which are elevating others around him; and if it is . . . harder for the colored man than any other, why, then let him work the harder, and, eventually, the summit will be attained."[12]

Although some historians have asserted that this strain of moral suasion was on its way out of vogue among black abolitionists by the 1840s, these leaders employed self-help arguments in a number of their writings into the 1850s and 1860s. And when some began to call for more militant action as their disenchantment with American racial policy grew throughout the 1850s, they never completely abandoned their arguments for racial elevation, and they consistently maintained their struggle to make whites accept them as equals. Products of white reform society, they served as transitional figures in the abolitionist movement, both influencing and learning from fugitive-slave leaders of the 1840s. Likewise, most of the fugitive slaves who assumed leadership positions in the black abolitionist crusade by the 1840s also insisted free blacks could earn white respect and further the cause of abolition by achieving intellectual, moral, and economic success through self-elevation.[13]

The concept of self-elevation had three main components—moral uplift, educational attainment, and economic self-sufficiency. White reform leaders of the day encouraged the white masses to strive for success in each of these areas, just as black leaders preached the tenets to the black masses. The crucial difference was that more was at stake for the black community. Self-elevation could lead to racial uplift that would force whites to accept racial equality. This, in turn, would lead to the abolition of slavery by defeating proslavery arguments that bondage alone kept blacks in line. Self-elevation was deeply ingrained in the philosophies of black leaders, and self-help arguments strongly punctuate their writings.

Throughout his career, Delany shared this obsession with perfecting black American society. Strongly influenced by the words of his mentor Lewis Woodson that "CONDITION and not *color*, is the chief cause of the prejudice, under which we suffer," he maintained throughout his career that racial uplift was the crucial first step to freedom and equality. Just as important, he insisted that blacks must achieve elevation without the help of whites.[14]

Like most other leaders of his time, both white and black, Delany firmly believed that blacks had to be prepared morally, intellectually, and economically to be productive members of society. Proud of his own restraint, Delany founded the first total abstinence society for blacks and urged others to "let your habits be strictly temperate." He emphasized his disapproval of "ardent liquid" in his novel *Blake*, characterizing one of the white slave traders as drunk and reckless while his main character, a black man, was sober and level-headed at all times. Likewise, he sought the highest level of education he could obtain.

By the mid-1830s, higher education was available to northern free blacks at schools such as Noyes Academy, the Oneida Institute, Wesleyan University, Oberlin College, and Dartmouth, but many avenues of opportunity remained closed. Many divinity schools also refused to admit black students, and quite a few American blacks turned to Europe for advanced degrees. James McCune Smith, a black abolitionist, followed this avenue and earned his medial degree in Glasgow. Impressed with Smith's achievement, Delany, who had been studying medicine under white doctors in Allegheny County, decided to follow suit and enjoyed a brief moment of hope after being accepted at Harvard Medical School in 1850. His acceptance at an American medical school was no small feat, since very few African Americans had managed to secure such training in the United States, and most had been under the auspices of the colonization society and under the promise that they would emigrate to Liberia and practice there. Hope soon turned to despair, however, as Delany's acceptance was rescinded, and he was asked to leave after white students protested. Delany's rejection occurred in the same year the Fugitive Slave Law was passed, and it surely helped push him in the direction of emigration, yet he remained unwilling to give up the racial uplift agenda.[15]

Despite his disappointment, Delany continued to push for black educational opportunity, but he also stressed the importance of material success, since economic self-sufficiency was as important as academic achievement. Many of his dispatches to the *North Star*, as well as much of his treatise *The Condition, Elevation, Emigration and Destiny of the*

Colored People of the United States, focused on the importance of economic self-sufficiency, celebrating black entrepreneurship by cataloging influential and successful black merchants and their achievements. Some leaders took this side of the agenda even further. Precursors to Booker T. Washington, they responded to segregation and exclusion of blacks from higher education by emphasizing the practical role of industrial education over traditional academic training, continuing the call for manual labor schools, which began with Forten in the 1830s.[16]

* * *

Given the American tradition of Jeffersonian thought and the opening of the West to farming ventures, some black leaders concluded that the best way to autonomy was through agriculture. Woodson had made this argument and even connected his agricultural emphasis with resettlement. Like Forten, he was a lifelong adherent to racial uplift and the self-help philosophy, and Woodson set out from December of 1837 to February of 1838 to explain the agenda in a series of letters to the *Colored American*. He insisted that, whether they liked it or not, blacks formed a "distinct class" in America and it was up to them to better their own condition. He compared the situation of black Americans to the Irish, Spanish, Turkish, and Russian people, who were stereotyped as "low, ignorant and degraded" even though "there may be found in all these countries, many who excel in whatever is elegant, polite and refined." It was the same with African Americans. "The few who have risen above the condition of the many, are not regarded; nor need they expect to be. Their virtues and attainments will never be fully appreciated, until the majority of the class with whom they are identified, have risen to something like a level with themselves." Therefore, the black community must seek a "*general* moral improvement," and it must be "a work of our own." Finally, he argued that such a "moral revolution" would be especially difficult for black Americans because "a thousand obstacles are thrown in the way." One of the most challenging obstacles was the need for "union and concert of action." "We are scattered over a vast surface of country, and settled in small communities at a great distance from each other, knowing little of each other, and feeling but little interest in each other's welfare."[17]

At some point within the next few months, Woodson decided that a black western settlement plan reminiscent of that proposed by Benezet years before would solve the dilemma of unity and foster the self-help agenda. Drawing on firsthand experience, since he had lived in Ohio in the early 1830s and his father still lived there, he cited more extensive black land ownership in both the country and the city in the lands west of the Allegheny Mountains. Especially in rural areas this meant increased opportunities since "a colored farmer has just the same chance of getting along that a white one has" because "nature has no prejudice in her heart" and lavishes "rewards on all who are willing to earn them." Further, this region saw "little prejudice against colored mechanics." The elder Woodson and his neighbors had their own church, day school, and Sabbath school, and they "cut their own harvests, roll their own logs, and raise their own houses." Thus, Woodson concluded that more blacks should head west and create similar communities. Closeness could foster the type of unity needed to push forward the self-help and racial uplift agenda and thus prove black equality. Crucially, however, for relocation to be part of self-help and racial uplift, "the *manner, time* and *place* of such removal should be exclusively matters of their own choice." Woodson pointed out that, given the racial climate in many eastern cities, "contact" must not necessarily foster friendship. Next, he insisted that groups such as the Quakers had separated from their own settlements within the larger communities they sought to influence. He insisted that there was a clear difference between "purchasing contiguous tracts of land from the Congress of our native country, and settling upon them so as to have society, churches, and schools of our own, without being subject to the humiliation of begging them from others" and being "*exiled* to the cheerless coast of Africa." What Woodson wanted to create in the West sounded much like what Delany would later seek in Africa—an asylum where a group of American blacks could succeed independently and prove their worth to white Americans, themselves, and their fellow African Americans.[18] Following his mentor, Delany would also tie independent settlement to the self-help, racial uplift agenda.

According to Ullman, Delany actually began considering emigration when black Pennsylvanians lost the vote a year after Woodson presented his plan. As we saw in our discussion of Forten, blacks who fulfilled the state's property qualifications had been allowed to vote since 1780, but in 1838 a Constitutional Convention amended the state charter by adding the word "white" to the section describing voter qualifications. Other states soon followed suit. That winter Delany took his first step on the path toward emigration by traveling south to investigate the suitability of the independent Texas republic as a safe haven for free blacks. After a journey of several months, during which he began to formulate his novel *Blake*, Delany concluded that Texas would make an ideal home for free blacks if it remained independent. He realized, however, that this was highly unlikely, so he abandoned this idea and returned to Pittsburgh, where he was elected to the board of managers of the Pittsburgh Anti-Slavery Society.[19]

Soon after his return, Delany served on a committee with Vashon, Woodson, and four other black leaders to organize a state convention to discuss strategies for regaining the vote. They began planning the meeting in January 1841, passing resolutions that criticized the general apathy blacks had shown since losing the franchise, and insisting "We owe it to ourselves, our friends, and our posterity to make at least some effort to silence the charge that has long been proffered against us of indifference to our rights." Unlike the Philadelphia conventions of the 1830s, this meeting was for blacks only, since, as Woodson pointed out in the *Pittsburgh Gazette*, "Every man knows his own affairs best, and naturally feels a deeper interest in them than anyone else, and therefore on that account ought to attend to them." Delany served on the agenda and arrangements committees before the convention and the publishing committee afterward. At Delany's suggestion, the delegates voted to establish a newspaper, but they failed to follow through. After waiting two years, Delany gave up and founded his own paper, the *Mystery*, which lasted four years, until he and Frederick Douglass joined forces in the *North Star* in 1847, the same year that Pennsylvania finally outlawed slavery completely and freed those still in bondage.[20]

Delany's affiliation with the *North Star* led him into the national anti-slavery crusade and eventually into conflict within the leadership ranks. As a traveling correspondent, he sent regular letters that addressed such topics as the hypocrisy of taxing blacks as citizens yet denying them the privileges that should go with it, the role of economic dependency in the "degraded" condition of many blacks, and the fate of fugitive slaves. He also wrote about the achievements of blacks he met and learned about, the particularly bad state of women in slavery, and the failings of black youth to live up to his injunctions for self-elevation. Repeatedly he also expounded on his favorite theme of the need for successful blacks to lead in the freedom struggle and his idea that slaves were waiting for such a leader. Though he stepped down as editor in 1849, he continued to send correspondence until the summer of 1850, when he and Douglass entered a heated exchange in the paper's columns after Douglass condemned Samuel R. Ward for speaking at a biracial meeting in which blacks were relegated to the balcony of their own church in Philadelphia. Douglass criticized Ward for conceding to racism for the benefit of reaching a larger audience, and Delany condemned Douglass for contributing to dissent and hostility in the black abolitionist ranks.[21]

* * *

Indeed, concession and dissent permeated the antislavery atmosphere in general, as the threat of secession forced many government officials, and even some abolitionists, to adopt a more conciliatory stance toward the southern slaveholders in the decades preceding the Civil War. As most political leaders sought at all costs to keep the union together, dedicated abolitionists fought in vain as a new and stronger fugitive slave law was passed and lawlessness in the territories threatened to make a mockery of popular sovereignty. Delany, like others, continued to blame social and political conditions, rather than blatant racism, for the setbacks that hampered the struggle. Indeed, he experienced firsthand the rejection embodied by the Dred Scott decision when he applied for a patent for an invention and was rejected due to his lack of citizenship. Still, he continued to believe that things would change if blacks could just prove that they were "more than equal." Proving that, however, became increasingly difficult as sectional tension and racial oppression grew. Indeed many antislavery politicians, represented after 1848 by the Free Soil Party, were antiblack and opposed slavery only because it dampened their hopes for a homogenous white republic. This type of antislavery, the political strand associated with Clay and Carey, was growing throughout the 1840s and 1850s, even as anti-abolition continued to assault the immediatists at every turn.[22]

Tepid abolitionists were especially challenged by the Fugitive Slave Law, which tested the loyalty of friendly whites by making it a federal offense to assist runaways. Delany was aware of the implications of white disregard for this law, and he knew what was at stake. He maintained that whites would not consider disobeying the law because its existence was "*necessary* to the continuance of the national compact. This law is the foundation of the Compromise [of 1850], remove it, and the consequences are easily determined." He also saw that northern fear for the stability of the Union gave the South a political advantage. "Let the South but *demand* it, and the North will comply as a *duty* of compromise."[23]

Many free blacks recognized the danger posed by the Fugitive Slave Law to their liberty. Because the law required nothing more than a sworn affidavit from a slave owner who wished to claim a black as renegade property, it tied free blacks directly to slaves by emphasizing their ethnic connection. This law brought about one of the most militant periods in the struggle for freedom and equality, as blacks saw the return of many fugitives, including Anthony Burns, to slavery despite public outcries from the black community. Many black leaders and white abolitionists alike began to encourage civil disobedience, and Delany, who realized that fugitive slaves were not the only ones who should fear for their freedom, warned the Pittsburgh mayor and a crowd of onlookers that he would fight efforts to invade his home. "My house is my castle; in that castle are none but my wife and my children. . . . If any man approaches that house in search of a slave . . . [h]e cannot enter that house and we both live." According to Delany the law was especially dangerous for northern free blacks because, unlike southern free blacks, they usually did not possess documentation of their status.[24]

The Fugitive Slave Law prompted an immediate mass exodus of free blacks to a number of locations beyond the borders of the United States. Estimates vary as to the number of refugees, but Vincent Harding contends that between 1850 and the Civil War fifteen to twenty thousand blacks, or between 4 and 5 percent of the northern free population, left the country. Peter Ripley contends that between 1830 and the Civil War, forty thousand American blacks left for the British North American Provinces alone, while an uncalculated number set sail for Great Britain, and Stanley Campbell contends that three thousand fugitive slaves escaped to Canada within three months after the signing of the Fugitive Slave Law. According to William Wells Brown, a contemporary of Delany's and one of the earliest black historians, "the subdued tone of the liberal portion of the press, the humiliating offers of northern political leaders of compromises, and the numerous cases of fugitive slaves being returned to their masters, sent a thrill of fear to all colored men in the land for their safety, and nearly every train going North found more or less negroes fleeing to Canada."[25]

Two years after the passage of the law, while William Pettit and John Durbin were delivering their appeal to the state legislature on behalf of the ACS, Delany began to make a name for himself as the chief supporter of emigration. That year he published *The Condition, Elevation, Emigration and Destiny of the Colored People of the United States*, a political treatise hailed by many historians as a radical emigrationist document. Floyd Miller argues that the views Delany presented in this work were "directly at odds" with his earlier optimism that self-elevation would allow blacks to achieve equality in the United States. At the same time, however, he admits that Delany held firmly to the belief that American whites' hostility was due to the condition, rather than the color, of their black neighbors.[26] Indeed, the book does embody the mix of hope and frustration that figured so prominently in the black abolitionist movement. Importantly, it devoted over one hundred pages to explaining why blacks should be accepted in America, but fewer than forty to emigration.

Using historical arguments and contemporary examples, Delany insisted throughout this treatise that blacks had contributed as much as whites to the creation of the country and were thus entitled to citizenship. "The legitimate requirement, politically considered necessary to the justifiable claims for protection and full enjoyment of all the rights and privileges of an unqualified freeman, in all democratic countries is, that each person so endowed, shall have made contributions and investments in the country." He and his associates had indeed made such contributions, and he wanted that to be recognized, insisting that Africans were not enslaved because of their color, or because whites had considered them racially inferior. On the contrary, he claimed that Europeans had discovered that Native Americans were unfit for slavery because they were "raised to the sports of fishing, the chase, and of war [and] were wholly unaccustomed to labor," whereas Africans were "known as an industrious people, cultivators of the soil." More than 120 years before Peter Wood's groundbreaking study of African contributions to American agriculture, Delany maintained that Africans, not Europeans, had brought the skills necessary for the cultivation of staple crops to the Americas and that Europeans of the colonial era appreciated the value of the slaves' intellectual contributions. Africans had been enslaved as a matter of policy, and the "absurd idea of natural inferiority of the African [was never] dreamed of until . . . adduced by the slave-holders and their abettors, in justification of their policy." Race was constructed as a justification for maintaining slavery, but blacks had not been enslaved because of racial inferiority.[27] Of course, not all blacks had reached self-elevation, so he pointed out that he was not advocating "the actual equal attainments of every individual." What he did want was the chance to lead other blacks to that point.

It is clear that much of Delany's irritation stemmed from the patriarchal attitudes shown by all abolitionists, gradual or immediate. He ran out of patience with even the immediatists in the early 1850s, and his *Condition, Elevation, Emigration* called them on the hypocrisy of professing support for abolition and racial justice yet refusing to offer blacks respected positions in their own freedom movement. Likely familiar with the relationship between Forten and William Lloyd Garrison, he reminded readers that "anti-slavery took its rise among *colored men*, just at the time they were introducing their greatest projects for their own elevation." White abolitionists were "converts of the colored men," but after joining the cause had co-opted the leading positions. Thus, within the established antislavery movement though blacks were the most dedicated and had the most at stake, they found themselves "occupying the very same position in relation to our anti-slavery friends, as we do in the relation to the pro-slavery part of the community—a mere secondary, underling position." When black leaders asserted their independence, they found themselves under personal attack by the very abolitionist press that was allegedly dedicated to racial equality.[28]

Delany's resentment grew when Harriet Beecher Stowe's widely read 1853 antislavery novel *Uncle Tom's Cabin* placed her in the spotlight of the abolition movement. At that time Delany chastised Douglass, the most popular and well-known black leader of the time, for consulting the white newcomer regarding matters of racial uplift. "In all due respect and deference to Mrs. Stowe, I beg leave to say, that she *knows nothing about us* . . . neither does any other white person—and, consequently, can contrive no successful scheme for our elevation; it must be done by ourselves." He asked "Why, in God's name, don't the leaders among our people make suggestions, and *consult* the most competent among *their own* brethren concerning our elevation?" Not only did Stowe presume to prescribe a remedy for uplifting a race she had no real connection to, she borrowed much of her story from existing slave narratives, showed contempt for the black republic of Haiti, called for white instructors to teach black children, treated blacks with a general indifference, and ended her work with a prescription that included emigration to the white-founded and white-controlled Liberia.[29]

Like Forten, Delany is remembered by many as a staunch critic of the ACS and Liberia, but he, like his predecessor, actually had an ambivalent relationship with the colonization movement. Though he denounced the colonization society in the *Mystery* in 1846, he admired the Chesapeake and Liberia Trading Company, a shipping company much like the one envisioned by Samuel Wilkeson. Indeed, this company, formed in 1845 under the direction of the Maryland State Colonization Society, may have been the result of Wilkeson's vision. More important, to Delany, it probably looked like the realization of Cuffee's dream. The venture only survived a few years and failed to serve as the avenue of black entrepreneurship intended by its founders, but while it lasted, Delany praised the opportunities it offered. He also praised Liberia when the colony achieved independence in 1847, but his praise rested on the young republic's determination "to exist without a *master* and *overseer.*" If it could survive without white leadership, Liberia, like Haiti, would serve as "evidence of the capacity of the colored man for self-government." Importantly, however, he insisted that blacks had to lead the efforts because "our elevation must be the result of *self-efforts*, and the work of our *own hands.*"[30]

His optimism, however, was ephemeral. By the time he wrote *The Condition, Elevation, Emigration, and Destiny of the Colored People of the United States* four years later, he had determined that Liberia was not an independent republic but rather "a poor *miserable mockery—a burlesque* on a government—a pitiful dependency on the American Colonizationists." Though Joseph J. Roberts was president in name, his real role was as "a mere parrot" of white colonizationists in Washington, namely Ralph Gurley and Elliot Cresson. To support his claim, he cited numerous cases in which Roberts sought permission from the ACS board before making decisions in Liberia. Thus, he concluded that Liberia maintained too many ties to the ACS to offer any real chance for black autonomy.[31]

Delany concluded that the safest places to go were the provinces of Central and South America and the Caribbean, places where people of color already made up the majority of the population. Not only was Mexico as easily accessible as Canada, but its large black population left it less desirable for annexation by the United States. After all, the Americans already had enough to worry about with the threat of an uprising among their own large population of slaves. Also, Delany insisted that the countries of Latin America, with a majority of black citizens, were less likely than Canada to allow themselves to be annexed by a nation known for racial subjugation. He called on blacks to emigrate to this region, where they could "become the producers . . . rather than the consumers" and uplift themselves through productivity and economic prosperity. Success in such endeavors would aid the slaves in the United States by helping prove black equality in general and the rights of freedom for all.[32]

By August 1854 a handful of black leaders had joined Delany in developing what Floyd Miller has described as "a well-articulated ideology," which still opposed the ACS and African resettlement but supported emigration to different points within the Western hemisphere. For some leaders Christianity played a large role in the dream of regeneration and resettlement, but Delany's focus remained on economic achievement and self-sufficiency. In the autumn of 1853 Delany issued a call for a convention in which emigrationists could come together and discuss such details. This call sparked a heated debate in the abolitionist press in both the United States and Canada, pitting Frederick Douglass and many leaders of the Canadian exile against Delany, James Theodore Holly, and Henry Bibb. Even so, delegates from eleven states, including six from slave states, and a number from Canada met in Cleveland as planned. As Miller has pointed out, however, almost half were from Pittsburgh and the surrounding area of western Pennsylvania. Indeed, only three, including Holly, were from areas east of Pittsburgh. Interestingly, one third of the delegates were women.[33]

During the meeting, Delany presented a Declaration of Sentiments as well as his Report on the Political Destiny of the Race on this Continent. Together these works argued that blacks would never gain equality until given a true voice politically. Not only must a true citizen be allowed to vote, but he or she must also have "the indisputable right of being chosen or elected as the representative of another." In short, blacks would not truly be citizens until "acknowledged as a necessary *constituent* in the *ruling element* of the country in which we live."[34]

Before disbanding, convention leaders formed a permanent National Board of Commissioners to aid those who wished to leave the United States. This board consisted of three committees, one each for foreign, financial, and domestic relations. Delany served on the foreign relations committee, whose job was to gather information about and correspond with countries that might serve as havens for black exiles from the United States.[35]

In the aftermath of the convention, debate continued among black leaders. George B. Vashon, the son of John B. Vashon, led the charge against emigration. He saw support for resettlement as a direct refutation of the efforts of his father and other black leaders who had fought the ACS so diligently in the 1830s. Of course, to the emigrationists, this argument was oversimplified. They too resisted, and continued to resist, the white colonization effort. In their minds, the key difference was that emigration independent of white leadership was a means to empowerment. It was an effort to resist, rather than cooperate with, the ACS.[36]

After the meeting, a number of talented black leaders came to support the cause, or at least to side with Delany over Douglass in the debate over emigration. An important convert was Mary Ann Shadd, a Canadian exile who was the main force behind the *Provincial Freeman* and who had denounced emigration to South America and Mexico in her 1852 *A Plea for Emigration or Notes of Canada West*. She had insisted that Canada made the best refuge for black American exiles and condemned the notion of emigrating to countries affiliated with the "Romish Church." She also insisted that Mexico was too greatly influenced by southern slaveholders. With both of their pamphlets appearing in the same year and advocating different destinations, Delany and Shadd had been at odds, but after the convention they became part of the same larger movement. Indeed, a number of blacks who had fled to Canada joined Delany's cause at this time, but the downside of this development was that it created competition for Delany as he struggled to maintain his position at the head of the movement. Arguments over the destination of America's black exiles persisted, but most continued to reject Africa. The main division remained that between secular emigrationists such as Delany and a growing number, led mainly by Holly, who sought to infuse a missionary element into emigration.[37]

At the same time Canadian emigrants began to join Delany's move-ment, he was also becoming more supportive of theirs. In his role as a member of the board of commissioners of the emigration movement, he issued a report favorable to Canadian settlement in August 1855. Impressed with the real estate holdings of blacks in Canada, he began to see the settlements there as offering hope for his dream of economic achievement and independence. He moved to Chatham, Ontario, in Feb-ruary of 1856 and opened a medical practice. By the time of the second emigration convention, held in August of 1856, as proslavery and anti-slavery forces fought over the status of the Kansas territory, Delany had become a valued member of the Canadian exile community.[38]

The second emigration convention showcased the disagreement among emigrationists as to the ideal destiny for black American exiles. At the first convention Holly had supported Haitian emigration with a focus on missionary work, and he used his ties with the Episcopal Church to advertise his ideas in the two years between the conventions. In 1855 he visited the republic as an official ambassador of the National Board of Commissioners, but on his own initiative he used the trip to scout for a location for a mission of the Protestant Episcopal Board of Foreign Missions. With this altered focus, Holly was beginning to lead his own faction of emigrationists, though Delany remained president of the National Board and headquarters was moved to Chatham.[39]

The Supreme Court's declaration through the Dred Scott case that no blacks could enjoy the privileges and protections of American citizen-ship caused a renewed interest in emigration. After the ruling, as we saw before, 110 Pennsylvania free blacks turned to the ACS for passage to Liberia.[40]

Though he had issued a scathing criticism of Liberia in 1855, Delany began to reconsider Africa in general by the spring of 1858, following the Dred Scott ruling. In response to Delany's criticism in *Condition, Elevation, Emigration,* the ACS renewed its struggle for black support, sending the Reverend Daniel H. Peterson to Liberia in 1853. Peterson published a favorable report, *The Looking-Glass: Being a True Report and Narrative of the Life, Travels, and Labors of the Rev. Daniel H. Peterson,* but another passenger on that voyage, William Nesbit, presented a different story in his *Four Months in Liberia; or, African Colonization Exposed.* Delany found Nesbit's argument more convincing and offered to write an introduction to his book. From Nesbit he learned details of the unsafe conditions and unhealthy climate of Liberia, a country that is "*daily* overflooded . . . by the *tide-water* from the ocean," the prevalence of slavery in the country, and "injurious effect" of white missionaries upon the indigenous population. He lamented the fact that money that should have been "spent in the proper education and preparation of young colored youths of both sexes, to carry the gospel to the foreign heathen," was instead "spent in support of pompous white men as missionaries; men who have neither interest, regard, nor respect for those races." This was unfortunate, since the presence of haughty white missionaries created the "impression that all great and good things are inherent in the whites, and, therefore, must necessarily emanate from them."[41]

He continued to resist the ACS, but Delany began increasingly to turn his attention to Africa. Perhaps because the American government had finally officially rejected them as citizens, more blacks became interested in the African dimensions of their identity, and a number began to consider emigration there, either with or without the assistance of whites. Two of the most prominent supporters of African emigration in the late 1850s were Delany and Henry Highland Garnet, another black abolitionist who shared Holly's desire to combine emigration and missionary work. Garnet was affiliated with the African Civilization Society, a group backed by white missionaries, but Delany tried to remain independent of whites, though even he fell short of this goal.[42]

Delany wanted whites to understand not only that blacks and whites were equal in general but that the black population contained its own leaders and did not need white guidance. Like the white reform leaders of his day, he firmly believed that educated, enlightened members of the upper classes were obligated to impart their cultural values and superior lifestyles to the downtrodden. His level of education and professional attainment obligated him to participate in the broader American reform movement just as his pure African bloodlines and royal lineage rendered him specifically responsible for uplifting the black "race." Indeed, he went so far as to insist that racial purity made him more qualified than light-skinned black leaders such as Frederick Douglass to represent African Americans, even if Douglass had experienced firsthand the horrors of the lash.[43]

Delany most fully develops the importance of racial purity among black leaders in his novel *Blake, or the Huts of America*. In this novel the hero, Henry Blake, is a "pure Negro—handsome, manly and intelligent . . . [a] man of good literary attainments." Born to a wealthy free black family and educated in the West Indies, Blake, after being kidnapped and sold into slavery, travels throughout the southern United States and Cuba plotting a large-scale slave revolt. A product of an elite background, he is one of the very few black characters in the novel to speak in proper English rather than dialect, and Delany makes it clear throughout the book that other blacks, degraded by a life of servitude, have been waiting for such an articulate, intelligent savior to lead them in their fight for freedom. He stresses Blake's pure African genetics as well as his intelligence, describing his hero in a manner that echoes his own self-perception.[44]

In the novel, white characters express admiration for Blake's intelligence, allowing Delany to further develop his idea that greed, rather than racism, is the driving force behind chattel slavery. One character admits that he "would just as readily hold a white as a black in slavery," adding that "it is all a matter of self-interest with me; and though I am morally opposed to slavery, yet while the thing exists, I may as well profit by it, as others." This character clearly represents Delany's vision of American slaveholders such as Andrew Jackson, who, he insisted, held slaves "as a policy, by which to make money—and would just as readily have held a white man, had it been the policy of the country." Furthermore, the white characters in his novel who develop close bonds with blacks begin to appreciate their talent and, in some cases, enter into relationships of mutual respect and even affection.[45]

Delany envisioned a world in which mutual respect would lead whites to acknowledge the authority of blacks of his class over their own racial community and allow them to serve as mediators between black and white society. White "politicians, religionists, colonizationists, and abolitionists" had "each and all, at different times, presumed to *think* for, dictate to, and *know* better what suited colored people, than they knew for themselves," and none of their plans had worked so far. Able black leaders, however, could put an end to the "moral . . . mental . . . [and] physical servitude" by keeping lower-class blacks in line while teaching whites the value of blacks historically and in contemporary society. This would ease white anxieties and leave more of them open to the idea of free black neighbors. Obviously, Delany had fallen into the same trap Forten had, expecting blacks to live up to the white American middle-class ideal and assuming whites would recognize and appreciate, rather than resent, their efforts.[46] By this time, he was beginning to believe that this might not be possible under the stifling racial climate of the United States, so he began to consider a new tactic—emigration to Africa.[47]

Most historians have emphasized Delany's "longstanding emotional attachment to Africa" as the chief reason for his change in focus. Of course, there were other factors as well. For one thing, Holly's focus on Haiti and the religious nature of his work bothered Delany, who continued to insist that emigration should involve self-sufficiency in an economic sense. Just as important, he believed that religion had played a part in keeping blacks subservient to whites, and reliance on white churches and missionary societies only transplanted the secondary status of American blacks to other parts of the world. Finally, since Haiti was already an established republic, it might be more difficult for black Americans to gain leadership roles. According to Miller, Delany began to reconsider a plan he developed during his early days in Pittsburgh to visit Africa and search for territory there to establish a colony.[48]

Once he set his sights on Africa in the spring of 1858, Delany proceeded to gain allies in the black community and secure the funds needed to explore the territory and establish his colony. He turned to his friend and previous supporter, Martin H. Freeman, first. Freeman, principal of Pittsburgh's Avery Institute for black youth, was intrigued by the idea but felt restricted by family ties and thus turned down the offer to join the exploring party. Delany then turned to physician James H. Wilson and artist Robert Douglass Jr., both of Philadelphia. Like Freeman, Wilson approved of Delany's idea but turned down his offer. Douglass, however, agreed to participate and suggested they also contact Robert Campbell, a West Indian native who now taught in Philadelphia. Campbell agreed to join the group if his family would be supported in his absence.[49]

The largest challenge was not in gaining support but in securing funding. Delany first tried to gain financial support from the black community, turning to Jonathan Myers, a Wisconsin grocer originally from Pennsylvania. At some point the two men created the "Mercantile

Line of the Free Colored People of North America," and Myers wrote to the Royal Geographic Society of England, Liberian president Stephen A. Benson, and Thomas Clegg, an English cotton merchant promoting cotton cultivation in West Africa, for information about the region. Desperate enough for financial support, Delany also turned to whites. He approached the American Missionary Association, a group affiliated with the American and Foreign Anti-Slavery Society and currently sponsoring a West African mission, promising that his settlement would help promote Christianity in the continent. Delany even went so far as to claim willingness to adhere to the AMA's evangelical principles when George Whipple, the group's secretary, indicated interest in his plan. Even so, the alliance failed to materialize.[50]

To gather support in the African American community, Delany called a third national emigration convention, held in Chatham in August 1858. This meeting lacked the cohesiveness of the previous meetings, and it became clear that Delany was no longer the leader of the group. Instead, William Howard Day assumed control and in turn offered only tepid support to Delany's African exploration committee. With a lack of black financial support, Delany turned again to whites to seek funding for this committee, which he called the Niger Valley Exploring Party.[51]

Affiliation between the Niger Valley Exploring Party and white colonizationists first developed out of a connection between Robert Campbell and ACS and PCS member Benjamin Coates, a man Delany had praised in both his *Condition, Elevation, Emigration* and his introduction to Nesbit's *Four Years in Liberia* as a genuine friend to both Africa and African Americans. Both men believed strongly that the primary importance of African colonization was the role it could play in producing cotton for the Free Produce movement. According to their plan, cotton could be produced more cheaply by free labor in Africa and would thus end American slavery by taking the market away from Deep South slaveholders.[52]

Campbell began cooperating with Coates and William Coppinger, the PCS secretary, who donated $60 to the exploration, and he tied Delany's party to Garnet's African Civilization Society by announcing in the press that the groups were working together. Soon afterward another member of the expedition, James W. Purnell, a nephew of the Philadelphia abolitionist William Whipper, visited Ralph Gurley, who insisted that the expedition visit Liberia before traveling to their destination of Yoruba. Purnell, Campbell, and eventually Delany, agreed to consult Liberian authorities before exploring the region. Delany also entered into a relationship with the African Civilization Society, which was heavily connected to the New York chapter of the colonization society. Hoping to tap their resources, he became friendlier toward a number of ACS officials. Even with his appeasement of ACS leaders, however, Delany remained committed to an independent, black-led expedition and the formation of an independent colony where blacks could truly lead and determine their own destiny.[53]

Turning to Africa added a whole new dimension to Delany's scheme and left him open to the charges that he committed the same patriarchal errors as the white colonizationists. Sounding like many of Elliott Cresson's associates, he began to argue that emigration there would create a "reflex influence" that would allow him to help in the uplift of blacks throughout the diaspora. Thus, his emigration plans, while motivated by heightened oppression in the United States, were in no way a rejection of Western culture. Rather, Delany's scheme was an attempt to prove that blacks were qualified to rule their own societies and, by extension, to fully participate in American democracy.[54]

Like his fellow emigrationists, Delany believed that the success of his plan required careful selection of participants. Whether in favor of Canada, Africa, or Haiti, most settlement advocates agreed with William J. Watkins, an abolitionist who supported Haitian emigration, that only "men of the right stamp" should participate. "Those who, in the States or in the Canadas, have been like driftwood washed down the stream, will be a valuable acquisition nowhere." Joining Haiti's struggle with American abolition, he concluded that "we go there to continue the warfare against that monstrous abomination, American Slavery—not to get rid of the conflict." Just as Puritans who went to New England embarked on a mission to save their home church, these emigrationists felt a loyalty to, and continued connection with, those who chose to stay home. Thus, antebellum emigrationists connected the freedom struggle in the United States with the interests of black self-government throughout the world, but their elitist outlook led them to insist that the leadership ranks must come from men like themselves who knew and understood Western culture.[55]

Delany, who planned to screen emigration applications carefully, believed his colony would provide a civilizing influence by teaching Africans European commercial values and Western agricultural skills. African farmers would then grow produce cultivated by former American slaves and thus meet the demands of world markets. In this respect, his colony would play a role in the free labor movement, which had long been popular in reform circles and was supported by a number of black abolitionists and emigrationists. Delany cited the cultivation he saw in Africa and the sophisticated agricultural division of labor as proof that Africans were qualified to become the producers of the world's wealth and help make slavery obsolete.[56]

What Africans needed was the same thing that African Americans needed—an opportunity to achieve self-sufficiency. If blacks on both continents could become self-sufficient, their success would then prove racial equality, make slavery obsolete, and even earn the international black community a starring role in the world economic scene. Elevation—moral, educational, and economic—was the key.

Though his plan was motivated primarily by a desire to gain acceptance for blacks in the United States and gave only secondary consideration to African interests, Delany did believe that his settlement would benefit all parties. Perhaps it was wishful thinking, but he saw Africans' enthusiasm for education and missionary assistance as evidence that his race, though held down by white oppression, was capable of reclaiming the cultural and economic dominance it once enjoyed. Maintaining that civilization actually began in Africa, he claimed that much of Western culture was borrowed from that continent. Among his claims for African cultural superiority was his assertion that Arabic numbers had originally been stolen from the Alexandrian Museum when the Saracens invaded in 146 A.D. and destroyed the "depository of the earliest germs of social, civil, political, and national progress." He also claimed that much of Western philosophy and theology had been borrowed from African mythology. Finally, he countered white assertions of black inferiority in civics by maintaining that national civil government was also borrowed from African society. Like the Arabs, Delany asserted, Europeans had stolen African ideas and innovations, deliberately destroying evidence of their deeds.[57]

Delany's version of black nationalism, then, sought to restore the greatness of Africa's past to gain legitimacy for people of African ancestry throughout the world. According to his plan, spreading Western culture to Africa would help Africans reclaim a position of leadership in the world economically by discouraging the slave trade and encouraging legitimate commerce. He sometimes used religious justification for his plan, but for the most part, he viewed religion as a stifling, conservative force that encouraged submissiveness in blacks. He also believed that white missionaries had already done a thorough job of planting Western religion in Africa, and he warned that black leaders needed to replace

Europeans there before the conservative force of religion aided white moneyed interests and government leaders in taking over Africa for selfish purposes. If that happened, he warned, Africans would be "shoved aside and compelled to take subordinate and inferior positions, if not, indeed, reduced to menialism and bondage." According to Delany, such a process had already begun, bringing "missionary efforts to their *maximum* and native progress to a pause."[58]

Delany insisted that only black Americans could aid Africans in the pursuit of cultural and economic advancement because of their unique position in the world. Unlike whites, they could identify with racial oppression, and they had a direct interest in the well-being of other blacks. As long as whites failed to make distinctions among blacks, the most "downtrodden" of the race would continue to be held up as the norm, so it was in the direct interests of men of Delany's position to uplift others.[59]

* * *

Because of their Western outlook, emigrationists who chose Africa made a number of grave errors. Emphasizing their racial connection to the indigenous people, they assumed a natural right to lead Africa's struggle to reclaim its ancient greatness. Seeking a natural affiliation with Africa, these early pan-Africans stressed the common ancestry of blacks and called on them to see a common oppression and unite in a larger struggle for freedom for all. Believing the reports of white explorers who wrote about Africa, they assumed that the continent needed to be uplifted and that they, because of their ancestry, possessed "those elements of power, mental and moral, which fit them to share in the glorious work of Africa's redemption." They also assumed that the "natives" shared their pan-African enthusiasm and truly wanted their help.[60]

Though Delany hoped to change some aspects of African culture, his main emphasis was on economic progress. Throughout his *Official Report*, which he wrote after returning from his exploratory trip to Africa, he discussed African agriculture and industry, praising some aspects and offering suggestions for improvements in others. He reported extensive cultivation of crops as well as industrial and commercial development and claimed that Africans themselves had already laid the groundwork for his regeneration efforts. Citing achievement in a number of areas, he claimed that their industrial and agricultural abilities were evidence of their potential. He called particular notice to their use of division of labor in the production and exportation of palm oil, and he defended them against erroneous travel narratives that described their methods as primitive. Such progress, according to Delany, demonstrated that Africa was on its way back to greatness. All that was needed was the assistance of "intelligent" leaders with knowledge of contemporary commerce and world politics to help bring it to the final stages of regeneration.[61]

Delany's reverence for Western culture caused him to fail to appreciate African culture and left him guilty of imperialistic behavior, as African historian Tunde Adeleke has argued. Like white colonizationists, Delany too easily managed to convince himself that Africans accepted his presence and welcomed his leadership. In his travel account he recounted instances of native merchants seeking his advice, and he described what he perceived as a pact between himself and a number of Abeokuta chiefs to create a pan-African partnership to fend off white corruption and imperialism. According to the agreement, "select and intelligent" members of the African American community would emigrate to Africa to ensure "the regeneration of our race from the curse and corrupting influences of our white American oppressors." If they could succeed, deliberate white suppression of black creativity and independence would be over after five hundred years.[62]

The treaty that Delany signed with the chiefs included elements of both partnership and autonomy for the settlers. The chiefs agreed to allow Delany's colonists to settle "in common" among them, and Delany promised that his settlers would be chosen from the most talented American blacks and would bring knowledge and practical skills to aid in African development. The settlers would respect native laws, and both parties would work together to settle matters that involved both groups. However, it stipulated that "all matters, requiring legal investigation among the settlers, [would] be left to themselves, to be disposed of according to their own custom." The ambiguous wording of the treaty leaves it unclear whether Delany actually planned for his settlers to disperse among the native population, or whether he truly planned to create a colony, which would by nature require not only self-government, but also possession of their own land, an idea foreign to native custom. As Robert Levine has pointed out, almost every aspect of Delany's plan, and, I would add, this treaty, duplicates "the European 'founding' of America, with all that it portended for natives and other subjugated groups." It is not likely that Delany saw this irony, though. Like white Americans who had been settling the western United States in earnest throughout his lifetime, he was on a mission backed by a belief in "Manifest Destiny."[63]

Like most paternalistic imperialists who think they have a higher purpose, Delany saw the regeneration of Africa as beneficial to Africans as well as to blacks throughout the international community. His emphasis on the talent and abilities of his elite settlers demonstrated the seriousness of his work. The sense of confidence that their accomplishments would engender in the black international community was crucial, Delany believed, because "people never entertain proper opinions of themselves until they begin to act for themselves."[64]

The best way to achieve self-sufficiency, according to Delany, was to grow cotton and enter into a trade partnership with Great Britain, the world's largest consumer of that that commodity. Of course, this plan led him to once again turn to whites. He had praised England as "the present masterpiece of the world" in a *North Star* article in 1848, portrayed the British as allies in the freedom struggle in *Blake*, and suggested in *Condition, Elevation, Emigration* that the English might be called upon for funding assistance. Even so, however, he remained ambivalent. Early in his *Official Report*, he showed irritation toward Campbell for seeking British financial assistance, claiming no knowledge of his partner's plans until after the fact. Perhaps influenced by Campbell's success, however, Delany began to allow himself to hope that the British, who had already abolished slavery in the empire, might prove a viable partner.

By this time he was in desperate need of funds to carry out his plans, and many American blacks, like Campbell, had enjoyed hospitality in Britain. Part of a transatlantic abolitionist crusade, these black leaders had all gone to Britain to seek support in a number of antislavery ventures, and most segments of the British population had been quite willing to help. The British attended lectures in impressive numbers, made generous donations to a number of causes, financed educations for blacks, bought freedom for fugitives, and rejected the ACS once American blacks convinced them that the group's main goal was not to end slavery. They had even shielded fugitive slaves William and Ellen Craft from American slave catchers, preventing them from becoming "the first victims . . . under the Fugitive Slave Law." Accordingly, as he had done throughout his career, Delany once again allowed his optimism to overshadow his understanding of the depth of white racism.[65]

Delany also let his faith in economics affect his judgment. A strong believer in the power of money, he had already decided that Britain and America were able to dominate the world because of their economic partnership, and he had always believed that capitalism was stronger than racism. Thus, he was able to convince himself that British economic ties to America were stronger than cultural ties, and that Britain continued to rely indirectly on bound labor only in the absence of a viable alternative. He had begun to formulate this idea in the early 1850s, arguing that "Great Britain is decidedly a commercial and money-making nation, and counts closely on her commercial relations with any country. That nation or people which puts the largest amount of money into her coffers, are the people who may expect to obtain her greatest favors." This perspective allowed him to believe that British racism could be overcome with the prospect of more advantageous commercial ties. Accordingly, he adopted the view he had once expressed in *Blake* that "the English . . . have sympathy for the Negro because he is oppressed: but never help those, in a general sense, who don't help themselves." Concluding that British help was merely auxiliary to his work, he claimed that "the English must see that something is done before they'll recognize the doer."[66]

Delany was overly optimistic, however, in his faith that the alliance he sought between black American leaders, African laborers, and British money would be an equal partnership. Stressing that British support was an investment rather than charity, he contended that "the British people have the fullest confidence in our integrity to carry out these enterprises successfully. . . . [T]here are to be nothing but business relations between us." Unfamiliar with, or eager to forget, the fate of black would-be leaders in Sierra Leone, he added that his new partners had "entire confidence . . . in the self-reliant, independent transaction of black men themselves." Perhaps to reassure himself as much as others, he added, "We are expected, and will be looked for, to create our own ways and means among ourselves as other men do." British imperialism in Africa, however, was already beginning, and his crusade for help did nothing more than support the arguments of British cotton interests that Africa was worth taking.[67]

The problems with Delany's proposed emigration scheme were multifaceted. The financial difficulties that forced him to rely on white support were only one factor in his lack of success. Despite support from the public in Britain, British racism remained an obstacle. By the time Delany arrived in Lagos, whites from a number of countries were already moving into Africa, and as soon as the treaty had been signed with the Egba of Abeokuta, Henry Townsend, a leader of the Church Missionary Society of Britain, began a campaign of opposition. Townsend, believing that blacks were not qualified to lead themselves, and unwilling to face competition, stressed that a colony such as Delany's would threaten

British missionary interests in the area. At the same time British cotton interests saw Delany's colony and its African laborers not as equal partners but as an exploitable source of labor.[68]

In addition to lacking monetary support, Delany's colony, like the ACS's, was planned on the faulty assumption that Western culture was superior and needed to be spread throughout the world. Building on his theory of worldwide conspiracy, he insisted that, by holding black progress down, whites had prevented them from enjoying the benefits of modernity, or "Western" civilization.[69]

For the most part Delany emphasized the need for economic rather than cultural change, but he did criticize some aspects of African culture. He believed that to become a world leader, Africa would have to dispense with those practices that elicited scorn from the rest of the world, including the practice of eating on the floor and wearing little clothing. Not only was such behavior considered unmannerly in his worldview, but his training as a physician may have led him to regard it as unhealthy. Indeed, his exploration account includes many comments on local sanitation. He also criticized ethnic conflicts in Africa that hindered trade, and he wrote scornfully of human sacrifice; he was more concerned, however, with erasing differences among blacks to create a unity that would bring the race back to a position of greatness.[70]

He was eager to include Africans as partners in his scheme, but he insisted that they would have to adopt the manners, lifestyle, and worldview essential to his cause. Because he was a product of a Western, middle-class worldview, he could not help but see some aspects of African culture as "primitive," and he feared that those aspects, like many of American slave culture, would reflect negatively on the international black community. Unlike whites, he did not have the luxury of recognized class and cultural distinctions within his ethnic community. Where he came from, a "degraded" white was seen as an exception, whereas a "degraded" black was seen as typical.

Delany's contempt was not reserved for African culture. As his emigration plans evolved, he always assumed that indigenous populations, whether Cuban, Haitian, or African, welcomed his leadership. Like his contemporaries, he failed to question the morality of cultural domination. Coming from a country that still sought the subjugation of Native Americans in the West and celebrated the European conquest of most of North America, Delany had learned to look on all "less advanced" cultures with scorn. Experience had taught him that independence relied on ownership of the means of production, and, encouraging his readers to emigrate, he told them to go "with the fixed intention—as Europeans came to the United States—of cultivating the soil, entering into mechanical operations, keeping of shops, carrying on merchandise, trading on land and water, improving property—in a word—to become the producers of the country instead of the consumers."[71] Because his goal was to "uplift" the entire race, he assumed that every member would enjoy benefits of his work.

Had Delany spent more than a few months in Africa, perhaps he would have come to appreciate indigenous cultures more and modified his Western outlook. Much of his writing reveals that contact with Africa heightened his racial pride, and he pointed out in a number of places that Africa was on the way back into the mainstream of historical progress. In fact, he praised African efforts at educational attainment in both *Condition, Elevation, Emigration* and his *Official Report*, maintaining that, "though benighted enough, even to an apparent hopeless degeneration, [Africa] is still the seat of learning, and must some day rise, in the majesty of ancient grandeur, and vindicate the rights and claims of her own children, against the incalculable wrongs perpetrated through the period of sixty ages by professedly enlightened Christians, against them." He further emphasized the unique role of Africans in bringing about an international uplift of their race in *Blake*, asserting that once they proved their equality with whites, American blacks of all shades would be seen as equals.[72]

* * *

Delany's antebellum emigration plan, based on the idea of select rather than mass emigration and intended to further black economic self-reliance and support for the Free Produce agenda, was, in the final analysis, a far-fetched scheme to prove black equality and self-leadership capability through an African "city on a hill." By also emphasizing the need to spread Western values and civilization, as well as legitimate commerce, throughout the world, Delany's plan shared much with Cresson's and Coates's version of colonization. It also differed from the ACS agenda. First, though the ACS as an organization remained ambiguous about whether all American blacks should go or not, Delany, like Forten before him, did not support the idea of mass exodus of blacks from the United

States. Also like Forten he remained adamant that any settlement geared to black uplift had to be led by black men. That is why even when it appeared he might support the ACS he ultimately chose not to. His plan, like the ACS's, was based on the idea that Western culture was the most advanced or "enlightened" and that Africa, though once great, needed to be regenerated, but in his view only blacks could lead in its restoration.

8 / "Maybe the Devil has got to come out of these people before we will have peace": Assessing the Successes and Failures of Pennsylvania's Competing Antislavery Agendas

According to a July 4 sermon delivered by William Henry Ruffner in 1852, Liberia had given blacks a place to succeed, free of racial prejudice, where their talent and merit were indeed recognized. Thanks to the progress of black Americans who were now succeeding in Liberia, "whole nebulae of phrenological speculations and scientific infidelities have thus been dissipated; and there, star-like, shines out the negro intellect, clear and bright." Black achievement was making it harder and harder for whites to justify slavery. At the same time, the outlet Liberia provided had encouraged many manumissions. Indeed, the years between 1841 and 1860 saw over twice as many American Colonization Society manumissions as had occurred between 1820 and 1840.[1]

From this assessment, the colonization society could be credited with helping both slaves and free blacks in the United States. Whether white Americans were any more willing to accept black equality in the 1850s than they had been in the 1820s was up for debate, though evidence such as the Dred Scott decision shows that it was highly unlikely. Sending conditionally freed settlers, however, had allowed philanthropists in the movement to convince themselves that they were contributing to the fight against human bondage. The specific-case tactic of telling donors exactly whom they helped free also carried a tremendous human-interest appeal. Whether the ACS or the Pennsylvania Colonization Society realized it, however, focusing on the enslaved had another important function. It allowed them to obtain colonists from the most

FIGURE 10. "A Printing Press Demolished," from the Anti-Slavery Almanac, 1839. (Courtesy of the Library Company of Philadelphia.)

likely source—those who had little choice. Thus the society could at least appear to thrive in the absence of voluntary free black emigrants, and colonizationists could keep telling themselves and others that their cause was successful. But was it?

As Eric Burin has shown, the efforts of the PCS and the Young Men's Colonization Society of Pennsylvania did foster manumission. By 1854 the group had helped send nearly five hundred blacks from other states to Liberia. Most of these were from the South and had been slaves before emigrating. Some of these bondspersons had been purchased by the PCS so they could go to Liberia with their families. Indeed, at this point, Pennsylvania colonizationists had funded the emigration of many more slaves than it had free blacks from Pennsylvania. Many had been owned by North Carolina Quakers who kept them in a state of semifreedom. Their situation was much milder than that most slaves faced, yet they were still owned legally as property. These Quakers faced the same situation that many others had throughout the years. In fact, many slave owners had been in touch with the Pennsylvania Abolition Society over the years, hoping the gradualists would help them find safe and legal ways to free slaves they no longer wanted to keep in bondage but could not legally free. The North Carolina group came into contact with the PCS primarily through Elliott Cresson, and, as we saw, much of his work with the PCS was for the benefit of Quaker-owned North Carolina slaves.[2] The antislavery work of the PCS, though minuscule in terms of the actual number of people freed, was "symbolically important, rhetorically valuable, and psychologically comforting."[3]

The PCS's change in focus from slaves to free blacks, however, changed the movement. Most obviously, it removed emancipation from the equation and essentially allowed Mathew Carey's vision of colonization to triumph over Cresson's. The focus on free emigrants also lent credence to the claim, made by immediatists, that the ACS supported compulsory removal. The evidence, however, does not clearly support this assertion. Free blacks, abolitionists, and some historians have repeatedly accused the colonizationists of wanting to forcefully remove free blacks all along, but the Pennsylvania group had been so busy focusing on manumission that this was not likely the case, especially in the early years. Nevertheless, James Forten and William Lloyd Garrison made this argument on several occasions and often managed to use it to win over former supporters of the ACS.[4]

Though abolitionists exaggerated the point, perhaps the idea of forced removal was not so far-fetched. William Freehling has argued that

Henry Clay and Abraham Lincoln both admired a scheme proposed by Thomas Jefferson that would have allocated federal land revenue to fund compulsory emancipation and colonization through a constitutional amendment. The 1820s saw a number of proposals for colonization to be funded by the sale of western land, and nine states passed resolutions for a program of gradual abolition and colonization. At the same time, several Presidents, beginning with Jefferson, pondered the fate of Native Americans until Andrew Jackson solved the issue by forcing the Native Americans of Georgia (most famously the Cherokees) off their valuable tribal lands and onto the less fertile "Indian Territory" of present-day Oklahoma. Slave insurrections made the black population more of a threat in the minds of southerners than the "civilized" tribes sent along the Trail of Tears, and removing the free and the more recalcitrant could indeed secure slavery. Indeed, Robert Forbes has argued that Indian removal "provided the template" for the treatment of free blacks and encouraged antiblack mobs to unleash their fury in Philadelphia, among other places. Coincidentally or not, 339 immigrants from Southampton County, Virginia, embarked for Liberia on December 9, 1831, the same year in which Nat Turner's rebellion had terrorized that very county. Even the PAS, though always more reluctant than immediatists to attack the colonization scheme, expressed a degree of concern. If conditions rendered life for blacks "irksome," the "avenues should be opened for their exportation to other climes." However, the gradualists protested "against compulsion, physical or moral, direct or consequential." As for northern colonizationists, most remained sure a day loomed on the horizon when blacks would want to go, and there is no evidence that they supported forced removal, even after they began to seek more free black emigrants.[5]

More realistically, however, abolitionists and free blacks also blamed colonizationists for trying to create just the type of "irksome" conditions the PAS referred to, in an effort to chase free blacks to Liberia. As for this charge, most northern colonizationists, including those in Pennsylvania, share an indirect culpability. Though there is no clear evidence that they participated in the terror tactics perpetrated by much of the public, much of their rhetoric helped justify the racist belief in America as a "white man's country." Kurt Kocher argues that the Pennsylvania group "never, at least in their writings, appealed to racist sentiment," but they did include pieces in the *Herald* that painted a bleak picture of the future of blacks in America.[6]

One of the most detailed articles described blacks as unqualified to

enjoy full citizenship in the United States and explained why their elevation was impractical. First, the number of blacks in the South and the
threat of "ambitious, unprincipled, and designing demagogues" taking
advantage of the situation provided serious hurdles. Handled improp-
erly, chaos, retribution, and anarchy would prevail. Also, social equality
would have to follow political equality, and though both races were of a
"common origin," distinct differences existed. Thus, there must either
be "continued distinction of colour" or "an intermixture, and confusion
of colours." According to the author, the idea of mixture repulsed even
the abolitionists, and the hope that the two populations could exist in
harmony was "utopian." If God wanted the colors to mix, he asked, then
why did he create the difference to begin with? Also, he pointed out that
those who did mix were generally of the less moral sort. Colonization,
however, would provide a real chance at uplift. In Liberia, the black's will
"shall operate as efficiently as any other in the enactment of laws and in
the appointment of officers." The settler's "way shall be unembarrassed
and open," which "is not a matter of reasonable expectation here." Even
better, God himself had sanctioned colonization when he delivered Israel
from Egyptian bondage. Other articles made similar claims but relied on
"scientific" or medical arguments.[7]

In some cases, even the most humanitarian colonizationists, though
not sanctioning terror tactics, expressed hope that oppression would lead
blacks to their cause. Though the *Colonization Herald* would later call for
the repeal of Ohio's Black Codes, which greatly discouraged blacks from
settling in the state by requiring them to post good-behavior bonds,
Cresson wrote to Gurley in 1829 that his feelings had "been much excited
by observing the expulsion of the blacks . . . and yet—by teaching them
that this is not the place of their rest—that here they can hope for no continuing city—it may be the means of directing the thoughts of these poor
people more generally to Africa." The ACS, he argued, should capitalize
on the situation by sending an agent to share with the exiles "the *views*
of the Colonization Society." At the same time perhaps it could convince
whites there to donate money "for transporting their disenfranchised
citizens to the colony." Two years later, when southern states began ex-
pelling free blacks, Gerrit Smith, still with the ACS, hinted that perhaps
such laws were not too severe.[8]

Kocher is right, however, in claiming that Pennsylvania colonizationists never called for forced compulsion. Immediatist William Jay also exonerated most colonizationists from the charge. He saw statements like
those above as evidence that good men who "would be horrified at the

idea of their agents scouring the country, and seizing men, women, and children, placing them on the rack, till as joint after joint was dislocated, the suffering wretches *consented* to go to Africa" had become numb "to the cruel persecution which their Society necessarily encourages." Even the author of the *Colonization Herald* article described above concluded that blacks would have to be convinced, rather than forced, to go. Describing northern blacks as content with menial jobs, he complained that "they do not value liberty, and the means of personal elevation and self-government." He added that they would gain incentive, however, once free blacks went to Liberia, succeeded, and set a good example. What Liberia needed most was a black William Penn or George Washington. Nevertheless, the type of legislation Cresson and Smith failed to condemn forced blacks to become "voluntary" emigrants.[9]

By not condemning exclusionary efforts, colonizationists also allowed others to commit atrocities in the name of the movement. One example was the Prudence Crandall case. Another occurred in Columbia, Pennsylvania. There citizens called a public meeting and adopted a series of resolutions. First, they pledged not to "purchase any articles that can be procured elsewhere, or give our vote for any office whatever, to any one who employs negroes to do that species of labor white men have been accustomed to perform." After that they resolved that "the Colonization Society ought to be supported by all the citizens favorable to the removal of the blacks from this country." A night or two after the meeting a mob assembled and destroyed a black home and lumber business. Jay attributed the unrest to the colonization society. By offering to transport all who would consent to go, the society only encouraged such acts, even if indirectly.[10]

The YMCSP responded with a lengthy rebuttal in the *Colonization Herald*. First, it argued that the ACS did not deliberately encourage racism but merely showed the "degraded" nature of blacks to gain support in its efforts to save them. Since it believed existing prejudices left equality unattainable, it had to use brutal honesty to awaken other white philanthropists to the cause. Before reading Jay's book, the group knew nothing of the Columbia resolutions, which it referred to as "unjust and cruel," and it expressed "no sympathy" for those who put them forth. The organization also chastised Jay for attributing the action to colonizationists and argued that though he showed that the perpetrators "had approved the society," he "failed to show that the society had countenanced the persecutors." The YMCSP conceded that "some men when engaged in acts of oppression have called on the name of colonization" but insisted that the movement was not "accessory to the crimes they committed." After all, "the greatest villainies have been perpetrated, in all ages, under pretense of the holiest sanctions."[11]

Jay did realize this distinction. As the immediatist cause gained ground in the 1830s, the public became increasingly agitated, and mob violence broke out in several places, including New York and Philadelphia. Since many agitators professed to support colonization, some abolitionists blamed the violence on the society without realizing that if so many truly supported the cause, the society's coffers would not be so empty. Still a colonizationist at the time, Gerrit Smith lamented, "There is a great deal of talking for our Society—but that is a cheap commodity." Jay realized that though many claimed to support the ACS, it did not make them active and contributing members, but he still found the ACS indirectly responsible. "That the pious, and respectable members of the Society detest the horrible outrages, recently committed upon these people in New York, Philadelphia, and elsewhere, it would be both foolish and wicked to doubt," yet "no one who candidly and patiently investigates the whole society can fail to be convinced that these outrages never would have happened, had the Society never existed."[12]

Historian Leonard Richards, however, tried to link the rioting more directly to the ACS. According to Richards, participants in most of the riots "openly identified with African Colonization" or "shouted colonization vows." Leaders of an 1835 uprising in Utica "included leading local colonizationists," and a Cincinnati mob of 1836 "included most of the city's prominent colonizationists." In few of his examples, however, did he identify specifically who all of these rioters were and how exactly they were affiliated with the ACS or any of its auxiliaries. The only clear example he offered is the case of James Watson Webb, a colonizationist editor from New York and instigator of the 1832 riot there. This was likely the only clear example Jay found as well, because he concluded that aside from "certain editors," there was no real evidence that the rioters were actual members of the colonization society.[13]

Linking the riots to colonization rather than general anti-abolition sentiment, however, Richards insisted that Garrison's denunciation of slavery drew little attention, but his criticism of the ACS sparked violence. When Garrison simply attacked slavery, "some colonizationists fumed secretly," but when he formed the New England Anti-Slavery Society and caused chaos for the colonization society, trouble began. Mass desertion of supporters, Cresson's defeat in England, Wilberforce's signing of the ACS denunciation, and falling July 4 collections led colonizationists to resort to mob action. According to his estimates, colonizationists constituted 50–70 percent of the mobs. Unlike Jay, however, Richards did not clearly account for the difference between professing colonizationist beliefs and actually being a member of the society. As the abolitionist cause met more and more resistance, it was easy for those who resisted to use colonization to legitimize their rioting, but certainly there were no Mathew Careys, Elliott Cressons, Leonard Bacons, Gerrit Smiths, or Benjamin Coateses in the mobs. Nor did anyone need to stir the masses into action. Anti-abolition was a grassroots movement of its own, and Richards admitted that some of his "supporters," such as Webb, never really were "true believers" in the cause. He even quoted Webb as admitting he supported colonization just because it provided a good barrier against abolition.

If abolitionist rhetoric drew fury on its own, then, would the riots have occurred in absence of the colonization society? The ACS gave the rioters a sense of legitimacy, but they would have attacked either way. Their quickly adopted colonization principles were just an afterthought. Furthermore, John Runcie, focusing on the Philadelphia riots, concluded that the city had no equivalent to Webb and that in the attack he studied "no prominent colonizationists took part in the riot, no rioters shouted colonization slogans as they destroyed negro property, and there is no proof that the society was responsible for organizing the mob."[14]

Other studies support the idea that the riots resulted from violent times made more dangerous by tense rhetoric. According to David Johnson, the era was "one of the most gang-plagued periods in urban history," a time in which "racial antagonism kept the ghetto area in turmoil for years." Runcie places the 1834 riot within this context by arguing that the mob included mostly the young and poor, many of whom had criminal records for offenses such as disorderly conduct. He concluded that labor tension motivated this unrest. Leonard Curry agrees that much mob activity in both Pittsburgh and Philadelphia resulted from "the resentment of abolitionist agitation and the ill-defined belief that the antislavery movement in some way constituted a threat to the white workingmen." As we saw in our discussion of Forten, social jealousy toward well-to-do blacks also played a role.[15]

The high tide of violent anti-abolition receded in 1837, but Philadelphia's most notorious incident occurred a year later with the attack on Pennsylvania Hall. The mob that attacked the hall and then turned its fury on the Quakers' Shelter for Colored Orphans and a black church was clearly motivated by anti-abolitionist sentiment as well as racial hatred. It was the PCS recorder, Richard Rush, however, who helped stop the crowd from attacking another black church.[16] The PCS expressed pride in Rush's actions and disgust with the mob's attack on the orphanage. As for the hall, colonizationists, irritated with what they saw as rashness and silliness displayed by both sides, expressed neither condemnation nor countenance. They attributed the violence to lower-class whites stirred up deliberately by abolitionists looking for a confrontation. As we saw earlier, Cresson served as foreman on the grand jury that investigated the incident. Attributing the affair to abolitionist agitation, they recommended not rebuilding the hall. Though not at all likely to have participated in the attack, Cresson helped prevent the owners from seeing justice served. In his mind, however, the immediatists caused the disturbance by the same rash and pushy behavior that had turned colonizationists like himself and Coates off from the beginning.[17]

In terms of coerced removal, then, colonizationists were indirectly culpable. Regardless of their motives, they had introduced a scheme easily co-opted by a wide variety of people for a large range of reasons. Their focus on the degraded condition of blacks fed into the growing racism of the time, and their removal scheme offered an established agenda to hide behind. Although the PCS shared in this blame because, like all other auxiliaries, it employed the degradation argument, it remained focused primarily on emancipation until 1857. Members such as Cresson and those he enlisted in this antislavery cause remained busy trying to collect donations of money and goods for the colonists and secure the freedom of slaves, in family units when possible. Free blacks were of secondary concern to them. Charles Sydnor concluded his study of Mississippi by arguing that "had there been no free negro class in Mississippi, the Mississippi Colonization Society would probably not have been created." Conversely, had there been no slaves in the United States, the PCS would never have gained the strength it did. Without the moral force of antislavery, it would never have become one of the most powerful auxiliaries in the nation.[18]

Also, when assessing the growth in racial antagonism, it must be realized that immediatists, though doing more than any other group to secure black equality and uplift in the United States, also inadvertently fed into the violent times. The PAS was more palatable to the public because gradualist work was more behind the scenes and, as a result, easier to ignore. Immediatists, however, worked hard to make sure they could not be ignored. Their calls, not only for black freedom, but also for true racial equality and integration, led the resistance to show the depths of its ugliness. Unfortunately, calls for social change often cause resistance from those who either have no reason to embrace the proposed changes or benefit from existing conditions. Also, radical stances, such as the immediatists' public displays of interracial unity and professed willingness to die for the cause, no matter how admirable when put forth for such an important cause, often alienated moderate supporters. As we saw with the attack on Pennsylvania Hall, rioters often set out to get abolitionists but then turned their wrath on the closest objects of abolitionist agitation—free blacks. Each movement set out to correct a terrible evil, but each fell victim to its own tactics.[19]

Although colonizationists called for change, they built their movement around conciliation. In doing so, they left too much room in their agenda. First, their refusal to attack slaveholders left them attractive to some with the sinister motive of removing only the free. Then, their refusal to label slavery a moral evil and prejudice a solvable problem left them attractive to "negrophobes" who tried to use the movement to sanction their terror tactics during what was a very violent time. Indeed, there is an impressive historiography on the anti-abolition climate and the resulting mobbings throughout the country. Many of these angry mobs shouted colonization rhetoric after the violence began and used colonization arguments to justify the attacks. Too often these statements have been taken at face value to conclude that the mobs were made up of colonizationists. I have found, at least in the case of Pennsylvania, that this was not true. What should be remembered is that these were *anti-abolition* mobbings; they took place because the public was resisting the type of changes immediatists wanted to make to the overall racial system.

At the same time, Garrisonians, though advocating moral suasion, peace, and passive resistance, built their movement on confrontation by trying to force Americans to realize that slavery was a sin. They left little room in their movement for conservative men such as Cresson and Coates, who considered themselves "prudent" and "judicious," two of many northern colonizationists' favorite words (and two qualities Garrison claimed to "hate" at the Pennsylvania Hall opening). They were brave enough to describe slaveholders not as victims of an inherited system but as "sinners." Their courage, however, left them unattractive to a broad spectrum and encouraged a level of fury manifested in anti-abolitionist attacks throughout the North. By appealing to emotion they aroused emotion.

Even so, it is easy to forgive immediatists for any role they may have had in escalating the violence. They realized that "sober" patience and case-by-case tactics were inadequate to the cause, and they deserve credit for being willing to put themselves in harm's way and fight in solidarity for black freedom. Thus, this violence served a very important function. It brought to light for the average citizen just what was at stake. Anti-abolition agitation, the murder of Elijah Lovejoy, the assaults on Garrison, the attacks on people who in any way crossed racial lines, and the destruction of Pennsylvania Hall showed the average northern citizen, step by step and little by little, that what was at stake was not just black freedom; it was liberty itself—freedom of speech, freedom of conscience, and freedom of action.

William Ellery Channing, who was a gradual abolitionist, illustrated this point well in an 1836 letter to an immediatist newspaper. He had written much to express his support of antislavery but also his "disapprobation" of immediatists' "spirit and measures." But the increasing violence of the time led him to rethink his position. "Had the abolitionists been left to pursue their object with the freedom which is guarantied to them by our civil institutions; had they been resisted only by those weapons of reason, rebuke, reprobation which the laws allow, I should have no inducement to speak of them again either in praise or censure." However, the violent resistance led him to reconsider by placing abolitionists "on the footing of an injured man" fighting a just fight. "In their persons the most sacred rights of the white man, and the free man have been assailed. They are sufferers for the liberty of thought, speech, and the press, and in maintaining this liberty amidst insult and violence, they deserve a place among its most honored defenders." Importantly, though they met violence, "they have refrained from opposing force to force." Though continuing to support gradual techniques himself and calling on immediatists to tone down their "intolerant tone," Channing concluded that the Garrisonians "stand up for rights which mobs, conspiracies, or single tyrants put in jeopardy."[20]

Immediatists, like civil rights activists of the early 1960s, built their movement on direct action and nonviolence but were brutally attacked by reactionaries in a way that brought each movement respect from whites who would otherwise not have noticed or not have cared. Howard Zinn, a New Left historian and civil rights activist who worked with the Student Nonviolent Coordinating Committee (SNCC) in the 1960s, saw the parallel between his associates and immediate abolitionists. He explained that "they believe, without inflicting violence, and while opening themselves to attack, in confronting a community boldly with the sounds and sights of protest." When considering if this would not inevitably encourage violence, Zinn turned to the words of James Bevel, affiliated with the Southern Christian Leadership Conference (SCLC) and SNCC. "Maybe the Devil has got to come out of these people before we will have peace."[21] That sentiment applies to those who resisted the immediate abolitionists just as well as it applied to southern resisters of civil rights a century later. Immediatists stirred a hornet's nest and encouraged those on the other side of the debate to turn increasingly to violence, but this was probably necessary for the overall antislavery movement to advance. Indeed, as James Loewen has pointed out about the twentieth-century movement, activists often "challenged an unjust law or practice in a nonviolent way," inciting resisters "to respond barbarically to defend 'civilization,' in turn appalling the nation and convincing some people to change the law or practice." This took courage and commitment on the part of both civil rights advocates and the abolitionists who came before them.[22]

Even most white immediatists, however, felt a need to lead in the freedom struggle and assumed that blacks needed their guidance. As Delany's story shows, even some of the most enlightened white antislavery leaders assumed that they would be in charge of the movement and that blacks, enslaved or free, would play auxiliary roles. Most recently, Edlie L. Wong has illustrated this patriarchal outlook in her examination of freedom suits and slave "rescues" in the North. As she has shown, well-meaning white abolitionists often acted on behalf of blacks without consulting them about their own desires. Describing the efforts of white immediatists to help enslaved blacks claim freedom as they traveled with their masters through northern states, Wong tells of cases in which the freedom claimed cost them important family ties. Although it seems logical that slaves would want to seize their freedom at the first opportunity, Wong illuminates a number of cases in which abolitionists gained a slave's freedom but failed to consider that he or she might have a spouse, parents, siblings, or children awaiting his or her return. Using contemporary press accounts, Wong shows that in some cases the media even realized the conundrum and likened abolitionist rescues of some slaves, especially children, to kidnapping. Of course, the abolitionists meant well, but they acted without seeing the results of their actions from the black perspective.[23]

Also, as the well-publicized tensions between Garrison and Frederick Douglass reveal, immediatists may have made a public show of pushing for black equality, but they often fell short of their own professed goals. Waldo E. Martin Jr. has pointed out that, although white abolitionists "were obviously less racist than most of their white con-temporaries . . . they still tended to see and to treat blacks as less than equal." He cites as evidence the fact that "very few blacks" were ever al-lowed prominent roles in either the American Anti-Slavery Society or the American and Foreign Anti-Slavery Society. Also, the "vituperative opposition" of white Garrisonians when Douglass chose to go his own way and express views counter to Garrison's "revealed not only deep disappointment and regret, but an unwillingness to allow Douglass, a black man, to speak his own mind." Douglass resented his treatment at the hands of the Garrisonians, and we saw how Delany regarded many self-appointed white leaders.[24]

Even so, when evaluating the sincerity of abolitionists, black leaders such as Forten unanimously chose immediatist abolitionists, though Delany and some of his colleagues cited Coates's vision of colonization as well-meant. Though suffering from their own patriarchal and often racially biased outlook, Garrisonians as a group made the most efforts to accept and promote black equality. Many black abolitionists rightly criticized their white counterparts for allowing them limited roles in the freedom struggle, but at least they made efforts to reach out. This is the most important respect in which the immediatists get the highest grade, but it would not be a perfect score. Coates shares this high mark for the respect he accorded blacks in general and Joseph J. Roberts and Henry Highland Garnet specifically.[25]

As for the charge of hampering black uplift, the verdict is equally am-biguous. Credit certainly goes to those who blamed colonizationists for spending resources on transporting blacks when the money would have been better spent on helping them gain educations and opportunities in the United States. As Hugh Davis has shown, "Their unwillingness to accept blacks as their equals or to risk censure and possible loss of status and influence by directly challenging the pervasive racism in American society," combined with their "fear of social disorder" and concomitant hatred of the abolitionists, severely limited their benevolent efforts. Yet the reformist group "clearly stood apart" from colonizationists such as Webb, and even Carey for that matter. Despite their shortcomings, hu-manitarian colonizationists "genuinely sympathized with the plight of free blacks and hoped to improve their condition in both Africa and the U.S."[26]

Coates and Cresson offer a case in point. As we have seen, Cresson considered the African Education Society crucial to the overall endeavor of colonization and black uplift, and when that group failed, he worked to encourage church leaders and women to carry its work forward. Cresson appealed to the Episcopal Church and left $5,000 to the mission aid schools that they had agreed to build in Port Cresson, Liberia. He also left $5,000 more to add a collegiate department, in addition to $1,000 to the PCS in general and $4,000 for "work in Liberia." Clearly, education remained his priority. Similarly, Coates joined both the Young Men's Colonization Society of Pennsylvania and the Pennsylvania Abolition Society because of their efforts to educate free blacks; he also contributed funds to the cause of black uplift and education, and these goals were a crucial part of his own colonization plan.[27]

The Presbyterians also contributed to Cresson's and Coates's dream of black higher education. Under their board of education, colonizationists such as Cresson's brother-in-law, John Miller Dickey, founded Ashmun Institute in Oxford, Pennsylvania, to educate future Liberian settlers as well as black preachers and teachers who wished to stay in the United States. The institute, now called Lincoln University, was modeled after the school proposed by the African Education Society in 1829, but it was also to serve the needs of Protestant missionaries in Africa. At a time when even immediatists focused on manual labor education for blacks, those who founded Ashmun emphasized liberal arts, classics, science, literature, and theology.[28]

The Ashmun Institute serves as an important example of colonizationist efforts at black uplift. Cortlandt Van Rensselaer, a New Jersey lawmaker and colonizationist who voted against the 1844 state constitution because it "refused to recognize the political rights of the free coloured population," spoke at the school's opening. Though the constitution he tried unsuccessfully to block left him convinced personally that blacks would never be treated fairly in the United States, he applauded Ashmun's goal of at least trying to help blacks who wanted to stay. "AFRICAN ELEVATION is the aim of the Institute," and "the home work of the Institute, as well as its foreign work is important." It was important, added Ashmun's first president John P. Carter, because even those who stayed were being forced out of white institutions, especially churches. Holding firmly to the colonizationist belief that slavery would eventually end, and that, unless planned and carefully managed, emancipation would bring chaos and destruction, he promised to do what he could for those who insisted on staying. But he also continued to express the importance of providing "a permanent and suitable home" for those hoping to live "beyond the reach of the white man's cupidity and competition."[29]

Of course, the PAS had offered education to free blacks all along, and its sustained efforts at black uplift earn it the most credit. In contrast to the other two groups, the PAS did little to make conditions worse for free blacks and much to improve their lot. It shared the patriarchal outlook of the colonizationists but the immediatists' faith that life could be made better for American blacks in their own homeland. Richard Newman has shown that instead of pronouncing slavery a sin and infuriating, or even scaring, whites of various opinions, the PAS called "for less antislavery talk and more . . . concrete solutions," in the form of laws and court decisions. As the other two groups dramatically fought it out, this group quietly sued for individual freedom on a case-by-case basis, presented memorials to Congress to abolish slavery in areas under its jurisdiction, and educated generations of free blacks, always with the hope that they could eventually gain acceptance in American society. The PAS fought for legislation to secure trial by jury for fugitive slaves, spent hours collecting census information to prove black worthiness, provided legal services in preparing freedom papers, and offered documentary testimony to defend kidnap victims. It also tried to intervene when the state constitution was being revised to disenfranchise blacks. As tensions grew in the 1840s, it renewed such efforts to defend individual freedom and to provide blacks with an education, and it continued this effort after the Civil War. Indeed, the PAS still offers scholarships to black students.[30]

In the overall balance sheet, the colonizationists deserve very low marks in one last category. Even the most humanitarian refused to let themselves see the extent of the mortality at the colony. This was one more area in which the strength of their vision deluded them. The society was made aware of the problem immediately by reports from Sierra Leone. The first American settlers had landed in the British colony and waited there while the ACS procured land for them in what would become Liberia. Fifteen of the eighty-seven settlers died in the first year. This included all but one of the whites on the voyage. As we have seen, the deaths of whites reinforced environmentalist assumptions that whites were not meant to live in Africa. But what of the blacks? After all, this was only the beginning, and mortality rates continued to skyrocket. Tom Schick found that between 1820 and 1843, 4,571 emigrants arrived but only 1,819 were still living there at the end of the period.[31]

The ACS and its auxiliaries all handled the mortality issue with a tragic sense of stubborn righteousness. In 1830 the parent group sent two doctors to try to alleviate some of the sickness. Even so, people kept dying, and word of the deaths began to trickle back to the general American population, sometimes hampering agents' efforts in the field. In late

1831, John Crosby, the agent in charge of Pennsylvania, wrote to ask Gurley if reports of recent mortality were true.[32]

Such reports were circulating in both the United States and England, and a Bristol man with experience in African shipping sent Cresson a prescription for alleviating the problem. His advice, reprinted by the society in 1832, had kept the crew of the *Cambridge* healthy for ninety days as they loaded cargo at Sierra Leone, even as men on nearby ships died. He warned that to be safe, people must go inside before the sun set and stay out of the night air. For those who had to be out at night, smoking tobacco could help fight illness. All would benefit from "liberal allowances" of coffee, and, perhaps most important, chloride of lime should be used to keep everything clean.[33]

To see for themselves, the society ordered their own medical investigation in 1832. The report blamed acclimatization, or "seasoning" for the high death rate and concluded that emigrants from northern states suffered the highest mortality because they would not have been exposed to malaria before. Other factors that encouraged mortality were arrival during the wet season and staying too close to the coast. As a result some colonizationists called for more careful planning of expedition arrival dates and the relocation of settlements further inland.[34]

At the same time, however, they downplayed the death rate. Personal correspondence, articles in the *Repository*, and speeches at annual meetings emphasized over and over that early settlers in Virginia fared even worse. Nevertheless, Crosby warned Gurley that the society should provide agents more realistic reports "to keep them from *extravagant representations*." Instead, Gurley and most others continued to convince themselves that Liberia had a healthful climate that just took adjusting to and prudent behavior from the settlers.[35]

The YMCSP tried to take steps to reduce mortality when founding their colony. Cresson researched possible locations and wrote that a colonial doctor described Bassa Cove as "very healthy," so that is where "*our* colony ought to be." When explaining to the public why they chose the area, the Pennsylvania group listed its healthy location first. Then, to show that their colony was safer, they kept careful records on causes of death and printed positive reports from those, like *Margaret Mercer* first mate Emanuel Elliott, who had been in Africa nearly seven years.[36]

As Schick argues, the problem lies not in the society's failure to solve the disease issue but rather in their refusal to stop sending people to what "came closer to being a death sentence than the start of a new life." As Schick and Burin have shown, colonizationists remained absolutely convinced they were doing God's work. Thus, states Burin, their "ideological rigidity left them impervious to evidence that conflicted with their preconceived views." Death became, in Schick's words, simply the "trials and tribulations" of God. Finally, the whole foundation of the project rested on success in Liberia and to admit the death rate would have been the end of the ACS.[37] Burin attributes colonizationists' refusal to reevaluate their agenda to the same psychological phenomenon Wong attributes to the immediatist disconnect from reality in the cases of the freedom suits—cognitive dissonance. According to Leon Festinger, the architect of this theory, cognitive dissonance occurs when people "find themselves. . . having opinions that do not fit with other opinions they hold." One way to deal with this situation is "selective exposure," which basically involves avoiding information that conflicts with the original theory.

In our example, both groups were fighting to end human bondage through the means they had identified as most viable. To colonizationists that means was resettlement. To immediatists it was direct action. Evidence should have led colonizationists to a number of new opinions about the effectiveness of their solution. Most obviously they should have considered the mortality rate at the colony. Similarly, as we saw with the Pennsylvania Hall incident, direct confrontation did not always lead to the "moral suasion" Garrison and his followers sought. Instead, it often led to attacks on abolitionists and on black bystanders, and as Wong shows, the familial separation that abolitionists often blamed slaveholders for causing. In both cases, advocates for the enslaved remained convinced that their solution was the best, but they were presented with evidence that should have caused them to reevaluate their theory. Instead, they overlooked the problems in their logic. At issue was the advocates' assumption that they knew what was best for others. What resulted were efforts to make decisions for, and in some cases seek to control, those they hoped to help "for their own good." This is well illustrated in my analysis of Delany's novel *Blake*.[38]

* * *

There are two other questions to address while considering the long-term effects of the colonization movement. First, was the effort to create a new life for black Americans in Liberia successful, despite the death rate? Second, how did the creation of Liberia affect the indigenous populations in the region and African development more generally?

In regard to the first question, early studies such as Dickson Bruce's and Mary Tyler McGraw's showed that, though blacks who came to embrace colonization did so out of hopes for independence and national identity, their hopes were not realized. Bruce concluded that "a 'national identity' was not something to be imposed by others, and . . . the Colonization Society sought to do just that." Similarly, McGraw argued that the interest blacks showed in the 1820s when they thought Liberia would offer them a chance at self-leadership dampened when negative reports began to indicate the lack of leadership opportunity for black settlers. At that point, she concludes, immigration began to dwindle, and most settlers were manumitted slaves. This brings us to Burin's main point, which is that colonization did bring freedom to six thousand people who would otherwise have remained in bondage.[39]

Claude Clegg also examined these questions in *The Price of Liberty: African Americans and the Making of Liberia* (2004). In terms of manumission he agrees with Burin that resettlement offered an outlet to many slave owners who wanted to free their slaves but could not, due either to their own fears or the laws of their states of residence. He also offers conclusions about Liberia that mirror in many ways Ellen Gibson Wilson's claims about Sierra Leone. Collectively these authors show that blacks who settled in these colonies took with them uniquely American attitudes about liberty that influenced the way they saw and dealt with their African neighbors. Importantly, Clegg focuses on the fact that the settlers who went to Liberia chose to do so, whether they started out enslaved or free, and, once there, worked to create a society that embodied their own American values.[40]

Basil Davidson has argued convincingly that this transfer of Western cultural bias to Africa was indeed quite harmful to indigenous populations. He showed that the recaptives who had been saved from slavers by the British ultimately embraced an idea of British superiority that caused them, and the nations they created in Africa, to suffer from an inferiority complex. According to Davidson, "The recaptives were all absolutely African in their origins; and yet they were divided from Africa by an acute experience of alienation. Africa had sent them into slavery," but Europe "had rescued and set them free." These Africans were exposed to European culture only briefly. Those who had spent their lives in North America were even more likely to venerate the Western culture they were reared in and to try to spread it to Africa, as Clegg and Wilson have shown.[41] The historiography on Martin Delany illuminates this point.

As a number of historians have shown, a Western cultural bias, shared by white and black Americans alike, led both races to participate in the cultural imperialism of their day. Tunde Adeleke, a historian from Nigeria, argued strongly that black Americans shared the guilt of American cultural imperialism. He accused them of seeking to "enhance the fortunes of the black American elite class . . . and the Europeans, at the expense of indigenous Africa." Another African historian, Monday Abasiattai, has been more forgiving. He explained that black emigrants in both Sierra Leone and Liberia emigrated in hope of achieving "unfettered freedom" and that Liberians were ultimately successful in this endeavor because the American government, unlike the British, did not interfere. He argued that "Liberia's success is due largely to the fact that the ACS was a philanthropic organization and the United Sates had disavowed colonialism," whereas "Britain was an outright imperial power and had no scruples whatever in colonizing Sierra Leone." Lamin Sanneh, another African historian, also approved of African American efforts, arguing that they brought a legacy from the American Revolution, which he called "antistructure." This new attitude led to the challenging of kings, the overthrow of the slave trade, and the modernization of Africa. Unlike Abasiattai, however, he maintained that efforts in Liberia did not go far enough. He argued that the British colony was ultimately more successful because of the role of the government.[42]

What is clear is that ultimately colonization, despite the different motives of supporters, changed Africa. Sanneh's optimistic argument that the change was for the better offers a relatively happy ending. The points of Adeleke and Davidson concerning the negative cultural effects are just as valid. The slave trade ended, and Western culture reached Africa. The end of the slave trade was unarguably a positive effect, but the spread of Western culture and influence was not necessarily good in the long run.

Remember that not only Carey, Cresson, and Coates but also Forten and Delany clearly sought to transform Africa in ways that they unquestioningly saw as beneficial. But the question is, who was to benefit the most from their visions of African settlement? Western cultural biases were not racially specific. In fact, Adeleke reserves his strongest criticism for "un-African Americans," such as Delany, who, even while looking toward Africa, remained focused on their American identities and citizenship. Robin D. G. Kelley has shown that when black leaders embraced emigration they generally did so after reaching "a point of profound pessimism" that led them to question, though not renounce, their American identities. When they thought about the consequences for Africa, their own patriarchal attitudes led them to see "the imminent return of African Americans as a kind of civilizing mission, bringing Christianity to the heathens and technology and knowledge to the backwards natives."[43]

In the end, what African settlement provided black intellectuals such as Delany, then, was a "freedom dream"—an ideal place where he could envision uplifting the race and exercising his leadership skills, in theory if not in reality. To dismiss it as unrealistic or impractical would be to miss the entire point. As Kelley explains, "Exodus represented dreams of black self-determination, of being on our own, under our own rules and beliefs, developing our own cultures, without interference." It would continue to serve this function for black intellectuals well into the twentieth century.[44]

An overall analysis of the Pennsylvania antislavery movement and its competing components, then, reveals a complicated antislavery environment. First, it is important to remember that all three movements competed for space within the state's (and the nation's) antislavery movement at the same time. It was not a matter of steps in which one replaced another. Sometimes their agendas and work overlapped, but often they conflicted quite publicly. Indeed, bickering between the immediatists and colonizationists led to violence and strife and often caused both groups to at least temporarily lose sight of their true goal—black freedom. Also, members of all three groups, blacks as well as whites, suffered from a degree of paternalistic thinking, but the Pennsylvania Anti-Slavery Society and Benjamin Coates at least made efforts at biracial cooperation while the PCS and most members of the PAS refused to break the conservative mold and challenge society in a more radical sense. In all cases, black Americans continued to push their white sympathizers to take the movement further and fight for both freedom and equality.

Epilogue

What does this story tell us about the relation between antislavery and the end of human bondage? It would seem logical on a superficial glance to assume that the fiery rhetoric of men such as William Lloyd Garrison led to the dissolution of the Union. After all, Garrisonians had been calling for "no union with slaveholders" for decades by the time the war broke out. Because of their more vocal and dramatic tactics, as both Richard Newman and Julie Roy Jeffrey have shown, immediatists did, after all, win the battle for historical memory. Indeed, when most non-historians think about abolition, they picture Garrison.

The immediatists truly did win the battle for historical memory and the right to the title "abolitionist." They were the ones brave enough to see a better social order and to fight for it, even when such a fight clearly put their very lives in danger. Importantly, however, as James Oakes showed by examining the life of Garrisonian-turned-political-abolitionist Frederick Douglass, these "radical abolitionists" played a smaller role than their historiographical presence would indicate because they refused to participate in the political drama that unfolded as the country expanded westward and leaders fought continually over the status of new territories. Instead, their type of antislavery and unqualified civil rights remained in the social arena of moral suasion.

Those who were the most influential in the long run were the ones who were adaptable to both social and political tactics and willing to explore a number of different antislavery avenues. Many of these were

FIGURE 11. "Freedom to the Slave." Philadelphia: Philadelphia Supervisory
Committee, 1863. (Courtesy of the Library Company of Philadelphia.)

African Americans. Though exclusionary antislavery made it to the forefront of the overall movement through the political arena in the 1840s and 1850s, black Americans were able to reshape the movement after the Civil War broke out and push, once and for all, for an immediate and unconditional end to slavery.[1]

What finally became worth fighting for, to the majority of white Americans, was the need to control the black population, not through colonization but through restricting their entrance into the new territories of the west. It was concern for white self-interest that reached the broader public, and the antislavery appeal that resulted gained support not through the American Colonization Society but through the Free Soil and Republican parties. What it shared with colonization was the political agenda pushed by Mathew Carey and Henry Clay, which focused first and foremost on protecting white society and white freedom.

As Matthew Mason has shown in his assessment of politics in the Early Republic, the debates over slavery did not quiet after the American Revolution but instead figured prominently in the years during and after the War of 1812. During this time "a sectionalist, political brand of antislavery was becoming an integral part of Northern sectional identity." Even so, although "almost every Northerner" disliked slavery, "they saw no need to convert opinion to organized action unless the evil they deplored somehow affected them." The first time it did clearly affect them was during Jefferson's presidency, when they became convinced that "slave representation" gave slaveholders a political advantage. At issue was the Three Fifths Clause in the Constitution, which allowed slave states to count their bound laborers as three-fifths of a person for purposes of determining the number of representatives the state would be allowed in the House of Representatives. Northern Federalists were able to point to this clause as evidence that slavery threatened the rights of white citizens even in free states. Mason ties the resentment that grew over this idea to the rise of the first secession threat at the Hartford Convention. Like political colonizationists, northern whites of all stripes, benevolent or merely selfish, could relate to this antislavery sentiment because it was born of what they perceived as their own disenfranchisement.[2]

In addition to this purely self-interested strain of antislavery, however, there was another that would have resonated with abolitionists, especially in border states such as New York and Pennsylvania. As we saw in the early chapters of this book, Quakers and members of the Pennsylvania Abolition Society hoped to distance themselves from the national sin of slavery, but, as Mason shows, the presence of slave dealers and kidnappers in their states made this quite difficult, and the situation made them choose either their antislavery convictions or party and national loyalty. In some cases northern Federalists and even some northern Republicans were willing to "give full vent to their detestation of slavery." As we saw through the experiences of Mathew Carey, however, colonization offered an outlet to many unwilling to go so far as to abandon party loyalty or their faith in the union. By supporting colonization, men such as Carey could be both antislavery and pro-union during the years surrounding the War of 1812, even as more and more people were becoming radicalized by the threat to northern rights posed by "slave representation," which, I would add, was the political version of the "Slave Power" theory. As Leonard Richards has shown, this theory gained prominence during the antebellum years as more and more northerners began to fear that slaveholders had become so corrupted by their power over slaves that they sought to extend physical power over anyone, white or black, who did not share their worldview.[3]

The sectional politics that germinated over the "slave representation" issue intensified as politicians and the public debated the expansion of slavery during the Missouri Crisis of 1819–21. Basically, even though northerners continued to resent slavery and the political power it gave southerners, most had seen Congress's 1808 banning of the slave trade as an important step toward the system's demise. "Received wisdom," as Robert Pierce Forbes has shown, "held that cutting off the supply of slaves was tantamount to ending slavery, since the brutal conditions under which slaves labored inevitably meant that they would soon die out." Whether that was the case or not, ending the trade was enough to appease most Americans who had no direct contact with the system. Once the United States acquired new land, however, slavery, or more precisely the spread of slavery, became central to U.S. politics once again. The debate over whether Missouri, and then other new states, would allow slavery served to highlight the fact that slave interests did indeed derive strength from a system that, if allowed to spread, would perpetuate not only human bondage but also that very same monopoly of power. As Forbes has shown, both leaders and the public in Pennsylvania, especially men who shared Carey's political outlook, "took a leading role in opposing the admission of new slave states."[4]

It should be no surprise, then, that Pennsylvania congressman David Wilmot led the drive to take the exclusionary antislavery we saw in the case study of Mathew Carey back into the political arena by suggesting a proviso that would keep slavery out of the territory gained by the

United States after the war with Mexico (1845 46). Antislavery though not abolitionist, Wilmot's plan gained support in the North, especially from those who had come to deeply resent the power of slave states in the national political arena. This support led to the organization of the Free Soil Party, which broadened the antislavery appeal by bringing together Whigs of the Carey and Clay type, antislavery crusaders of different sorts, and a variety of northerners who had come to resent the power of the South.[5]

In the years following Wilmot's Proviso, exclusionary political antislavery perhaps reached its height through the Know Nothing party, which combined anti-Catholicism, anti-immigration, and antislavery to win support from moderates who wanted the Missouri Compromise reinstated, as well as conservative ex-Whigs who placed preservation of the union above all else. Tyler Anbinder has shown that the latter held numerical advantage in lower North states such as Pennsylvania, where efforts to present themselves as a moderate antislavery alternative would have appealed to political colonizationists. According to Anbinder, it was the firm stance northern members took against the extension of slavery that led to Know Nothing success. Like many other moderates and exclusionary antislavery supporters, most Know Nothings eventually moved into the Republican Party.[6]

If the blatantly exclusionary type of antislavery entered the political arena through resistance to the spread of slavery, the more radical abolition found political expression through the Liberty Party, under the leadership of Gerrit Smith, the New York colonizationist turned immediatist. It began when Smith challenged William Lloyd Garrison by arguing that the Constitution could be read as an antislavery document. Garrison, in contrast, had argued that the Constitution was proslavery and that the government it created was thus illegitimate; therefore, to participate in politics under it was to compromise with evil. Through the Liberty Party, political abolitionists fused Garrison's moral crusade for an end to slavery in all parts of the country with Smith's reinterpretation of the Constitution to offer a new tactic—exercising the vote to choose antislavery leaders.

Few Americans supported Garrison's or Smith's aim of ending slavery throughout the nation, but when antislavery was packaged as a means of defending northern whites from the power of southern slaveholders, it gained a broader appeal. For example, as Reinhard Johnson has shown, political expediency led many Liberty Party supporters to ultimately embrace the Free Soil movement by 1848. These supporters articulated a fear that they shared with the Federalists who organized the Hartford Convention. Whereas the earlier generation had focused on the expanded political powers of slaveholders, many antebellum northerners broadened their critique of southern "Slave Power" to include fear of physical force as well as political power. Much of this fear was a product of the violent anti-abolition climate that fostered the attacks on the press, including the murder of Elijah P. Lovejoy, the attack on Pennsylvania Hall, and the caning of Massachusetts congressman Charles Sumner by South Carolina's representative Preston Brooks on the Senate floor. The violent times led more and more otherwise ambivalent members of the general populace to see abolitionists as the lesser evil and left them more interested in antislavery, even if not abolition itself.[7]

* * *

If the story ended there, the Civil War victory would have been for the exclusionary ideals of Free Soil and the Republicanism that Abraham Lincoln embraced when he ran for the presidency. The quest to control black Americans would then have lived on in further efforts to remove them from the country. But black Americans were unwilling to let that happen. As it was, black leaders were more practical than many white Garrisonians and were willing to participate in an important coalition that allowed them to force Lincoln to change the war goal from that of preserving the union to that of ending human bondage.

Even if southern white Americans distrusted Lincoln for his abolitionist stance, the truth is that he, like the Free Soilers, was antislavery but not abolitionist. He began his career as an avowed supporter of Henry Clay's American System and the brand of antislavery we saw in our discussion of Carey. In 1854, his opposition to the Kansas-Nebraska Act's repeal of the Missouri Compromise heightened his opposition to slavery. Though he repeatedly spoke of his personal dislike for the system and his belief that all humans shared basic rights despite their skin color, what he focused on politically was an exclusionary antislavery that aimed to keep slavery confined to the South. And he often spoke in favor of colonization.[8]

The limitations of Lincoln's antislavery views resulted, not from racial dislike per se, but from his interpretation of the Constitution and political expediency. Lincoln's views on the Constitution were between Garrison's and Smith's. For Lincoln, the Constitution left enough room for the national government to confine slavery to the areas in which it already existed, but it protected slavery in the South. As for his views on colonization, he saw removal to Central America or Africa as a necessary corollary to gradual emancipation. In December 1861, he urged border states to allow the federal government to buy their slaves and free them. To prevent the government from having to care for large numbers of freed dependents he proposed that Congress create colonies for the freed to emigrate to voluntarily. By August of 1862 he had begun to advocate colonization to Central America but continued to insist that emigration must be voluntary rather than compulsory. By the time of his death, however, Lincoln had discarded his colonization plans.[9]

Lincoln was influenced in many ways by American blacks who were unwilling to be controlled by masters or the government. Black abolitionists including Sojourner Truth, Frederick Douglass, and Martin R. Delany all met with the President at different times throughout the war to boldly offer suggestions and advice. Delany's story is of particular interest for our purposes. He abandoned his emigration scheme, partly due to a lack of funding but even more importantly because he saw the Civil War early on as a chance for blacks to earn their own freedom and control their own destiny. Despite initial claims that it would be a war for the union rather than a war to end slavery, he, like most blacks, saw its potential.

Delany had allowed himself all along to indulge in the hope that black uplift might have a chance in America. After all, in his 1854 address at Cleveland he had called for emigration only because he believed that the Fugitive Slave Law had cast into law dangerous legal distinctions based merely on race. He had insisted that the situation could "never be changed except by legislation," and that it was "the height of folly to expect such express legislation, except by the inevitable force of some irresistible internal political pressure." Like other African American intellectuals, he had already cited black service in past wars as a claim to citizenship and equality, and when the Civil War produced the type of pressure he had been hoping for, he extended his self-help philosophy to the battlefield. Seeing that pressure from blacks could influence the goals and outcome of the war, he began to hope that African Americans could prove their worth by actively fighting to enjoy the privileges of American citizenship. Only blacks could make this a successful war for freedom because "the rights of no oppressed people have ever yet been obtained by a voluntary act of justice on the part of the oppressors."[10]

Although the war did not become a war for black freedom until Lincoln issued the Emancipation Proclamation on January 1, 1863, Delany and most other blacks saw it that way from the beginning. The politically minded realized that the brand of antislavery that spurred the war was quite different from the abolition they sought, but they realized that a coalition could be a good start to pushing the issue further. Most leaders determined that blacks had a unique opportunity, as well as an obligation, to turn the fight to preserve the union into a fight against slavery and the war to contain slavery into a war for genuine freedom and equality.[11]

Though initial enthusiasm was dampened by exclusionary policies aimed at keeping them out of the struggle, blacks remained determined to take part. Minor victories during the war years, such as the abolition of slavery in Washington, D.C., the diplomatic recognition of Haiti and Liberia, and the acceptance of black troops, fueled their optimism. As the events of the war unfolded, most blacks began to put aside the persecution of the past decade, becoming determined to contribute to the war effort in a number of ways. Building on black service in previous wars, they pushed for the government to adopt emancipation as a war goal and extend the right to blacks to participate on the battlefield. Some also offered their skills as laborers, scouts, and spies. Finally, after the war was opened to black participation, they expanded their decades-long struggle to employ self-help in the crusade for racial uplift by fighting for the Union and assisting in efforts to educate the freedmen and prepare them for the future. Pennsylvania blacks played important roles in recruiting for, and fighting in, the famous Massachusetts 54th Regiment, and, all in all, 8,612 black Pennsylvanians fought in Union blue. By the end of the war, eleven regiments of the United States Colored Troops had trained in the state at Camp William Penn, the only training camp set up exclusively for black troops.[12]

Even though Abraham Lincoln was not the "Great Emancipator" mythologized in popular history, a number of policies under his administration gave black Americans hope for acceptance in the United States even before emancipation. Delany told his earliest biographer that he immediately saw the potential in the Lincoln administration. As early as 1861 Delany had begun considering the ways in which blacks could contribute to the war effort, and after Lincoln issued the Emancipation Proclamation, Delany made his ultimate decision to stay and fight rather than continue pursuing his unrealistic, utopian dream of moral suasion through emigration. Seeing black leadership as the key, he wrote to Frederick Douglass proclaiming that "the recent recognition of Haiti and Liberia, was due more to the presence of intelligent black representatives from Liberia at Washington than a thousand whites." Optimistically, he added, "If I have one great political desire more than another it is that the black race manage their own affairs instead of entrusting them to others."[13]

Delany's self-help agenda and his recruiting efforts earned him the official leadership role he had pursued throughout his life. He became the first black to be granted a field officer's commission after approaching Lincoln with a plan that would have allowed him to live out the fantasies embodied by his character Blake. According to this scheme, like Blake, Delany would follow the Underground Railroad throughout the South liberating slaves and organizing them in a large-scale uprising against the Confederate States.[14]

In presenting his plans to Lincoln and Secretary of War Edwin M. Stanton, Delany emphasized that he was offering his assistance rather than asking a favor. He had determined that "to wait upon the president at such a time to obtain anything from him could only be realized by having something, [a] plan, to offer the government." He had also decided that to ask "Mr. President, what have you to give me?" would elicit the response "Sir, what have you to offer me?" and he was equipped with the answer. Aware of the barriers to appointing black officers, he suggested "an army of blacks, commanded entirely by black officers . . . to penetrate through the heart of the South, and make conquests, with the banner of Emancipation unfurled, proclaiming freedom as they go, sustaining and protecting it by arming the emancipated [and] taking them as fresh troops." He told Lincoln that his black-led liberation army would "give confidence to the slaves, and retain them to the Union, stop foreign intervention, and speedily bring the war to a close." Although he emphasized what his plan would do for the country when presenting it to Lincoln, he was most concerned with what it would do for African Americans.[15]

* * *

Delany shared this story with his biographer during an optimistic time— a time that had yet to see the resurgence of southern power and the painful death of Reconstruction. By the time Delany was dictating his life story to his biographer, the PAS and Pennsylvania State Anti-Slavery Society were both still working for black civil rights and sharing a growing number of common members. Importantly, the PAS took a major step forward by accepting black members, beginning with the induction of James Forten's son-in-law Robert Purvis in 1842. Through the PAS connection, Purvis and Coates began working together, furthering the cross-racial nature of Pennsylvania's antislavery movement. Coates also worked with the black abolitionist William Still, a PAS member since 1866, in a PAS-sponsored effort to desegregate Philadelphia trolley cars. Even so, he remained dedicated to Africa and African education, especially once his friend and associate Joseph Jenkins Roberts became the president of Liberia College. Indeed, education remained the one positive legacy of colonizationist efforts—whether through Liberia College in Africa or Pennsylvania's Ashmun Institute, renamed Lincoln University in 1866. Though the colonization movement and the PCS still lived on, the idea of African resettlement had been given a serious blow by the state's abolitionists, who fought hard to consolidate civil rights gains in the postwar years and push the movement ever forward.[16]

As Delany looked back on the abolition struggle, his emigration plans, and his wartime service, he must have felt that African Americans had come a long way, and indeed they had. They had participated in all aspects of the antislavery movement. Forten and his generation had worked with gradualists to develop and promote the self-help agenda that Delany's life at this point seemed to personify. Forten's generation and Delany's each considered, and ultimately rejected, colonization and white control of their destiny. Finally, black Americans had played crucial roles in shaping the goals and outcome of the Civil War by forcing the federal government to accept them as citizens and allow them to fight for their own freedom. Though Carey's exclusionary antislavery was what had finally captured the nation's attention, blacks had taken a very active role in pushing for freedom without the condition of removal. Indeed, as Steven Hahn has argued, they may very well have managed to turn the war into "the greatest slave rebellion in modern history."[17] Freedom had been achieved, and, for the time being at least, black leaders could celebrate the triumph of being able to control their own destiny.

Notes

Notes to Prologue

1. Those fire companies that were listed as present by their own records and those of other companies were Columbia Hose Company, Pennsylvania Fire Company, Schuylkill Fire Company, Washington Fire Company, Philadelphia Fire Company, Southwark Engine Company, Hibernia Fire Company, and Northern Liberties Hose Company. The records of the Hibernia Company also list a "Good Intent" Hose Company, but that was likely the Goodwill Fire Company that was later instrumental in saving the Home for Colored Orphans. This list was compiled using the records of the Pennsylvania Fire Company, Washington Fire Company, Philadelphia Fire Company, and Hibernia Fire Company, all available at the Historical Society of Pennsylvania.

2. For a full account of the proceedings, see Samuel Webb, *History of Pennsylvania Hall, Which was Destroyed by a Mob, on the 17th of May 1838* (Philadelphia: Merrihew and Gunn, 1838).

3. Philadelphia Anti-Slavery Society, *First Annual Report of the Board of Managers of the Philadelphia Anti-Slavery Society* (Philadelphia, 1835); Pennsylvania Abolition Society Minutes, 1825–1847, available at the Historical Society of Pennsylvania; Ira V. Brown, *Pennsylvania Reformers: From Penn to Pinchot* (University Park: Pennsylvania Historical Association, 1966), 11–12; Ira V. Brown, "Racism and Sexism: The Case of Pennsylvania Hall," *Phylon* 37, no. 2 (1976):12.

4. PAS Minutes, 1825–47, 271–72.

5. *National Enquirer*, 3 August 1836, 31 August 1836, 2 November 1837, 9 November 1837, 10 June 1837, 24 June 1837.

6. Webb, *History of Pennsylvania Hall*, 22, 31, 33.

7. Ibid., 70, 71, 72.

8. Ibid., 75, 99–100, 74.

9. Ibid., 136.

10. Ibid., 140; *Pennsylvanian*, 18 May 1838, 19 May, 1838; *American Sentinel*, 19

May 1838; *Alexander's Weekly Messenger*, 23 May 1838; Hibernia Fire Company, Record of Fires; Philadelphia Fire Company, Account of Fires.

11. *U.S Gazette*, 23 October 1838.

12. Brown, "Racism and Sexism," 135.

Notes to Introduction

1. Doug Rossinow, *Visions of Progress: The Left-Liberal Tradition in America* (Philadelphia: University of Pennsylvania Press, 2008), 3. I owe a special gratitude to Dan Horowitz for introducing me to Rossinow and his concept of the left-liberal coalition.

2. Herman von Holst, *The Constitutional and Political History of the United States*, vol. 1 (Chicago: Callaghan, 1889), 331; Paul Goodman, *Of One Blood: Abolitionism and the Origins of Racial Equality* (Los Angeles: University of California Press, 1998), 18, 16; Stanley Harrold, *American Abolitionists* (New York: Longman, Pearson Education, 2001), 26.

3. Daniel Walker Howe, *What Hath God Wrought: The Transformation of America, 1815–1848* (New York: Oxford University Press, 2007), 260–61; P. J. Staudenraus, *The African Colonization Movement, 1816–1865* (New York: Columbia University Press, 1961), vii, 28; Hugh Davis, *Leonard Bacon: New England Reformer and Antislavery Moderate* (Baton Rouge: Louisiana State University Press, 1998); Hugh Davis, "Northern Colonizationists and Free Blacks, 1823–1837: A Case Study of Leonard Bacon," *Journal of the Early Republic* 17, no. 4 (1997); George M. Frederickson, *The Black Image in the White Mind: The Debate on Afro-American Character and Destiny, 1817–1914* (New York: Harper and Row, 1971; reprint, Hanover, N.H.: Wesleyan University Press, 1987). All page numbers are to the reprint edition.

4. Davis, *Leonard Bacon*, 35, 56; Davis, "Northern Colonizationists and Free Blacks," 651–77; Eric Burin, *Slavery and the Peculiar Solution: A History of the American Colonization Society* (Gainesville: University Press of Florida, 2005).

5. In addition to his book, see Eric Burin's article, "Rethinking Northern White Support for the African Colonization Movement: The Pennsylvania Colonization Society as an Agent of Emancipation," *Pennsylvania Magazine of History and Biography* 27, no. 2 (2003).

6. Douglas Egerton, "'Its Origin Is Not a Little Curious': A New Look at the American Colonization Society," *Journal of the Early Republic* 5, no. 4 (1985): 463–80; Douglas Egerton, "Averting a Crisis: The Proslavery Critique of the American Colonization Society," *Civil War History* 43, no. 2 (1997): 142–57.

7. Benjamin Franklin, "Observations Concerning the Increasing of Mankind, Peopling of Countries, etc." (Boston: S. Kneeland, 1755).

8. For more on Jefferson and slavery, see the seminal studies—Robert McColley, *Slavery and Jeffersonian Virginia* (Urbana: University of Illinois Press, 1964), and John Chester Miller, *The Wolf by the Ears: Thomas Jefferson and Slavery* (New York: Free Press, 1977). For Jefferson's own words on the subject, see, among other printed collections, Julian Boyd, *The Papers of Thomas Jefferson* (Princeton: Princeton University Press, 1950–1990). For the Jefferson quote, see Thomas Jefferson to John Holmes, 22 April 1820. This letter can be found in all major collections of Jefferson's writings, and also at the Library of Congress website at http://memory.loc.gov/master/mss/mtj/mtj1/051/1200/1238.jpg .

9. Edward R. Turner, *The Negro in Pennsylvania: Slavery, Servitude, Freedom,*

1639–1861 (Washington, D.C.: American Historical Association, 1911). As a Progressive historian, Turner celebrated efforts to improve society through mild tactics. What he calls "abolition," however, modern historians call "emancipation." For the social historians of the later twentieth century, those who called for immediate emancipation are "abolitionists," whereas the gradualists, including colonizationists, are "emancipationists." Thomas E. Drake, *Quakers and Slavery in America* (New Haven: Yale University Press, 1950); A. Leon Higginbotham Jr., *In the Matter of Color: Race and the American Legal Process: The Colonial Period* (New York: Oxford University Press, 1978); Jean R. Soderlund, *Quakers and Slavery: A Divided Spirit* (Princeton: Princeton University Press, 1985); Gary B. Nash and Jean R. Soderlund, *Freedom by Degrees: Emancipation in Pennsylvania and Its Aftermath* (New York: Oxford University Press, 1991); David Brion Davis, *The Problem of Slavery in Western Culture* (Ithaca, N.Y.: Cornell University Press, 1966).

10. Larry E. Tise, *Proslavery: A History of the Defense of Slavery in America, 1701–1840* (Athens: University of Georgia Press, 1987); Joanne Pope Melish, *Disowning Slavery: Gradual Emancipation and "Race" in New England, 1780–1860* (Ithaca, N.Y.: Cornell University Press, 1998) 163.

11. For an example of this, see Beverly Tomek, "'From motives of generosity, as well as self preservation': Thomas Branagan, Colonization, and the Gradual Emancipation Movement," *American Nineteenth Century History* 6, no. 2 (2005): 121–47.

12. James Walvin, *The Black Presence: A Documentary History of the Negro in England, 1555–1860* (New York: Schocken Books, 1972), 12; Peter Wilson Coldham, *Emigrants in Chains: A Social History of Forced Emigration to the Americas, 1607–1776* (Bath, Avon: Bath Press, 1992); A. Roger Ekirch, *Bound for America: The Transportation of British Convicts to the Colonies, 1718–1775* (Oxford: Clarendon Press, 1987). For comparisons between convict and African transportation, see Cassandra Pybus, "Bound for Botany Bay: John Martin's Voyage to Australia," in *Many Middle Passages: Forced Migration and the Making of the Modern World*, ed. Emma Christopher, Cassandra Pybus, and Marcus Rediker (Berkeley: University of California Press, 2007), 92–108, esp. 93–94. See also from the same volume Emma Christopher, "'The Slave Trade Is merciful Compared to [This]': Slave Traders, Convict Transportation, and the Abolitionists," 109–28.

13. Howard Temperley, *White Dreams, Black Africa: The Antislavery Expedition to the River Niger, 1841–42* (New Haven: Yale University Press, 1991); James Walvin, *England, Slaves, and Freedom,1776–1838* (Jackson: University Press of Mississippi, 1986); Mavis Campbell, *Back to Africa: George Ross and the Maroons from Nova Scotia to Sierra Leone* (Trenton, N.J.: Africa World Press, 1993); John Peterson, *Province of Freedom: A History of Sierra Leone, 1787–*1870 (Evanston, Ill.: Northwestern University Press, 1969); James Walker, *The Black Loyalists: The Search for a Promised Land in Nova Scotia and Sierra Leone, 1783–1870* (New York: Dalhousie University Press, 1976); Ellen Gibson Wilson, *The Loyal Blacks: The Definitive Account of the First American Blacks Emancipated in the Revolution, Their Return to Africa, and Their Creation of a New Society There* (New York: G. P. Putnam's Sons, 1976).

14. Richard S. Newman, *The Transformation of American Abolitionism: Fighting Slavery in the Early Republic* (Chapel Hill: University of North Carolina Press, 2002), 23, 25, 4–6, 31. For the role of the French Revolution, see Tise, *Proslavery*.

15. Staudenraus, *African Colonization Movement*, vii, 28; Frederickson, *Black*

Image in the White Mind, 15; Early Lee Fox, *American Colonization Society, 1817–1840* (Baltimore: Johns Hopkins University Press, 1919), 151.

16. Franklin was PAS president while a delegate to the Constitutional Convention. He took a PAS petition calling for an end to the slave trade with him to the convention but chose not to present it when he saw how South Carolina and Georgia reacted to another delegate's proposal to tax imports. Thus, as historian Thomas E. Drake claims, "The Constitution and the Union held more importance than the slavery question." Drake, *Quakers and Slavery in America*, 102. For a general assessment of Whig politics see Daniel Walker Howe, *The Political Culture of the American Whigs* (Chicago: University of Chicago Press, 1979). Egerton also discusses this connection in "Averting a Crisis" and "'Its Origin Is Not a Little Curious.'" For Franklin's role in particular, see David Waldstreicher, *Runaway America: Benjamin Franklin, Slavery, and the American Revolution* (New York: Hill and Wang, 2004).

17. Newman, *Transformation of American Abolitionism*, 2.

18. James Brewer Stewart, *Holy Warriors: The Abolitionists and American Slavery* (New York: Hill and Wang, 1976), 52–66.

19. See Lawrence J. Friedman, *Inventors of the Promised Land* (New York: Alfred A. Knopf, 1975), and Eric Foner, *Free Soil, Free Labor, Free Men: The Ideology of the Republican Party before the Civil War* (New York: Oxford University Press, 1995).

20. Floyd J. Miller, *The Search for a Black Nationality: Black Colonization and Emigration, 1787–1863* (Urbana: University of Illinois Press, 1975); Dickson D. Bruce Jr., "National Identity and African-American Colonization, 1773–1817," *Historian* 58, no. 1 (1995): 15–28; Mary Tyler McGraw, "Richmond Free Blacks and African Colonization, 1816–1832," *Journal of American Studies* 21, no. 2 (1987): 209–22; James Wesley Smith, *Sojourners in Search of Freedom: The Settlement of Liberia by Black Americans* (New York: University Press of America, 1987); Julie Winch, *A Gentleman of Color: The Life of James Forten* (New York: Oxford University Press, 2002).

Notes to Chapter 1

1. For the PAS report, see the Pennsylvania Abolition Society Papers, available in manuscript form at the Historical Society of Pennsylvania and on microfilm. This particular report is also reprinted in Edward Needles, *An Historical Memoir of the Pennsylvania Society, for Promoting the Abolition of Slavery; The Relief of Free Negroes Unlawfully Held in Bondage, and for Improving the Condition of the African Race* (Philadelphia: Merrihew and Thompson, 1848); reprint edited by James McPherson and William Loren Katz (New York: Arno Press, 1969), 63–65. The original text is available in the PAS Papers as well. For the apathy the group faced and their difficulty in reaching quorum, see the PAS records: General Meeting Minutes, Series I, Reels 1, 9, 10; Correspondence, Series I, Reels 11, 12, 13. I viewed the manuscript papers at the HSP, but still needed the reel numbers to locate the boxes. All PAS records at the HSP are AmS HSP No. 490. See also Arthur Zilversmit, *The First Emancipation: The Abolition of Slavery in the North* (Chicago: University of Chicago Press, 1967).

2. Higginbotham, *In the Matter of Color*, 267; Nash and Soderlund, *Freedom by Degrees*, 11, 80, 99, 115, 138; John Newton Boucher, ed., *A Century and a Half of Pittsburg and Her People*, vol. 1 (Chicago: Lewis Publishing, 1908), 533; Robert L. Hall, "The Meaning of Slavery in the North: An Introduction," in *The Meaning of Slavery in the North*, ed. David Roediger and Martin H. Blatt (New York: Garland, 1998), xvii–xxiv.

3. Henry J. Cadbury, "Another Early Quaker Document," *Journal of Negro History* 27, no. 2 (1942): 210–15. For slavery and the founding of Pennsylvania, see Nash and Soderlund, *Freedom by Degrees*, 12, and Higginbotham, *In the Matter of Color*, 270–72. Gary Nash, "Slaves and Slaveowners in Colonial Philadelphia," *William and Mary Quarterly* 30, no. 2 (1973): 254. See also Darold D. Wax, "The Demand for Slave Labor in Colonial Pennsylvania," *Pennsylvania History* 34 (1967): 331–45.

4. Higginbotham, *In the Matter of Color*, 267. The Germantown Protest, reprinted in the *Pennsylvania Magazine of History and Biography* 4 (1880): 28–30. Zilversmit also discusses the Germantown Petition, *First Emancipation*, 55–56. For good timelines of Quaker antislavery efforts, see Soderlund, *Quakers and Slavery*, 18–23, and David Brion Davis, *The Problem of Slavery in the Age of Revolution, 1770–1823* (Ithaca, N.Y.: Cornell University Press, 1975), 215–17.

5. *An Exhortation & Caution to Friends Concerning Buying or Keeping of Negroes* (New York, 1693), reprinted in the *Pennsylvania Magazine of History and Biography* 13 (1889): 265–70.

6. Cadbury, "Another Document," 211.

7. Nash and Soderlund, *Freedom by Degrees*, 45; Soderlund, *Quakers and Slavery*, 20–23.

8. Nash and Soderlund, *Freedom by Degrees*, 42; Cadbury, "Another Document," 214; Editorial note in Joe William Trotter Jr. and Eric Ledell Smith, eds., *African Americans in Pennsylvania: Shifting Historical Perspectives* (University Park: Pennsylvania State University Press, 1997), 42.

9. James A. Rawley with Stephen D. Behrendt, *The Atlantic Slave Trade: A History*, rev. ed. (Lincoln: University of Nebraska Press, 2005), 145; W. E. B. Du Bois, *The Suppression of the African Slave Trade to the United States of America, 1638–1870* (new impression, New York: Longmans, Green, 1904), 10–14, 25, 38.

10. Zilversmit, *First Emancipation*, 57–58. Nash and Soderlund, *Freedom by Degrees*, 44; Soderlund, *Quakers and Slavery*, 4, 13. Drake makes a similar point about Quaker moderation in *Quakers and Slavery in America*. See also Lois Horton, "From Class to Race in Early America: Northern Post-Emancipation Racial Reconstruction," *Journal of the Early Republic* 19, no. 4 (1999): 629–49. Michael Goode is currently examining the connection between Quaker nonviolence and antislavery, focusing particularly on Keith and his followers. Currently titled "In the Kingdom but Not of It: The Quaker Peace Testimony and Atlantic Pennsylvania, 1681–1720," his project is forthcoming as a PhD dissertation from the University of Illinois at Chicago history department.

11. Nash and Soderlund, *Freedom by Degrees*, 44, 48, 71–72. Davis, *Problem of Slavery in Western Culture*, 251–52, 313, 307–9, 325. Graham Russell Hodges, *Slavery and Freedom in the Rural North: African-Americans in Monmouth County, New Jersey, 1665–1865* (Madison, Wisc.: Madison House Books, 1997), offers a detailed look at Quakers' exclusionary views toward slaves and the limits of their antislavery.

12. Winthrop Jordan, *White over Black: American Attitudes toward the Negro, 1550–1812* (Chapel Hill: University of North Carolina Press, 1968), 357; Zilversmit, *First Emancipation*, 85, 90; Nash and Soderlund, *Freedom by Degrees*, 52; Drake, *Quakers and Slavery*, 91. Roberts Vaux, *Memoirs of the Life of Anthony Benezet* (New York: Burt Franklin, 1817), 92.

13. Anthony Benezet, *A Short Account of that Part of Africa, Inhabited by the*

Negroes (Philadelphia: W. Dunlap, 1762), 43–46, 53–56, 78, 67, 29, 41; Anthony Benęzet, *Some Historical Account of Guinea, Its Situation, Produce, and the General Disposition of Its Inhabitants, With an Inquiry Into the Rise and Progress of the Slave Trade, Its Nature, and Lamentable Effects* (London: J. Phillips, 1771), 110–14.

14. Benezet, *Short Account*, 29, 49–50, 52–53, 56–58, 64–65, 68, 39, 78–80; Anthony Benezet, *Caution and Warning to Great Britain and Her Colonies, on the Calamitous State of the Enslaved Negroes in the British Dominions*. Reprinted in *Views of American Slavery, Taken a Century Ago: Anthony Benezet, John Wesley* (Philadelphia: Association of Friends for the Diffusion of Religious and Useful Knowledge, 1858), 48; Zilversmit, *First Emancipation*, 85–86; Vaux explains that the idea that God's law superseded man's was a long-acknowledged part of English Common Law, *Memoirs*, 49–50.

15. Benezet, *Short Account*, 42, 70–71, and *Guinea*, 117–18; Zilversmit, *First Emancipation*, 86.

16. Vaux, *Memoirs of Anthony Benezet*, 31; Drake, *Quakers and Slavery*, 86; Benezet, *Guinea*, 116–17; Zilversmit, *First Emancipation*, 87. Benezet's need to speak out against the idea of African resettlement reveals that such a current of thought already existed among gradual abolitionists and that at least some Americans saw race-based colonization as a way to encourage emancipation. Later colonizationists would try to invoke Benezet's name in support of their plans, but a closer reading of Benezet's correspondence reveals his support not for colonization but for something more along the lines of reparations. See Henry Noble Sherwood, "Early Negro Deportation Projects," *Mississippi Valley Historical Review* 2, no. 4 (1916): 485–87; *Laws of Pennsylvania* (Lancaster, Penn., 1801), 1:45, 46; Edmund S. Morgan also saw black deportation as an outgrowth of the English tradition of colonizing lower-class whites. Morgan, "Slavery and Freedom: The American Paradox," *Journal of American History* 59 (June 1972). See also Davis, *Problem of Slavery in the Age of Revolution*, 261, for further discussion.

Job Tyson, "A Discourse Before the Young Men's Colonization Society of Pennsylvania, Delivered October 24, 1834" (Philadelphia: Printed for the Society, 1834), 43–44; Benezet to John Fothergill, 28 April 1773, printed in Vaux, *Memoirs of the Life of Anthony Benezet*, 29–32; Davis, *Problem of Slavery in the Age of Revolution*, 230. For Benezet's opposition to African colonization, see Benezet, *Short Account*, 69–70; Benezet, *Guinea*, 116–18.

Herbert Aptheker, *American Negro Slave Revolts* (New York: International Publishers, 1943), 172–73; Gary Nash, *Forging Freedom: The Formation of Philadelphia's Black Community, 1720–1840* (Cambridge: Harvard University Press, 1988), 140, 173–76, 181–82.

17. Nash and Soderlund, *Freedom by Degrees*, 58–62, 65–66, xi, 69–71; Soderlund, *Quakers and Slavery*, 27.

18. Nash and Soderlund, *Freedom by Degrees*, 83, 54; Davis, *Problem of Slavery in Western Culture*, 330–31; Soderlund, *Quakers and Slavery*, 31; Zilversmit, *First Emancipation*, 74.

19. "Estimated Population of the American Colonies," available at web.viu.ca/davies/H320/population.colonies.htm; Gary B. Nash, "The Social Evolution of Preindustrial American Cities, 1700–1820," in *The Making of Urban America*, 2nd ed., ed. Raymond A. Mohl (Lanham, Md.: Rowman and Littlefield, 1997), 15–36, see esp. 19; 71.

20. Nash and Soderlund, *Freedom by Degrees*, 78, 80; Soderlund, *Quakers and*

Slavery, 103, 7; Turner, *Negro in Pennsylvania*, 79, 113–14; Nash and Soderlund, *Freedom by Degrees*, 153, xiv, 156, 12, 43, 54, 13; Higginbotham, *In the Matter of Color*, 270–72, 285; see also Edward R. Turner, "The Abolition of Slavery in Pennsylvania," *Pennsylvania Magazine of History and Biography* 36 (1912): 129–42; Pennsylvania Archives, 8th Series VI. 5191, 5196, 5197, 5204, 5205–6, 521–14, 5215, 5217. Zilversmit also describes the provisions of the act but adds that the marriage ban and vagrancy laws were later removed (*First Emancipation*, 127–28). For information on the economic side of gradual abolition, see Robert William Fogel and Stanley L. Engerman, "Philanthropy at Bargain Prices: Notes on the Economics of Gradual Emancipation," *Journal of Legal Studies* 3 (1974): 377–401. Fogel and Engerman argue that the greatest fear expressed during debates over emancipation in the Northeast centered on the concern that nonslaveholders would be hurt financially by emancipation.

21. Vaux, *Memoirs of the Life of Anthony Benezet*, 49–50, 92–93; Drake, *Quakers and Slavery*, 119; Staughton Lynd, *Intellectual Origins of American Radicalism*, new ed. (1968; New York: Cambridge University Press, 2009), 114.

22. Zilversmit, *First Emancipation*, 82–83, 174; Drake, *Quakers and Slavery*, 94; Nash and Soderlund, *Freedom by Degrees*, 115; Boucher, ed., *Century and a Half*, 533; Needles, *Historical Memoir*, 41–42. For more on the connection between Quakers and the PAS see Davis, *Problem of Slavery in the Age of Revolution*, 216–17, and Jordan, *White over Black*, 359.

23. "Minute Book of the Committee for Improving the Condition of the Free Blacks, with Material on Social Conditions, Race Discrimination, Crime Education, etc., 1790–1803," PAS papers at the HSP. See also loose documents in the PAS Manuscript Collection Volume II, pp. 41, 45, 47, 87, 95–101, 193. See also Needles, *Historical Memoir*, 31; Zilversmit, *First Emancipation*, 158; Soderlund, *Quakers and Slavery*, 181. For efforts to protect blacks from kidnapping, see Daniel E. Meaders, ed., *Kidnappers in Philadelphia: Isaac Hopper's Tales of Oppression, 1780–1843* (New York: Garland, 1994).

24. Needles, *Historical Memoir*, 47.

25. Rush, "To the Citizens of Philadelphia," 28 March 1787, in *Letters of Benjamin Rush*, ed. Lyman Butterfield (Princeton: Princeton University Press, 1951), 1:412–15. See also Drake, *Quakers and Slavery*, 120. For the prevalence of environmentalist ideology, see Jordan, *White over Black*, 365; Joanne Pope Melish, "The 'Condition' Debate and Racial Discourse in the Antebellum North," *Journal of the Early Republic* 19, no. 4 (1999): 655; Davis, *Problem of Slavery in the Age of Revolution*, 252–53, 305; *Minutes of the Proceedings of the Twelfth American Convention for Promoting the Abolition of Slavery and Improving the Condition of the African Race: Assembled at Philadelphia, the Ninth day of January, One thousand eight hundred and nine.* (Philadelphia: J. Bouvier, 1809), 17.

26. Benezet, *Short Account*, 40, 65–55; Benezet, "Caution and Warning," 38, 39, 55–56, 58–59, 65, 31, 38, 39, 55–56, 58–59, 65, 31; Benezet, *Guinea*, 112.

27. Jordan, *White over Black*, 357; James Mease, *The Picture of Philadelphia, Giving an Account of its Origin, Increase and Improvement sin Arts, Science, Manufactures, Commerce and Revenue, with a Compendious View of its Societies, Literary, Benevolent, Patriotic, and Religious. It's Police—The Public Buildings—the Prison and Penitentiary System—Institutions, Monied and Civil—Museum* (Philadelphia: B & T Kite, 1811), 262–63; Vaux, *Memoirs of the Life of Anthony Benezet*, 21.

28. Benezet to "E.G." reprinted in Vaux, *Memoirs of the Life of Anthony Benezet*, 111; Benezet to "S,N " reprinted in Vaux, *Memoirs of the Life of Anthony Benezet*,114.

29. Vaux, *Memoirs of the Life of Anthony Benezet*, 125, 107; Soderlund, *Quakers and Slavery*, 181; Davis, *Problem of Slavery in the Age of Revolution*, 305. For more details on the effort to educate the freed, see Jean R. Soderlund, "Black Women in Colonial Pennsylvania," in *African Americans in Pennsylvania*, ed. Trotter and Smith, 84.

30. Pennsylvania Society for Promoting the Abolition of Slavery, "Plan for Improving the Condition of the Free Blacks" (Philadelphia, 1789); Pennsylvania Society for Promoting the Abolition of Slavery, "An Address to the Public from the Pennsylvania Society for Promoting the Abolition of Slavery, and the Relief of Free Negroes, Unlawfully Held in Bondage" (Philadelphia: Francis Bailey, 1789). Zilversmit also discusses this plan in *First Emancipation*, 163–64.

31. Richard S. Newman, *Freedom's Prophet: Bishop Richard Allen, the AME Church, and the Black Founding Fathers* (New York: New York University Press, 2008), 5, 55–57, 173.

32. Leonard Curry, *The Free Black in Urban America, 1800–1850: The Shadow of the Dream* (Chicago: University of Chicago Press, 1981), 1–2, 26–30, 86.

33. Nash, *Forging Freedom*, 137, 173, 180–81; Nash and Soderlund, *Freedom by Degrees*, 32. For population statistics, see Mease, *Picture of Philadelphia*, 35–37, 53.

34. Curry, *Free Black in Urban America*, 1–2, 26–30; Stuart M. Blumin, "Residential Mobility within the Nineteenth-Century City," in *The Peoples of Philadelphia: A History of Ethnic Groups and Lower-Class Life, 1790–1940*, ed. Allen F. Davis and Mark H. Haller (Philadelphia: Temple University Press, 1973), 49; See also Davis's introduction to this volume, 7.

35. Nash, *Forging Freedom*, 155–56, 157–58; Curry, *Free Black in Urban America*, 114–17; Turner, *Negro in Pennsylvania*, 158. John Alexander points out that 68.3 percent of the criminals convicted were either born in Ireland or were black, and *Gale's Independent Gazetteer* made a similar point in 1797. John K. Alexander, "Poverty, Fear, and Continuity: An Analysis of the Poor in Late Eighteenth-Century Philadelphia," in *Peoples of Philadelphia*, ed. Davis and Haller, 13–35. For the most comprehensive article-length study of blacks in Walnut Street Prison, see Leslie Patrick-Stamp, "Numbers That Are Not New: African Americans in the Country's First Prison, 1790–1835," *Pennsylvania Magazine of History and Biography* 119 (January/April 1995): 95–128.

36. Pennsylvania Abolition Society, "An Address from the Pennsylvania Abolition Society to the Free Black People of the City of Philadelphia and its Vicinity" (Philadelphia: John Ormrod, 1800), 3–7, 4, 5, 7–8. See also the minutes and records of the Committee to Oversee the Colored Population in the PAS Records at the HSP. For the role of black leaders, see Newman, *Freedom's Prophet*, 153–54.

37. Turner, *Negro in Pennsylvania*, 251, 149–50; Nash, *Forging Freedom*, 173, 180–81.

38. Tise, *Proslavery*; Melish, *Disowning Slavery*, 163.

39. Newman, *Freedom's Prophet*, 155.

40. For the role of the PAS in fighting kidnappers, see Nash and Soderlund, *Freedom by Degrees*, 196–99. Needles, *Historical Memoir*, 47–49, 59, 62–64, 54–56; Drake, *Quakers and Slavery*, 114; Jordan, *White over Black*, 373; Christopher Densmore, "Seeking Freedom in the Courts: The Work of the Pennsylvania Society for Promoting the Abolition of Slavery and for the Relief of Negroes Unlawfully Held in Bondage

and for Improving the Conditions of the African Race," *Pennsylvania Legacies* 5, no. 2 (2005): 16–20.

41. Turner, *Negro in Pennsylvania*, 123; Needles, *Historical Memoir*, 54–56.

42. Minutes of the Proceedings of the 12th American Convention, 15–16. See also Needles, *Historical Memoir*, 56–57; Zilversmit, *First Emancipation*, 224, 207–8. Minutes from all Abolition Convention meetings can also be found in the PAS records at the HSP.

43. Benjamin Rush to the President of the Pennsylvania Abolition Society, [1794?], in *Letters of Benjamin Rush*, vol. 2: *1793–1813*, ed. Lyman Butterfield.

44. John Parrish, *Remarks on the Slavery of the Black People: Addressed to the Citizens of the United States, particularly to those who are in legislative or executive stations in the general or state governments; and also to such individuals as hold them in bondage* (Philadelphia, 1806); see also Staudenraus, *African Colonization*, 4. Jesse Torrey Jr., *A Portraiture of Domestic Slavery, in the United States: With reflections on the practicability of restoring the moral rights of the slave, without impairing the legal privileges of the possessor; and a project of a colonial asylum for free persons of colour; including memoirs of facts on the interior traffic in slaves, and on kidnapping* (Philadelphia, 1817).

45. Newman, *Freedom's Prophet*, 185–206. Quote from 186.

46. Minutes of the Proceedings of the Fourteenth American Convention for Promoting the Abolition of Slavery, and Improving the Condition of the African Race (Philadelphia: W. Brown, 1816), 32, 28–29. These minutes are also available in the PAS papers at the HSP.

47. Ibid., 32–33. For the group's attempts to seek English advice, see Joshua Civin, "The Revival of Antislavery in the 1820s at the Local, National, and Global Levels," a paper presented at Yale University, Third Annual Gilder Lehrman Center International Conference, Sisterhood and Slavery: Transatlantic Antislavery and Women's Rights, 25–28 October 2002.

48. Minutes of the Proceedings of the Fifteenth American Convention for Promoting the Abolition of Slavery, and Improving the Condition of the African Race (Philadelphia: Merritt, 1817), 30–31.

49. Newman, *Freedom's Prophet*, 203–4.

50. Minutes of the Proceedings of the Fifteenth American Convention for Promoting the Abolition of Slavery, and Improving the Condition of the African Race, 18.

51. Ibid., 48–50, 68.

52. Report of the Committee, in Relation to the Subjects of the Second Resolution of the Committee of Arrangement, in *Minutes of the Sixteenth American Convention for Promoting the Abolition of Slavery, and Improving the Condition of the African Race* (Philadelphia: William Fry, 1819), 50–56, 58. *Minutes of the Seventeenth Session of the American Convention for Promoting the Abolition of Slavery, and Improving the Condition of the African Race* (Philadelphia: Atkinson and Alexander, 1821), 42–43. See also PAS papers at the HSP, Box 37B and reel 15 on the microfilm edition.

53. For the proslavery critique of the American Colonization Society, see von Holst, *Constitutional and Political History of the United States*, 331; Goodman, *Of One Blood*, 16–18; Harrold, *American Abolitionists*, 26.

54. Henry Noble Sherwood, "The Formation of the American Colonization Society," *Journal of Negro History* 2, no. 3 (1917): 209–28; Fox, *American Colonization Society*; Frederic Bancroft, *The Colonization of American Negroes, 1801–1865*, in *Frederic*

Bancroft, Historian, ed. Jacob Ernest Cooke (Norman: University of Oklahoma Press, 1957); Staudenraus, *African Colonization Movement;* Fredrickson, *Black Image in the White Mind,* Egerton, "'Its Origin Is Not a Little Curious'"; Egerton, "Averting a Crisis." For PAS concerns about the consequences of emancipation, see the Cox, Parrish, Wharton papers at the HSP and PAS Papers AMS 02, folders 1, 2, 9, 11, 12, and 15 at the HSP.

Notes to Chapter 2

1. *Philadelphia in 1824; or, a Brief Account of the Various Institutions and Public Objects in this Metropolis: Being a Complete Guide for Strangers and an Useful Compendium for The Inhabitants. To which is prefixed, an Historical and Statistical Account of the City. With a Plan of the City, View of the Water-Works, and other Engravings* (Philadelphia: H. C. Carey and I. Lea, August, 1824), 131; Mease, *Picture of Philadelphia,* 262–64; R. A. Smith, *Philadelphia as it is, in 1852: Being a Correct Guide to all the Public Buildings; Literary, Scientific, and Benevolent Institutions; and Places of Amusement; Remarkable Objects; Manufactories; Commercial Warehouses; and Wholesale and Retail Stores in Philadelphia and its Vicinity. With Illustrations and a Map of the City and Environs* (Philadelphia: Lindsay and Blakiston, 1852), 13, 141–45, 153, 45; Curry, *Free Black in Urban America,* 150–53, 163–64; Nash and Soderlund, *Freedom by Degrees,* 52; J. Thomas Scharf and Thompson Westcott, *History of Philadelphia, 1609–1884,* 3 vols. (Philadelphia: L. H. Everts, 1884), 3:1922; Alexander ("Poverty, Fear, and Continuity," 13–35) argues for the social control aspect of these endeavors; for Benjamin Rush on the role of education, see "To the Citizens of Philadelphia," 28 March 1787, cited on page 20 of Alexander's essay.

Daniel Bowen, *A History of Philadelphia, with a Notice of Villages, in the Vicinity, Embellished with Engravings, Designed as a Guide to Citizens and Strangers, Containing a Correct Account of the City Improvements, Up to the Year 1839: Also, the State of Society, in Relation to Science, Religion, and Morals; with an Historical Account of the Military Operations of the Late War, Including the Names of Over Two Thousand Patriotic Officers, and Citizen Soldiers, Who Volunteered their Services in Defense of this City, When Threatened by a Hostile Army. In 1812, -13, & -14* (Philadelphia: Daniel Bowen, 1839), 180–81; Sharf and Westcott, *History of Philadelphia,* 2:1455; Smith, *Philadelphia in 1852,* 13, 141; Negley Tetters, "The Early Days of the Philadelphia House of Refuge," *Pennsylvania History* 27 (April 1960): 165–87.

2. For more on this reform movement, see Steven Mintz, *Moralists and Modernizers: America's Pre-Civil War Reformers* (Baltimore: Johns Hopkins University Press, 1995), and Ronald G. Walters, *American Reformers, 1815–1860* (New York: Hill and Wang, 1978). For the social control aspect, see John K. Alexander, *Render Them Submissive: Responses to Poverty in Philadelphia, 1760–1800* (Amherst: University of Massachusetts Press, 1980), and Simon P. Newman, *Embodied History: The Lives of the Poor in Early Philadelphia* (Philadelphia: University of Pennsylvania Press, 2003). ACS, *First Annual Report,* 11. For statistics on Philadelphia's black population, see Nash, *Forging Freedom,* 136–37, 143, and Curry, *Free Black in Urban America,* 6, 86. Turner, *Negro in Pennsylvania,* 167.

3. Newman, *Freedom's Prophet,* 108.

4. Egerton, "'Its Origin Is Not a Little Curious,'" 479. For black interest in colonization see Newman, *Freedom's Prophet,* 183–206.

5. Staudenraus, *African Colonization Movement*, 15-30; ACS, *Second Annual Report*, 3; Newman, *Freedom's Prophet*, 188-89.

6. Staudenraus, *African Colonization*, 39-40, 6.

7. ACS, *First Annual Report*, 20, 4; Staudenraus, *African Colonization*, 49-51, 39-40, 69-79, 168-69; ACS, *Third Annual Report*, 17-18, 20, 143; ACS, *Fifth Annual Report*, 112-13.

8. Staudenraus, *African Colonization*, 170, 85-86, 117-19; ACS, *Seventh Annual Report*, 30-31, 10; ACS, *Eight Annual Report*, 14, 47-50; ACS, *Third Annual Report*, 2; ACS, *Third Annual Report*, 7; Boucher, *Century and a Half*, 1:535.

9. Egerton, "Averting a Crisis," 144; Staudenraus, *African Colonization Movement*, 150.

10. ACS, *Seventh Annual Report*, 94-95; Staudenraus, *African Colonization Movement*, 100.

11. Staudenraus, *African Colonization*, 125-26, 33, 26; Gurley to John Kennedy, 12 October 1826; William B. Davidson to Gurley, 2 December 1826; Gurley to Kennedy, 25 October 1826, 30 October 1826; Benjamin O. Peers to Gurley, 20 September 1826; all in ACS Papers.

12. Leonard Bacon, "Plea for Africa," *African Repository* 1, no. 6 (August 1825) (New York: Kraus Reprint, 1967), 169-75; Staudenraus, *African Colonization*, 126, 26; John H. Kennedy, "Sympathy, its foundation and legitimate exercise considered, in special relation to Africa: A discourse delivered on the Fourth of July 1828, in the 6th Presbyterian Church, Philadelphia," (Philadelphia: W. F. Geddes, 1828).

13. ACS, *First Annual Report*, 8; *African Repository* 4, no. 12 (March 1829): 363; ACS, *Third Annual Report*, 100; *African Repository* 4, no. 9 (November 1828): 258-59.

14. Reprinted in ACS, *Seventh Annual Report*, 98; *African Repository* 1, no. 2 (April 1825): 34.

15. *African Repository* 1, no. 12 (February 1826): 384; "The Degraded Character of the Coloured Population," *African Repository* 2, no. 7 (July 1826): 153; *Philadelphia in 1824; or, a Brief Account of the Various Institutions and Public Objects in this Metropolis: Being a Complete Guide for Strangers, and an Useful Compendium for the Inhabitants. To which is prefixed, An Historical and Statistical Account of the City. With a Plan of the City, View of the Water-Works, and Other Engravings* (Philadelphia: H. C. Carey and I. Lea, 1824), 144. For a breakdown on the prison population and their crimes, see 143. For further analysis of the black prison population and the white tendency to exaggerate the numbers, see Curry, *Free Black in Urban America*, 113; ACS, *Tenth Annual Report*, 22.

Jonathan Nash, a PhD candidate at SUNY-Albany, is currently researching prisons during this era and has found a number of connections between black imprisonment and the growth of colonization sentiment among reformers. In addition to his forthcoming work, see the William Parker Foulke Papers and the American Philosophical Society as well as the *First Annual Report of the Board of Managers of the Prison Discipline Society, Boston, June 26, 1826* (Boston: T. R. Marvin, Printer, 1828), 38.

16. ACS, *First Annual Report*, 140; "African Colonization. An Enquiry into the Origin, Plan and Prospects of the American Colonization Society; Being an extract from an article in the December number of the *American Quarterly Review*, for 1828" (Frederickburg, Virginia: Arena Office, 1829), 14-16, 22.

17. Higginbotham, *In the Matter of Color*, 273-74, 285; Turner, *Negro in*

Pennsylvania, 194–96; Gary Nash, *Red, White, and Black: The Peoples of Early North America* (Englewood Cliffs, N J · Prentice Hall, 1992), 287.

18. Aptheker, *American Negro Slave Revolts*, 172–73, 184, 22, 239–40; Nash, *Forging Freedom*, 140. For information about Prosser's rebellion, see Douglas R. Egerton, *Gabriel's Rebellion: The Virginia Slave Conspiracies of 1800 and 1802* (Chapel Hill: University of North Carolina Press, 1993); ACS, *Seventh Annual Report*, 91–93, 42.

19. David Robertson, *Denmark Vesey: The Buried History of America's Largest Slave Rebellion and the Man Who Led It* (New York: Alfred A. Knopf, 1999), 6–9; Silas McKeen, "A Sermon Delivered at Montpelier, October 15, 1828, Before the Vermont Colonization Society" (Montpelier, 1828), 19–22; *Christian Spectator* article reprinted in the ACS, *Seventh Annual Report*, 92–94.

20. McKeen, "Sermon," 19, 22; "Prospectus," *African Observer*, April 1827, 2; ACS, *Ninth Annual Report*, 6–8.

21. *African Repository* 2, no. 9 (1826): 287, 291–92; *African Repository* 3, no. 10 (December 1827): 310; W. Paxton to Gurley, 7 July 1829, and Ralston to Gurley, 10 January 1829, both in ACS Papers; "Prospects in Pennsylvania," *African Repository* 3, no. 3 (May 1827): 93–94.

22. *African Repository* 4, no. 12 (March 1829): 363; ACS, *Tenth Annual Report*, 46, 83, 90–100; William B. Davidson to Ralph Gurley, 2 December 1826; George Cookman to Gurley, 22 December 1826; Connelsville Chapter to Parent Society, 18 December 1826; all in ACS Papers.

23. PCS, *The First Report of the Board of Managers, of the Pennsylvania Colonization Society* (Philadelphia: T. Town, 1827), 3, 4–5, 7.

24. Ibid., 5, 7–8.

25. Ibid., 8; Ralston to Gurley, 23 February 1827; Resolution of the Lutheran Synod, 30 September 1827, both in ACS Papers; Staudenraus, *African Colonization Movement*, 125.

26. W. Paxton to Gurley, 7 July 1829; Miller to Gurley, 16 July 1829, both in ACS Papers.

27. The name of the author is missing from the letter, but evidence points to Josiah F. Polk. The letter was written to Gurley on 28 August 1829, ACS papers; Lewis de Schweinitz to ACS, 6 July 1829, in *African Repository* 5, no. 7 (September 1829).

28. Davidson to Gurley, 28 September 1827, in ACS Papers; "Minutes for a Regular Meeting of 9-27-1827," PAS Papers Reel 2; Drake, *Quakers and Slavery*, 118–32; "Prospectus," *African Observer*, April 1827, 4; *African Observer*, May 1827, 37–39; *African Observer*, July 1827, 139–40; *African Observer*, September 1827, 173–75; *African Observer*, June 1827, 121–24. The newspaper lasted only a year, and all page numbers are from the bound volume, *The African Observer. A Monthly Journal, Containing Essays and Documents Illustrative of the General Character, and Moral and Political Effects, of Negro Slavery* (Westport, Conn.: Negro Universities Press, 1970); Needles, *Historical Memoir*, 85–86, 72–76; Turner, *Negro in Pennsylvania*, 227–33.

29. ACS, *Third Annual Report*; *African Repository* 4, no. 10 (December 1828): 317; *African Repository* 5, no. 7 (September 1829): 218–19; Staudenraus, *African Colonization*, 116; *The First Report of the Board of Managers of the Pennsylvania Colonization Society* (Philadelphia: T. Town, printer, 1827), 7.

30. "African Colonization," 23; No, 196 Senate File, "An Act to Aid the American Colonization Society," 9 March 1827, in ACS Papers; *African Repository* 3, no. 10

(December 1827); *African Repository* 3, no. 12 (February 1828): 368; *African Repository* 5, no. 2 (April 1829); *African Repository* 5, no. 10 (December 1829): 306–7.

31. Carey to *African Repository*, 8 November 1828, in *African Repository* 4, no. 10 (December 1828): 300–303.

32. PAS Papers, 1775–75, reel 2; *African Repository* 4, no. 10 (December 1828): 298; *African Repository* 4, no. 12 (March 1829).

33. *African Repository* 4, no. 10 (December 1828): 299; PCS, *[Third] Report of the Board of Managers of the Pennsylvania Colonization Society* (Philadelphia: Thomas Kite, 1830), 4.

34. *African Repository* 5, no. 11 (January 1830): 342; Ralston to Gurley, 31 October 1829, in ACS Papers; PCS, *[Third] Report of the Board of Managers*, 4–5, 6, 7; Staudenraus, *African Colonization*, 135.

35. Bayard to Gurley, 7 December 1829, in ACS Papers; PCS, *[Third] Report of the Board of Managers*, 8–9; *African Repository* 5, no. 12 (February 1830): 373–77.

36. PCS, *[Third] Report of the Board of Managers*, 9, 13; Sherman to PCS, 4 June 1830; see also appendix A–D of the 1830 annual report.

37. Most of these joined during the 1829 drive. One example was Sarah Grimké, who gave $10. I have arrived at these statistics by comparing the financial records and membership lists in the PCS reports with a master list of all PAS members, published in the Pennsylvania Abolition Society, *Centennial Anniversary of the Pennsylvania Society, for Promoting the Abolition of Slavery, the Relief of Free Negroes Unlawfully Held in Bondage: And for Improving the Condition of the African Race* (Philadelphia: Grant, Faires and Rodgers, 1875), 51–66. In some cases this was difficult, as a person would be listed by first and last name in one place but by first and middle initial and last name in another. If the name varied but other factors such as occupation seemed to indicate that one person was the same on both rosters, though listed with slight variation, I classified the person as "likely," but not "clearly," the same person; *African Repository* 5, no. 12 (February 1830): 382–83.

38. ACS, *Fifth Annual Report*, 1822, 24; *African Repository* 4, no. 12 (March 1829): 376–77; PAS Microfilm Reel 13.

Notes to Chapter 3

1. Mathew Carey to Ralph Gurley, 8 November 1828, *African Repository and Colonial Journal* 4, no. 9 (November 1828): 270–71; Mathew Carey to Ralph Gurley, 25 June 1833 [*sic*, all indications show that the date should be 1832], American Colonization Society Papers. The Gerrit Smith Plan was a program whereby Smith challenged others to match his commitment to donate $100 a year for ten years.

2. Glyndon G. Van Deusen, *The Jacksonian Era, 1828–1848* (New York: Harper and Brothers, 1959; reprint. New York: Harper Torchbooks, 1963), 18, 51; Edward Carlos Carter, "The Political Activities of Mathew Carey, Nationalist, 1760–1814," PhD diss. (Bryn Mawr, 1962), 337, 150; A. D. H. Kaplan, *Henry Charles Carey, A Study in American Economic Thought* (1931; New York: AMS Press, 1982), 11, 21.

3. Davis, *Problem of Slavery in the Age of Revolution*, 240–41; Egerton, "Averting a Crisis," 147; Lawrence J. Friedman, "Purifying the White Man's Country: The American Colonization Society Reconsidered, 1816–40," *Societas* 6, no. 1 (1976): 1–24. For Carey's importance as ACS publicist see Staudenraus, *African Colonization*, 215.

4. Carter, "Political Activities," 2, 7; Jane F. Hindman, *Mathew Carey, Pamphleteer*

for Freedom (New York: P. J. Kenedy and Sons, 1960), 15, 23, 30–31. See also Mathew Carey, *Autobiographical Sketches, In a Series of Letters Addressed to a Friend* (Philadelphia, 1829), and Kenneth Rowe, *Mathew Carey: A Study in American Economic Development* (Baltimore, 1933); James N. Green, *Mathew Carey, Publisher and Patriot* (Philadelphia: Library Company of Philadelphia, 1985).

5. Carter, "Political Activities," 6.

6. Ibid., 7–11.

7. Ibid., 11–13.

8. Ibid., 29–30. Thanks to Jim Green for correcting the factual error in which Carey cited 1779 as the year of publication and exile. As Jim pointed out, an advertisement in the *Dublin Journal* places publication at 1781, and records in the Benjamin Franklin papers place Carey in Passy in 1781–82 rather than 1779. *The Urgent Necessity* was printed almost in its entirety but never published. What is perhaps the only surviving copy can be found at the Library Company of Philadelphia, along with the handbill, *Advertisement to the Roman Catholics of Ireland.*

9. Carter, "Political Activities," 36; Hindman, *Mathew Carey*, 69–77.

10. Carter, "Political Activities," 49, 60; Earl Bradsher, *Mathew Carey, Editor, Author and Publisher* (New York: AMS Press, 1966), 3–4; Eugene F. J. Maier, "Mathew Carey, Publicist and Politician," *Records of the American Catholic Historical Society of Philadelphia* 39 (1928): 71–154; Rowe, *Mathew Carey*, 16.

11. "Postscript," *Pennsylvania Evening Herald* 1, no. 46 (2 July 1785): 2.

12. Ibid., 2, no. 3 (3 August 1785): 2. See also Carter, "Political Activities," 62.

13. A Friend to Equality of Freedom and Learning in Pennsylvania, "To Those INHABITANTS of PENNSYLVANIA, who are, either by birth or descent, GERMANS," *Pennsylvania Evening Herald* 2, no. 6 (13 August 1785): 3.

14. "Postscript," *Pennsylvania Evening Herald* 2, no. 5 (10 August 1785): 2; David M. Streifford, "The American Colonization Society: An Application of Republican Ideology to Early Antebellum Reform," *Journal of Southern History* 45, no. 2 (1979): 201–20.

15. "An Enquiry into the most advantageous Occupations to be followed by Persons emigrating to America," *Columbian Magazine* 1, no. 14 (October 1787): 698–702; "Reflections on the Subject of Emigration from Europe, with a View of settlement in the United States; Containing Brief Sketches of the Moral and Political Character of this Country," 1826. Reprinted in Mathew Carey, *Miscellaneous Essays* (New York: Burt Franklin, 1830), 119–47; "Emigration from Ireland, and Immigration into the United States," 18 July 1828, Reprinted in *Miscellaneous Essays*, 321–25.

16. Carter, "Political Activities," 118–20; Streifford, "American Colonization Society," 202–20.

17. Andrew Shankman, *Crucible of American Democracy: The Struggle to Fuse Egalitarianism and Capitalism in Jeffersonian Pennsylvania* (Lawrence: University Press of Kansas, 2004), 230–31; Howe, *Political Culture*, 20.

18. "A Summary View of the Slave Trade; and the probable consequences of its abolition—On the inhumanity and injustice of the Negro trade—Slaves acquired by means of war," Supplement to *The Columbian Magazine*, Volume I; W. Elford, Chairman of the Plymouth Committee, "Remarks on the Slave Trade," extracted from the *American Museum* for May 1789 (Philadelphia: Mathew Carey, 1789).

19. "Postscript," *Pennsylvania Evening Herald* 1, no. 42 (June 18, 1785): 2; "Postscript," *Pennsylvania Evening Herald* 1, no. 44 (June 25, 1785): 2; "The State of Slavery

in Virginia and other parts of the Continent, from the Marquis de Chastellur's Travels in America," *Columbian Magazine*1, no. 10 (June 1787): 479–80.

20. "State of Slavery in Virginia," 480.

21. Ibid.

22. "Chronicle of the Year 1850," *Columbian Magazine* 1, no. 1 (September 1786): 5.

23. Mathew Carey, "To The Editors of the Philadelphia Daily Papers," 8 April 1829, in *Miscellaneous Essays*, 405–8, quote from 405; For more on Carey's self-funding of his charitable essays, see Mathew Carey to (possible investors?), 11 October 1832, and Carey to Ralph Gurley, 26 July 1832, both in ACS Papers; Van Deusen, *Jacksonian Era*, 18; George Dangerfield, *The Awakening of American Nationalism, 1815–1828* (New York: Harper Torchbooks, 1965), 278.

24. Mathew Carey, "To the Public," 12 April 1830, in *Miscellaneous Pamphlets*, collected in April 1831 and available on microfilm. There are no continuous page numbers; Mathew Carey, "The Infant School," 28 December 1827, in *Miscellaneous Essays*, 313–17; Mathew Carey, "Essays on the Public Charities of Philadelphia, Intended to Vindicate the Benevolent Societies of this City from the Charge of Encouraging Idleness," 5th ed., 1828. Reprinted in *Miscellaneous Essays*, 153–203; Mathew Carey, "Extract from the First Report of the Society for the Encouragement of Faithful Domestics," 20 October 1830, in *Miscellaneous Essays*, 455–57; Carter, "Political Activities," 114–15, iv.

25. Carey, "Essay on Public Charities," 161, 172. For more on the plight of working women, see various articles in *Miscellaneous Essays*, 266–88.

26. Mathew Carey, "Address to the Liberal and Humane," May 1829, in *Miscellaneous Essays*, 272–76; Mathew Carey, "Address on Benevolent Societies," 29 June 1829, in *Miscellaneous Essays*, 276–78; "Appeal to the Rich," *Liberator* 1, no. 2 (8 January 1831); "Admonitory Sentence," *Liberator* 1, no. 8 (19 February 1831).

27. Streifford, "American Colonization Society," 201–20; Carey to Gurley, 26 July 1832, in ACS Papers; Egerton, "'Its Origin Is a Little Strange,'" 468–70; David J. Rothman, *The Discovery of the Asylum: Social Order and Disorder in the New Republic* (Boston: Little, Brown, 1971); Friedman, "Purifying the White Man's Country," 4.

28. Mathew Carey, "A Short Account of the Malignant Fever Which Prevailed in Philadelphia, In the Year 1793, With a Statement of the Proceedings that Took Place on the Subject in Different Parts of the United States," 1830, reprinted in *Miscellaneous Essays*, 10–97; Absalom Jones and Richard Allen, "A Narrative of the Proceedings of the Black People, During the Late Awful Calamity in Philadelphia, in the Year 1793; and a Refutation of some Censures, Thrown Upon Them in Same Late Philadelphia" (Philadelphia: William W. Woodward, 1794), 13; Mathew Carey, "Address to the Public," 4 April 1794; Phillip Lapsansky, "'Abigail, a Negress': The Role and the Legacy of African Americans in the Yellow Fever Epidemic," in *A Melancholy Scene of Devastation: The Public Response to the 1793 Philadelphia Yellow Fever Epidemic*, ed. J. Worth Estes and Billy G. Smith (Philadelphia: Science History Publications, 1997), 61–78. See also Sally F. Griffith, "'A Total Dissolution of the Bonds of Society': Community Death and Regeneration in Mathew Carey's *Short Account of the Malignant Fever*," in *Melancholy Scene of Devastation*, ed. Estes and Smith, 45–59.

29. Frederickson, *Black Image in the White Mind*, 2–5. See also the "SHA Roundtable Discussion," *Journal of the Early Republic* 18, no. 2 (1998). This discussion features James Brewer Stewart's "The Emergence of Racial Modernity and the Rise of the

White North, 1790–1840," as well as comments by Jean L. Soderlund, James Oliver Horton, and Ronald G. Walters; Howe, *Political Culture*, 135.

30. George Morgan, "An Essay, exhibiting a plan for a Farm-Yard, and method of conducting the same," *Columbian Magazine* 1, no. 1 (October 1786): 77–81. Volume 1 was bound and printed in Philadelphia by Seddon, W. Spotswood, C. Cist, and J. Trenchard; "Postscript," *Pennsylvania Evening Herald* 1, no. 17 (22 March 1785): 3; "Postscript," *Pennsylvania Evening Herald* 1, no. 23 (April 12, 1785): 3.

Carter, "Political Activities," 137, iii; Van Deusen, *Jacksonian Era*, 19; Mathew Carey, "Address to those on whom Heaven has bestowed the goods of fortune, and, what is more valuable, hearts to make a proper use of them for the public benefit," delivered in Philadelphia, 11 October 1824, printed in *Miscellaneous Essays* (Philadelphia: Carey and Hart, 1830). (Reprint, New York: Burt Franklin, 1966), 325–28.

See also William Strickland, "Reports on Canals, Railways, Roads and Other Subjects, Made to 'The Pennsylvania Society for the Promotion of Internal Improvements'" (Philadelphia: H. C. Carey and I. Lea, 1826), and Mathew Carey, "Brief View of the System of Internal Improvements of the State of Pennsylvania; Containing a Glance at its Rise, Progress, Retardation;—the Difficulties it Underwent,—Its Present State,—and its Future Prospects" (Philadelphia: Lydia R. Bailey, 1831), 13–14, 10–20.

31. Carey, "Brief View," vi–vii, 29–30; Pennsylvania Society for the Promotion of Internal Improvements, *The First Annual Report of the Acting Committee of the Society for the Promotion of Internal Improvement in the Commonwealth of Pennsylvania* (Philadelphia: Joseph R. A. Skerrett, 1826), 5.

32. Howe, *Political Culture*, 140; David Hackett Fisher, *The Revolution of American Conservatism: The Federalist Party in the Era of Jeffersonian Democracy* (New York: Harper and Row, 1965), 175; Mathew Carey, *The Olive Branch: Or, Faults on Both Sides, Federal and Democratic. A Serious Appeal on the Necessity of Mutual Forgiveness and Harmony* (Philadelphia: Published by the Author, 1815), 269–73, 366–67; Mathew Carey, *A Calm Address to the People of the Eastern States, on the Subject of the Representation of Slaves; the Representation in the Senate; and the Hostility to Commerce Ascribed to the Southern States* (Philadelphia: M. Carey, 1814); Matthew Mason, *Slavery and Politics in the Early American Republic* (Chapel Hill: University of North Carolina Press, 2006).

33. Carey, *Olive Branch*, 138–46, 114, 173, 56, 87, 50–51. For just how close the nation came to Civil War, see Richard Buel Jr., *America on the Brink: How the Political Struggle over the War of 1812 Almost Destroyed the Young Republic* (New York: Palgrave Macmillan, 2005).

34. Mathew Carey, "Emancipation of the Slaves in the United States," 1827, in *Miscellaneous Essays*, 222–32; Mathew Carey, *Autobiographical Sketches in a Series of Letters Addressed to a Friend* (Philadelphia, 1829), 143–33; Mathew Carey, *Common Sense Addresses, to the Citizens of the Southern States*, 4th ed. (Philadelphia: Clark and Raser, 1829), vi; Mathew Carey, *Prospects on the Rubicon, Letters on the Prevailing Excitement in South Carolina, Addressed to the Honorable Henry Clay*, 2nd ed. (Philadelphia: Clark and Raser, 1832), v; Mathew Carey, *Look Before You Leap: Address to Southern State, Being a Solemn Warning Against the destructive Doctrine of a Separation of the Union* (Philadelphia: Haswell and Barrington, 1835); Carey, *Prospects on the Rubicon*, iv; Mathew Carey, *The New Olive Branch: or, an Attempt to Establish an Identity of Interest Between Agriculture, Manufactures, and Commerce*, 2nd ed.

(Philadelphia: M. Carey and Son, 1821); Mathew Carey, *The Tocsin: A Solemn Warning against the Dangerous Doctrine of Nullification*, 3rd ed. (Philadelphia: William F. Geddes, 1832); Mathew Carey, *Essays on the Ruinous Effects of the Policy of the United States, on the Three Classes, Farmers, Planters, and Merchants* (Philadelphia: Joseph R. A. Skerrett, 1826).

35. Mathew Carey, *The Olive Branch Once More* (Philadelphia, 1833), 7–8; Carey, *Look Before You Leap*, ii; "Postscript," *Pennsylvania Evening Herald* 2, no. 20 (1 October 1785): 3.

36. "Postscript," *Pennsylvania Evening Herald* 2, no. 21 (5 October 1785): 3; "To the Editor of the *Columbian Magazine*," *Columbian Magazine* 1, no. 4 (December 1786): 182; "Postscript," *Pennsylvania Evening Herald* 1, no. 37 (1 June 1785): 3; "Postscript," *Pennsylvania Evening Herald* 1, no. 38 (4 June 1785): 2; "Postscript," *Pennsylvania Evening Herald* 1, no. 44 (25 June 1785): 2; "Postscript," *Pennsylvania Evening Herald* 1, no. 46 (2 July 1785): 2; "Postscript," *Pennsylvania Evening Herald* 1, no. 48 (9 July 1785): 2; See the September 1786, February 1787, and supplementary volume to the *Columbian Magazine* for a few examples; Van Deusen, *Jacksonian Era*, 18.

37. Van Deusen, *Jacksonian Era*, 19; Carey, *Olive Branch*, 27; Mathew Carey, *Essays on the Protecting System* (Philadelphia: Mifflin and Parry, 1830); Mathew Carey, *The New Olive Branch: Addressed to the Citizens of South Carolina* (Philadelphia: Clark and Raser, 1831), vi, viii.

38. Mathew Carey, *A Warning Voice to the Cotton and Tobacco Planters, Farmers, and Merchants of the United States on the Pernicious Consequences to Their Respective Interests of the Existing Folly of the Country* (Philadelphia: H. C. Carey and I. Lea, 1824); Mathew Carey, *Twenty-One Golden Rules to Depress Agriculture, Impede the Progress of Manufactures, Paralize Commerce, Impair National Resources, Produce a Constant Fluctuation in the Value of Every Species of Property and Blight and Blast the Bounties of Nature* (reprint, Salem: Warwick Palfray, 1824); Mathew Carey, *Address Delivered Before the Philadelphia Society for Promoting Agriculture at its Meeting on 20 July 1824*, 2nd ed. (Philadelphia: Joseph R. A. Skerrett, 1824); Mathew Carey, *Address to the Farmers of the United States, on the Ruinous Consequences to their Vital Interests, of the Existing Policy of this Country* (Philadelphia: M. Carey and Son, 1821), 5–6; Edward Pessen, *Jacksonian America: Society, Personality, and Politics* (Homewood, Ill.: Dorsey Press, 1969), 20.

39. "Thoughts on the present Situation of the Federal Government of the United States of America," *Columbian Magazine* 1, no. 4 (December 1786); Carter, "Political Activities, 73. The Constitution was completed in September of 1787, and Carey included it in that month's edition, *Columbian Magazine* 1, no. 13 (September 1787); "Of Politics—Rules for seeing with ones own eyes—Knowledge of History—Of Government—Philosophy—A good Heart—Advantages which result form a conviction that two and two make four," *Columbian Magazine* 1, no. 16 (December 1787): 819–22; "Preface," *Columbian Magazine* 1, no. 1 (September 1786): 1; Mathew Carey, "Remarks on the Tragedy of Hamlet," 30 November 1811, reprinted in *Miscellaneous Essays*, 408.

40. Mathew Carey, "To the Freemen of the Commonwealth of Pennsylvania," *Pennsylvania Evening Herald*, 24 August 1785; Carter, "Political Activities, 322, 131, 197, 141; David Hackett Fisher, *The Revolution of American Conservatism: The Federalist Party in the Era of Jeffersonian Democracy* (New York: Harper and Row, 1965), 202. Shankman, *Crucible*, 41; Carter, "Political Activities, 199–200, 193–94, 254; Fisher,

Revolution, 163; Matthew Mason, *Slavery and Politics in the Early American Republic* (Chapel Hill: University of North Carolina Press, 2008), 52, 54, 62, 66.

41. Shankman, *Crucible,* 74, 96–98, 108–9, 122, 184; Howe, *Political Culture,* 109; Drew McCoy, *The Elusive Republic: Political Economy in Jeffersonian America* (Chapel Hill: University of North Carolina Press, 1980), 226.

42. Shankman, *Crucible,* 222–23. E. Malcolm Carroll, *Origins of the Whig Party* (Gloucester, Mass.: Peter Smith, 1925; reprint, Duke University Press, 1964); Howe, *Political Culture,* 2, 138–39, 16, 210, 76–78, 18–20. For Whigs on race see Howe, *Political Culture,* 39.

43. Mathew Carey, "Slave Labour Employed in Manufactures," 2 October 1827, in *Miscellaneous Essays,* 232–34.

44. "Hamilton," *African Repository* 5, no. 7 (September 1829). For an in-depth look at the issue of comity, see Paul Finkelman, *An Imperfect Union: Slavery, Federalism, and Comity* (Chapel Hill: University of North Carolina Press, 1981).

45. Mathew Carey, "Emancipation of the Slaves in the United States," 26 November 1827, in *Miscellaneous Essays,* 222–32.

46. Streifford, "American Colonization Society," 201; ACS, *Tenth Annual Report,* 18–22.

47. Carey, "African Colonization," in *Miscellaneous Essays,* 214–15; Mathew Carey, *Letters on the Colonization Society; with a View of its Probable Results* (Philadelphia: Young, 1832) 2nd ed., 14; 4th ed., 12.

48. Carey, *Letters on the Colonization Society,* 2nd ed.; Mathew Carey, *Reflections on the Causes That led to the Formation of the Colonization Society: With a View on its Probable Results* (Philadelphia: William F. Geddes, 1832); Mathew Carey, "African Colonization," 1830, reprinted in *Miscellaneous Essays,* 214–22; Mathew Carey to [publisher?], 26 March 1832, ACS Papers.

49. Carey, *Letters on the Colonization Society,* 4th ed., 27–28; Carey, *Reflections,* 16.

50. Carey, *Reflections,* 16.

51. Carey, *Letters on the Colonization Society,* 4th ed., 17–20; Carey, "African Colonization," in *Miscellaneous Essays,* 216; Carey, *Reflections,*11–15, 19, 2, 16.

52. Carey, *Reflections,*16–20, 8; Carey, *Letters on the Colonization Society,* 2nd ed., 30–31, 7; 4th ed., 29–30, 9, 14.

53. Carey, *Letters on the Colonization Society,* 4th ed., 26–27; Carey, "African Colonization," in *Miscellaneous Essays,* 218; Finkelman, *Imperfect Union,* 9.

54. Carey to Gurley, 21 December 1829, and Carey to "Sir," 26 March 1832, both in ACS Papers; Carey, *Letters on the Colonization Society,* 4th ed., 5–6; 2nd ed., 6; Carey, "African Colonization," in *Miscellaneous Essays,* 218.

55. Carey, *Reflections,*3; Carey, "African Colonization," in *Miscellaneous Essays,* 218–20. For more on population statistics, see Carey, *Letters on the Colonization Society,* 4th ed., 12–13; 2nd ed., 14–15.

56. Carey, *Letters on the Colonization Society,* 4th ed., 13; 2nd ed., 16, 7; Carey, "African Colonization," in *Miscellaneous Essays,* 216.

57. Carey, *Letters on the Colonization Society,* 4th ed., 9, 17–19, 31–32, 9–14; Carey, *Reflections on the Colonization Society,* 1, 10, 5; Carey, "African Colonization," 216; Egerton, "Averting a Crisis," 148; Howe, *Political Culture,* 136; Burin, *Slavery and the Peculiar Solution,* 23; William Freehling, *The Road to Disunion: Secessionists at Bay, 1776-1854* (New York: Oxford University Press, 1990); Staudenraus, *African*

Colonization, 169–87; Frederickson, *Black Image in the White Mind*, 26; Mathew Carey to Ralph Gurley, 21 December 1829, in ACS Papers. See also Herman Hailperin, "Pro-Jackson Sentiment in Pennsylvania, 1820–1828," *Pennsylvania Magazine of History and Biography* 1 (July 1926), and Henry R. Mueller, *The Whig Party in Pennsylvania* (New York: Columbia University Press, 1922).

58. Pessen, *Jacksonian America*, 247, 175, 242; Shankman, *Crucible*, 216–19; John H. Kennedy to Ralph Gurley, 27 November 1827, ACS Papers Series I, Volume 7, Reel 3.

59. Carey, *Letters on the Colonization Society*, 4th ed., iv; Carey to Gurley, 25 June 1833 [*sic*], 23 July 1832, and 9 July 1832, all in ACS Papers; Carey to [unknown], 7 May 1832, in *Miscellaneous Essays of Matt Carey*, assembled from a private collection of Samuel Breck, available at the Library Company of Philadelphia; ACS, 15th Annual Report, 39–46; Mathew Carey to Ralph Gurley, 7 September 1829, 15 April 1832, 14 April 1832, 9 April 1832, 3 April 1832, 23 March 1832, 24 May 1832, 25 June 1833 [likely 1832], 1 May 1832, 2 May 1832, 30 April 1832, 20 April 1832, all in ACS Papers; ACS, 23rd Annual Report; Mathew Carey, *Philosophy of Common Sense* (Philadelphia, 1835); Carey to Gurley, 22 September 1832, in ACS Papers; Staudenraus, *African Colonization*, 187.

60. Friedman, *Inventors of the Promised Land*, 236–43; Michael F. Holt, *The Fate of Their Country: Politicians, Slavery Extension, and the Coming of the Civil War* (New York: Hill and Wang, 2004); Staudenraus, *African Colonization*, 229.

61. Henry C. Carey, *The Slave Trade, Domestic and Foreign* (Philadelphia, 1856), 57–58; Henry C. Carey, *The Harmony of Interests, Agricultural, Manufacturing and Commercial* (New York, 1856), 145; Mathew Carey, *Past, Present, Future*, 320; Frederickson, *Black Image in the White Mind*, 6; Robert Engs and Randall Miller, Introduction to *The Birth of the Grand Old Party: The Republican's First Generation* (Philadelphia: University of Pennsylvania Press, 2002); Michael F. Holt, "Making and Mobilizing the Republican Party, 1854–1860," in *Birth of the Grand Old Party*, ed. Engs and Miller, 29–59; Eric Foner, "The Ideology of the Republican Party," in *Birth of the Grand Old Party*, ed. Engs and Miller, 8–28; Leonard L. Richards, *The Slave Power: The Free North and Southern Domination, 1780–1860* (Baton Rouge: Louisiana State University Press, 2000); Robert V. Remini, *The Legacy of Andrew Jackson: Essays on Democracy, Indian Removal, and Slavery* (Baton Rouge: Louisiana State University Press, 1988); Jonathan H. Earle, *Jacksonian Antislavery and the Politics of Free Soil, 1824–1854* (Chapel Hill: University of North Carolina Press, 2004); Frederick J. Blue, *The Free Soilers: Third Party Politics, 1848–1854* (Urbana: University of Illinois Press, 1973); Foner, *Free Soil, Free Labor, Free Men*, 36, 59, 61, 72; Eric Foner, *Politics and Ideology in the Age of the Civil War* (New York: Oxford University Press, 1980).

62. Frederickson, *Black Image in the White Mind*, 25; Carey, "Essay on Public Charities," 181, 187.

Notes to Chapter 4

1. *Colonization Herald*, 17 October 1835, contains several articles about the attack. Quote is from William I. Weaver, the superintendent of Edina, to officials in Monrovia, dated 11 June 1835, reprinted in *Colonization Herald*, 3.

2. "To the Christian Public," *Colonization Herald*, 17 October 1835, 3.

3. ACS, 13th Annual Report, 17, 53–55; ACS, 14th Annual Report, 2–3, v, 15; *African Repository* 6, no. 9 (November 1830): 282–83; *African Repository* 6, no. 8 (October

1830): 248; *African Repository* 7, no. 2 (April 1831): 59, 45–46; *African Repository* 7, no. 8 (October 1831): 251; *African Repository* 7, no. 9 (November 1831): 284; ACS, 15th Annual Report, 11–12; *African Repository* 8, no. 5 (July 1832): 155; Burin, *Slavery and the Peculiar Solution*, 35.

4. Joseph Samuel Hepburn, "Special Report on the Life and Works of Elliott Cresson," *Journal of the Franklin Institute* 281, no. 3 (1966): 263, 264; Horace Mann Bond, *Education for Freedom: A History of Lincoln University, Pennsylvania* (Princeton: Princeton University Press, 1976), 3–4, 114; "Elliott Cresson, [obituary]," *Colonization Herald*, new series, no. 45, March 1854, 2; R. J. M. Blackett, *Building an Antislavery Wall: Black Americans in the Atlantic Abolitionist Movement, 1830–1860* (Baton Rouge: Louisiana State University Press, 1983), 54.

5. Staudenraus, *African Colonization*, 125; William B. Davidson to Gurley, 24 March 1827, and Cresson to Gurley, 23 August 1828, both in ACS Papers.

6. Cresson to Gurley [heading missing], August 1828, 23 August 1828, all in ACS Papers; PCS, 3rd Annual Report, 10; Kurt Lee Kocher, "'A Duty to America and Africa': A History of the Independent African Colonization Movement in Pennsylvania," *Pennsylvania History* 51, no. 2 (1984): 124; Winch, *Gentleman of Color*, 236; Burin, *Slavery and the Peculiar Solution*, 36.

7. *African Repository* 5, no. 11 (January 1830): 342–43; *African Repository* 6, no. 5 (July 1830): 159; *African Repository* 6, no. 9 (November 1830): 267; Boyd to Gurley, 2 November 1833, in ACS Papers.

8. Elliott Cresson, *American Colonization Society. Liberia*, 1831.

9. Burin, *Slavery and the Peculiar Solution*, 83, 96; Burin, "Rethinking Northern White Support," 199–200, 224–25; Captain Sherman to the PCS, 4 June 1830, printed in the *African Repository* 6, no. 5 (July 1830): 142–43; Cresson, address at the ACS 14th Annual Convention, 14th Annual Report, v.

10. Staudenraus, *African Colonization*, 4–7, 13–16, 18–19.

11. Ibid., 19–20; Frederickson, *Black Image in the White Mind*, 6; "Colonization Meeting," *Colonization Herald*, 25 June 1836, 1; R. R. Gurley, *Address at the Annual Meeting of the Pennsylvania Colonization Society, November 11, 1839* (Philadelphia: Herman Hooker, 1839), 8; John H. B. Latrobe, *Liberia: Its Origin, Rise, Progress, and Results. An Address Delivered Before the American Colonization Society, January 20th, 1880*, 2nd ed. (Washington, D.C.: Printed for the Society, 1883), 5; Cresson to Gurley, 30 April 1832, in ACS Papers; Andrew E. Murray, "The Founding of Lincoln University," *Journal of Presbyterian History* (Winter 1973): 393.

12. *African Repository* 14, no. 5 (May 1838): 151–52; ACS. 14th Annual Report, 12–14; *African Repository* 8, no. 3 (May 1832): 73–74.

13. ACS, 14th Annual Report, iv; Edward Everett, Address to the ACS 15th Annual Convention, xii–xxii; "Effects of the Colonization Scheme on the Slave Trade," ACS, 15th Annual Report, 45–46; Cresson to Gurley, 10 March 1831, 11 November 1830, 4 December 1829, 23 June 1831, 29 July 1831, 24 February 1831, 6 September 1831, all in ACS Papers; "Effects of Colonization on Slavery," *Colonization Herald*, 10 January 1837; *Colonization Herald*, 19 March 1836, 2; Cresson, *Liberia*, 1831; Cresson to Gurley, 4 December 1829, 18 November 1830, both in ACS Papers.

14. ACS, 15th Annual Report, 6–7; ACS, 14th Annual Report, 5–11; ACS, 13th Annual Report. For information on Devany's visit, see ACS, 14th Annual Report, 5–6, and for Russwurm's paper see 10.

15. Blackett, *Building an Antislavery Wall*, 56, citing the *Patriot*, 18 July and 1 August 1832.

16. Cresson to Gurley, date illegible but indications point to February 1829, ACS Papers.

17. Cresson to Gurley, 6 September 1831, ACS Papers.

18. Cresson to Gurley [date illegible but answered 12 March 1828], 23 August 1828, refers to school opened by Fortens and Douglasses, both in ACS Papers; see also Winch, *Gentleman of Color*, 116, 401; Cresson to Gurley, 11 November 1829, 4 March 1828, both in ACS Papers.

19. Davis, "Northern Colonizationists and Free Blacks," 653, 662; Cresson to Gurley, 25 September 1830, 5 August 1830, 26 August 1830, 10 September 1830, all in ACS Papers.

20. Henry Clay, "Appendix F," PCS 3rd Annual Report, 28; Job R. Tyson, *A Discourse Before the Young Men's Colonization Society of Pennsylvania Delivered October 24, 1834 in St. Paul's Church* (Philadelphia: Printed for the Society, 1834); Burin, *Slavery and the Peculiar Solution*, 22. For more on colonizationists and their racial views, see Frederickson, *Black Image in the White Mind*, 13–16. See also F. Freeman, *Yaradee: A Plea for Africa, In Familial Conversations on the Subject of Slavery and Colonization* (Philadelphia: J. Whetham, 1836).

21. Reverend John P. Carter, *Address of Rev. John P. Carter delivered at his installation as President of the Ashmun Institute, December 31, 1856* (Philadelphia, 1857), 5, 7.

22. Cortlandt Van Rensselaer, *God Glorified by Africa: An Address Delivered on 31 December 1856, at the Opening of the Ashmun Institute, Near Oxford, Pennsylvania* (Philadelphia: J. M. Wilson, 1859), 34, 24–25, first published in 1857 in the *Presbyterian Magazine*; Joseph Ingersoll, *Address of Joseph R. Ingersoll at the Annual Meeting of the Pennsylvania Colonization Society, October 25, 1838* (Philadelphia: William Stavely, 1838), 10; Burin, *Slavery and the Peculiar Solution*, 22.

23. Van Rensselaer, *God Glorified*, 6–8, 10.

24. "Prospectus," *Colonization Herald*, 4 April 1835, 1.

25. Davis, "Northern Colonizationists and Free Blacks," 656, 663; *African Repository* 5, no. 4 (April 1830): 46–47; Bond, *Education for Freedom*, 169. See also Vincent P. Franklin, "Education for Colonization: Attempts to Educate Free Blacks in the United States for Emigration to Africa, 1823–1833," *Journal of Negro Education* 43, no. 1 (1974): 91–103.

26 Bond, *Education for Freedom*, 169; Cresson to Gurley, 29 January 1830, 6 July 1830, 26 May 1830, 20 February 1832, [heading missing], and 25 September 1830, all in ACS Papers; Davis, "Northern Colonizationists and Free Blacks," 663; Boyd, *Education for Freedom*, 164.

27. William Jay, *An Inquiry into the Character and Tendency of the American Colonization and American Anti-Slavery Societies* (Boston: Crocker and Brewster; 3rd ed., New York: Leavitt, Lord, 1835), 28–29.

28. Jay, *Inquiry*, 30–33; Bruce Rosen, "Abolition and Colonization, the Years of Conflict: 1829–1834," *Phylon* 33, no. 2 (1972): 190; Leonard L. Richards, *Gentlemen of Property and Standing: Anti-Abolition Mobs in Jacksonian America* (1970; New York: Oxford University Press, 1974), 38–40.

29. Rosen, "Abolition and Colonization," 188–89, 191, 190.

30. Cresson to Gurley, 11 June 1834, ACS Papers.

31. For immediatist use of the media, see Newman, *Transformation*, 12; Peers to Gurley, 4 October 1826, in ACS Papers; Davis, "Northern Colonizationists and Free Blacks," 6/2–73. For donation list, see ACS, 13th Annual Report, 55; Cresson to Gurley, 3 August 1829, 12 April 1830, and Josiah Polk to Gurley, 7 July 1830, all in ACS Papers.

32. For Russwurm's role as superintendent, see ACS, 13th Annual Report, 11; Winch, *Gentleman of Color*, 202, 205, 236; Cresson to Gurley, 1 January 1828, in ACS Papers.

33. Cresson to Gurley, 1 January 1828, in ACS Papers.

34. For Quaker women and reform, see Bruce Dorsey, "Friends Becoming Enemies: Philadelphia Benevolence and the Neglected Era of American Quaker History," *Journal of the Early Republic* 18, no. 3 (1998): 400. ACS, 14th Annual Report, 15; Josiah Polk to R. R. Gurley, 23 July 1830, and Dr. Beaton Smith, manager of Columbia Pennsylvania Colonization Society to Josiah Polk, 20 July 1830, both in ACS Papers; *African Repository* 5, no. 12 (February 1830): 384; *African Repository* 8, no. 6 (August 1832): 191; *Colonization Herald*, 29 May 1836, 1; *African Repository* 6, no. 3 (May 1830): 87; *African Repository* 6, no. 2 (April 1830): 63; John Crosby to Gurley, 23 December 1831; L. Fletcher of Chester County, Pennsylvania, to Gurley, 17 July 1832; and Leonard Fletcher to Gurley, 4 September 1833; all in ACS Papers; Rev. John Crosby, ACS agent, to Gurley 23, December 1831, in *African Repository* 7, no. 12 (February 1832): 378; ACS, 20th Annual Report, 17; *African Repository* 5, no. 12 (February 1830): 382; *African Repository* 8, no. 6 (August 1832): 190; ACS, 18th Annual Report, 15; *Colonization Herald* 4 July 1835, 4.

35. Bruce Dorsey, "A Gendered History of African Colonization in the Antebellum United States," *Journal of Social History* 34, no. 1 (2000): 80; ACS, 13th Annual Report, x–xi, 17.

36. Cresson to Gurley, 9 June 1832; John Crosby to Gurley, 6 July 1832, 19 July 1832; Eliza Jones to Gurley, 26 July 1832; and Crosby to Gurley, 16 October 1832; all in ACS Papers; "Ladies Liberia Association," *Colonization Herald*, 4 April 1835, 2, 3.

37. Cresson to Gurley, 8 April 1830, 4 December 1829, 15 April 1831; and Jackson Kemper to Gurley, 6 May 1831; all in ACS Papers; *African Repository* 13, no. 9 (September 1837): 293–35; ACS, 21st Annual Report, 25.

38. *African Repository* 5, no. 12 (February 1830): 375–77; Mary Beth Norton, *Liberty's Daughters: The Revolutionary Experiences of American Women, 1750–1800* (Ithaca, N.Y.: Cornell University Press, 1996); Alisse Portnoy, *Their Right to Speak: Women's Activism in the Indian and Slave Debates* (Cambridge: Harvard University Press, 2005); Dorsey, "Gendered History," 82.

39. Staudenraus, *African Colonization*, 135; Appendix 10, in ACS, 13th Annual Report, 53–55, 17; ACS, 14th Annual Report, v, 2–3, 15; PCS, 3rd Annual Report, 8–10; *African Repository* 6, no. 2 (April 1830): 62; *African Repository* 6, no. 8 (1830): 248; *African Repository* 6, no. 9 (November 1830): 282–83; *African Repository* 7, no. 2 (April 1831): 59, 45–46; ACS, 15th Annual Report, 11–12; *African Repository* 7, no. 8 (October 1831): 251; *African Repository* 7, no. 9 (November 1831): 284.

40. J. W. Bayard to Gurley, 2 December 1829; Cresson to Gurley, 23 November 1829; Hanson to Gurley, 7 December 1829, 19 December 1829; and Ralston to Gurley, 30 December 1829; all in ACS Papers.

41. Ralston to Gurley, 30 December 1829, 3 January 1830; Cresson to Gurley, 3 January 1830; Ralston to Gurley, 25 January 1829 [*sic*], 5 February 1830; all in ACS Papers.

42. Cresson to Gurley, 13 February 1830; Ralston to Gurley, 5 March 1830; Cresson

to Gurley, 22 February 1830, 4 March 1830, 5 March 1830; Ralston to Gurley, 5 March 1830; George Edwards to Gurley, 12 March 1830; John Kennedy to Gurley, 13 March 1830; D. J. Burr to Gurley, 12 March 1830; Cresson to Gurley, 26 May 1830; and Polk to Gurley, 1 September 1830; all in ACS Papers.

43. Cresson to Gurley, 27 March 1830, 3 June 1830, 6 July 1830, 5 August 1830, 10 September 1830, 11 November 1830, 12 September 1830, 10 March 1831, 19 March 1831, all in ACS Papers.

44. Cresson to Gurley, 10 July 1830; Orr to Gurley, 15 July 1830; Cresson to Gurley, 10 September 1830, 15 March 1833; all in ACS Papers.

45. Cresson to Gurley, 17 May 1830, 20 June 1830, 30 June 1830, 5 August 1830, 10 September 1830, 25 September 1830, 24 February 1831, all in ACS Papers.

46. Cresson to Gurley, 4 December 1829, 27 March 1830, both in ACS Papers.

47. Ralston to Gurley, 15 December 1829, 19 December 1829; Cresson to Gurley, 30 September 1830, 4 October 1830, 18 November 1830, 13 March 1831; all in ACS Papers.

48. Cresson to Gurley, 19 March 1831; PCS Board of Managers to Gurley; 31 March 1831, Cresson to Dr. Field, 8 April 1831; Cresson to Gurley, 12 April 1831; PCS Board to Gurley, 15 April 1831; Davidson to Gurley, 21 July 1831; James Bayard to Gurley, 25 August 1831, 31 August 1831; Cresson to Gurley, 7 May 1832; Kennedy to Gurley, 23 October 1832, 24 October 1832; and Cresson to Gurley, 11 June 1834; all in ACS Papers.

49. Cresson to Gurley, 3 August 1829, 12 September 1830, November 1830, 6 July 1832, all in ACS Papers; ACS, 15th Annual Report, 14; Staudenraus, *African Colonization*, 216; ACS, 15th Annual Report, 49; ACS, 16th Annual Report, 22–23; ACS, 17th Annual Report, 14–15, 43–46; *African Repository*, 8, no. 9 (November 1832): 257; *African Repository* 8, no. 11 (January 1833): 344–45; *African Repository* 7, no. 9 (November 1831): 280–81; *African Repository* 7, no. 10 (December 1831): 320; *African Repository* 7, no. 12 (February 1832): 385; *African Repository* 8, no. 3 (May 1832): 77–80; *African Repository* 8, no. 5 (July 1832): 155; Cresson to Gurley, 9 June 1832, ACS Papers.

50. Burin, "Rethinking Northern White Support," 208; Blackett, *Antislavery Wall*, 55–60; Anthony Barker, *Captain Charles Stuart, Anglo-American Abolitionist* (Baton Rouge: Louisiana State University Press, 1986).

51. Cresson to Gurley, 16 April 1832, 31 May 1831, 6 October 1831, 23 June 1831, all in ACS Papers; Blackett, *Antislavery Wall*, 55; Cresson to Gurley, [heading missing], and 23 June 1831, both in ACS Papers.

52. Blackett, *Antislavery Wall*, 56–57; Staudenraus, *African Colonization*, 217; Cresson to Gurley, 6 September 1831 and 16 April 1832, both in ACS Papers.

53. Cresson to *Albion*, April 1832, sent with letter to Gurley, 30 April 1832, in ACS Papers.

54. Cresson to Gurley, 6 January 1832, 20 June 1831, 5 December 1831; and Cresson to *Morning Post*, 20 December 1831; all in ACS Papers.

55. Blackett, *Antislavery Wall*, 58; Cresson to Gurley, 22 May 1832 and 10 November 1832, both in ACS Papers.

56. *Liberator* 3, no. 10 (9 March 1833); Cresson to Gurley, 28 June 1833 and 15 August 1833, both in ACS Papers; Jay, *Inquiry*, 123; Paul to Garrison, 22 January 1834, in *Liberator*, 4, no. 15, 12 April 1834. For more on Allen, see *African Repository* 9, no. 7 (September 1833): 211–15; *African Repository* 9, no. 9 (November 1833): 257–58; ACS, 17th Annual Report, xi.

57. Cresson to Gurley, 6 September 1831, 25 July 1832, 28 January 1833, 25 August 1832, 6 September 1831, 6 July 1832, 14 January 1832, 6 January 1832, 10 September 1830, all in ACS Papers.

58. Cresson to Gurley, 20 June 1831, 22 July 1831, 6 September 1831, 15 March 1833, all in ACS Papers.

59. Cresson to Gurley, 18 November 1830, 29 July 1831, 6 October 1831, [heading missing]; Ralston to Gurley, 5 December 1831, Cresson to Gurley, 10 December 1831, [heading missing, likely September 1832]; all in ACS Papers.

60. Cresson to Gurley, 2 November 1833, 10 November 1832, 28 June 1833, all in ACS Papers.

61. Cresson to Gurley, 6 August 1831, ACS Papers.

62. Cresson to Gurley, 6 July 1832, 29 July 1831, 22 July 1831, 28 January 1833, 10 November 1832, 29 July 1831, 16 April 1832, 25 July 1832, all in ACS Papers.

63. Cresson to Gurley, 16 June 1832, ACS Papers.

64. Cresson to Gurley, 15 August 1833, 5 December 1831, 2 November 1833; and Cresson to "Gentlemen," 2 November 1833; all in ACS Papers; Blackett, *Antislavery Wall*, 64; Davis, "Northern Colonizationists and Free Blacks," 666.

65. Cresson to Gurley, 15 August 1833, ACS Papers.

66. Cresson to Gurley, 5 August 1830, 26 August 1830, 6 July 1832, 2 November 1833, 10 November 1832, 28 December 1831, 10 November 1831, 10 September 1830, 26 August 1830, 30 September 1830, 28 December 1831, 14 January 1832, 22 May 1832, all in ACS Papers.

67. Cresson to Gurley, [date illegible but apparently January of 1829], 27 March 1830, 6 August 1831, 5 December 1831, 22 May 1832, 9 June 1832, 13 February 1834, 11 June 1834, 26 August 1830, 24 February 1831, 11 November 1830, 26 March 1831, all in ACS Papers.

68. Cresson to Gurley, 18 November 1830, 24 February 1831, 12 April 1831, 16 June 1832, all in ACS Papers; Blackett, *Antislavery Wall*, 59; Cresson to Gurley, 21 December 1833, ACS Papers.

69. Cresson to Gurley, 21 December 1833, 11 June 1834, 9 June 1830; and Gurley to Yates, 1 April 1834; all in ACS Papers.

70. Cresson to Gurley, 13 February 1834, and Cresson to Gentlemen, 20 November 1833, both in ACS Papers; Staudenraus, *African Colonization*, 223.

71. Miles White to Gurley, 28 September 1830; Cresson to Gurley, 10 March 1831, 13 March 1831; George Blight to Gurley, 28 May 1832; Cresson to Gurley, 26 April 1832, 6 September 1831; and Ralston to Gurley, 18 January 1833; all in ACS Papers.

72. Staudenraus, *African Colonization*, 178–82; Tise, *Proslavery*, 71–73; Thomas R. Dew, *Review of the Debate in the Virginia Legislature of 1831 and 1832* (Richmond: T. W. White, 1832). See also Kenneth M. Stampp, "An Analysis of T. R. Dew's Review of the Debates in the Virginia Legislature," *Journal of Negro History* 27, no. 4 (1942): 380–87.

73. Walsh to Gurley, 19 September 1832, ACS Papers; [Leonard Bacon], "Review of Pamphlets on Slavery and Colonization" (Boston: Baldwin and Ellis, 1833), originally published in *Quarterly Christian Spectator*, March 1838, 2nd separate edition, 22–23.

74. Staudenraus, *African Colonization*, 221; William Lloyd Garrison, *Thoughts on African Colonization; or an Impartial Exhibition of the Doctrines, Principles and Purposes of the American Colonization Society* (Boston: Garrison and Knapp, 1832), 2, 5, 7; Stewart, *Holy Warriors*, 31; Stewart, "Racial Modernity," 211.

75. Cresson to Gurley, 4 March 1830, 18 November 1830; Vaux to ACS Board of Managers, 9 June 1832; and Vaux to Gurley, 21 June 1832; all in ACS Papers; Gurley to Vaux, 27 June 1832, reprinted by the temperance society, flyer at HSP; *African Repository* 6, no. 11 (January 1831): 333–34; *African Repository* 8, no. 4 (June 1832): 128; ACS, 15th Annual Report, 8; *African Repository* 9, no. 7 (September 1832): 205–6.

76. Eli Seifman, "The United Colonization Societies of New York and Pennsylvania and the Establishment of the African Colony of Bassa Cove," *Pennsylvania History* 35, no. 1 (1968): 31; Cresson to Gurley, 11 November 1830, ACS Papers; *Liberator*, 3, no. 14 (6 April 1833); *African Repository* 9, no. 3 (May 1833): 66–68.

77. Staudenraus, *African Colonization*, 128; Smith to Gurley, 8 February 1831, ACS Papers; ACS, 14th Annual Report, xi–xiv; Seifman, "United Societies," 33–34; Staudenraus, *African Colonization*, 213; ACS, 17th Annual Report; *African Repository* 10, no. 1 (March 1834): 17–19, 8; Frankie Hutton, "Economic Considerations in the American Colonization Society's Early Effort to Emigrate Free Blacks to Liberia, 1816–36," *Journal of Negro History* 68, no. 4 (1983): 382; ACS, 18th Annual Report, 18; Merton L. Dillon, *The Abolitionists: The Growth of a Dissenting Minority* (New York: W. W. Norton, 1974), 93; *Colonization Herald* 1, no. 18 (19 December 1835).

78. Jay, *Inquiry*, 124; ACS, 15th Annual Report, ix; Bacon, "Review," 18, 5, 19–22.

79. ACS, 16th Annual Report; Staudenraus, *African Colonization*, 208–9.

80. ACS, 16th Annual Report, 41–42; ACS, 17th Annual Report, xviii–xix; Seifman, "United Societies," 35–36.

81. Fox, *American Colonization Society*, 110–12; Cresson to P. Fendall, 13 September 1833, and Cresson to Gurley, 21 December 1833, both in ACS Papers; ACS, 17th Annual Report, x–xi; Seifman, "United Societies," 34.

82. Cresson to Gurley, 24 February 1831, 12 April 1831; Gurley to Fendall, 27 September 1833; and Cresson to Gurley, 15 August 1833; all in ACS Papers; ACS, 17th Annual Report, 16–17; *African Repository* 9, no. 3 (May 1833): 89–91; *African Repository* 11, no. 4 (April 1834): 102–3; Staudenraus, *African Colonization*, 232–33; Seifman, "United Societies," 33–36; Gurley to Fendall, 23 November 1833, ACS Papers; Kocher, "Duty," 127–28; Cresson to Gurley, 21 December 1833, and Gurley to Fendall, 2 December 1833, both in ACS Papers.

83. Gurley to Fendall, 27 November 1833, and Gurley to Yates, 31 March 1834, both in ACS Papers; Seifman, "United Societies," 37; *African Repository* 10, no. 5 (July 1834): 151; *African Repository* 10, no. 7 (September 1834): 193–98; Cresson to Gurley, 5 May 1834, ACS Papers; ACS, 18th Annual Report,1; Fox, *American Colonization Society*, 61; Kocher, "Duty," 140–41, 128–29; Staudenraus, *African Colonization*, 234–35; Tyson, *Discourse*, 6, 20, 43, 31; YMCSP, 1837 Annual Report, 12; YMCSP, 1838 Annual Report, 45.

84. Taylor to Gurley, 30 April 1831, in ACS Papers.

Notes to Chapter 5

1. For Forten's life and family background, see Winch, *Gentleman of Color*.

2. Ibid., 36.

3. Ibid., 37, 41–43, 49; W. Jeffrey Bolster, *Black Jacks: African American Seamen in the Age of Sail* (reprint, Boston: Harvard University Press, 1998).

4. Winch, *Gentleman of Color*, 61.

5. Ibid., 73–75, 85, 89, 116.

6. Leon F. Litwack, *North of Slavery: The Negro in the Free States, 1790–1860*, 5th ed. (1961; Chicago: University of Chicago Press, 1969), 15.

7. Winch, *Gentleman of Color*, 132–36; Nash, *Forging Freedom*, 175.

8. Carey, "Short Account of the Malignant Fever"; Jones and Allen, "Narrative of the Proceedings of the Black People"; Newman, *Freedom's Prophet*, 78–127.

9. Winch, *Gentleman of Color*, 152.

10. Ibid., 153. Apparently the original petition has been lost.

11. Ibid., 155–56.

12. Winch, *Gentleman of Color*, 156; Nash and Soderlund, *Freedom by Degrees*, 131–34; Zilversmit, *First Emancipation*, 203–4.

13. Winch, *Gentleman of Color*, 161–62.

14. Nash, *Forging Freedom*, 134–71, 173–76, 180–81. See also Carl Oblinger, "New Freedoms, Old Miseries: The Emergence and Disruption of Black Communities in Southeastern Pennsylvania, 1780–1860," PhD diss., Lehigh University, 1988.

15. Nash, *Forging Freedom*, 182.

16. James Forten, *Letters from a Man of Colour, on a Late Bill Before the Senate of Pennsylvania* (Philadelphia, 1813), 1–2, 10–11.

17. Ibid., 2.

18. Ibid., 11.

19. Patrick Rael, *Black Identity and Black Protest in the Antebellum North* (Chapel Hill: University of North Carolina Press, 2002), 213–14.

20. Emma Jones Lapsansky, "'Since They Got Those Separate Churches': Afro-Americans and Racism in Jacksonian Philadelphia," in *African Americans in Pennsylvania: Shifting Historical Perspectives*, ed. Joe William Trotter Jr. and Eric Ledell Smith (Philadelphia: Pennsylvania State University Press, 1997), 93–122, 101–2; Nash, *Forging Freedom*, 254–59.

21. Lapsansky, "'Since They Got Those Separate Churches," 111–12; James O. Horton and Lois E. Horton, *In Hope of Liberty: Culture, Community and Protest among Northern Free Blacks, 1700–1860* (New York: Oxford University Press, 1997), 204–7. To compare the process of black community formation in New England and New York, see William D. Pierson, *Black Yankees: The Development of an Afro-American Subculture in Eighteenth-Century New England* (Amherst: University of Massachusetts Press, 1980), and Kathryn Grover, *Make a Way Somehow: African-American Life in a Northern Community, 1790–1965* (Syracuse, N.Y.: Syracuse University Press, 1994).

22. Litwack, *North of Slavery*, 18.

23. For thwarted attempts of blacks to control their own struggle, see Nash, *Forging Freedom*, 109, 191–202, 205–11, 218–19, 230–31. For the declining status of free blacks in Philadelphia, see also Horton, "From Class to Race in Early America," esp. 644–46, and Theodore Hershberg, "Free Blacks in Antebellum Philadelphia," in *Peoples of Philadelphia*, ed. Davis and Haller, 111–34.

24. Wayne Ackerson, *The African Institution (1807–1827) and the Antislavery Movement in Great Britain* (Lewiston, Me.: Edwin Mellen Press, 2005), 59–76; For an overview of British abolition and Sierra Leone, see Walvin, *England, Slaves, and Freedom*, and Christopher Fyfe, *A History of Sierra Leone* (London: Oxford University Press, 1961).

25. Lamont D. Thomas, *Paul Cuffee: Black Entrepreneur and Pan-Africanist* (Urbana: University of Illinois Press, 1988), 19, 33–35; Winch, *Gentleman of Color*,

178–80; James Pemberton to Paul Cuffee, 8 June 1808, in, *Captain Paul Cuffee's Logs and Letters, 1808–1817: A Black Quaker's "Voice from within the Veil,"* ed. Rosalind Cobb Wiggins (Washington, D.C.: Howard University Press, 1996), 77–78; James Pemberton to Paul Cuffee, 27 September 1808, in Wiggins, 79–80; Henry Noble Sherwood, "The Redemption of Africa," *Journal of Negro History* 8, no. 2 (1923): 167–73. This entire issue of the *Journal of Negro History* showcased Sherwood's work on Cuffee in a series of articles that traced his life. Pemberton is discussed on 167–70. See also Sherwood, "Paul Cuffee and his Contribution to the American Colonization Society," *Proceedings of the Mississippi Valley Historical Association for the Year 1912–1913, Volume VI,* Benjamin F. Shambaugh, editor (Cedar Rapids, Iowa: Torch Press, 1913), 370–402; Ackerson, *African Institution,* 72–76; Horton and Horton, *In Hope of Liberty,* 181, 179.

26. Paul Cuffee to Nathan G. M. Senter, 7 March 1814, in Wiggins, 276–77; Cuffee to John James and Alexander Wilson, 10 June 1809, in Wiggins, 80–81; James and Wilson to William Dillwyn, 21 June 1809, in Wiggins, 81–82; Thomas, *Paul Cuffee,* 59, 40, 46; Cuffee to Christopher McPharson [*sic*], 25 April 1813, in Wiggins, 245–46; Cuffee to Laban Wheaton [*sic*], 20 April 1814, in Wiggins, 281–82; Cuffee to Nathan Lord, 19 April 1815, in Wiggins, 341–42; Cuffee to William Allen, 1 April 1816, in Wiggins, 408–11; Cuffee to Cato Sawyer, 17 February 1814, in Wiggins, 271–72.

27. Zacharay Macaulay to William Dillwyn, 29 August 1809, quoted in Thomas, *Paul Cuffee,* 44; Thomas, *Paul Cuffee,* 54, 59. See also editorial comments as well as correspondence between Cuffee and Allen throughout Wiggins.

28. Walker, *Black Loyalists*; Wilson, *Loyal Blacks.*

29. Thomas, *Paul Cuffee,* 61.

30. Ibid., 77, 96; African Institution of Philadelphia, "Voyage to Africa," *Poulson's Daily American Advertiser,* 20 September 1815.

31. Philadelphia African Institution to parent society, 15 November 1815, in African Institution, *Tenth Report,* 70–71. According to Thomas, the letter also appeared in the *Boston Recorder* on 18 March 1817. See Thomas, *Paul Cuffee,* 152 n12. Cuffee to Forten, 29 May 1816, in Wiggins, 413; Cuffee to William Allen, 1 April 1816, in Wiggins, 408–10; Thomas, *Paul Cuffee,* 102, 98; For information on the settlers, see Winch, *Gentleman of Color,* 185; Horton and Horton, *In Hope of Liberty,* 178, 186.

32. Cuffee to Gardner Wainer, 14 August 1814, in Wiggins, 297; Cuffee to Samuel J. Mills, 15 March 1814, in Wiggins, 279–80; Cuffee to Forten, 27 January 1815, in Wiggins, 308–9; Cuffee to Forten, 27 March 1815, in Wiggins, 330–31; Cuffee to Richard Allen, 27 March 1815, in Wiggins, 331.

33. Cuffee to Peter Williams Jr., 14 June 1816, in Wiggins, 414–15; John James to Paul Cuffee, 7 June 1816, in Wiggins, 416–17; Samuel Aiken to Cuffee, 23 July 1816, in Wiggins, 427–28; Cuffee to Mills, 15 March 1814, in Wiggins, 279–80; Cuffee to Mills, 30 April 1814, in Wiggins, 283; Nathan Lord to Cuffee, 12 April 1815, in Wiggins, 349–50; Cuffee to Lord, 19 April 1815, in Wiggins, 341–31; Thomas, *Paul Cuffee,* 94. For Mills's background, see Staudenraus, *African Colonization,* 18.

34. Horton and Horton, *In Hope of Liberty,* 182; Cuffee to Lord, 19 April 1815, in Wiggins, 341–43; Thomas, *Paul Cuffee,* 68.

35. See Thomas, *Paul Cuffee,* 104, for Cuffee's abandonment by the institution, and 113–19, for his relationship with the American Colonization Society. See also Henry Noble Sherwood, "The Formation of the American Colonization Society," *Journal of*

Negro History 2, no. 3 (1917): 209–28, and Henry Noble Sherwood, "A Friend in Need," *Journal of Negro History* 8, no. 2 (1923): 211–20.

36. Edward Scobie, *Black Britannia: A History of Blacks In Britain* (Chicago: Johnson Publishing, 1972), 67; James Walvin, *The Black Presence: A Documentary History of the Negro in England, 1555–1860* (New York: Schocken Books, 1972); Olaudah Equiano, *The Life of Olaudah Equiano*, ed. Paul Edwards (Essex, Eng.: Longman Group UK, 1988), xv, 187; Robert J. Allison, preface to Olaudah Equiano, *The Interesting Narrative of the Life of Olaudah Equiano, Written by Himself* (New York: Bedford Books of St. Martin's Press, 1995), 187; Cassandra Pybus, *Epic Journeys of Freedom: Runaway Slaves of the American Revolution and their Global Quest for Liberty* (Boston: Beacon Press, 2007), 84–86, 104–6. See also Vincent Carretta, *Equiano, the African: Biography of a Self-Made Man* (New York: Penguin, 2007); Ottobah Cugoano, *Thoughts and Sentiments* (London, 1787) in Walvin, *Black Presence*, 85–86.

37. Rael, *Black Identity*, 209–12.

38. Sherwood, "Friend in Need," 212–14; Thomas, *Paul Cuffee*, 113; Cuffee to Forten, 8 January 1817, in Wiggins, 493–94; Forten to Cuffee, 25 January 1817, in Wiggins, 501–3; Horton and Horton, *In Hope of Liberty*, 188.

39. For an account of the meeting, see Benjamin Quarles, *Black Abolitionists* (New York: Oxford University Press, 1969; reprint, New York: Da Capo Press, 1991), 3–5; James Forten and Russel Parrott, *To the humane and benevolent Inhabitants of the city and country of Philadelphia*, reprinted in *Minutes of the Proceedings of a Special Meeting of the 15th American Convention for Promoting the Abolition of Slavery* (Philadelphia: Hall and Atkinson, 1818); Winch, *Gentleman of Color*, 192–97.

40. Forten and Parrot, *To the humane and benevolent*.

41. Ibid.

42. Richard Peterson Jr., "Circular Address to the Abolition and Manumission Societies in the United States of America," 15 December 1818, *Minutes of the Proceedings of a Special Meeting of the Fifteenth American Convention for Promoting the Abolition of Slavery, and Improving the condition of the African Race* (Philadelphia: Hall and Atkinson, 1818), 60–68; PAS papers, HSP manuscript collections, vol. 6, box 10A. See also microfilm PAS papers, reel 15.

43. Nash, *Forging Freedom*, 241; Miller, *Search for a Black Nationality*, 60–61; McGraw, "Richmond Free Blacks," 210; Bruce, "National Identity," 15–28; Horton and Horton, *In Hope of Liberty*, 188. For a more thorough analysis of the agency of blacks in deciding whether to go to Liberia, see Claude A. Clegg III, *The Price of Liberty: African Americans and the Making of Liberia* (Chapel Hill: University of North Carolina Press, 2004).

44. William B. Davidson to Gurley, 6 February 1827, in ACS Papers.

45. Winch, *Gentleman of Color*, 197; George W. Brown, "Haiti and the United States," *Journal of Negro History* 8, no. 2 (1923): 135–37.

46. Prince Saunders, *Memoir Presented to the American Convention for Promoting the Abolition of Slavery, and Improving the Condition of the African Race*, 11 December 1818 (Philadelphia: Dennis Heartt, 1818), 8, 10–12, 16, 19.

47. C. L. R. James, *The Black Jacobins: Toussaint L'Ouverture and the San Domingo Revolution*, 2nd ed. (New York: Vintage Press, 1989); Winch, *Gentleman of Color*, 210.

48. Winch, *Gentleman of Color*, 214–15.

49. Ibid., 217–19.

50. Horton and Horton, *In Hope of Liberty*, 194 95; Clegg, *Price of Liberty*, 44–49.

51. Louis R. Mehlinger, "The Attitude of the Free Negro Toward African Coloniza-
tion," *Journal of Negro History* 1, no. 3 (1916): 287; Ella Forbes, "African-American
Resistance to Colonization," *Journal of Black Studies* 21, no. 2 (1990): 210–23; Winch,
Gentleman of Color, 197.

52. For the report, see the *Liberator* 1, no. 50 (10 December 1831), reprinted from
the *United States Gazette*; "A Colored Philadelphian," "Men Must Be Free," *Liberator*
1, no. 34 (20 August 1831).

53. Winch, *Gentleman of Color*, 237, 285, 287. For more on the legislature's attempts
to bar black emigration, Oblinger, "New Freedoms, Old Miseries," 118–19; "Sydney,"
"Violent Measurers," *Liberator* 1, no. 50 (10 December 1831).

54. [William Whipper and Robert Purvis], "A Remonstrance Against the Proceed-
ing of a Meeting, Held November 23rd, 1831, at Upton's in Dock Street, Philadelphia,"
[Philadelphia, 1832], 2; see also the *Liberator* 2, no. 15 (14 April 1832).

55. Winch, *Gentleman of Color*, 237–38, 315; Howard H. Bell, *A Survey of the Negro
Convention Movement, 1830–1861* (New York: Arno Press, 1969), 15; American Society
of Free Persons of Color, "Constitution of the American Society of Free Persons of
Colour, for improving their condition in the United States; for purchasing lands, and
for the establishment of a settlement in Upper Canada," (Philadelphia: J. W. Allen,
1831); James Forten, "An Address Delivered Before the Ladies' Anti-Slavery Society of
Philadelphia, On the Evening of the 14th of April 1836," (Philadelphia: Merrihew and
Gunn, 1836), 4.

56. Staudenraus, *African Colonization Movement*, 230.

57. Staughton Lynd, *Intellectual Origins of American Radicalism*, new ed. (1968;
New York: Cambridge University Press, 2009), xxvi.

58. Ibid., xxxiv, 4, 23, 44–46, 52–56, 59–60, 100, 96, 110.

59. Ibid., 103.

60. Asa Earl Martin, "Pioneer Anti-Slavery Press," *Mississippi Valley Historical
Review* 2, no. 4 (1916): 509–28; Winch, *Gentleman of Color*, 241; Wendell P. Garrison,
William Lloyd Garrison, 1805–1879, vol. 1 (New York: Century, 1885), 223.

61. Winch, *Gentleman of Color*, 242; "Mortality at Liberia," *Liberator* 1, no. 48 (26
November 1831); "Errata," *Liberator* 1, no. 47 (19 November 1831); Cato, "The Colo-
nization Crusade," *Liberator*, 1, no. 11 (12 March 1831); A Colored Philadelphian,
"A Few Words," *Liberator* 1, no. 12 (19 March 1831); Forten to *Liberator* 1, no. 4 (22
January 1831); Oneas, "Vindicatory," *Liberator* 1, no. 15 (9 April 1831); A Colored
Philadelphian, "Men Must Be Free," *Liberator* 1, no. 34 (20 August 1831); A Colored
Philadelphia, "Men Must Be Free," *Liberator* 1, no. 36 (3 September 1831); From the
Philadelphia Friend, "Free People of Color," *Liberator* 2, no. 15 (14 April 1832); "People
of Color," *Liberator* 5, no. 16 (18 April 1835); Goodman, *Of One Blood*.

62. Winch, *Gentleman of Color*, 250–51.

63. Ibid., 254; Forten to *Liberator*, 13 January 1831, printed as "Spirited Sentiments," *Liberator* 1, no. 4 (22 January 1831); "Important Testimony," *Liberator* 5, no.
31 (1 August 1835).

64. Winch, *Gentleman of Color*, 255–57; Gurley to Fendall, 3 December 1833, in
ACS Papers; *Liberator* 3, no. 15 (13 April 1833); Janice Sumler-Lewis, "The Forten-
Purvis Women of Philadelphia and the American Antislavery Crusade," *Journal of
Negro History* 66, no. 4 (1981–82): 281–88.

65. Winch, *Gentleman of Color*, 295–300. See also Alexander Keyssar, *The Right to Vote: The Contested History of Democracy in the United States* (New York: Basic Books, 2000), 54–60.

66. "Appeal of Forty Thousand Citizens, Threatened with Disfranchisement, to the People of Pennsylvania," (Philadelphia: Merrihew and Gunn, 1838), 4.

67. Ibid., 10–11; Hershberg, "Free Blacks," 112–14.

68. Rael, *Black Identity*, 211–13.

69. Winch, *Gentleman of Color*, 220, 307; Nash, *Forging Freedom*, 267–73; Horton and Horton, *In Hope of Liberty*, 208–9; Melish, "'Condition' Debate," a 659; Philadelphia Friend, "People of Color," *Liberator* 5, no. 16 (18 April 1835).

Notes to Chapter 6

1. W. P. Garrison, "Free Produce among the Quakers," *Atlantic Monthly*, October 1868, 485–94; Carol Faulkner, "The Root of the Evil: Free Produce and Radical Antislavery, 1820–1860," *Journal of the Early Republic* 27 (Fall 2007): 377–405.

2. ACS, 18th Annual Report, 11–12; For Gurley's address, see ACS, 21st Annual Report, 34–36; response by Mr. Garland, 36.

3. Cresson to Gurley, 23 September 1831, in ACS Papers; ACS, 15th Annual Report, 9; Cresson to Gurley, 6 October 1831, 5 December 1831, both in ACS Papers.

4. Ralph Gurley, *Address at the Annual Meeting of the Pennsylvania Colonization Society, November 11, 1839* (Philadelphia: Herman Hooker, 1839), 17–18; "A Southern Abolitionist" to the *Colonization Herald* 1, no. 12 (19 September 1835); Cresson speech reprinted in *Colonization Herald* 1, no. 3 (17 January 1838): 2; "The Union," *Colonization Herald* 1, no. 4 (24 January 1838): 2; "Be Alert and Doing," *Colonization Herald* 1, no. 2 (30 May 1838): 2.

5. "To the Friends of Colonization," *African Repository* 14, no. 5 (May 1838): 158–59; Fox, *American Colonization Society*, 114.

6. PCS Minute Book, 27 December 1838 and 9 May 1839; Coates to Wilkeson, 26 March 1840, ACS Papers.

7. Kocher, "Duty," 139; PCS Minute Book 5 June 1838; "Articles of Association of American Colonies in Africa," *African Repository* 15, no. 12 (1838); 205–7; Staudenraus *African Colonization*, 235–39; Seifman, "United Societies," 43. For the new constitution, see *African Repository* 14, no. 10 (October 1838): 227, 288–89; Fox, *American Colonization Society*, 115; *Colonization Herald* 1, no. 52 (26 December 1838): 2; PCS Minute Book, 27 December 1838.

8. Kocher, "Duty," 143; Fox, *American Colonization Society*, 114–23.

9. Wilkeson to [ACS?], 7 March 1838, in ACS, 21st Annual Report, 45–48. See also ACS, 22nd Annual Report, 9–10; *African Repository* 14, no. 5 (May 1838): 128–30.

10. *African Repository* 15, no. 19 (November 1839): 318; ACS, 23rd Annual Report, 7; *African Repository* 15, no. 1 (January 1839): 29; ACS, 22nd Report, 8.

11. *African Repository* 15, no. 16 (September 1839), 269–70; Ralph Gurley, *Address at the Annual Meeting of the Pennsylvania Colonization Society, November 11, 1839* (Philadelphia: Herman Hooker, 1839), 6–7, 30.

12. Calvin Colton, *Colonization and Abolition Contrasted* (Philadelphia: Herman Hooker, 1839), 2–12.

13. David Paul Brown, *Eulogium Upon Wilberforce: With a Brief Incidental Review*

of the Subject of Colonization. Delivered at the Request of the Abolition Society, March 10, 1834 (Philadelphia: T. K. Collins, 1834), 15, 18–19, 20.

14. Kocher, "Duty," 144; PCS Minute Book 2 July 1839 and 7 July 1839.

15. Emma J. Lapsansky-Werner and Margaret Hope Bacon, *Back to Africa: Benjamin Coates and the Colonization Movement in America, 1848–1880* (University Park: Pennsylvania State University Press, 2005), 18; Ryan P. Jordan, *Slavery and the Meetinghouse: The Quakers and the Abolitionist Dilemma, 1820–1865* (Indianapolis: Indiana University Press, 2007).

16. Lapsansky-Werner and Bacon, *Back to Africa*, 26.

17. Ibid., 28.

18. Ibid., 31; Coates to McClain, 16 May 1851, Coates to Lugenbil, 18 June 1851, Coates to McClain, 10 January 1852, all in Lapsansky-Werner and Bacon, *Back to Africa*.

19. Ibid., 31, 39; Coates to Douglas, 27 June 1850, Wagoner to Coates, 8 January 1859, William Whipper to Coates, 24 February 1859, Cary to Coates, 14 June 1859, Coates to Coppinger, 6 June 1866, in Lapsansky-Werner and Bacon, *Back to Africa*, 60–67, 114–116, 122–23, 131, 190–92. See also 41. See also the next chapter of this work for more on Delany's views.

20. Coates to Wilkeson, 7 November 1839, 8 January 1840, 13 February 1840, 17 June 1840, and 19 June 1840, all in ACS Papers.

21. Margaret Hope Bacon, *But One Race: The Life of Robert Purvis* (Albany: State University of New York Press, 2007), 122.

22. Lapsansky-Werner and Bacon, *Back to Africa*, 21–22.

23. Ibid., 22.

24. Kocher, "Duty," 145; Staudenraus, *African Colonization*, 240–41.

25. *Colonization Herald* 1, no. 4 (April 1839); *Colonization Herald* 1, no. 36 (March 1848): 2; *Colonization Herald*, new series, no. 5 (November 1850); *Colonization Herald*, new series, no. 17 (November 1851); *Colonization Herald*, new series, no. 32 (February 1853): 2; Burin, *Slavery and the Peculiar Solution*, 29.

26. Burin, *Slavery and the Peculiar Solution*, 46; PCS, *To the Friends of the African Race.—An Appeal in Behalf of the Pennsylvania Colonization Society* (Philadelphia: By Order of the Board, 1853).

27. Burin, "Rethinking Northern White Support," 226–27; *Colonization Herald* 1, no. 26 (16 April 1836).

28. Young Men's Colonization Society of Pennsylvania, *Annual Report of the Board of Managers of the Young Men's Colonization Society of Pennsylvania: Read February 22, 1837* (Philadelphia: William Stavely, 1837).

29. *Addresses Delivered in the Hall of the House of Representatives, Harrisburg, Pa. On Tuesday Evening, April 6, 1852, by William V. Pettit, Esq., and Rev. John P. Durbin, D.D.* (Philadelphia: W. F. Geddes, 1852), 4–5.

30. Ibid., 20, 21, 22.

31. *Colonization Herald* 1, no. 26 (16 April 1836); *Colonization Herald* 1, no. 21 (6 February 1836): 3; *Colonization Herald* 3, no. 58 (12 August 1837): 4.

32. *Colonization Herald* 3, no. 65 (18 November 1837): 4.

33. Van Rensselaer, *God Glorified by Africa*.

34. For a general look at the fugitive slave law, see Stanley W. Campbell, *The Slave*

Catchers: Enforcement of the Fugitive Slave Law, 1850–1860 (New York: W. W. Norton, 1970). For an analysis the Dred Scott case and its effects, see Don Fehrenbacher, *Slavery, Law, and Politics: The Dred Scott Case in Historical Perspective* (New York: Oxford University Press, 1981).

35. Holt, *Fate of Their Country*; Mason, *Slavery and Politics*; Robert Pierce Forbes, *The Missouri Compromise and Its Aftermath: Slavery and the Meaning of America* (Chapel Hill: University of North Carolina Press, 2007), 4; Cresson to Gurley, 10 November 1831, 5 December 1831, 10 November 1832, 29 January 1833, and 15 March 1833, all in ACS Papers.

36. For the best example of this uncomfortable union, see James Oakes, *The Radical and the Republican: Frederick Douglass, Abraham Lincoln, and the Triumph of Antislavery Politics* (New York: W. W. Norton, 2007), 16–25.

37. Richards, *Gentlemen*, 163; Harrold, *American Abolitionists*, 64; Davis, "Northern Colonizationists and Free Blacks and Free Blacks," 670; Leon Litwack, "The Abolitionist Dilemma: The Antislavery Movement and the Northern Negro," *New England Quarterly Review* 34 (March 1961): 50–73; Lawrence J. Friedman, *Gregarious Saints: Self and Community in Antebellum American Abolitionism, 1830–1870* (Cambridge: Cambridge University Press, 1982), 160–65; Jane H. Pease and William H. Pease, "Antislavery Ambivalence: Immediatism, Expediency, Race," *American Quarterly* 17 (Winter 1965): 689–92, 695; Dorsey, "Gendered History," 82.

38. PCS, "At a Meeting of the Board of Managers of the Pennsylvania Colonization Society, held January 13, 1857," Report of a Committee of Six (Philadelphia, 1857); Tom W. Schick, "A Quantitative Analysis of Liberian Colonization from 1820 to 1843 with Special Reference to Mortality," *Journal of African History* 12, no. 1 (1971): 47; Burin, *Slavery and the Peculiar Solution*, 52.

39. Kenneth Stampp, *America in 1857: A Nation on the Brink* (New York: Oxford University Press, 1990), viii; Burin, *Slavery and the Peculiar Solution*, 229, 81; Burin, "Rethinking Northern White Support," 228; PCS Papers, vol. 2, 1 April 1859, 8 November 1859, 10 January 1860, 14 February 1860.

40. For a list of PAS members, see Pennsylvania Abolition Society, *Centennial Anniversary of the Pennsylvania Society, for Promoting the Abolition of Slavery, the Relief of Free Negroes Unlawfully Held in Bondage: and for Improving the Condition of the African Race* (Philadelphia: Grant, Faires and Rodgers, Printers, 1875), and for names of immediatists, see Brown, *Pennsylvania Reformers*, 6–16; Pennsylvania Anti-Slavery Society, *Twenty-First Annual Report Presented to the Pennsylvania Anti-Slavery Society, by its Executive committee, October 6th, 1858, with the Resolutions of the Annual Meeting, Constitution of the Society and Declaration of Sentiments* (Philadelphia: Merrihew and Thompson, 1858), 13, 6–7.

41. Jordan, *Slavery and the Meetinghouse*, 28.

42. Faulkner, "Root of the Evil," 377–405; W. P. Garrison, "Free Produce," 485–94.

43. Blackett, *Building an Antislavery Wall*, 70–73; Lapsansky-Werner and Bacon, *Back to Africa*, 33.

44. Benjamin Coates, *Cotton Cultivation in Africa, Suggestions on the Importance of the Cultivation of Cotton in Africa, in Reference to the Abolition of Slavery in the United States, through the Organization of an African Civilization Society* (Philadelphia: C. Sherman and Son, 1858), 5.

45. Ibid., 7–8.

46. Ibid , 8–9, 21.

47. Ibid., 19, 14.

48. Ibid., 11.

49. Ibid., 15.

50. Lapsansky-Werner and Bacon, *Back to Africa*, 33; Joel Schor, *Henry Highland Garnet: A Voice of Black Radicalism in the Nineteenth Century* (Westport, Conn.: Greenwood Press, 1977), 154–55; Henry Highland Garnet, "African Civilization Society" (New York, 1859). This flyer is available at the Historical Society of Pennsylvania.

Notes to Chapter 7

1. Robert Levine, *Martin Delany, Frederick Douglass, and the Politics of Representative Identity* (Chapel Hill: University of North Carolina Press, 1997), 65–55; Robin D. G. Kelley, *Freedom Dreams: The Black Radical Imagination*, new ed. (Boston: Beacon Press, 2003), 17.

2. Stuckey, *Ideological Origins of Black Nationalism*; Victor Ullman, *Martin R. Delany: The Beginnings of Black Nationalism* (Boston: Beacon Press, 1971); Dorothy Sterling, *The Making of an Afro-American: Martin Robison Delany, African Explorer, Civil War Major, and Father of Black Nationalism* (New York: Da Capo Press, 1971); Vincent Harding, *There Is a River: The Black Struggle for Freedom in America* (New York: Harcourt Brace Jovanovich, 1981) and *The Other American Revolution* (Los Angeles: University of California at Los Angeles, 1980); Harold Cruse, *The Crisis of the Negro Intellectual* (New York: William Morrow, 1967); Louis Rosenfeld, "Martin Robison Delany: Physician, Black Separatist, Explorer, Soldier," *Bulletin of the New York Academy of Medicine*, 2nd series, 65, no. 7 (1989).

Theodore Draper, "The Father of American Black Nationalism," *New York Review of Books*, 12 March 1970, and Theodore Draper, *The Rediscovery of Black Nationalism* (New York: Viking Press, 1970); Wilson Jeremiah Moses, *The Golden Age of Black Nationalism, 1850–1925* (New York: Oxford University Press, 1978), 7; Miller, *Search for a Black Nationality* vii; Blackett, *Building an Antislavery Wall;* R. J. M. Blackett, *Beating against the Barriers: The Lives of Six Nineteenth-Century Afro-Americans* (Ithaca, N.Y.: Cornell University Press, 1986); R. J. M. Blackett, "Martin R. Delany and Robert Campbell: Black Americans in Search of an African Identity," *Journal of Negro History* 62 (January 1977): 1–24; R. J. M. Blackett, "Return to the Motherland: A Jamaican in Early Colonial Laos," *Phylon* 40 (December 1979): 375–87.

Tunde Adeleke, *UnAfrican Americans: Nineteenth-Century Black Nationalists and the Civilizing Mission* (Lexington: University Press of Kentucky, 1997), 64–66, 6; Tunde Adeleke, *Without Regard to Race: The Other Martin Robison Delany* (Jackson: University Press of Mississippi, 2003).

3. Ullman, *Martin R. Delany*, 4–5, Sterling, *Making of an Afro-American*, 2–4.

4. Ullman, *Martin R. Delany*, 6, 74; Martin R. Delany, correspondence in the *North Star*, 12 May 1848, 2; David Smith, "On the Edge of Freedom: The Fugitive Slave Issue in South Central Pennsylvania, 1820–1870," PhD diss., Pennsylvania State University, 2006.

5. Ullman, *Martin R. Delany*, 10.

6. Ibid.,12–13, 18, 31, 40–44, 25–28.

7. Ibid., 29–31; Curry, *Free Black in Urban America*,100; Frank A. Rollin, *Life and Public Services of Martin R._Delany* (Boston: Lee and Shepard, 1883; reprint, New York: Arno Press, 1969), 94; Sterling, *Making of an Afro-American*, 58.

8. Horton and Horton, *In Hope of Liberty*, 117; Nash, *Forging Freedom*, 247–52; James O. Horton and Lois E. Horton, *Black Bostonians: Family Life and Community Struggle in the Antebellum North* (Teaneck, N.J.: Holmes and Meier, 2000), xi, 10.

9. Blackett, *Building an Antislavery Wall*, 166–68; Pessen, *Jacksonian America*, 63.

10. Frederickson, *Black Image in the White Mind*, 72.

11. Ibid., 73–75. For examples, see the *American Journal of the Medical Sciences* 19 (January 1850) and 20 (July 1850).

12. Ullman, *Martin R. Delany*, 22; Dorothy Sterling, ed., *Speak Out in Thunder Tones: Letters and Other Writings by Black Northerners, 1787–1856* (New York: Da Capo Press, 1973), 81; William C. Nell, *The Colored Patriots of the American Revolution with Sketches of Several Distinguished Colored Persons: To Which is Added a Brief Survey of the Condition and Prospects of Colored Americans* (Boston: Robert F. Wallcut, 1855), 158, 360.

13. Sterling *Speak Out*, 161; C. Peter Ripley, *Black Abolitionist Papers Volume III: The United States, 1830–1846* (Chapel Hill: University of North Carolina Press, 1991),14–15, 20; Carleton Mabee, *Sojourner Truth: Slave, Prophet, Legend* (New York: New York University Press, 1995); Nell Irvin Painter, *Sojourner Truth: A Life, A Symbol* (New York: W. W. Norton, 1997); Waldo Martin Jr., *The Mind of Frederick Douglass* (Chapel Hill: University of North Carolina Press, 1984). Also see Frederick Douglass's writings throughout Milton Meltzer, ed., *Frederick Douglass in His Own Words* (New York: Harcourt Brace, 1995).

14. Augustine, *The Colored American*, 16 February 1839. For expressions of Delany's views on self-elevation, see his letters in the *North Star*, 28 January 1848, 2; 28 April 1848, 2; 26 May 1848, 2; 9 June 1848, 2–3; 16 June 1848, 2; 28 July 1848, 2–3; 4 August 1848, 2–3; 17 November 1848, 2; 1 December 1848, 2; 15 December 1848, 2–3; and 1 January 1849, 2–3; Litwack, *North of Slavery*, 170–71, 74.

15. J. K. Mitchell to Ralph Gurley, 13 June 1828, ACS Papers; *African Repository* 8, no. 9 (November 1832): 285–86; Ullman, *Martin R. Delany*, 113–18.

16. Martin R. Delany, *Official Report of the Niger Valley Exploring Party* (1860), reprinted in Howard Bell, *Search for a Place: Black Separatism and Africa, 1860* (Ann Arbor: University of Michigan Press, 1969), 93; Martin R. Delany, *Blake, or the Huts of America*, was first published in serialized form in *The Anglo-African Magazine* and *The Weekly Anglo-African* between January 1859 and May 1862. Reprinted in novel form by Beacon Press of Boston, 1970, 220.

Sterling, *Speak Out*, 93–95; Frank A. Rollin, *Life and Public Services of Martin R. Delany*, (Millwood, N.Y.: Kraus Reprint Company, 1969), 41; Shadd, Hamilton, and Whipper, address to the annual black convention, 13 June 1832, in *Black Abolitionist Papers*, 3:109–13; Barbara Ann Steward to Frederick Douglass, 29 May 1855, in *Black Abolitionist Papers*, 4:295; Herbert Aptheker, ed., *A Documentary History of the Negro People in the United States* (New York: Citadel Press, 1951), 361–63; Ripley, *Black Abolitionist Papers*, 4:193–94.

Martin R. Delany, The *Condition, Elevation, Emigration, and Destiny of the Colored People of the United States. Politically Considered* (1852; reprint, Ithaca, N.Y.: Cornell University Press), 85–137; *North Star*, 28 January 1848, 28 April 1848, 9 June 1848, 16 June 1848, 28 July 1848, 4 August 1848, 1 December 1848, 15 December 1848, 5 January 1849; Nell, *Colored Patriots*. Lester to William Still, 30 November 1859, in *Black*

Abolitionist Papers, 2:421–23, John N. Still to Henry Bibb, 3 February 1852, in *Black Abolitionist Papers*, 4:108–9.

17. "Augustine" to the *Colored American*, 2 December 1837, 9 December 1837, 10 February 1838. Woodson outlined his views on moral uplift and self-help in a series of letters to the editor of the *Colored American*. Signed Augustine, these letters were printed in the 2 December 1837, 9 December 1837, 30 December 1837, 13 January 1838, 27 January 1838, 10 February 1838, 28 July 1838, 9 February 1839, 16 February 1839, and 13 March 1841 editions. They are reprinted in Stuckey, ed., *Ideological Origins of Black Nationalism*, 118–48.

18. Woodson to the *Colored American*, 28 July 1838. See also Adeleke, *Without Regard*, 32–33; Miller, *Search for a Black Nationality*, 104–5; Levine, *Martin Delany, Frederick Douglass*, 24–25; Floyd Miller, "'The Father of Black Nationalism': Another Contender," *Civil War History* 17 (1971); Lewis Woodson to Samuel E. Cornish, 7 February 1838, in *Black Abolitionist Papers*, 3:256–60.

19. Pessen, *Jacksonian America*, 62–63; Ullman, *Martin R. Delany*, 35–38.

20. Ullman, *Martin R. Delany*, 42–45.

21. For the exchange, see Delany to Samuel Ringold Ward, and an editor's note addressing Delany's comments, *North Star*, 27 June 1850, 2, and Delany to Douglass, *North Star*, 11 July 1850, 2.

22. This quote is used as the title of the Martin R. Delany website (www.wvu. edu/~library/delany/fugitive.htm). Accessed on 23 July 1998; Blackett, "Martin R. Delany and Robert Campbell," 7–8; Adeleke, *UnAfrican Americans*, 34–35; Harding, *There Is a River*, 157; Stanley W. Campbell, *The Slave Catchers: Enforcement of the Fugitive Slave Law, 1850–1860* (New York: W. W. Norton, 1970).

23. Delany, *Condition, Elevation, Emigration*, 157; Delany, "Political Destiny," in Rollin, *Life and Services*, 360.

24. Delany to Pittsburgh Mayor Hugh Fleming and a large crowd at the Pittsburgh Market House in Allegheny, 30 September 1850. Quoted in Ullman, *Martin R. Delany*, 112; Sterling, *Making of an Afro-American*, 120; William Katz, *Eyewitness: A Living Documentary of the African American Contribution to American History* (New York: Simon and Schuster, 1967), 189–90; Harding, *There Is a River*, 158–59; Nell, *Colored Patriots*, 18; Delany, *Condition, Elevation, Emigration*, 155–56, and his 1854 speech to the Cleveland Emigration Convention. Now called "Political Destiny of the Colored Race on the American Continent," it is reprinted in Rollin, *Life and Services*, 327–67, quoted from 359–60; Horton and Horton, *In Hope of Liberty*, 237–39; Solomon Northup, *Twelve Years a Slave* (Baton Rouge: Louisiana State University Press, 1968).

25. Harding, *There Is a River*, 161, 176; Ripley, *Black Abolitionist Papers*, 2:3, and 1:4–5; Campbell, *Slave Catchers*, 62–63; William Wells Brown, *The Negro in the American Rebellion* (Boston: A. G. Brown, 1880), 51, 41.

26. Miller, *Search for a Black Nationality*, 126.

27. Delany, *Condition, Elevation, Emigration*, 21–22, 53; Peter Wood, *Black Majority: Negroes in Colonial South Carolina from 1670 through the Stono Rebellion* (New York: W. W. Norton, 1974).

28. Delany, *Condition, Elevation, Emigration*, 26–27; Miller, *Search for a Black Nationality*, 128–30; Jane H. Pease and William H. Pease, "Ends, Means, and Attitudes: Black-White Conflict in the Antislavery Movement," *Civil War History* 18, no. 2 (1972): 17–28.

29. Robert Levine included the exchange between Delany and Douglass in *Martin R. Delany: A Documentary Reader* (Chapel Hill: University of North Carolina Press 2003), 224–35.

30. Miller, *Search for a Black Nationality*, 119; Delany to Douglass, 21 January 1848, in *North Star*, 4 February 1848, 2; Delany, *Condition, Elevation, Emigration*, 45.

31. Delany, *Condition, Elevation, Emigration*, 169–70.

32. Miller, *Search for a Black Nationality*, 127–28; Delany, *Condition, Elevation, Emigration*, 178–88, 205.

33. Miller, *Search for a Black Nationality*, 134, 137.

34. Ibid., 149.

35. Ibid., 153.

36. Ibid., 155.

37. Ibid., 157; Jane Rhodes, *Mary Ann Shadd Cary: The Black Press and Protest in the Nineteenth Century* (Bloomington: Indiana University Press, 1998), 43–45.

38. Miller, *Search for a Black Nationality*, 158–59; Rhodes, *Mary Ann Shadd Cary*, 117–20; James A. Rawley, *Race and Politics: "Bleeding Kansas" and the Coming of the Civil War* (Philadelphia: J. B. Lippincott, 1969); Fehrenbacher, *Slavery, Law, and Politics*.

39. Miller, *Search for a Black Nationality*, 165–69.

40. Staudenraus, *African Colonization* 245.

41. Martin R. Delany, introduction to William Nesbit, *Four Months in Liberia; or African Colonization Exposed* (Pittsburgh: J. T. Shryoch, 1855). Reprinted in Wilson Jeremiah Moses, *Liberian Dreams: Back-to-Africa Narratives from the 1850s* (University Park: Pennsylvania State University Press, 1998), 79–178. Quotes from 81–84.

42. Miller, *Search for a Black Nationality*, 170–71.

43. Rollin, *Life and Public Services*; Levine, *Martin Delany, Frederick Douglass*.

44. Delany, *Blake*, 16–17, 64 of the Beacon Press volume; Delany, *Condition, Elevation, Emigration*, 81–82.

45. Hugh Gloster, *Negro Voices in American Fiction* (Chapel Hill: University of North Carolina Press, 1948).

46. Delany, *Condition, Elevation, Emigration*, 10.

47. Ibid., 49, 66, and "Political Destiny," in Rollin, *Life and Services*, 327–67.

48. Miller, *Search for a Black Nationality* 171–72.

49. Ibid., 172–74.

50. Ibid., 175–79.

51. Ibid., 180–93.

52. Delany, *Condition, Elevation, Emigration*, 35; Delany, introduction to *Four Years in Liberia* in Moses, *Liberian Dreams*, 82.

53. Miller, *Search for a Black Nationality*, 190–98, quote from 98; *Frederick Douglass' Paper*, 3 December 1858, 3; *North American and U.S. Gazette*, 3 December 1858, 1; PCS Minutes, 14 December 1858; Pinney to Gurley, 8 February 1859, and Campbell and Purnell to Harvey Lindsly, 17 February 1859, both in ACS Papers; *New York Colonization Journal*, October 1859; Benson to Gurley, 1 August 1859, ACS Papers.

54. For an analysis of the "reflex influence," see Howard Bell, *Search for a Place: Black Separatism and Africa, 1860* (Ann Arbor: University of Michigan Press, 1969).

55. Delany, *Condition, Elevation, Emigration*, 42; Delany used the word "intelligent" throughout his writings to describe any black whom he considered worthy of

note. William J. Watkins, speech delivered before the Provincial Association for the Education and Elevation of the Colored People at Sayer Street British Methodist Episcopal Church, Toronto, Canada, 12 August 1861, in *Black Abolitionist Papers*, 2:446–48; Barbara Bair, "Pan-Africanism as Process," in *Imagining Home: Nationalism in the African Diaspora*, ed. Sidney Lemelle and Robin D. G. Kelley (New York: Verso Press, 1994), 122; Paul Gilroy, *The Black Atlantic: Modernity and Double Consciousness* (Cambridge: Harvard University Press, 1993), 25–27; Blackett, *Beating against the Barriers*, 172; Blackett, *Building an Antislavery Wall*, 170–72, 156; Moses, *Golden Age of Black Nationalism*, 42. McCoy, *Elusive Republic*; Moses, *Golden Age of Black Nationalism*, 20–21. See also Alexander Crummell's writings, especially a speech delivered before the British and Foreign Anti-Slavery Society at Freemasons' Hall, London, England, 19 May 1851, in *Black Abolitionist Papers*, 1:276–82.

56. Delany, *Official Report*, 70, 72–73, 113–19, 108.

57. Rollin, *Life and Services*, 18; Delany, *Condition, Elevation, Emigration*, 163, 168; Delany, "International Policy of the World towards the African Race," in Rollin, *Life and Services*, 324–25, 317, 321, 319, 326; Delany, "International Policy," in Rollin, *Life and Services*, 314–16.

58. Delany's novel *Blake* serves as an indictment on religion, and he discussed the stifling aspects of religion in articles to the *North Star*. Delany, *Blake*; *North Star*, 16 February 1849, 23 March 1849, 13 April 1849, 20 April 1849. For an analysis of Delany's religious views, see Gilroy, *Black Atlantic*, 28–29; Ullman, *Martin R. Delany*, 202–3; Moses, *Golden Age of Black Nationalism*, 152; and Miller, *Search for a Black Nationality*, 122–23; Delany, *Official Report*, 108–9.

59. Delany, "International Policy," in Rollin, *Life and Services,* 313–27, and "Political Events," *Chatham Provincial Freeman*, 5 July 1856; Adeleke, *UnAfrican Americans*, 50–51.

60. Moses, *Golden Age of Black Nationalism*, 20; Michael A. Gomez, *Exchanging Our Country Marks: The Transformation of African Identities in the Colonial and Antebellum South* (Chapel Hill: University of North Carolina Press, 1998), 212, 219–21; Gilroy, *Black Atlantic*, 27–28; William H. Watkins, "Pan-Africanism and the Politics of Education: Towards a New Understanding," in *Imagining Home,* ed. Lemelle and Kelley, 223; Henry Highland Garnet, "Circular by the African Civilization Society," February 1859, in *The Black Abolitionist Papers*, 5:3–6.

61. Delany, *Official Report*, 65, 86, 89, 92–97, 100–106, 133–34, 139; Adeleke, *UnAfrican Americans*, 58–59, 70–73.

62. Robert Levine does a particularly good job of describing Delany's elitism, capitalism, and reverence for Western culture in *Martin Delany, Frederick Douglass*, 9, 16, 63, 64, 66; Delany, letter to the editor of the *Chatham Planet*, 29 November 1859; Delany, *Official Report*, 77; This estimate was calculated using Delany's claim in *Condition, Elevation, Emigration* that white oppression of blacks began in 1442.

63. A. H. M. Kirk-Greene, "America in the Niger Valley: A Colonization Centenary," *Phylon* 23, no. 3 (1962): 235; Blackett, *Beating against the Barriers*, 162–66; Levine, *Martin Delany, Frederick Douglass*, 67.

64. Blackett, *Building an Antislavery Wall*, 119.

65. Delany to the editor, *Chatham Planet*, 15 January 1861; Delany, *Blake*, 262; Blackett, *Building an Antislavery Wall*, 119; Clapham to Gurley, December 1833, ACS Papers; Delany, *North Star*, 10 February 1848; *Blake*, 263, 225–60; *Condition,*

Elevation, Emigration, 212; *Official Report*, 42–46; Blackett, *Beating against the Barriers*, and "Return to the Motherland"; Kirk-Greene, "America in the Niger Valley," 232. Blackett provides the best description of this campaign in *Building an Antislavery Wall*. See also Ripley, *Black Abolitionist Papers*, vol. 2; Rollin, *Life and Services*, 55.

66. Delany, "Political Destiny," in Rollin, *Life and Services*, 364; and Delany, *Blake*, 184.

67. Delany, *Official Report*, 137–38; Blackett, *Building an Antislavery Wall*; Walvin, *England, Slaves, and Freedom;* Martin Klein, "Slavery, the International Labour Market and the Emancipation of Slaves in the 19th Century," *Slavery and Abolition* 15, no. 2 (1994): 197–220; Seymour Drescher, "The Slaving Capital of the World: Liverpool and National Opinion in the Age of Abolition," *Slavery and Abolition* 9, no. 2 (1988): 128–43; James Smith, "The Liberals, Race, and Political Reform in the British West Indies, 1866–1874," *Journal of Negro History* 79, no. 2 (1994): 131–40; Blackett, *Beating against the Barriers*, 161–73.

68. Blackett, *Building an Antislavery Wall*, 190–208, and *Beating against the Barriers*, 160–70; Miller, *Search for a Black Nationality*, 213, 217–18.

69. Blackett, *Building an Antislavery Wall* .

70. Gilroy, *Black Atlantic*, 27–28; Delany, *Official Report*, 65, 89, 92–97, 100–106, 133–34, 139; Adeleke, *UnAfrican Americans*, 58–59.

71. Delany, *Condition, Elevation, Emigration*, 187.

72. Rollin, *Life and Services*, 20–21, 96, 129; Delany, *Condition, Elevation, Emigration*, 161–62; *Blake*, 261–62.

Notes to Chapter 8

1. *Colonization Herald* 1, no. 4 (April 1839); *Colonization Herald* 1 no. 36 (March 1848): 2; *Colonization Herald*, new series, no. 5 (November 1850); *Colonization Herald*, new series, no. 17 (November 1851); *Colonization Herald*, new series, no. 32 (February 1853): 2; William Henry Ruffner, *Africa's Redemption: A Discourse on African Colonization in its Missionary Aspects, and in its relation to Slavery and Abolition: Preached on Sabbath Morning, July 4th 1852, in the Seventh Presbyterian Church, Penn Square, Philadelphia* (Philadelphia: William S. Martien, 1852), 43; Burin, *Slavery and the Peculiar Solution*, 45.

2. A number of letters in the PAS files at the HSP pertain to slaves being freed provided they be relocated to western territories such as Illinois or Indiana or to Philadelphia. See the PAS papers that correspond to reels 13 and 15 of the microfilmed collection. They can be found at the HSP, call number AmS02, folders 1, 2, 9, 11, and 12. This correspondence includes information regarding a trip Benjamin Lundy took to Haiti to explore the option of resettlement there. See also the Cox, Parrish, Wharton Papers at the HSP. For more about the North Carolina slaves and the PCS see Clegg, *Price of Liberty*, which chronicles their journey from North Carolina to Liberia.

3. Burin, "Rethinking Northern White Support," 226, 215.

4. Christian Soldier, "Important Correspondence," *Liberator* 2, no. 13 (31 March 1832); *Liberator* 2, no. 11 (17 March 1832); Jay, *Inquiry*, 61–69; "With Their Own Consent," *Liberator* 3, no. 24 (15 June 1833); Cresson to Gurley, 9 March 1833; Padmore to Simpson, 18 July 1833; Cresson to Gurley, 10 November 1831, 6 July 1832; all in ACS Papers.

5. Howe, *What Hath God Wrought*, 255–56, 264–65, 339–500; Forbes, *Missouri*

Compromise, 12. William Freehling, *The Reintegration of American History: Slavery and the Civil War* (New York: Oxford University Press, 1994), 190; Jay, *Inquiry*, 49–51

6. Kocher, "'Duty to America and Africa,'" 148.

7. "Dr. Mconaughy," *Colonization Herald* 1, no. 11 (5 September 1835): 1; "Harrisburg Meeting," *Colonization Herald* 1, no. 12 (19 September 1835): 3; "Varieties of Mankind," *Colonization Herald* 1, no. 31 (1 August 1838): 1.

8. *Colonization Herald* 3, no. 59 (26 August 1837): 4; Cresson to Gurley, 3 August 1829, in ACS Papers; ACS, 14th Annual Report, xiii.

9. Kocher, "'Duty to America and Africa,'" 148; Jay, *Inquiry*, 48; "Dr Mconaughy," *Colonization Herald* 1, no. 11 (5 September 1835): 1.

10. Jay, *Inquiry*, 52–53.

11. *Colonization Herald* 1, no. 2 (18 April 1835): 7; *Colonization Herald* 1, no. 5 (30 May 1835): 1.

12. ACS, 17th Annual Report, 28; Jay, *Inquiry*, 47–48. See also Davis, *Leonard Bacon*, 76–78 .

13. Richards, *Gentlemen*, 29–30, 114; Jay, *Inquiry*, 118.

14. Richards, *Gentlemen*, 30, 36; John Runcie, "'Hunting the Nigs' in Philadelphia: The Race Riot of August 1834," *Pennsylvania History* 38, no. 2 (1972): 196–97, 211.

15. David R. Johnson, "Crime Patterns in Philadelphia, 1840–70," in *Peoples of Philadelphia*, ed. Davis and Haller, 97; Runcie, "'Hunting the Nigs,'" 211; Curry, *Free Black in Urban America*, 100.

16. Brown, *Pennsylvania Reformers*, 12; Nash, *Forging Freedom*, 227; Curry, *Free Black in Urban America*, 105; *Colonization Herald* 1, no. 21 (23 May 1838): 2.

17. *Colonization Herald* 1, no. 42 (17 October 1838): 2; *Colonization Herald* 1, no. 44 (31 October, 1838): 2–3.

18. Charles Sydnor, *Slavery in Mississippi* (Baton Rouge: Louisiana State University Press, 1966), 204.

19. Davis does an excellent job of showing that Leonard Bacon feared just such a situation and thus rejected immediatism. Davis, *Leonard Bacon*, p. 2. For a detailed look at Quaker disdain for immediatist tactics, see Jordan, *Slavery and the Meetinghouse*, esp. 27–29.

20. William Ellery Channing to James G. Birney, reprinted in the *National Enquirer and Constitutional Advocate of Universal Liberty*, 31 December 1836, 1.

21. Howard Zinn, *SNCC: The New Abolitionists* (1964; Cambridge, Mass.: South End Press, 2002), 14. Raymond Arsenault notes in *Freedom Rides: 1961 and the Struggle for Racial Justice* that twentieth-century civil rights leaders often wrote their wills before participating in activities such as the Freedom Rides because they knew what they faced and were prepared to die for the cause (New York: Oxford University Press, 2006). It would be interesting to see if similar wills exist in the papers of immediatists.

22. James W. Loewen, *Lies My Teacher Told Me: Everything Your American History Textbook Got Wrong* (1995; New York: Touchstone, 2007), 241.

23. Edlie L. Wong, *Neither Fugitive nor Free: Atlantic Slavery, Freedom Suits, and the Legal Culture of Travel* (New York: New York University Press, 2009), 92, 107–15.

24. Martin, *Mind of Frederick Douglass*, 27; Frederick Douglass, *My Bondage and My Freedom*, reprint, edited by John David Smith (New York: Penguin Books, 2003), xli–xlii.

25. John Stauffer, *The Black Hearts of Men: Radical Abolitionists and the*

Transformation of Race (Cambridge: Harvard University Press, 2002); Goodman, *Of One Blood*; Newman, *Transformation*.

26. Davis, "Northern Colonizationists and Free Blacks," 675.

27. Cresson to Gurley, 15 August 1833; Kocher, "'Duty to America and Africa,'" 124–25.

28. Board of Education of the Presbyterian Church, *Thirty-Fifth Annual Report of the Board of Education of the Presbyterian Church in the United States of America, Presented to the General Assembly, May 1854* (Philadelphia: Published by the Board, 1854), 33–35; Carter, *Address*, 3; Bond, *Education for Freedom*, 164, 3; Murray, "Founding," 397–98, 400; An Act to Incorporate the Ashmun Institute, Passed by the Legislature of Pennsylvania at the Session of 1854, HSP, Leon Gardiner Collection on Negro History, ANHS box .1G f.8, 1.

29. Van Rensselaer, *God Glorified by Africa*. 15, 43; Carter, *Address*, 11.

30. Newman, *Transformation*, 20; Needles, *Historical Memoir*, 91–97, 102–5; PAS, *Centennial Anniversary of the PAS*, 82.

31. Schick, "Quantitative Analysis," 58, 55.

32. ACS, 14th Report, 14–15; John Crosby to Gurley, 1 December 1831, in ACS Papers.

33. Joseph Reynolds to Cresson 3 November 1831, in ACS Papers, also in ACS, 15th Report, 51–52.

34. Schick, "Quantitative Analysis," 56.

35. Crosby to Gurley, 6 July 1832, in ACS Papers; ACS, 16th Annual Report, 4; Staudenraus, *African Colonization*, 102–3; Schick, "Quantitative Analysis," 57–58; ACS, 17th Annual Report, 4–6.

36. Cresson to Gurley, 11 June 1834, in ACS Papers; "Ezekiel Skinner to Elliott Cresson," 15 December 1835, in *Colonization Herald* 1, no. 4 (1835); Kocher, "'Duty to America and Africa,'" 134; *Colonization Herald* 1, no. 4 (1835).

37. Schick, "Quantitative Analysis," 58; Burin, "Rethinking Northern White Support," 200.

38. Wong, *Neither Fugitive nor Free*, 92. The theory of cognitive dissonance was developed by Leon Festinger, a Stanford University psychologist, and presented in *A Theory of Cognitive Dissonance* (Stanford, Calif.: Stanford University Press, 1957), 4; Dieter Frey, "Recent Research on Selective Exposure to Information," in *Advances in Experimental Social Psychology*, vol. 19, ed. Leonard Berkowitz (Orlando: Academic Press, 1986), 41–80.

39. Bruce, "National Identity and African-American Colonization," 28; McGraw, "Richmond Free Blacks," 216–17; Burin, *Slavery and the Peculiar Solution*, 170.

40. Clegg, *Price of Liberty*, 6; Wilson, *Loyal Blacks*.

41. Basil Davidson, *The Black Man's Burden: Africa and the Curse of the Nation-State* (New York: Random House, 1992), 25; Clegg, *Price of Liberty*, especially chap. 7.

42. Adeleke, *UnAfrican Americans*, 144; Lamin Sanneh, *Abolitionists Abroad: American Blacks and the Making of Modern West Africa* (Cambridge: Harvard University Press, 1999).

43. Kelley, *Freedom Dreams*, 17–18, 21.

44. Ibid., 17.

Notes to Epilogue

1. Newman, *Transformation of American Abolition*, 4; Julie Roy Jeffrey, *Abolitionists Remember: Antislavery Autobiographies and the Unfinished Work of Emancipation* (Chapel Hill: University of North Carolina Press, 2008); James Oakes, *The Radical and the Republican: Frederick Douglass, Abraham Lincoln, and the Triumph of Antislavery Politics* (New York: W. W. Norton, 2007); See also Frederick J. Blue, *No Taint of Compromise: Crusaders in Antislavery Politics* (Baton Rouge: Louisiana State University Press, 2005).

2. Mason, *Slavery and Politics*, 4–5, 52, 51. See also Tomek, "'From motives of generosity.'"

3. Mason, *Slavery and Politics*, 7, 62; Richards, *Slave Power*.

4. Forbes, *Missouri Compromise*, 4–5, 7.

5. Oakes, *Radical and Republican*, 16–17. For a discussion of Wilmot's primary concerns in opposing slavery, particularly his concern first and foremost for his small farming constituents, see Blue, *No Taint of Compromise*, 10, 184–212. See also Earle, *Jacksonian Antislavery and the Politics of Free Soil*.

6. Tyler Anbinder, *Nativism and Slavery: The Northern Know Nothings and the Politics of the 1850s* (Cambridge: Oxford University Press, 1994), 192, 195, 190–93.

7. Elizabeth Varon, *Disunion!: The Coming of the American Civil War, 1789–1859* (Chapel Hill: University of North Carolina Press, 2010), 147–48; Reinhard O. Johnson, *The Liberty Party, 1840–1848* (Baton Rouge: Louisiana State University Press, 2009), 88.

8. John Stauffer, *Giants: The Parallel Lives of Frederick Douglass and Abraham Lincoln* (New York: Twelve, 2008), 185.

9. Oakes, *Radical and Republican*, 153, 192–93; Stauffer, *Giants*, xiii, 184, 242, 263, 265, 268, 269.

10. Delany, "Political Destiny," in Rollin, *Life and Services*, 355.

11. Donald Yacovone, *A Voice of Thunder: A Black Soldier's Civil War* (Urbana: University of Illinois Press), 26–33; James McPherson, *The Negro's Civil War: How American Negroes Felt and Acted during the War for the Union* (New York: Pantheon, 1965), 11; David Walker, *Walker's Appeal, in Four Articles; Together with a Preamble, to the Coloured Citizens of the World, But in Particular, and Very Expressly, to Those of The United States of America, Written in Boston, State of Massachusetts, September 28, 1829* (Boston: David Walker, 1830); Henry Highland Garnet, "An Address to the Slaves of the United States of America" (Rejected by the National Convention held in Buffalo, N.Y., 1843), in Stuckey, *Ideological Origins of Black Nationalism*, 165–73; George Lawrence Jr. in the *Weekly Anglo-African*, 13 April and 27 April 1861, in Ripley, *Black Abolitionist Papers*, 5:110–12.

12. Yacovone, *Voice of Thunder*, 26–57; Donald Scott Sr. and Donald Scott Jr., *Camp William Penn (Images of America: Pennsylvania)* (Mount Pleasant, S.C.: Arcadia, 2008); Mark Lardas, *African American Soldiers in the American Civil War: USCT 1862–66* (New York: Osprey, 2006).

13. Rollin, *Life and Services*, 137, 39–40, 128–29; Ullman, *Martin R. Delany*, 263, 268. Levine maintains that Delany held on to emigration after the outbreak of the Civil War simply to maintain his status as leader. Levine, *Martin Delany, Frederick Douglass, and the Politics of Representative Identity*, 189. In the light of Delany's own interviews with his biographer, this may be true. Perhaps, however, his glowing

optimism at that time was a product of hindsight developed during the optimistic period of Reconstruction. Ullman's assertion that Delany became the voice of black authority, speaking to packed audiences does support Levine, though. Ullman, *Martin R. Delany*, 278. Harding accuses Delany of selling out his cause by joining the Civil War struggle, but this is unfair. Delany was simply employing a new method, physical force, to his lifelong crusade for racial uplift. Harding, *There Is a River*, 240–41. William Wells Brown, *The Rising Son; or, the Antecedents and Advancement of the Colored Race* (Boston: A. G. Brown, 1874), 348; Delany to Douglass, *Douglass' Monthly*, September 1862.

14. J. W. C. Pennington to Editor, *Weekly Anglo-African*, 15 April 1865, describing a 28 March 1865 speech by Delany; Rollin, *Life and Services*, 159–60, 185.

15. Rollin, *Life and Services*, 158, 162, 166; Delany to Stanton, 15 December 1863, in Ripley, *Black Abolitionist Papers* 5:261–64; Rollin, *Life and Services*, 168–69. Harding contends that Delany's participation in the war was a surrender of his militant dreams, maintaining that "brilliant black men [like Delany] were standing outside the ruling element, organizing other blacks to fight for the purposes of the white ruling class" just when they were needed the most. Harding, *There Is a River*, 238. This is incorrect, however. To Delany, he was taking an active leadership role in fighting to end slavery and prove racial equality.

16. Winch, *Gentleman of Color*, 355; Hope-Bacon and Lapsansky-Werner, *Back to Africa*, 50–51; Hope-Bacon, *But One Race*, 95.

17. Steven Hahn, *The Political Worlds of Slavery and Freedom* (Cambridge: Harvard University Press, 2009), 55–114.

Index

Page numbers in italics refer to illustrations.

About the Author

Beverly C. Tomek is an instructor of history at Wharton County Junior College and Resident Lecturer at the University of Houston-Victoria.